CGI

By

EXAMPLE

que

Robert Niles and Jeffry Dwight

CGI by Example

Copyright© 1996 by Que™ Corporation

Library of Congress Catalog No.: 96-69964

ISBN: 0-7897-0877-9

99 98 97 96   4 3 2 1

Interpretation of the printing code: the rightmost double-digit number is the year of the book's printing; the rightmost single-digit number, the number of the book's printing. For example, a printing code of 96-1 shows that the first printing of the book occurred in 1996.

President: *Roland Elgey*

Publisher: *Joseph B. Wikert*

Editorial Services Director: *Elizabeth Keaffaber*

Managing Editor
Sandy Doell

Director of Marketing
Lynn E. Zingraf

Publishing Manager
Jim Minatel

Acquisitions Manager
Cheryl Willoughby

Acquisitions Editor
Stephanie Gould

Product Director
Benjamin Milstead

Production Editor
Andy Saff

Copy Editor
Kelly Oliver

Product Marketing Manager
Kim Margolious

Assistant Product Marketing Manager
Christy Miller

Technical Editors
Louis Masters, S. Jon Sahaydak, and Glenn Smith

Technical Specialist
Nadeem Muhammed

Book Designer
Barb Kordesh

Graphic Image Specialists
Stephen Adams, Debra Bolhuis, Daniel Harris, and Laura Robbins

Production Team
Mona Brown, Jason Hand, Mike Henry, Donna Martin, Bobbi Satterfield, Laura A. Smith, Mark Walchle

Indexer
Erika Millen

Acquisitions Coordinator
Angela C. Kozlowski

Operations Coordinator
Patricia J. Brooks

Composed in *Palatino* and *MCPdigital* by Macmillan Computer Publishing.
Screen reproductions in this book were created by means of the program Collage Plus from Inner Media, Inc., Hollis, NH.

Dedication

To my wife, Kimberly.

—Robert Niles

To my brothers, Phil, Ken, and Tim. (This is your Christmas present.)

—Jeffry Dwight

About the Authors

Robert Niles is a systems administrator and Web programmer for InCommand, Inc., a company located in Yakima, Washington, that specializes in Internet and intranet applications.

Robert loves all things Internet, especially the Web, and CGI in particular. He has been online since 1983, exploring the very nature of the online world. In 1984, he entered the military service as a communications specialist, taking a one-year intensive course at the Presidio of Monterey as a Czech linguist. After completing military service, he returned to his home in the Yakim Valley.

Currently Robert can usually be found with his head almost stuck to a montitor—no matter where he is. He specializes in the UNIX environment, Perl, and SQL. Previously, he was a contributing author to Que's *Special Edition Using CGI*.

Robert lives in Selah, Washinton (apple country) with his wife, Kimberly, his son, Michael, and his daughter, Shaela. You can find him on the Web at **http://www.sehal.net/** or by e-mail at **rniles@imtired.selah.net**.

Jeffry Dwight is CEO of Greyware Automation Products, a consulting firm specializing in custom applications and Internet-related utilities. He is a confirmed Windows NT bigot, and his firm produces NT software almost exclusively. In 1990, he founded Greyware, a firm that has since become an important resource to the Windows NT community. Jeffry is a certified engineer with expertise in dozens of operating systems and programming languages.

Jeffry also writes poetry and fiction, and is active in the science fiction community. He chaired the Nebula Awards Novel Jury for the Science Fiction Writers of America (SFWA) in 1993 and 1994, and Greyware provides home pages for many SFWA authors—as well as SFWA itself. The Horror Writers Association, several genre magazines, and many other authors all make their homes at Greyware, too. It's the "in" place for science fiction, fantasy, and horror on the Internet.

Jeffry's computer background, combined with his professional writing skills, lets him bring a unique blend of knowledge and readability to his books. He is currently unmarried, has no pets, and lives in Dallas, Texas. He seldom refers to himself in the third person when writing things other than book-cover blurbs. He enjoys programming and writing fiction, but would much rather give it all up in favor of mucking about with a guitar and a drink somewhere cool, quiet, and dark.

Acknowledgments

I would like to thank my wife Kimberly for her love and support during the time I locked myself away to write this book. I thank my two children, Michael and Shaela, just for being kids and making me smile. I would like to thank my mom, who has been wonderfully supportive and kind. I also would like to thank Melissa, who is dear to my heart. To the crew at InCommand in Yakima—John, Mike, Pablo, Jon, Diane, Ken, and JC—thank you all! They were quite helpful by giving me time off to write the book, by answering questions, and by helping with some of the graphics within the book (thanks again Mike!). Thanks also for being a strange, fun, but quite professional crew to work with. I can't forget Nem (Ryun) Schlecht, who provided me with valuable information on dbm databases, and to Rasmus Lerdorf for answering my questions on PHP/FI.

Last, I would also like to thank Jeffry Dwight, Stephanie Gould, Benjamin Milstead, Andy Saff, Kelly Oliver, Louis Masters, and everyone else at Que. Thank you all for giving me a chance to write this book, and making sure that this book is the best that it could possibly be.

—Robert Niles

Thanks go to Robert Niles, Michael Erwin, Matt Wright, and Matthew Healy, for providing background material or examples; to Steve Ratzlaff, for putting up with me; to Stephanie Byrd and Cindy Carnes, for handling my FedEx woes; to Tom Melms, for his advice and encouragement; to Stephanie Gould and Valerie Smith, for failing to declare war; to Susan Dunn, for her exceedingly delicate touch with the red pen; to my father, for missing a holiday with me so I could work on the book; and to Benjamin Milstead, for his supervision.

Thanks also go to my family, for accepting my strange ways; and to my imaginary pet parakeet, Vozo the Brave, for keeping his beak closed at the right times.

—Jeffry Dwight

Trademark Acknowledgments

All terms mentioned in this book that are known to be trademarks or service marks have been appropriately capitalized. Que cannot attest to the accuracy of this information. Use of a term in this book should not be regarded as affecting the validity of any trademark or service mark.

Overview

Contents

Part II Basic CGI Applications

Contents

Contents

Part VI Server Administration Issues

Contents

Part VIII CGI Resources Online

Appendixes

B Contents of the CD-ROM   429

Index   435

We'd Like To Hear From You!

As part of our continuing effort to produce books of the highest possible quality, Que would like to hear your comments. To stay competitive, we *really* want you, as a computer book reader and user, to let us know what you like or dislike most about this book or other Que products.

You can mail comments, ideas, or suggestions for improving future editions to the address below, or send us a fax at (317) 581-4663. For the online inclined, Macmillan Computer Publishing now has a forum on CompuServe (type **GO QUEBOOKS** at any prompt) through which our staff and authors are available for questions and comments. The address of our Internet site is **http//:www.mcp.com** (World Wide Web).

In addition to exploring our forum, please feel free to contact me personally to discuss your opinions of this book. You can find me on CompuServe at **102121,1324** or on the Internet at **bmilstead@que.mcp.com**.

Thanks in advance—your comments will help us to continue publishing the best books available on computer topics in today's market.

Benjamin Milstead
Product Director
Que Corporation
201 W. 103rd Street
Indianapolis, Indiana 46290
USA

Introduction

The Common Gateway Interface, or CGI as it is commonly known, provides you with the means to deliver information that is rich, dynamic, and most importantly, interactive.

CGI is the muscle behind the World Wide Web. Using CGI, you can interact with visitors to your site. They can ask you questions, leave information for others who visit your site at a later date, or provide information from your organization's database. If the information in the database changes, your Web pages automatically change to reflect this new information. Where your pages previously were "static" or nonchanging, CGI enables you to present Web pages that constantly change—pages that are *dynamic*.

About *CGI by Example*

CGI by Example was written to provide you the means to learn as you read. Everything within this book is meant to be "hands-on." When reading through a chapter, or dealing with the scripts within this book, you should type each script yourself. This will help you get a feel for how each script works. It will also help you to remember how the script works, so that the next time you can do it on your own. We've found that the best way to learn how to create effective CGI scripts is by example.

The scripts within this book are just tools to help you learn how CGI works. After you have learned a script, feel free to modify it—adding a little here, removing a little there. This will help you understand what happens when you change something within a script. Also, consider each script as just an idea or a starting point. You can add on to each script, making it do precisely what you want or need it to do.

Who Should Use This Book?

This book is for anyone who wants to create more interactive or dynamic Web pages. If you have created a Web page and have been wondering how to make it more interesting, CGI is the next step.

CGI can help any Webmaster at any level, from the individual who wants to place a counter on his or her page, to the business that wants to provide information to everyone on the Internet or just to those within the organization.

You probably have seen counters on a Web page. Maybe you have visited a site that enables you to keep track of items selected, placing them into a virtual shopping cart. Perhaps you have visited a site that provides up-to-the-minute information on the current location of a package that you shipped. If you have ever wondered how all these features work, and how you can incorporate them into your Web pages, this book is for you.

What Do You Need To Write CGI Scripts?

Because so many different kinds of platforms host Web sites, the tools that you need to develop CGI applications vary. No matter which platform you use, however, you need three things to create CGI scripts:

♦ A Web server that has CGI. Fortunately, almost every Web server provides CGI, whether you are using an Amiga, Macintosh, Windows, or UNIX machine. Some of these servers are free, and others can be purchased from vendors or the company that created the server.

♦ A language in which to program. Web servers run on a variety of machines, so developers have created a means by which you can use almost every language to create CGI scripts. In this book, most of the scripts are in either Perl or C. Both of these languages are freely available for all the major operating systems. Other languages include Visual Basic, TCL, C++, the UNIX shell, and AppleScript. Just about every computer language available has been used to create CGI scripts.

♦ A connection to a network. The network can be connected only within an office or organization, or connected to the Internet. Of course, you could create CGI applications that are limited to a single computer, but that would defeat the purpose of CGI. After all, you want to provide information to a group of people or to the world.

What Do You Need To Know To Create CGI Scripts?

This book assumes that you already have a working knowledge of HyperText Markup Language (HTML) and generally how the Internet works.

You should also know how to program in any of the commonly available languages. Although we describe in detail how each script works, this book's purpose isn't to teach you how to program. Even so, we try to explain how a script performs a specific function. Using this information, you can effectively create scripts in any language.

How To Use This Book

This book is intended to be a tutorial on how to create CGI applications. The best way to learn from this book is to read each chapter, starting with Chapter 1. As you proceed through the book, type the example scripts and then execute them through your Web server. At the same time, feel free to move from one chapter to another, reading about a particular script and then trying it out.

Most chapters cover a specific task. The chapter explains how a script or program works, and then walks you through the script, describing what is being done at any given point. As you progress through each chapter, you see more of what you have learned being implemented as you explore new concepts.

After reading through the book, you'll want to keep it as a reference guide. You can refer to a section if you get stuck and need help figuring out how to accomplish a particular task. You can also find ideas for your own CGI scripts. We cover many topics not found in some of the other CGI books on the market.

Conventions Used in This Book

You might find that the same words used within the Internet can mean different things, and at times different words are used that mean the same thing. To avoid confusion, we try to use the same terminology whenever possible. Throughout this book, you will see the following terms:

♦ *Visitor.* This term refers to a user visiting your site.

♦ *Server.* This term refers to the Web server rather than the various other servers that might be running on your site.

♦ *Machine.* This term refers to the physical machine on which a program, script, or server is running.

♦ *Browser.* This term refers to the program that a visitor is using to view your Web documents. Within the Internet, you also see this program referred to as a *client.*

♦ *Scripts.* Although not all CGI scripts are actually "scripts," it is common to refer to them as such. This book refers to all CGI scripts as *scripts.* Any time you see the word *script,* you can assume that we are referring to any program that runs in the background preparing information for the visitor.

Being one of the largest publishers of computer-related books on the market, Macmillan Computer Publishing has developed a set of conventions that help make reading and learning easier. Throughout this book, we use the following conventions to make important points stand out:

♦ To introduce new terms or to emphasize a particular point, we use the *italic* typeface.

♦ Programming code and commands are presented in a `monospaced` font.

♦ When presenting syntax, we indicate parameters, placeholders, or variables by using `monospaced italics`.

♦ If you are required to type in text at a prompt, the text indicates that information in **boldface** type. Uniform Resource Locators (URLs) also appear in boldface.

Pseudocode

To explain code or concepts that might be difficult to grasp, we use *pseudocode*—an English-language description of what normally is represented in programming code. The icon in the margin alerts you when we are using pseudocode.

Overview

This book consists of eight parts. Each part covers a particular topic in detail.

Part I, "Introducing CGI"

The first part briefly introduces the World Wide Web, HyperText Transport Protocol (HTTP), HTML, and CGI.

Chapter 1, "The World Wide Web," explains how the Web emerged and how it works. You learn how a client and server communicate with each other. Chapter 2, "The Common Gateway Interface (CGI)," describes how the client, server, and the CGI script communicate with each other. It also covers various platform considerations, including some of the languages used for CGI scripting.

Part II, "Basic CGI Applications"

Part II covers HTML codes that you can use to create forms that enable your site's visitors to interact with your CGI scripts. You also see how to create a couple of simple CGI scripts that incorporate your knowledge of the form tags, and how to tie the scripts together.

Chapter 3, "Using Forms To Collect Input," deals with HTML forms. You learn about each form tag—where you can use each tag, and which tags are most useful under various circumstances. Chapter 4, "A Simple Guestbook," then shows you how to create an application that enables a visitor to your site to interact with past *and* future visitors. Chapter 5, "An Online Order Form," demonstrates how to create an order form that enables a visitor to order a product online.

Part III, "User Interaction"

Part III introduces more advanced scripts. These scripts demonstrate how you can control user-entered information, and how you can make your scripts react to certain circumstances.

Chapter 6, "Advanced Scripts," shows you how to trap and correct errors. You see examples demonstrating how to check the information that the visitor entered, to ensure your data's integrity or your script's proper execution. Chapter 7, "A More Complex Guestbook," expands on Chapter 6, incorporating this information with the guestbook script initially introduced in Chapter 4. Chapter 8, "A Shopping Cart Script," ties all this information together, demonstrating how you can create a shopping cart script that enables a visitor to your site to select items and have the script "remember" that information.

Part IV, "Database Connectivity"

Part IV deals with databases and how you can use various kinds of databases to store and retrieve information.

Chapter 9, "Collecting Information," explains how to collect information from the visitor and from the server, and how you can use this information to build statistics on your site and its visitors. Chapter 10, "Storing Information in Flat Files," discusses how you can save information that a visitor supplies within a text file, commonly referred to as a flat file. Chapter 11, "Storing Information in Databases," deals with dbm databases and how you can use them to store information, speeding up the storage and retrieval process. The chapter also introduces you to various relational databases and explains their benefits. Finally, Chapter 12, "Common Database Solutions," covers some common solutions for database problems. The chapter describes the Microsoft SQL Server and its use with the Microsoft Internet Information Server. Chapter 12 also introduces you to GSQL, a program that helps you create Web pages based on the information contained within a database. You then create a scheduling script that stores and retrieves information from one of the commonly available database programs.

Part V, "Web Indexing"

Part V covers indexing methods that enable a visitor to search your pages for information.

Chapter 13, "Introduction to Indexing," introduces you to various search mechanisms in use on the Internet. Chapter 14, "Indexing Your Own Site," goes into more detail, showing you how you can index your own site using FreeWAIS and SWISH.

Part VI, "Server Administration Issues"

Part VI provides information on how you can run your scripts on an Internet service provider (ISP), use Server-Side Includes (SSI), handle security issues, and more.

Chapter 15, "Enabling and Configuring Servers To Use CGI," shows you how you can activate your server to enable the use of CGI with most major Web servers. Chapter 16, "Server-Side Includes," explains the benefits of using SSI and the concerns that you should have. Chapter 17, "Security Issues," covers the security concerns that you should address for CGI scripts.

Part VII, "CGI Alternatives"

Part VII looks briefly at alternatives to CGI.

Chapter 18, "JavaScript," covers the JavaScript scripting language. You learn how to perform simple tasks with JavaScript, a language that you use within your HTML documents. Chapter 19, "Using PHP / FI," covers another language that you can use within an HTML document. Chapter 20, "Using Visual Basic," shows you how you can use Visual Basic scripts within your HTML documents.

Part VIII, "CGI Resources Online"

One way to learn about CGI is to look at how others have used it to create their scripts. Part VIII provides you with various Internet resources that might aid you in developing your CGI scripts.

Chapter 21, "Finding Help on the Internet Itself," covers the various places on the Internet in which you can find additional information on or help with CGI scripts. Chapter 22, "The Best CGI Collections on the Web," describes some of the best sites on the Internet to find good CGI scripts that are either freeware or shareware.

Glossary of Terms

The book includes a glossary of terms commonly associated with CGI and the World Wide Web.

Appendix A, "Answers to the Review Questions"

Most of the chapters in this book include review questions and exercises. Appendix A provides the answers to the review questions. If you get stuck on a particular question, look up the answer here. Then find where the chapter referenced the issue that the question addresses, to find out why it is important to know the answer.

Appendix B, "Contents of the CD-ROM"

The accompanying CD-ROM provides most of the scripts and programs that this book covers. Appendix B describes each script and program—what it accomplishes, the programming language in which it is written, and the platform on which it runs.

Entering the World of CGI Programming

Now you should be ready to enter the world of CGI programming. If you are interested in enlivening your Web documents, this book will show you how to do it, and provide you with the resources to turn your ideas into reality.

The World Wide Web is young and extremely exciting. To be a part of nurturing the Web in its infancy is a truly astounding opportunity. How the Web develops depends completely on the ideas of programmers who are introducing new concepts to the Web, and to the Internet in general. By the time you finish this book, you should have your own ideas on what you can do to make the World Wide Web even more interesting, and perhaps to make your mark on this new global information superhighway.

Part I

Introducing CGI

The World Wide Web

When you watch television or listen to the radio, the information that you get is one-way. You get only the information that the media want to give you—when they want to give it to you. Of course, you can always change the channel, an option that gives you a little more control over the content that you receive, but the conversation remains one-sided.

Originally, the World Wide Web (WWW) was much the same way. You received only information that others wanted you to see. The WWW simply offered many more channels. The Web added another feature that you couldn't get from radio or television: the ability to control when you receive the information, and the order in which you receive it. However, the problem of one-sided communication remained.

Soon Web pages began providing links that you could click, and if you had a browser that supported the mailto: anchor, you could send e-mail to the Web author or other individuals. Although this method of communication was arcane, it worked. For the first time, the Web surfer could provide feedback—day or night, seven days a week.

Then the Common Gateway Interface (CGI) emerged. CGI is simply a gateway between the Web server and your script. The CGI specification tells the server how to send information to a script, and what the server should do after receiving information from a script. Using CGI, Web authors could create scripts that enabled the user to provide feedback, even if the user lacked a browser or an e-mail address. Then authors could create scripts that enabled visitors to interact with people who had previously visited the pages. You could also interact with people who hadn't yet visited the page.

Now CGI seems to have become more powerful than anyone could have imagined. For example, some sites keep track of packages. From the moment that your package leaves your hands until it reaches its destination, you can track the package every step of the way. You can enter physical symptoms concerning an illness and get a response indicating the probable cause. You can even find out how many Pepsi cans are left in a machine down the hall in some building thousands of miles away.

Before you learn how CGI makes this possible, you first need to understand the World Wide Web and how it works.

Client/Server—Browsers and Servers

In 1989, Tim Berners-Lee, then working for the European Particle Physics Laboratory (CERN), devised a way in which you could access documents locally within a small network, or remotely, whether the information was across the street or across the ocean. His intention was to create a method by which people could share information on a global level.

Berners-Lee (also known as TBL) was also considering the use of hypertext and multimedia in this application. In October 1990, he began building the protocols and methods used for creating the first World Wide Web client and server. He had to develop a means by which to piece these hyperlinks and multimedia applications together. The requirements for this World Wide Web of information were as follows:

♦ Information had to be available remotely across networks. Transmission Control Protocol/Internet Protocol (TCP/IP), an existing protocol for retrieving information, was already commonly in use among universities and government organizations.

♦ People had to be able to access the same data no matter which platform they were using to access that data. The idea was to create an open system using the client/server model. By doing so, a Macintosh user could access the same data as a VAX user or a PC user.

♦ Information had to be accessible even if the data were stored on different machines at different locations. The larger an information base becomes, the more likely information is decentralized. Also, a series of hypertext links were necessary to make global, collaborative efforts possible.

♦ The hypertext system had to be capable of accessing currently available information. To minimize the need to convert documents, the client needed to be able to view existing documents where possible.

♦ Hypertext documents had to be capable of easily incorporating graphics, animations, and sound to enhance the documents' look and feel.

By December 1990, Berners-Lee had his hypertext protocol installed and in use for the first time at CERN. Later, his creation was finally introduced to the Internet community. Although his creation grew within the Internet community during the next few years, the Web didn't take off sprinting until late 1994—it hasn't slowed down since.

Many people believe that Berners-Lee's creation is the reason for the popularity of the Internet. Because UNIX was the Internet's backbone, the Internet was cumbersome to use. Although the Internet stored tons of information, accessing that information was difficult unless you had a good working knowledge of UNIX and the tools necessary for roaming the Internet. The Web changed all that. Now, with a simple mouse click, you could FTP files, browse information on a Gopher server, send e-mail, read the UseNet newsgroups, and view documents.

HTTP is merely the method by which the client and server—your browser and the Web server to which you are connected—talk to each other. To understand how CGI works, you first must understand how HTTP works. That means understanding how the client and the server communicate with each other.

As with any media, using HTTP requires an act of communication in which two or more parties share information among each other. Even your day-to-day contacts with other people involve this process of communication, through which everyone expresses his or her thoughts to someone else.

Suppose that a coworker at your office wants to talk with you. To begin that communication process, your coworker might give you a certain look or a greeting. At that point, your coworker has established a communication link. He or she makes a statement or a request, and then you reply. This method of communication continues until either you or your coworker closes it. Figure 1.1 illustrates these steps.

Figure 1.1

The communication process for HTTP is much like the process followed in any medium of communication.

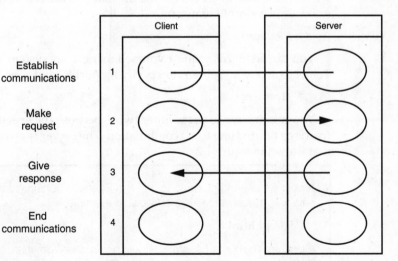

		Client	Server
Establish communications	1		
Make request	2		
Give response	3		
End communications	4		

HTTP tells the Web applications in use how this conversation is going to take place. Although this process can become a bit more complicated, HTTP usually uses the same four steps:

- ◆ Establish communications
- ◆ Make a request
- ◆ Give a response
- ◆ End communications

The Connection

The connection between the client (often called a browser, although it can be any entity that accesses your Web document, such as a Web robot) and the server starts when the client makes a request to the port on which the server resides. Usually this is port 80 (the default) or port 8000 if the server cannot be started under root, using a Transmission Control Protocol (TCP) connection, but it can be any port that the server administrator specifies.

The Request

After the connection is established, the client sends to the server either a full or simple request for information.

A simple request is simply the *method* that you are using and the Request-URI, which is the path and name of the file that you are requesting. The following is an example of a simple request:

```
GET /cgi.html
```

You can send this request yourself using your system's Telnet command. Use Telnet to access a Web server specifying port 80 and type the following request:

```
GET /index.html
```

You might have to press Enter twice, because the specification requires a CrLf (carriage return/line feed) combination. The server returns output that resembles that shown in figure 1.2.

> **Note:** A Uniform Resource Identifier (URI), as it pertains to the Web, is simply a path to a document, as in the following example:
>
> **/cgi/cgi.html**
>
> A Uniform Resource Locator (URL) is part of the Web, in that it not only points to the URI, but specifies the protocol (such as HTTP, FTP, or Gopher) and the document's location. The following is an example of a URL:
>
> **http://www.selah.net/cgi.html**

Figure 1.2

Sample output
from a simple
request made
through a Telnet
session.

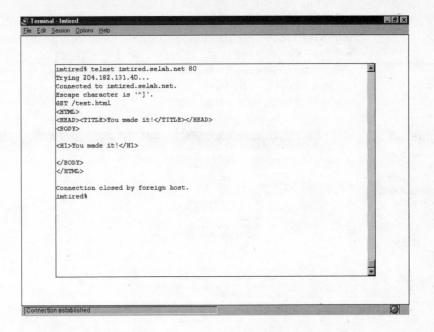

```
imtired% telnet imtired.selah.net 80
Trying 204.182.131.40...
Connected to imtired.selah.net.
Escape character is '^]'.
GET /test.html
<HTML>
<HEAD><TITLE>You made it!</TITLE></HEAD>
<BODY>

<H1>You made it!</H1>

</BODY>
</HTML>

Connection closed by foreign host.
imtired%
```

A full request is a complete request that tells the server not only the method and requested URI, but also the HTTP version being used. To format a full request, you use the following syntax:

METHOD / Request-URI HTTP/version/ CrLf

The following is an example of a full request:

GET /test.html HTTP/1.0

GET is the only method that can use the simple request. Any other method must use a full request. In HTTP, you commonly use three methods:

♦ The GET method. Normally you use this request method to issue a request for a Web page. GET simply tells the server to return the requested information to the client.

♦ The HEAD method. This method is useful because it returns to the client only the header information. You can use this method to determine whether a page has been updated before you have the client take the time to request the full document.

♦ The POST method. This method tells the server that it is to send information to the URI as a subprocess of that URI, without any interpretation by the server. This method is often used with HTML forms.

Various clients and servers can use other methods, but these three methods within the HTTP specification are the ones most commonly used. The only method that a server must use is GET. If the server doesn't support a requested method, the server returns an error code of 400, which indicates a bad request, along with a brief explanation as to why the server considered the request bad. Figure 1.3 shows an example of such an explanation.

Figure 1.3

If a server doesn't support a requested method, the server should provide a brief note explaining why it doesn't.

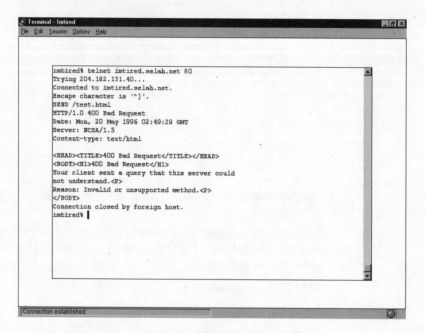

The next portion of the request consists of the request fields. These fields provide the server with information about the client, or about a query (if, for example, the visitor submitted a form). The most common request fields are Referrer, User-Agent, and Accept.

The *Referrer* Field

The Referrer field tells the server which site and document provided a link to your document. This tool is useful in helping you to determine who is providing links to one or more of your pages. When using a CGI script, you can call this field by using the environmental variable HTTP_REFERRER. Chapter 2, "The Common Gateway Interface (CGI)," covers additional environmental variables that you can use in your scripts.

The *User-Agent* Field

The User-Agent field indicates which client a visitor is using. The field usually has the following format:

```
User-Agent: client/version, library/version
```

The following is an example of the User-Agent field:

```
User-Agent: Mosaic/1.1, libwww/1.0
```

This field isn't specific to Web browsers. Web spiders and robots also send the server a User-Agent field.

The *Accept* Field

The Accept field tells the server which Multipurpose Internet Multimedia Extensions (MIME) the client is willing to accept. Every browser is supposed to be capable of handling text/plain and text/html, but a browser can also supply others. The following line demonstrates the use of the Accept field:

```
Accept: image/gif, image/x-bitmap, image/jpeg, */*
```

In this instance, the Accept field tells the server that the client is willing to accept .GIFs, bitmap images, and JPEG images. */* indicates that if none of the specified MIME extensions is available, the server should send any extensions.

The Response

The response consists of four parts:

♦ The status line

♦ The response header fields

♦ The entity type

♦ The entity body

The status line tells the client the status of the client's request. The line consists of the HTTP protocol's version, the document's status code, and a brief explanation of the status code. The status line's format is as follows:

```
HTTP-version CODE CODE-description
```

The following is an example of a status line:

```
HTTP/1.0 200 OK
```

Table 1.1 lists all the available status codes.

Table 1.1   Response status codes and their descriptions

Status Code	Description
200	OK
201	Created
202	Accepted
204	No content
300	Multiple choices
301	Moved permanently
302	Moved temporarily
304	Not modified
400	Bad request
401	Unauthorized
403	Forbidden
404	Not found
500	Internal server error
501	Not implemented
502	Bad gateway
503	Service unavailable

You can change the description for any error code if the server configuration files allow such changes. However, the meaning of the code remains the same. The codes that you will most likely encounter when writing CGI scripts are 200 (everything is OK), 204 if you did not provide any information back to the client, and error 500 (internal server error). You get an error code 500 if you write a script that does not return the Content-type to the server before the rest of the body.

The response header fields give the client additional information about the server that you cannot place within the status line. The Date and Server information shown in figure 1.4 are just a couple of examples.

Figure 1.4

Each response must have a status line; the rest of the response depends on the requested information.

Response header fields

Entity type

Entity body

Status line

```
imtired% telnet imtired.selah.net 80
Trying 204.182.131.40...
Connected to imtired.selah.net.
Escape character is '^]'.
GET /test.html HTTP/1.0
HTTP/1.0 200 Document follows
Date: Mon, 20 May 1996 21:01:43 GMT
Server: NCSA/1.5
Content-type: text/html

<HTML>
<HEAD><TITLE>You made it!</TITLE></HEAD>
<BODY>

<H1>You made it!</H1>

</BODY>
</HTML>

Connection closed by foreign host.
imtired%
```

The entity type is simply a MIME type, which specifies the type of file being sent. For an HTML document, you would see the following entity type:

```
Content-type: text/html
```

If you were sending a .GIF image, the Content-type would be image/gif. Other common MIME types include the following:

MIME Type	Description
audio/basic	Covers sound files ending with au or snd
audio/x-wav	Covers .WAV files
image/jpeg	Sends JPEG images
image/tiff	Sends TIFF images
image/x-xbitmap	Sends X Window bitmapped images
video/mpeg	Sends MPEG videos
video/quicktime	Sends QuickTime vidoes
text/plain	Sends plain ASCII text documents

If you are using the NCSA server, you can take a look at the file MIME types located in the server root's CONF directory.

The entity body consists of the requested information, whether it is an HTML document, an image, or any other type of file.

The Closure

Finally, the connection closes. Either party can close the connection at any time, but it is usually terminated when the requested information has been transmitted to the client.

When the request is for an HTML document, the document most likely includes images and other bits and pieces. If so, the entire communication process starts all over again, until the client finally retrieves everything within the document.

The HyperText Markup Language

The HyperText Markup Language (HTML) in use on the Web today describes a document's logical structure and attributes rather than the method by which the document is to be processed.

An HTML document consists mainly of two parts: the <HEAD> and the <BODY>. The HTML Document Type Definition (DTD) specifies what each part is supposed to contain. You don't put the <H1> tag inside the <HEAD>, and you don't place a <TITLE> tag inside the <BODY>.

HTML doesn't describe how to display a particular tag on your screen, but only the tag's purpose for being on the screen. For example, you use the <EM> tag on text that you want to emphasize. HTML does not specify whether that emphasis is to be conveyed with boldface, italics, or any other method. Instead, HTML lets the software that is reading the HTML document—such as your browser—determine how to emphasize the text. For this reason, HTML documents do not have to be system- or application-specific.

HTML derives from the Standard Generalized Markup Language (SGML). Dr. Charles F. Goldfarb originated the SGML standard in the early 1980s at IBM.

The Standard Generalized Markup Language

Most word processors mark up text to give documents a certain look and feel. SGML was originally meant to be a standard that everyone could use, but as Goldfarb attempted to add each variance of typesetting into the standard, problems arose. For this reason, Goldfarb ultimately developed SGML as a language that enabled its users to create another language specific to their work. HTML is an example of such a language.

SGML provides several benefits:

◆ *SGML is application-independent.* This independence makes it possible to view an HTML document using Lynx, Mosaic, or Netscape, or a typical word processor such as WordPerfect 6.0.

◆ *SGML is nonproprietary.* You can use the language on any platform. Any computer can display an HTML document, whether its platform is Windows, Amiga, Macintosh, or any flavor of UNIX.

♦ *SGML defines only the logical structure of a document.* The standard specifies the elements, the contents within a delimiter (< >, for example), as well as entities, bullets, special characters, and so on. The HTML tags <BODY>, <EM>, and <LI> are examples of the elements. SGML also describes where you can use each element within a document. Here's an example of SGML's use in HTML:

```
<HTML>

<HEAD>
<TITLE>Smitget's Gum Factory News</TITLE>
</HEAD>

<BODY>
<H1> Smitget's Gum Factory News v1.01</H1>
<UL>
<LI> Increase of gum found under tables</LI>
<LI> How to deal with sidewalk gum on hot days</LI>
</UL>
</BODY>

</HTML>
```

♦ *SGML is general, not procedural.* The preceding example lists the listed item (<LI>) with SGML. The standard doesn't specify how the document displays the list. It just knows that the list is an unordered list as specified by the <UL> tag. One browser might display the list by using bullets, while another might use a dash.

♦ *SGML is descriptive.* The tags are descriptive and understandable by humans as well as computers. Any person should easily guess what the following section should be:

```
<TITLE>Smitget's Gum Factory News</TITLE>
```

The International Standards Organization (ISO) has adopted SGML, making it an international standard (ISO-8879), which is the highest and most stringent level of standardization.

Two good sources for additional information are available. You can find the SGML primer at the following address:

http://www.sq.com/sgmlinfo/primbody.html

You can find an introduction to SGML at the following address:

http://www.brainlink.com/~ben/sgml/

The Current Version of HTML

Although this book's purpose isn't to show you how to develop HTML documents, you need to know what is happening with the HTML specification.

After Tim Berners-Lee wrote the original HTML specification, Dan Connolly, working with TBL, later revised and submitted the specification as a working draft. They received input from others on the mailing list **www-talk**, and used that input to continue revising and improving the HTML specification by adding elements and removing unused sections.

The HTML specification is constantly being revised as people continue to push the specification's current limits. The current version of HTML is 2.0 (RFC 1866), which you can find at the following address:

ftp://ds.internic.net/rfc/rfc1866.txt

HTML DTD 2.0 provides tools that manipulate text better and handle such graphics as forms, imagemaps, and meta information. The specification also introduces the line break tag, <BR>.

The Mozilla DTD

Netscape Communications Corporation expanded the HTML 2.0 specifications considerably. While the Internet Engineering Task Force (IETF) was proposing the level 3 DTD for HTML, Netscape promoted its Mozilla DTD to the public. This DTD extends the existing HTML standard to provide even better text and graphics handling for Web pages.

The Mozilla DTD expands HTML's existing elements as follows:

◆ Its <BODY> element enables you to add colors and graphics to a page's background

◆ Its <HR> element enables you to set the horizontal rule's width and length

The Mozilla DTD also adds several new elements:

◆ The <CENTER> element, which centers text and graphics within an HTML document

◆ The capability to right- or left-align pictures

◆ The use of tables

◆ The <FONT> element, which specifies color and relative size

◆ The capability to create frames within an HTML document

Although Netscape wasn't the only organization to develop a variance of the official standard, its DTD has become the most popular. Other organizations building Web browsers found themselves trying to incorporate the Mozilla DTD into their clients.

HTML 3.2

Netscape's efforts paid off. On May 7, 1996, World Wide Web Consortium (W3C), Institut National de Recherche en Informatique et Automatique (INRIA), Netscape, IBM, Microsoft, Sun, Novell, and other interested parties agreed on a proposal for HTML 3.2, named Wilbur. The proposal included most of the additions that Netscape had already incorporated into its DTD. Here are some of HTML DTD 3.2's features:

- Additions to the `<HEAD>` tag, including `<STYLE>` and `<SCRIPT>` elements

- Additions to the `<BODY>` element, including `BACKGROUND`, `BGCOLOR`, `VLINK`, and `ALINK`

- Additions to the block- and text-level elements, including the capability to align the `<HEADING>`, `<P>`, `<HR>`, and `<DIV>` (document division) elements

- The capability to assign values to `<LI>` elements

- The `<APPLET>` `element`, which enables you to embed Java applets into HTML documents

- The `<FONT>` element, which enables you to control a font's color and size

- The `<MAP>` element, which makes client-side imagemaps possible

Summary

By now you should understand a little about the history of the World Wide Web, and how HTTP and HTML make the WWW work. HTTP is the method that enables the client and the server to communicate, and HTML is the language that enables you to communicate your thoughts to others around the world. Although the Web is still in its infancy, it is growing up at an incredible rate. A difficult decision for the Web developer is which DTD to follow. A bad choice can send you back to the drawing board and force you to revise your Web documents and CGI scripts.

When developing your CGI applications, keep the information from this chapter in mind. This information can help you create scripts that work properly and are pleasing to the visitor.

Review Questions

1. What are the four basic steps of communication and how do they relate to the HTTP protocol?

2. What is the default port for HTTP connections?

3. Name three of the most common methods that you use when requesting information from a server.

4. What is a Uniform Resource Locator?

5. Describe a typical situation in which you would use the POST method to request a document.

6. If possible, use Telnet to connect to a Web server and use the request method SEND. What happens? Why?

7. What comprises the HTTP response?

8. What is the current official HTML DTD?

## CHAPTER 2

The Common Gateway Interface (CGI)

The Common Gateway Interface (CGI) is simply a method by which the server interacts with external scripts or programs. The interface is precisely what it is called: a gateway. It receives the information from the server and creates a child process that handles or stores this information for the CGI script.

CGI enables you to add applications to your Web pages so that visitors to your site can interact with your Web pages, retrieve real-time data, communicate with other individuals, and more. If the HyperText Transport Protocol (HTTP) and HyperText Markup Language (HTML) are the backbone of the World Wide Web, CGI is the muscle.

With CGI, you can provide a method by which visitors to your site can access your databases, store information, and execute external programs (such as sendmail and archie). CGI helps you transform your Web pages from simply providing static information to supplying real-time or dynamic information.

Without CGI, you could only place pages on the Web for readers to read. The only changes to those pages would be those that you had to do by hand, tediously writing and rewriting every sentence and HTML code, just to keep the information current. However, with CGI, you can create a script that interfaces with a database and displays that information to the user in an ever-changing state—and that is only one small example of how CGI can help you or your organization.

To take advantage of these benefits, however, you first need to know how CGI works with the client and the server, which is the subject of this chapter.

How CGI Works

Depending on the method that the client requests, the server gathers the information provided by the client and then sends that information to the CGI script. The CGI script then processes the information and returns the result to the server. Then the server parses the information and sends the result to the client. Figure 2.1 illustrates how this process works.

Figure 2.1

The interaction among the client, server, and the CGI script.

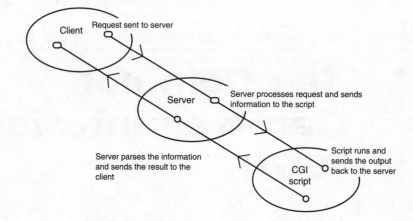

The client can call a script using either the GET, POST, or HEAD method. The way in which the information is presented to the script depends on the method that you use. This section covers the methods GET and POST in more detail, because they pertain to CGI scripts more than the HEAD method does.

Environmental Variables

When you make a request or call a CGI script, your client as well as the server stores certain pieces of information into environmental variables. Either the server or your scripts can use these variables. Later, this chapter discusses some of the things that you can do with these environmental variables, but this section provides a brief overview to give you an idea of the purpose of each variable.

There are three types of environmental variables: server information, client information, and script information.

Server Information Variables

The server provides information about itself that you can use within your scripts. This information includes the server software and the version of the software used, the server name, the server protocol and the protocol's version, the server port, and the gateway interface.

Although some of the information about the server might not be useful in most circumstances, you will most likely find yourself using this information at some point.

The *SERVER_SOFTWARE* Variable
The SERVER_SOFTWARE variable simply states the server software's name and version. For example, you might see this variable set as NCSA/1.5.

The *SERVER_NAME* Variable
The SERVER_NAME variable states the name of the server to which you are connecting. This name usually is a full domain name, but can also be the IP address. Examples include **hoohoo.ncsa.uiuc.edu** or **www.in-command.com**.

This information can be quite useful if you are hosting virtual Web sites. Suppose that your site is hosting Web pages for **www.foo.com** and **www.bar.com**. You could create a script that reacts differently depending on the server name used. The following should give you an idea of how to do so.

*Is the server_name **www.foo.com**?*

*If so, display the message "Welcome to **www.foo.com**."*

Is the SERVER_NAME ***www.bar.com**?*

*If so, display the message "Welcome to **www.bar.com**."*

Although this example is very simple, it should give you an idea of how you could use this variable within your scripts.

The *GATEWAY_INTERFACE* Variable
The GATEWAY_INTERFACE variable holds the CGI interface's name and version. CGI/1.1 is the latest version that most UNIX Web servers use.

The *SERVER_PROTOCOL* Variable
The SERVER_PROTOCOL variable shows the server's protocol and version. An example is HTTP/1.0.

The *SERVER_PORT* Variable
The SERVER_PORT variable holds the port on which the server is running. The default setting is port 80, but it can be any port that the server administrator specifies.

Client Information Variables
Along with the server, the client also provides information about itself. The client variables can provide you with information about a visitor to your site, the Web

browser that he or she is using, and where the visitor is from. This information might include the Internet Protocol (IP) address that the visitor is using, the domain name of the site that the visitor is on, the username that the visitor entered if the accessed page is password protected, and possibly the visitor's username. This section looks briefly at some of the information available about the client.

The *REMOTE_HOST* Variable

The REMOTE_HOST variable holds the full domain name of the client requesting access to the server. An example setting is **sheala.itm.com**. If the server doesn't receive the domain name, this variable is set as NULL.

> **Note:** In general programming lingo, NULL means nothing. If a string or variable has a length of zero (0), it is NULL.

The *REMOTE_IP* Variable

The REMOTE_IP variable holds the IP address of the client requesting access to the server. An example of an IP address is **204.182.131.40**.

The *REMOTE_USER* Variable

If a document is protected, the REMOTE_USER variable displays the username that visitors use when the Username and Password Required dialog box prompts them to enter to gain access to a protected area (see fig. 2.2).

Figure 2.2

The username that the visitor enters into the Username and Password Required dialog box passes to the CGI script.

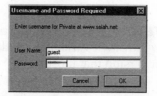

The *REMOTE_IDENT* Variable

The REMOTE_IDENT variable contains the username used by the visitor on the remote host. To retrieve this information, you must configure the server to do so. Because of delayed delivery times and server overhead, activating the server to request the visitor's identity is rarely done. Also, an ident daemon must be running on the system from which the visitor is making the request.

> **Note:** Although the server can log the username provided by an ident daemon—and that username would most likely be correct—you should use this username for informational purposes only. With knowledge and resources, someone can easily falsify the information returned by an ident daemon.

The *HTTP_***** Variable

The HTTP_**** variable holds extra information that the client provides as part of the HTTP protocol. **** represents the actual request header fields sent by the client.

Here are some examples of request header fields with the HTTP_ prefix:

HTTP_USER_AGENT	The name and version of the client software. Examples include Mozilla/2.01 and wwwlib/.011.
HTTP_REFERER	The URL that contains a link to the file being requested on your server.
HTTP_ACCEPT	The accept parameters sent by the client. Examples include image/gif and image/jpeg. (See Chapter 1, "The World Wide Web," for more information on the Accept field.)

Script Information Variables

Variables also hold information about your form and the script. For example, your form contains information that the server receives. The server places this information into environmental variables, which makes it easy for your CGI scripts to use the information. A few of the more common variables are QUERY_STRING (which contains the information that the visitor entered), CONTENT_TYPE (which tells the server what kind of information it is receiving), and CONTENT_LENGTH (which specifies the length of the information entered by the user). This section explores each of these and other script information variables.

The *REQUEST_METHOD* Variable

The REQUEST_METHOD variable contains information that the client is using to request information. The information includes the method specified within the form that you create. In the following example, the REQUEST_METHOD variable contains the value POST:

```
<FORM ACTION="/cgi-bin/test-cgi" METHOD="POST">
```

You can use quite a few methods to request information from the server. GET, POST, PUT, and HEAD are a few. CGI supports only GET, POST, and in rare instances, HEAD.

The *PATH_INFO* Variable

If the Uniform Resource Indicator (URI) provides additional path information, the PATH_INFO variable holds that information. For example, if **http://www.selah.net/cgi-bin/web-sql/cgi/cgi.html** is the URI request, PATH_INFO's setting is **cgi/cgi.html**.

The *PATH_TRANSLATED* Variable

The PATH_TRANSLATED variable holds the actual path to the PATH_INFO. For the example cited in the last section, the path is **/usr/local/etc/httpd/htdocs/cgi/cgi.html**.

The *SCRIPT_NAME* Variable

The SCRIPT_NAME environmental variable holds the name of the CGI script that the client calls within the URI.

The *QUERY_STRING* Variable

The QUERY_STRING environmental variable holds information about the query if the GET method was used. If the URI requested was **/cgi-bin/cgi.pl?name=John+Doe**, the query string is the information located after the question mark (?). The plus sign (+) identifies a space (commonly called a *whitespace*).

The *CONTENT_TYPE* Variable

If a form using the POST method sends a request to the server, the CONTENT_TYPE variable contains the following value:

application/x-www-form-urlencoded

Otherwise, the CONTENT_TYPE variable is usually set to NULL.

The *CONTENT_LENGTH* Variable

The CONTENT_LENGTH variable holds the query's actual length, which the POST method uses. Make sure that your script does not read STDIN more than the length provided within the CONTENT_LENGTH environmental variable; otherwise, your script continues to read data that has nothing to do with your script or the information entered by the visitor, and thus corrupts the input.

The *DOCUMENT_URI* Variable

The DOCUMENT_URI variable holds the document's path and name. For example, if the URL is **http://www.selah.net/cgi-bin/cgi.pl**, the DOCUMENT_URI would be **/cgi-bin/cgi.pl**.

You can use this variable within your scripts if you need information from the server, the client, or the script itself. Likewise, if you want to put together a log file (which is a good idea if you don't have access to the server's logs), you could easily do so using only the environmental variable. Listing 2.1 shows a short "hello" script.

Listing 2.1   HELLO.PL—a Small Hello Script

```
#! /usr/bin/perl
print "Content-type: text/plain \n\n";
if($ENV{'REMOTE_HOST'}) {
  print "Hello user from $ENV{'REMOTE_HOST'}!<br> \n";
  }
print "Your IP is: $ENV{'REMOTE_IP'} \n";
print "This page is $ENV{'DOCUMENT_URI'}, \n";
print "which was referred by, $ENV{'HTTP_REFERER'} \n";
exit;
```

Occasionally some of the fields might be empty because the client is not required to send this information to the server. The client sends HTTP_REFERER only if the previous site or document that the visitor was on had a link to your site. You might add some error checking to check whether some of the environmental variables are empty; if they are, react appropriately as in the preceding example: Use the if statement to check REMOTE_HOST's contents.

This script simply outputs the information provided from visitors and returns it so that they can view it. You can also send the information to a file, as shown in listing 2.2.

> **Note:** You must call the following script with the `<!--#exec cgi=""-->` tag. You also must activate Server-Side Includes (SSIs) for the directory in which the script resides. Also, there are some precautions that you might want to take when enabling or using SSI. See Chapter 16, "Server-Side Includes," for more information about SSI.

Listing 2.2   LOG.PL—Sending Access Information to a Log File

```
#!/usr/bin/perl
print "Content-type: text/plain \n\n";
open ( LOG, ">>access.log") || die "Can't open log file";
print LOG "Remote Host: $ENV{'REMOTE_HOST'} \n";
print LOG "Remote IP  : $ENV{'REMOTE_IP'} \n";
print LOG "Page Requested: $ENV{'DOCUMENT_URI'} \n";
print LOG "Referred from: $ENV{'HTTP_REFERER'} \n";
print LOG "\n";
exit;
```

This simple log takes the information from the environmental variables and stores it in the file ACCESS.LOG. You can, of course, add more information, such as the date, or any other environmental variables. The USER_AGENT variable might be a good addition to keep track of the most popular browsers hitting your site.

The Command Line

Only a query using the <ISINDEX> attribute can use the command line. When using the <ISINDEX> tag without an equal sign (=) within the query string, the server enables you to send the query to a system command and have the results returned to you. Note the following example:

http://hoohoo.ncsa.uiuc.edu/cgi-bin/finger

The server checks the QUERY_STRING environmental variable to see whether an equal sign exists. If the equal sign does exist, the server disallows the command-line query and sends the visitor the default query form.

When you use the command line, the query passes to the command line with argv (argument value) and argc (argument count). For example, suppose that you pass the following URI to the server:

/cgi-bin/find?john+doe

The server splits this string at the plus sign (+) and assigns the arrays argc as 2 and argv as john doe. The line then executes as follows:

```
find john doe
```

When the HTTP specification was written, this method was considered safe. Since then, a few problems have been found—namely, the ability to gain root access to your site. You should use the method only if necessary.

STDIN and *STDOUT*

Every program has STDIN (standard in) and STDOUT (standard out). Suppose that you enter the following on a UNIX system:

```
% ls ¦ more
```

ls sends its STDOUT to the STDIN of more, which displays its STDOUT to the screen. The following is an MS-DOS example:

```
type config.sys ¦ more
```

In this example, the type command sends the contents of its STDOUT to more, which then processes the contents and sends its STDOUT to the screen.

CGI's STDIN is the server's STDOUT. The CGI program processes the information and sends the results to STDOUT. The server receives the results through its STDIN and sends the results to the client through its STDOUT. If this sounds confusing, examine figure 2.3.

The method POST, which this chapter discusses in detail later, uses STDIN and STDOUT, but the method GET gets its query information from the environmental variable QUERY_STRING, unless the query is an <ISINDEX>.

Figure 2.3

Notice the flow of traffic between the script and the server.

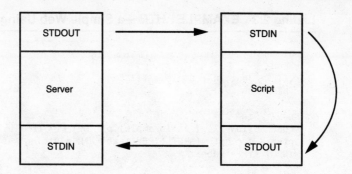

The *GET* Method

The GET method is best used when you are doing simple queries in which the query string consists of less than 255 characters. When you use the GET method, you place the query string into the environmental variable QUERY_STRING. An environmental variable has a limit of 255 characters, including spaces.

The server knows that anything after the first question mark (?) is the query string. Using that information, the server creates an environmental variable QUERY_STRING and places the query into the variable. For example, examine the following line:

```
http://www.cgistuff.com/cgi-bin/test.cgi?This+is+a+test.
```

The client breaks this query into various parts and places the string following the question mark, This+is+a+test, into the QUERY_STRING variable.

The *POST* Method

The method POST can also use the environmental variables, but the method sends most information to a CGI script through STDIN and STDOUT.

After receiving information from a visitor using a form that uses the POST method, the server spools the information to the server's STDOUT, which is the CGI script's STDIN. The script then must decode and process the information, and then send the result to STDOUT. Listing 2.3 shows a form using the method POST.

Listing 2.3   EXAMPLE1.HTM—a Simple Web Using the Method *POST*

```
<HTML>
<HEAD>
<TITLE> Just an example </TITLE>
</HEAD>

<BODY>
<FORM ACTION="/cgi-bin/example1.pl" METHOD="POST">
Enter a string: <INPUT TYPE="text" NAME="string"><p>
<INPUT TYPE="submit">
</FORM>
</BODY>

</HTML>
```

This code creates a form that looks like that shown in figure 2.4. If you enter **This is a test** on the input line, the server receives that information and then sends the string to the script's STDIN. The script is responsible for checking the CONTENT_LENGTH and receiving the information from STDIN, depending on the size of the CONTENT_LENGTH environmental variable.

Figure 2.4

A short form that sends the entered string to a script.

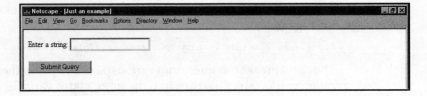

When receiving information from STDIN, the information is basically one big glob containing the information that the visitor entered. Your script must split the information that it received from STDIN into key and value pairs, making it easier to handle the visitor-provided data.

Listing 2.4 shows an example of a CGI script that processes the information from STDIN and then displays the query to the user.

Listing 2.4   EXAMPLE1.PL—a Simple Script That Uses the Method *POST*

```
#!/usr/bin/perl

# example1.pl

if ($ENV{'REQUEST_METHOD'} eq 'POST')
{
 read(STDIN, $buffer, $ENV{'CONTENT_LENGTH'});
 @pairs = split(/&/, $buffer);
 foreach $pair (@pairs)
```

```
  {
    ($name, $value) = split(/=/, $pair);
    $value =~ tr/+/ /;
    $value =~ s/%([a-fA-F0-9][a=fA-F0-9])/pack("C", hex($1))/eg;
    $form{$name} = $value;
  }
}

print "Content-type: text/html\n\n";
print "<HTML>";
print "<HEAD>";
print "<TITLE>Results from Example 1 </TITLE>";
print "</HEAD>";
print "<BODY>";
print "<H1> Example 1 results </H1>";
print "This is the string that you entered, \"$form{'string'}\" ";
print "</BODY>";
print "</HTML>";

exit;
```

First, EXAMPLE1.PL checks to ensure that REQUEST_METHOD is the method POST. Next the script reads STDIN with the size CONTENT_LENGTH. The EXAMPLE1.PL script then checks whether more than one name/value pair exists; if so, the script splits them. Finally, EXAMPLE1.PL assigns each name/value pair to a string, which the script then prints and returns to the server, which in turn sends the result to the visitor's browser.

The POST method is the most frequently used method in CGI programming. The method doesn't have the limitations of the GET method.

Languages Used for CGI Scripts

You can use any programming language to write CGI scripts. What you decide to use depends completely on the application that you are building and the programming languages that you have available. This section takes a quick look at some of the most common languages used to create CGI applications and explains some of the benefits of each.

Perl

The Practical Extraction and Report Language (Perl) is undoubtedly the best language overall to use for creating CGI scripts. The Perl syntax is easy to learn and follow, making it easier to learn than C, Tcl, or many of the other languages available. The Internet has many examples demonstrating various ways to use Perl to develop CGI scripts. Larry Wall originally created Perl to handle data and create reports. After some additional development, Perl has become a full-blown language. It's available for UNIX, Windows NT, Windows 95, OS2/Warp, and VMS, as well as the Macintosh and the Amiga. If you have already searched the Internet for CGI scripts, you probably have encountered quite a few scripts written in Perl.

You can find Perl on just about any FTP server as well as from any of the Web search engines, but check out the UseNet newsgroup **comp.lang.perl** or visit the Perl Web site at **http://www.perl.com/perl/**.

C

Probably the most used programming language, C has found its niche in the CGI market. C is much harder to learn than Perl, but C programs run faster than Perl programs, and the C language is flexible enough to enable you to do just about anything. One of C's disadvantages is that C code is hard to debug. To make any changes to a C program, you have to have the source code and then recompile it. Changes to a script that are normally quick and simple to make can become a hassle in a C program.

UNIX Shells

UNIX shells provide a way to create quick, simple CGI scripts. Of course, you could create extremely complicated scripts with a shell, but you might find yourself pulling out all your hair before you even finish your project. However, shells can be extremely efficient for writing small scripts. UNIX shells enable you to use system commands to process information from a query, which makes creating scripts easy if you are already familiar with UNIX.

Various shells are available on UNIX systems. Four of the most popular shells are `sh`, `csh`, `bash`, and `tcsh`.

Tcl

The Tool Command Language (Tcl, pronounced *tickle*) is available for MS-DOS and Macintosh as well as UNIX. The language is easy to learn if you're familiar with C, because Tcl's syntax is similar to C's. Tcl is still in its infancy as far as CGI scripts are concerned, but its popularity is growing. Tcl isn't very portable, because it can use direct system calls, which are machine-specific.

Visual Basic

Visual Basic is an excellent language for creating CGI applications. The language is easy to learn, making it a good choice for new programmers. Although still a newcomer in the CGI world, Visual Basic is starting to make its mark as increasingly more Windows NT and Windows 95 Web servers are introduced on the Internet. Visual Basic is a BASIC programming language that can be compiled. Although not as fast as a binary compiled with C, Visual Basic does have an enormous advantage in that it is quite popular with Microsoft operating systems. The disadvantage is that only Microsoft operating systems can run Visual Basic scripts. If you are running Web servers on a Microsoft system, Visual Basic is a good language to consider for developing CGI scripts.

Other Languages To Consider

Although this section has discussed the most popular languages for CGI scripts, others are starting to gain notice.

Sun Microsystems' Java is one. Java enables you to create small applications called applets. A browser receives the applets as binaries and handles their execution. The fact that the browser must handle execution causes problems, because most browsers currently do not handle Java. Fortunately, however, the most widely used browser, Netscape, does.

> **Note:** Also, Java still poses major security concerns. Because an applet is a small program that transfers to the client and runs on the client side, clients leave themselves wide open to attacks. No wonder Netscape lists the option to turn Java on or off as a security option.

C++ is another language that you can use for CGI scripts. C++ is an object-oriented programming language. You can use parts of C++ source code with other parts to make development a little easier and less redundant.

AppleScript is a great language for building CGI scripts for Macintosh-based Web servers. The language is quite easy to understand and powerful for smaller applications. AppleScript can also communicate with existing Macintosh programs, like the finder. This capability gives you even more flexibility when writing CGI scripts.

The Future of CGI

The current CGI specification has a few inherent problems. Because a CGI script spawns as a separate process under a Web server, sites with much traffic can have considerable overhead. Although CGI is the strongest method for running external applications with a Web server, a few aspects of CGI could be improved.

A few groups have started writing different application programming interfaces (APIs) and are trying to create solutions that reduce some of the overhead:

♦ *FastCGI* is a promising alternative to CGI. Created by Open Market, FastCGI provides a way to increase the speed at which a server communicates with external programs, and reduces the server's load when performing CGI operations. FastCGI is language-independent, so you can use any existing language with it. Like CGI, FastCGI runs applications separate from the Web server, and thus is server-independent. Designed to enable its applications to run on a foreign system, FastCGI frees the server's system to concentrate on HTTP requests and perform authentication and authorization checks.

For more information on FastCGI, visit the following site:

http://www.fastcgi.com

◆ The *ILU Requestor* was designed to solve the same problems of the existing CGI's high load and slow response times, especially on busy servers. The ILU Requestor is not language-specific, but portable and fast.

For more information on the ILU Requestor, visit the following address:

http://www.w3.org/hypertext/WWW/TR/WD-ilu-requestor

◆ *Internet Server Application Programming Interface (ISAPI),* developed by Process Software and Microsoft, is a promising candidate to replace CGI at least for servers running on Windows-based machines. ISAPI is based on the idea of using dynamic link libraries (DLLs), making back-end applications quicker. ISAPI has Microsoft's backing, which will help this API get running.

For more information on ISAPI, visit the following site:

http://www.process.com/news/spec.htp

Various other APIs exist, including one for Netscape's servers, the Apache server, and Spry's server. Each of these APIs makes back-end applications quicker and reduces the system's load. The problem is that the APIs are system- and server-dependent, which makes porting their programs difficult.

It's hard to anticipate whether a viable replacement for CGI will ever be developed. For now, the existing CGI standard will have to do. It's tested and true, and more versatile than any other alternative.

Summary

In this chapter, you have seen how the client, server, and CGI scripts communicate and share information. Knowing this will help you build your scripts. Most of this book's scripts require various information about the client and the server. Also, you will see in more detail how to pass information among your script, the server, and the client, and various things that you can do to take full advantage of that information.

You have learned what the various environmental variables are and how you can use them. By checking the contents of an environmental variable, you can make your script create different Web documents depending on the environmental variable's contents. You can use them to ensure the integrity of the information being passed to your script.

The chapter introduced <ISINDEX> and explained the differences between the POST and GET methods. You have also seen some of the various languages used for writing scripts. Finally, you peeked into the future of CGI and some of the alternatives to CGI that are available. However, as the computer industry changes, the state of the Web and the interfaces change as well. You never know what will be the most popular gateway in the future.

Review Questions

1. How do you use environmental variables?

2. What happens if you enter the query **name=john** into an <ISINDEX> query?

3. What type of query can use the command line?

4. From where does a CGI script's STDIN come? Where does its STDOUT go?

5. What limitations exist when using the GET method?

Review Exercises

1. Create an HTML form and script that enables visitors to enter their name and location.

2. Using the information from the first review exercise, create a script that displays to the visitors the information that they entered into the form.

Part II

Basic CGI Applications

## CHAPTER 3

Using Forms To Collect Input

A HyperText Markup Language (HTML) form provides the only method by which a visitor can interact with your CGI scripts. Without a form, a visitor cannot sign your guestbook, use a CGI e-mail script, or even make an order to purchase your products. HTML forms provide visitors a means by which to interact with your site. Throughout this chapter, you build on a form in which visitors to your site can register a software product that they purchased from your company. To do so, you explore the HTML tags and attributes that you need to create an HTML form. Understand, however, that this book's purpose isn't to instruct you on the use of HTML. To learn about that topic, you can find many good books already on the market.

The *<FORM>* Attribute

Like the <HTML> tag, a <FORM> tag has an opening and closing tag. You have to let the visitor's browser know what parts of your pages are a <FORM> and which are just another part of your document. The browser needs this information because more than one form can be open on any given page. To start a second form, you simply repeat the process that you used to create the first form.

The beginning of the form

The form's contents

The end of a form

With HTML, you give the browser this information by using the <FORM> tag. The <FORM> and </FORM> tags specify that the contents between them are part of the form. Within the <FORM> tags, you can use any HTML tag except another <FORM>. For example, your form can include the <HR>, <PRE>, or </PRE> tags. Adding additional HTML tags enhances the form's layout, transforming a somewhat sloppy site to one with an outstanding professional appearance.

Within a form are additional tags and attributes, all of which have rules. These tags tell the browser when to start a section and when to stop, and ensure that the items display exactly as you intended. Within the <FORM> tag, you can use the attributes ACTION, METHOD, and ENCTYPE.

The *ACTION* Attribute

The ACTION attribute tells the server which CGI script is to process the form. Double quotation marks enclose the attribute's value, which specifies the Uniform Resource Locator (URL) to the script that is to process the form. Here are a few examples:

```
<FORM ACTION="register.pl">
<FORM ACTION="/cgi-bin/register.pl">
<FORM ACTION="http://www.yakima.net/cgi-bin/register.pl">
```

> **Note:** Double quotation marks are not required to assign values to attributes unless the value of an attribute contains a space or other special characters. Even so, you should use double quotation marks because they make your HTML easier to read.

If you don't provide a value to the ACTION attribute, the browser assumes that you are specifying the URL that you are currently on. For example, suppose that you are looking at the following URL:

http://www.yakima.net/register.pl

The form would then assume that the ACTION type is the following:

```
ACTION="http://www.yakima.net/register.pl"
```

> **Note:** Calling a script while already viewing that script isn't too uncommon. Many scripts produce HTML documents, which can also be forms. The forms that the script creates can call the script again (often when a script is checking for user input errors).
>
> If you choose to call a script that you are viewing, be careful. You could easily receive a server error if you use the wrong METHOD type or if your script cannot handle the information that it receives. Also, you get an error if your script creates a form that incorrectly calls the script again.

The *METHOD* Attribute

The METHOD type specifies which method you are using to communicate with the server and script. You can use any method that your server supports, but most likely your server supports only the methods POST and GET. When writing your scripts, you want your script to check which type of method is being used, because a script has to get information differently depending on the METHOD type that the form is using.

Here's an example of a <FORM> attribute with each METHOD type:

```
<FORM ACTION="http://www.in-command.com/register.pl" METHOD="GET">
<FORM ACTION="/cgi-bin/register.pl" METHOD="POST">
```

If you don't specify which METHOD type to use, the default is GET.

The method POST is probably the most versatile METHOD type. As you learned in Chapter 2, "The Common Gateway Interface (CGI)," the GET method limits you to less than 255 characters, and thus limits the amount of information that you can allow a user to enter. POST does not have this limitation, because the information from the form passes directly to the server using STDIN.

The *ENCTYPE* Attribute

CGI doesn't actually support the ENCTYPE attribute yet; this section covers the attribute briefly in case you happen to encounter it, because ENCTYPE is becoming increasingly popular with the advent of file uploads using a Web browser. You can use this attribute only when using the method POST, and currently the attribute has only one value:

```
application/x-www-form-urlencoded
```

When you use the POST method, this value is the default type anyway.

In the future, you might be able to use ENCTYPE to specify the type of file that you are sending, whether you are uploading a file, or something similar. Currently, however, you can't really do anything with ENCTYPE.

Examples of *<FORM>* Tag Usage

Here are a few examples using the <FORM> tag:

```
<FORM ACTION="http://www.selah.net/cgi-bin/register.pl"> ... </FORM>

<FORM ACTION="/cgi-bin/register.pl" METHOD="POST"> ... </FORM>

<FORM ACTION="register.pl" METHOD="POST"> ... </FORM>

<FORM> ... </FORM>
```

Each of these examples is valid. After you place some elements between the opening and closing tags, you can present them to your site's visitors.

The *<INPUT>* Tag

Probably the most important item that you can put inside a <FORM> is the <INPUT> tag. When designing your form, you will find that most of the information that you want a potential visitor to enter will be placed within the <INPUT> tag. The <INPUT> tag doesn't have a closing tag like the <FORM> or <BODY> tag does. <INPUT> works much like the <IMG> tag. Within the <INPUT> tag, you can have several different <TYPE> values. This variety of TYPE values gives <INPUT> its power and flexibility. The TYPE values include the following:

- text
- password
- checkbox
- radio
- submit
- reset
- hidden

The next few sections explore each of these TYPE values in more detail as you build a registration page that enables visitors to your site to register their products.

The *text* Input Type

The value text simply creates a box in which the visitor can enter text. Usually the box provides only one row, although the box was originally designed to handle more. You can use this box to prompt visitors to enter their name, address, birth date, or any other piece of information that you want.

Examine the following lines:

```
<FORM ACTION="/cgi-bin/register.pl" METHOD="POST">
<INPUT TYPE="text" NAME="name">
</FORM>
```

This code produces a text box in which a user can enter text (see fig. 3.1).

You can control the size of the text box using the SIZE attribute, and specify the size as SIZE=*width* or SIZE=*width,height*, as in the following examples:

```
SIZE=4

SIZE=12,2
```

Normally you don't use *height*; if you need a larger area, you use the <TEXTAREA> tag (which is discussed later in this chapter). If you don't specify the size, the default setting is SIZE=20. Figure 3.2 shows a few examples that use the SIZE attribute.

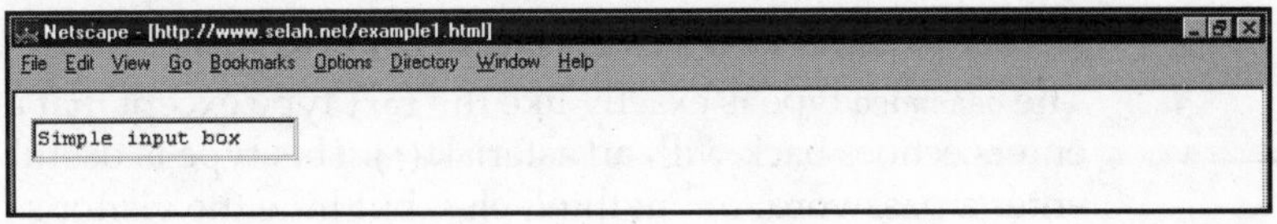

Figure 3.1

The default input line using the input type `text`.

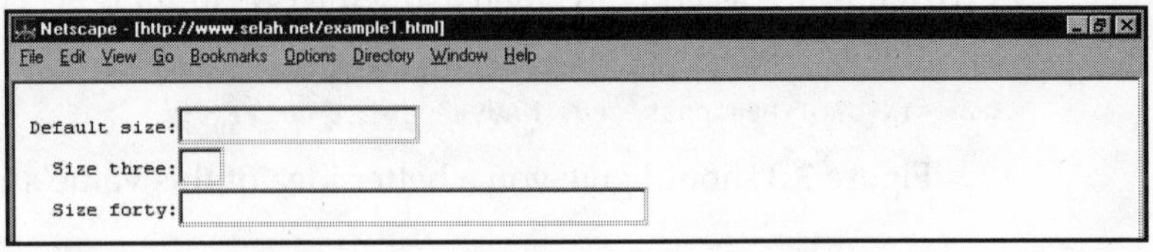

Figure 3.2

Using the SIZE attribute, you can control the size of a text or password box.

You can use the SIZE attribute only with the input types `text` and `password`, but by controlling the text box's size, you can control your page's look and feel. You don't need a text box that is 40 characters long if its purpose is simply to hold a date.

You might also use the VALUE attribute to enter a value into a text box. The VALUE attribute enables you to add a default value to the text box. Here's an example:

```
<FORM>
<INPUT TYPE="text" SIZE=25 NAME="test3" VALUE="Enter your address">
</FORM>
```

You set the default value just in case the visitor doesn't enter anything. For example, you could have your page automatically enter the date, but still enable the visitor to change the date. If you can easily provide needed information automatically, setting a default can free the visitor from having to enter information.

Finally, you can control the maximum number of characters that a text box allows the visitor to enter. This control is useful when you are building a script in which you want a field to send only a specific number of characters. Here's an example:

```
<FORM>
<INPUT TYPE="text" NAME="City" SIZE=25 MAXLENGTH=25>
</FORM>
```

This example lets the visitor enter only 25 characters. If you don't specify the MAXLENGTH setting, the visitor can enter an unlimited number of characters.

Although the input type value `text` is probably the TYPE value that you will use most often, other types are available.

> **Note:** When you create your CGI scripts, you want your script to check and ensure that the user actually entered the expected information. If you fail to check for the expected information, your script might behave badly, perhaps corrupting information stored in a database or flat file. Chapter 6, "Advanced Scripts," covers various methods that you can use to perform this checking, and Chapter 17, "Security Issues," covers other security concerns.

The *password* Input Type

The password type is exactly like the text type except that anything that the visitor enters echoes back with an asterisk (*). This type is useful if you want the user to enter a password, or anything else, but hide the visitor's entry from people with access to the visitor's screen. You can even set a default value by using the VALUE attribute, just as you can when using the text input type. Here's an example of the password value in use:

```
<INPUT TYPE="password" NAME="serial_no">
```

Figure 3.3 should give you a better idea of this value's use and purpose.

Figure 3.3

You can use the password type to hide a visitor's entry from prying eyes.

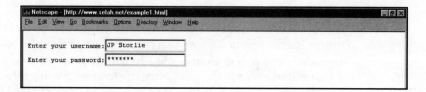

The *hidden* Input Type

Use the hidden input type when you want the form to contain information that the visitor cannot change. For example, to create a form that accesses an e-mail script to enable the visitor to send you feedback, you can enter To: as a hidden field. When you use the hidden input type, the visitor cannot access or change this information. In fact, the visitor can't even see the information.

For example, a visitor cannot see the following information on the screen:

```
<INPUT TYPE="hidden" name="to_email" value="rniles@selah.net">
```

Caution: The hidden input type isn't completely hidden from the visitor. If the visitor uses his or her browser to view the source, the hidden fields display on the HTML source. The hidden input type does have its value, but the user can manipulate that value if he or she saves the HTML document as a file.

The *checkbox* Input Type

The checkbox value works much like a simple on/off switch. If the check box is selected, the script receives the box's value. If the visitor doesn't place a check in the box, the NAME attribute is disregarded and not sent to the script at all. Within an input type checkbox, you can have the following attributes:

Attribute	Description
NAME	As with the TEXT input type, you must define a value for the NAME attribute. Your script receives this name as part of the name/value pair.

Attribute	Description
VALUE	Specifies the entry's value. The default value is on.
CHECKED	Checks the check box by default. If you set this attribute, the check box that the visitor sees is automatically selected, although the visitor can turn it off. Setting this default is a good idea if most visitors are more likely to choose the check box.

Regarding the form for your software company, consider the following example:

```
<FORM>
<INPUT TYPE="checkbox" NAME="programs1" VALUE="Graphics"
➥ CHECKED>Graphics
<INPUT TYPE="checkbox" NAME="programs2" VALUE="Internet"
➥ CHECKED>Internet
<INPUT TYPE="checkbox" NAME="programs3" VALUE="Games">Games
<INPUT TYPE="checkbox" NAME="programs4" VALUE="Programming">Programming
<INPUT TYPE="checkbox" NAME="programs5" VALUE="Business">Business
</FORM>
```

Figure 3.4 shows the resulting form. You can specify that the form display the check boxes side by side or stacked on top of one another. You can even set a check box between words within your form.

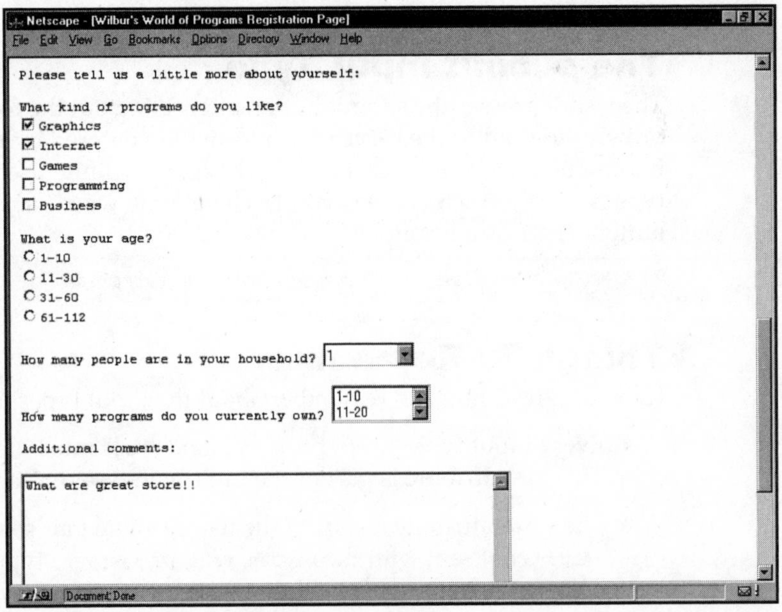

Figure 3.4

Using check boxes, you can enable the user to select specific choices.

The *radio* Input Type

The radio input type is much like the checkbox input type, except that a radio button enables a visitor to select one item from a list of several. The radio input type should have the same NAME attribute, but different values for the VALUE attribute. Therefore, the user can select only one item in the list.

Take a look at the following example:

```
<FORM>
<INPUT TYPE="radio" NAME="come_again" VALUE="Yes" CHECKED>Yes
<INPUT TYPE="radio" NAME="come_again" VALUE="No">No
<INPUT TYPE="radio" NAME="come_again" VALUE="Maybe">Maybe
</FORM>
```

In this example, the visitor can select either Yes, No, or Maybe, with the Yes radio button being selected by default. This example doesn't enable visitors to select two or more choices, as they can with the checkbox type.

The *reset* Input Type

The reset input type enables the visitor to reset the form completely. When you completely reset the form, you clear it and reset the default values. The only attribute used within the reset type is VALUE, which displays the label for the reset button. If you don't specify VALUE, the label is "Reset" by default. Examine this example of the reset button:

```
<INPUT TYPE="reset" VALUE="Clear the form!">
```

The *submit* Input Type

The visitor presses the submit button after filling out the form. This event tells the browser to send to the server the information entered by the visitor; in turn, this information goes to the CGI script. The only attribute used with the submit input type is VALUE, which enables you to change the word *submit* that appears on the button. Here is an example:

```
<INPUT TYPE="submit" VALUE="Send the registration!">
```

Things To Remember

Here are a few things to remember about the input types used within forms:

♦ Every input type except for submit and reset must have a NAME attribute set. The NAME attribute is part of the information sent as a name/value pair

♦ The VALUE attribute is part of the name/value pair sent to the script. If the VALUE is not sent with the hidden, text, or password types, the script receives only name=. If not set for either the checkbox or radio types, the VALUE attribute is completely discarded and not sent to your script at all.

♦ You can use the CHECKED attribute only on the checkbox and radio input types. By default, the checkbox input type enables the visitor to select more than one item.

♦ If you are using the MAXLENGTH attribute and the size is smaller than MAXLENGTH's value, the text scrolls as the user enters information longer than specified by the SIZE attribute.

The *<SELECT>* Tag

The <SELECT> tag enables the user to select an item from either a pull-down menu or a scrolling menu. The <SELECT> attribute has both an opening tag (<SELECT>) and closing tag (</SELECT>), between which can only be <OPTION> tags.

Within the <SELECT> tag, you must set a NAME attribute. You can also set SIZE and MULTIPLE attributes.

The SIZE attribute enables you to specify the number of items visible to the visitor. The default value is 1. If you want to display more than one item, the available options are displayed as a list, showing only the amount of options specified. By changing the SIZE attribute, you enable the visitor to scroll through a list rather than opening the list like a pull-down menu. Figure 3.5 shows examples of both a pull-down menu and a scrolling list.

Figure 3.5

When using the <SELECT> tag, you can display options within either a scrolling list or a pull-down menu.

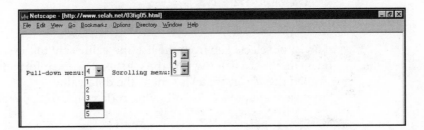

You can use the MULTIPLE attribute to enable the visitor to select more than one item from a list. Unless you use this attribute, the visitor can select only one item.

Between the opening and closing <SELECT> tags, you can have only the <OPTION> tag:

```
<OPTION> Option
```

You can have as many <OPTION> tags as you want within the <SELECT> tags. Within an <OPTION> tag, however, you can use only two attributes: SELECTED and VALUE.

The SELECTED attribute enables you to define which option is the default. SELECTED is like the CHECKED attribute that you use within the input types radio and checkbox. Here's an example:

```
<FORM>
<SELECT NAME="recommend">
<OPTION> Yes
<OPTION SELECTED> No
<OPTION> Maybe
</SELECT>
</FORM>
```

This example first displays the option No to the visitor. The visitor can select another option, but this one is the default.

The second attribute that you can define within an <OPTION> tag is VALUE. The VALUE attribute enables you to specify the data value. Suppose that you are creating an option list that displays the first three letters of the month, but you are working with a database that takes only numbers for the month. The VALUE tag can solve this problem as follows:

```
<FORM>
<SELECT NAME="test">
<OPTION VALUE="1"> Jan
<OPTION VALUE="2"> Feb
...
<OPTION VALUE="11"> Nov
<OPTION VALUE="12"> Dec
</SELECT>
</FORM>
```

If a visitor selects Feb from the list, the value sent to the server is 2.

If you don't set a value within the <OPTION> tag, the information after the <OPTION> tag (called the *display value*) is sent as the data value.

Suppose that you use the following code rather than the preceding example:

```
<FORM>
<SELECT NAME="test">
<OPTION> Jan
<OPTION> Feb
...
<OPTION> Nov
<OPTION> Dec
</SELECT>
</FORM>
```

In this case, the script receives the name/value pair as test=Jan and so on.

The <SELECT> tag is handy when you have a large list of options from which you want visitors to choose one option. You can have visitors select the day of the month as well as the months of the year. You can even provide a list of all 50 states.

For your software company's form, you can ask how many programs the visitor currently has by enabling the visitor to select from a list of ranges:

```
<FORM>
<SELECT NAME="amount">
<OPTION> 1-10
<OPTION> 11-20
<OPTION> 21-40
<OPTION> 41-80
<OPTION> 81-200
<OPTION> 201 or more
</SELECT>
</FORM>
```

The <*TEXTAREA*> Tag

Suppose that you want to enable visitors to enter a large amount of information. The best way to do so is to create a text box by using the <TEXTAREA> tag. Using the <TEXTAREA> tag, you can define the input box's size and width, letting the user add more information than would be appropriate if you use the text input type box. The <TEXTAREA> attribute must have both opening and closing <TEXTAREA> and </TEXTAREA> tags.

To use the <TEXTAREA> tag, you must define a NAME attribute along with the size of the box set by the amount of columns and rows. To define the columns, you use the COLS attribute; to define the rows, you use the ROWS attribute. Examine the following example:

```
<TEXTAREA NAME="test" COLS=25 ROWS=6> </TEXTAREA>
```

Between the <TEXTAREA> tags, you can enter any text that you want to display in the visitor's browser. For instance, the following example creates the display shown in figure 3.6:

```
<TEXTAREA NAME="comments" COLS=40 ROWS=10>
What a wonderful place to shop!
</TEXTAREA>
```

The visitor can edit the information that you place in the text box, and can also add information. You provide a scrollbar so that the user can scroll up or down to view the information within the text box.

Figure 3.6

You can define the
<TEXTAREA>
attribute by size
and then input
information into
the text box.

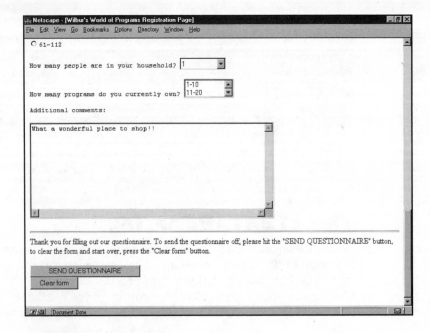

Creating a Form

Now that you are familiar with each tag, and the attributes that go with each tag,
you can put together your form like that shown in listing 3.1. Recall that the form
is to enable visitors to register the product that they purchased from your software
company.

Listing 3.1 WILBUR.HTM—a Full Document Using Forms

```
<HTML>
<HEAD>
<TITLE> Wilbur's World of Programs Registration Page </TITLE>
</HEAD>
<BODY>
<CENTER>
<IMG SRC="HTTP://KOZMO.YAKIMA.NET/cgi-bin/animate?/
➥~mike/anim/anim.dat">
<H1> Wilbur's World of Programs </H1>
</CENTER>
<P>
<H2> Welcome to our Registration Page!</H2>
Thank you for purchasing our product. If you could,
please complete the form.
If you do so, you help us gain a better understanding of
our customers, allowing us to serve you better.
<p>
<FORM ACTION="/cgi-bin/register.pl" METHOD="POST">
```

```
<PRE>
Enter your name:<INPUT TYPE="text" NAME="name" SIZE=40>
         Address:<INPUT TYPE="text" NAME="address" SIZE=40>
            City:<INPUT TYPE="text" NAME="city" Size=20>
           State:<INPUT TYPE="text" NAME="state" SIZE=14>
             Zip:<INPUT TYPE="text" NAME="zip" SIZE=6>
<hr>
What is the name of the product that you are registering?<BR>
<INPUT TYPE="text" NAME="product" SIZE=40 VALUE="WebInit"><BR>
What is the registration number of your product:
<INPUT TYPE="password" NAME="product_id" SIZE=40><BR>
<INPUT TYPE="hidden" NAME="storename" VALUE="wilburworld">
<HR>
Please tell us a little more about yourself:<p>
What kind of programs do you like?
<INPUT TYPE="checkbox" NAME="programs1" VALUE="Graphics"
➥CHECKED>Graphics
<INPUT TYPE="checkbox" NAME="programs2" VALUE="Internet"
➥CHECKED>Internet
<INPUT TYPE="checkbox" NAME="programs3" VALUE="Games">Games
<INPUT TYPE="checkbox" NAME="programs4" VALUE="Programming">Programming
<INPUT TYPE="checkbox" NAME="programs5" VALUE="Business">Business
<P>
What is your age?
<INPUT TYPE="radio" NAME="age" VALUE="1-10">1-10
<INPUT TYPE="radio" NAME="age" VALUE="11-30">11-30
<INPUT TYPE="radio" NAME="age" VALUE="31-60">31-60
<INPUT TYPE="radio" NAME="age" VALUE="61-112">61-112

How many people are in your household? <SELECT NAME="household">
<OPTION> 1
<OPTION> 2
<OPTION> 3
<OPTION> 4
<OPTION> 5
<OPTION> 6
<OPTION> 7 or more
</SELECT>
<P>
How many programs do you currently own? <SELECT NAME="programs" SIZE=2>
<OPTION> 1-10
<OPTION> 11-20
<OPTION> 21-30
<OPTION> 31-40
<OPTION> 41-60
<OPTION> 61-80
<OPTION> 81 or more
</SELECT>
<P>
Additional comments:<BR>
<TEXTAREA NAME="comments" ROWS=10 COLS=60>
What a wonderful place to shop!!
</TEXTAREA>
```

continues

Listing 3.1   Continued

```
</PRE>
<HR>

Thank you for filling out our questionnaire. To send the questionnaire
off, please hit the "SEND QUESTIONNAIRE" button, to clear the form and
start over, press the "Clear form" button.
<p>

<INPUT TYPE="submit" VALUE="SEND QUESTIONNAIRE"><BR>
<INPUT TYPE="reset" VALUE="Clear form">

</FORM>
</BODY>
```

Figure 3.7 shows the finished form's appearance.

Figure 3.7

By adding a few graphics, you transform a bland form into a more attractive one.

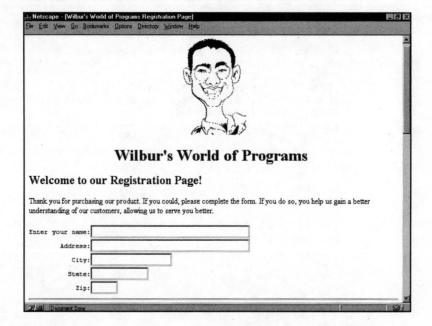

Now you've created your first form. Consider other applications that you can build, and try to create a form interface for them.

Summary

Forms provide the only interface that the visitor to your site can use to interact with your CGI scripts. The forms specification has been well thought out and should provide any tool that your page needs to receive a wide variety of input from your visitors. In this chapter, you have learned how to use the various input types, the <SELECT> tag, and the <TEXTAREA> tag. This chapter should get you started creating your own forms. With a background, a few pictures to touch up the page, and possibly a table to aid you in formatting the page, you can create a top-notch, professional-looking page.

Review Questions

1. Which tags within a form must have both an opening and closing tag?

2. Which METHOD is the default?

3. What are the input types allowed within the <INPUT> tags?

4. In addition to submit and reset, what attribute do you have to place within all input types?

5. What attribute do you use to mark a check box or radio button as selected?

6. What attributes are allowed within the <SELECT> tag?

7. How many characters are allowed within a <TEXTAREA> box?

Review Exercises

1. Create a form that prompts visitors to enter their mail address. Place the state within a <SELECT> tag.

2. Suppose that you are creating a form that enables a visitor to enter information that will be placed into a guestbook. Create a list of information that you would like the visitor to enter, and then create a form that enables the visitor to enter the desired information.

3. Create a form that enables a visitor to enter comments that will be mailed to someone selected from a list. Create a list of three names from which the visitor can choose the e-mail message's recipient. Next create a list in which the visitor chooses an item to include in the Subject line. Finally, enable the visitor to enter his or her name, e-mail address, and a comment.

## CHAPTER 4

A Simple Guestbook

In Chapter 3, "Using Forms To Collect Input," you learned how fill-in forms are structured and the kinds of input that you can collect. You also learned how to format the information and pass it from the server to your CGI script.

In this chapter, you put that knowledge to use by creating a simple guestbook script. A Web-based guestbook is much like a paper-based guestbook; visitors sign the book when they stop by, leaving their names and perhaps brief comments.

The program that you develop in this chapter is called SGB1 (*simple guestbook number 1*). Chapter 7, "A More Complex Guestbook," presents another guestbook called SGB2. The numerals make it easier to distinguish these two programs, both in your mind and on the accompanying CD-ROM.

What SGB1 Does

Figures 4.1, 4.2, and 4.3 show the various possible SGB1 screens that a visitor might see. Figure 4.1 shows SGB1 in action, with a visitor named Karla Borden just about to sign the book.

Figure 4.2 shows the thank-you screen that the visitor sees after signing the book. The screen also displays the visitor's entry so that she can see what it will look like in the guestbook. Notice that her name is underlined; because Karla supplied both her name and her e-mail address, SGB1 thoughtfully made an `<a href=mailto...>` link from the information.

Figure 4.1

SGB1 in action, ready to accept input from a visitor named Karla Borden.

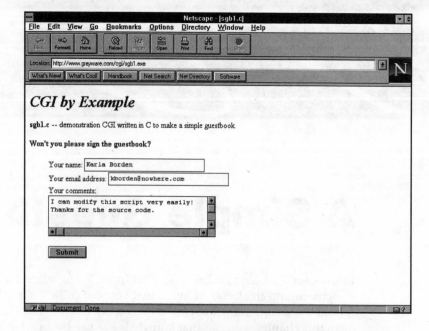

Figure 4.2

The screen that Karla sees after clicking the Submit button.

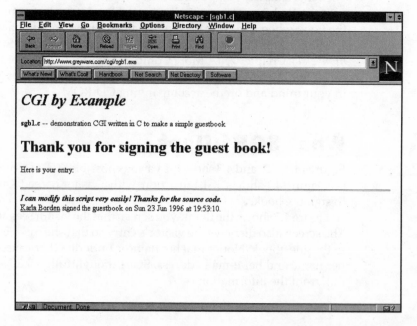

Figure 4.3 shows the same screen as figure 4.1, but after several more visitors have signed the book. Notice that the guestbook records visitors who don't supply a name or e-mail address, but records them only as "Anonymous Visitor." Also notice that the form for signing the book is still available at the top of the screen. This enables visitors to scroll through the entire list before deciding whether to sign.

Figure 4.3

The guestbook after several more visitors have signed it.

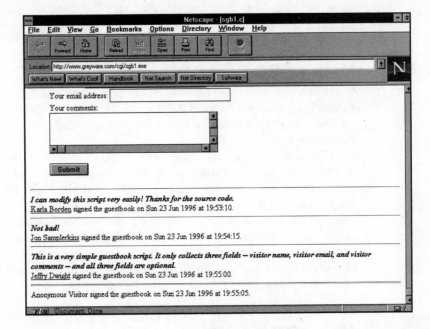

This chapter walks you through a complete CGI script written in C. The code is heavily commented, so large sections of it are not explained in detail. However, the text describes and explains the procedures and choices that are of particular interest to CGI programmers.

Creating the HTML File To Invoke SGB1

The HTML file to invoke SGB1 is simple. Because the script creates its own forms on the fly, all you need is an `<a href...>` link somewhere on one of your pages. Suppose that you installed SGB1 in your /SCRIPTS directory. Listing 4.1 shows some sample HTML code that would be appropriate.

Listing 4.1   Sample HTML To Invoke SGB1

```
<html>
<head><title>Invoking SGB1</title></head>
<body>
<h1>Invoking SGB1</h1>
<a href="/scripts/sgb1.exe">View or Sign the Guestbook</a>
</body>
</html>
```

Using SBG1

When invoked with the GET method (as shown in listing 4.1), SGB1 displays a screen similar to figure 4.3. That is, SGB1 does all the work necessary to create and display a fill-in form for signing the book, and automatically displays the entries in the guestbook at the same time.

When invoked with the POST method, SGB1 processes the input, adds a new record to the guestbook data file, and then displays a screen similar to figure 4.2.

You don't need to write a separate HTML form for visitors to use when signing the guestbook (although you could do so). In fact, if you run SGB1 and view the source code, you see that the fill-in form is already created for you. After running under the GET method once, SGB1 has all the information necessary to create a form to call itself again using the POST method. This is exactly what happens normally. A visitor clicks the View or Sign the Guestbook link from listing 4.1, and SGB1 takes over from there.

How SGB1 Works

This section describes in detail how SGB1 accomplishes its tasks. In particular, this section reviews the parts of the code that set up the initial environment, decide what to do, and process the input.

The *main()* Routine

All programs start *somewhere*. That is, a program must have a defined entry point to which control transfers when the operating system first loads the program. In some development environments, you have no control over where the program starts. DOS batch files and UNIX shell scripts, for example, always start at the first line.

Compiled programs can start anywhere. In the C language, convention and syntax usually require that the program start at the main() routine. Also by convention, the main() routine is at the end of the source file. This convention seems to be the opposite of top-down design, because the program's execution sequence doesn't match the source code's organization. In C programs, however, the order of the subroutines doesn't matter, other than to avoid a *forward reference*. A forward reference is a reference to something further down in the source code. Because the `main()` routine calls the other subroutines, positioning it as the last routine makes some sense. All the routines that `main()` references precede it, and therefore you won't have any forward references.

> **Tip:** You can work around the problem of forward references in several ways. The most popular is to use *function prototypes*, or declarations about routines that appear later in the source code.
>
> A better solution is to have the compiler run two passes through the source code—the first to note all the references, and the second to compile the code. Unfortunately, although low-level languages such as assembler and some high-level languages such as Visual Basic enable you to use this solution, C does not.
>
> Unless you have a good reason for arranging your C subroutines out of order, don't use function prototypes. Put your subroutines in the order appropriate for their use. Function prototypes are a half-baked solution that ultimately forces you to make changes in *two* places whenever you need to edit a function definition.

Listing 4.2 shows the SGB1's `main()` subroutine in its entirety. This routine embodies the basic logic behind CGI script processing. Almost all of your C programs will have code similar to listing 4.2. All CGI scripts must handle some fundamental tasks, and if you organize your program efficiently, you can control the entire program flow from the `main()` routine.

Listing 4.2   SGB1's *main()* routine

```
// The script's entry point

void main() {

    char * pRequestMethod;  // pointer to REQUEST_METHOD

    // First, set STDOUT to unbuffered

    setvbuf(stdout,NULL,_IONBF,0);

    // Zero out the global variables

    ZeroMemory(szEmail,sizeof(szEmail));
    ZeroMemory(szComments,sizeof(szComments));
    ZeroMemory(szName,sizeof(szName));
```

continues

Listing 4.2　Continued

```
// Figure out how we were invoked, and determine what
// to do based on that

pRequestMethod = getenv("REQUEST_METHOD");

if (pRequestMethod==NULL) {

    // No request method; must have been invoked from
    // command line.  Print a message and terminate.

    printf("This program is designed to run as a CGI script, "
           "not from the command-line.\n");

}

else if (stricmp(pRequestMethod,"GET")==0) {

    // Request-method was GET; this means we should
    // print out the guestbook

    PrintMIMEHeader();      // Print MIME header
    PrintHTMLHeader();      // Print HTML header
    PrintForm();            // Print guestbook form
    PrintGBEntries();       // Print contents of guestbook
    PrintHTMLTrailer();     // Print HTML trailer
}

else if (stricmp(pRequestMethod,"POST")==0) {

    // Request-method was POST; this means we should
    // parse the input and create a new entry in
    // the guestbook

    PrintMIMEHeader();      // Print MIME header
    PrintHTMLHeader();      // Print HTML header
    GetPOSTData();          // Get POST data to szBuffer
    ProcessPOSTData();      // Process the POST data
    PrintHTMLTrailer();     // Print HTML trailer
}

else
{

    // Request-method wasn't null, but wasn't GET or
    // POST either.  Output an error message and die

    PrintMIMEHeader();      // Print MIME header
    PrintHTMLHeader();      // Print HTML header
    printf("Only GET and POST methods supported.\n");
    PrintHTMLTrailer();     // Print HTML trailer
```

```
    }

    // Finally, flush the output & terminate

    fflush(stdout);
}
```

The `main()` routine first allocates storage for local variables. In this case, only one local variable is relevant to `main()`'s tasks: `pRequestMethod`. `main()` uses `pRequestMethod` to point (hence the `p`) to the `REQUEST_METHOD` environment variable. As you saw in Chapter 3, this environment variable tells your script which method invoked it.

Before evaluating `pRequestMethod`, however, `main()` does some generic house-keeping chores. First, it sets the `STDOUT` stream to *unbuffered*. Even though this script doesn't mix output methods, and thus is unlikely to be subject to scrambled output, you should always set your streams to raw mode before running the rest of your script. (See the sidebar "Changing Buffers in the Middle of the Stream" for more information about streams, buffering, and raw versus cooked mode.) The last bit of housekeeping is to *zero out* some global variables—that is, to fill the bytes of the strings with binary zeros. Zeroing out such variables can help you avoid some problem-checking later when you use the variables.

After finishing this housekeeping, `main()` can move on to the heart of the program: deciding what to do based on how it was invoked.

Changing Buffers in the Middle of the Stream

In the UNIX world, a character *stream* is a special kind of file. By default, `STDIN` and `STDOUT` are character streams. The operating system helpfully parses streams for you, ensuring that everything is proper seven-bit ASCII or an approved control code.

Fortunately, HTML codes can all be expressed in seven bits. However, if your script sends graphical data, using a character-oriented stream results in instant death. The solution is to switch the stream to binary mode. In C, you can make this switch by using the `setmode()` function:

```
    setmode(fileno(stdout), O_BINARY)
```

You can change modes in midstream with the following complementary statement:

```
    setmode(fileno(stdout), O_TEXT)
```

A typical graphics script outputs the headers in character mode, then switches to binary mode for the graphical data.

In the Windows NT world, streams behave the same way, for compatibility reasons. A simple `\n` in your output is converted to `\r\n` when you write to `STDOUT`. This conversion doesn't occur with regular Windows NT system calls, such as `WriteFile()`; you must specify `\r\n` explicitly if you want `CRLF`.

UNIX programmers frown at the term CRLF, whereas programmers who use other platforms might not recognize \n or \r\n. \r enables C programmers to specify a carriage-return (CR) character, and \n enables them to specify a line-feed (LF) character. (In BASIC, Chr$(10) is the equivalent of LF, and Chr$(13) is the equivalent to CR.)

Other words for character mode and binary mode are *cooked* and *raw*, respectively. Those in the know use these terms rather than the more common ones.

Whichever terms and platform you use, streams pose a problem: By default, they're *buffered*. Therefore, the operating system hangs on to the data until it encounters a line-terminating character, the buffer fills up, or the stream closes. For this reason, if you mix buffered printf() statements with unbuffered fwrite() or fprintf() statements, the output probably will be jumbled even though the statements might all write to STDOUT. printf() uses a buffer to write to the stream; file-oriented routines output directly. The result is an out-of-order mess.

You might blame this problem on the need for backward-compatibility. Beyond the existence of many old programs, streams have no reason to default to buffered and cooked. You should have to turn on these options when you want them, instead of having to turn them off when you don't. Fortunately, the following statement handles all the backward-compatibility problems by turning off all buffering for the STDOUT stream:

```
setvbuf(stdout, NULL, IONBF, 0)
```

Another solution is to avoid mixing types of output statements. However, even this solution won't make your cooked output raw, so you should turn off buffering anyway. Many servers and browsers are cranky and dislike receiving input in drabs and twaddles.

The decision-making process actually presents very few options. First, main() sets pRequestMethod to point at the environment variable REQUEST_METHOD. The function then examines this pointer to determine the environment variable's contents. Only four options are possible:

♦ The REQUEST_METHOD isn't set at all. A user probably executed the script from the command line. If you want to print version information or a help screen, you should do so while writing the code to handle this case.

♦ The REQUEST_METHOD equals GET. The GET method invoked the script, and GET-type processing should occur. This setting tells SGB1 to display the fill-in form and the entire contents of the guestbook file.

♦ The REQUEST_METHOD equals POST. The POST method invoked the script (probably because a user clicked the Submit button on the form generated by the GET method). If POST invokes SGB1, it gathers input from STDIN and writes a new record to the guestbook file.

◆ The REQUEST_METHOD is something other than GET or POST. Other possibilities are HEAD or PUT, but the script doesn't care. Because SGB1 supports only the GET and POST methods, main() simply issues an error message and dies.

Common Subroutines

You might notice in listing 4.2 that the routines supporting the GET, POST, and unknown methods all share a few things in common. Specifically, all of them call these three routines:

```
PrintMIMEHeader();      // Print MIME header
PrintHTMLHeader();      // Print HTML header
PrintHTMLTrailer();     // Print HTML trailer
```

Like the main() routine itself, most of your programs will have routines like these three. The structure of the generated HTML is mostly the same, whether you are outputting an error message or a complete guestbook file.

Listing 4.3 shows these three routines in their entirety. The exact syntax of these three routines changes from script to script, but their functions remain the same. All scripts need a MIME header. Well-formed HTML always has a header including <html>, <head>, <title>, and <body> tags, and always finishes with a trailer providing matching </body> and </html> tags. The trailer is also a handy place to put copyright notices or other standard text that you want to include.

Listing 4.3   The *PrintMIMEHeader()*, *PrintHTMLHeader()*, and *PrintHTMLTrailer()* Routines

```
// PrintMIMEHeader:  Prints content-type header

void PrintMIMEHeader() {
    // This is the basic MIME header for the
    // CGI.  Note that it is a 2-line header,
    // including a "pragma: no-cache" directive.
    // This keeps the page from being cached,
    // and reduces the number of duplicate
    // entries from users who keep hitting the
    // submit button over and over
    printf("Content-type: text/html\n");
    printf("Pragma: no-cache\n");
    printf("\n");

}

// PrintHTMLHeader:  Prints HTML page header

void PrintHTMLHeader() {
    printf(
        "<html>\n"
```

continues

67

Listing 4.3 Continued

```
            "<head><title>SGB1.c</title></head>\n"
            "<body "
                "bgcolor=#FEFEFE "
                "text=#000000 "
                "link=#000040 "
                "alink=FF0040 "
                "vlink=#7F7F7F"
                ">\n"
            "<h1><i>CGI by Example</i></h1>\n"
            "<b>SGB1.c</b> — demonstration CGI written "
            "in C to make a simple guestbook <p>\n"
            );
}

// PrintHTMLTrailer:  Prints closing HTML info

void PrintHTMLTrailer() {
    printf(
        "</body>\n"
        "</html>\n"
        );
}
```

Reading the Input

When you invoke the script with the POST method (that is, from a form), you still get some information from environment variables, but most of the input comes from STDIN (standard input). The CONTENT_LENGTH variable tells you how many characters you need to retrieve. Listing 4.4 shows a simple loop to retrieve input from STDIN and place the input in a global buffer called, appropriately enough, szBuffer.

Listing 4.4 A Routine To Read *POST* Data from *STDIN*

```
// GetPOSTData:  Read in data from POST operation

void GetPOSTData() {
    char * pContentLength;  // pointer to CONTENT_LENGTH
    int  ContentLength;     // value of CONTENT_LENGTH string
    int  i;                 // local counter
    int  x;                 // generic char holder

    // Retrieve a pointer to the CONTENT_LENGTH variable

    pContentLength = getenv("CONTENT_LENGTH");
```

```
    // If the variable exists, convert its value to an integer
    // with atoi()

    if (pContentLength != NULL)
    {
      ContentLength = atoi(pContentLength);
    }
    else
    {
      ContentLength = 0;
    }

    // Make sure specified length isn't greater than the size
    // of our statically allocated buffer

    if (ContentLength > sizeof(szBuffer)-1)
    {
      ContentLength = sizeof(szBuffer)-1;
    }

    // Now read ContentLength bytes from STDIN

    i = 0;
    while (i < ContentLength)
    {
      x = fgetc(stdin);
      if (x==EOF) break;
      szBuffer[i++] = x;
    }

    // Terminate the string with a zero

    szBuffer[i] = '\0';

    // And update ContentLength

    ContentLength = i;
}
```

Parsing the Input

After reading data sent from STDIN by the POST method and storing the data in a local
buffer, you need to loop through the data, splitting each pair of name=value items. In
C, this process is simply a matter of searching for each ampersand character (&) to
delimit the pair and then finding the equal sign (=) within the string to split the
variable name from the variable value.

Here's a snippet of code extracted from the `ProcessPostData()` routine, which demonstrates using the C `strtok()` routine to parse the ampersands:

```
char    * pToken;            // pointer to token separator

// Find the first "&" token in the string

pToken = strtok(szBuffer,"&");

// If any tokens in the string

while (pToken != NULL)
{
    // Process the pair of tokens (var=val)
    ProcessPair (pToken);

    // And look for the next "&" token
    pToken = strtok(NULL,"&");
}
```

The `ProcessPostData()` routine calls the `ProcessPair()` routine for each pair of `var=val` items found. The action that your own script might take with each `var=val` item depends on your script's purpose. SGB1, however, is interested in only three possible variables: `name`, `email`, and `comments`. The fill-in form created during the GET process provides these three variables, which are the only ones that SGB1 uses when creating the guestbook entries.

To keep the code understandable, you use global variables to hold the data from the `name`, `email`, and `comments` variables. In a real-life program, you would probably process the data within the `ProcessPair()` routine, and use local variables only. However, by having `ProcessPair()` only identify the variables and save them, you can group functional processes together with the data that they use, even if you lose some encapsulation.

Validating the Input

Only one more feature of SGB1 needs explanation. SGB1 is careful to validate the input data before using it. In particular, SGB1 ensures that the data isn't too long for the reserved space, and that no stray HTML tags can remain in the input.

This validation is easier than it might sound. First, any program knows the size of the space that it has reserved for a particular variable. SGB1 uses the C routine `strncpy` to copy up to the maximum number of bytes. If the source string is shorter than the maximum, you do no harm; you copy only the bytes up to and including the terminating zero. If the source string is longer than the maximum, however, you copy only the maximum number of bytes and discard the rest of the source string.

You can see this protection in action in listing 4.5, within the `ProcessPair()` subroutine.

If you remove an HTML tag from a string, the resulting string is always shorter than the original. This happy circumstance enables SGB1 to edit strings *in place*—

that is, without having to copy them to temporary storage, and without having to reallocate the original storage length.

SGB1 doesn't want to let any HTML tags in the input wind up in the output. Because all HTML tags start with a left angle bracket, finding the beginning of a tag is fairly easy. SGB1 then continues parsing the string, looking for a right angle bracket. After finding this character, the script simply shortens the string, copying it right over itself and eliminating the HTML tag entirely. To see how you accomplish this process, see the `FilterHTML()` routine in listing 4.5.

Putting It All Together

Listing 4.5 contains the complete SGB1 program source code. In previous chapters, you learned about URL decoding and HTML syntax, so none of the routines to accomplish these tasks demonstrate anything conceptually new. You've learned in this chapter about those parts of the code that are new, or that demonstrate particularly desirable functions. It's time to dive in and start programming.

Feel free to use any of these routines—or the whole program—either as is or as seed for your own projects. Designed for Windows NT, this code includes a few NT-centric functions, particularly the file input/output (I/O) and date/time formatting. If you want to use this code on a UNIX machine, you must adapt those parts to use pure ANSI C run-time routines rather than the faster and more efficient Windows API calls.

> **Note:** In Chapter 10, "Storing Information in Flat Files," you learn all about flat file organization and access methods. SGB1 uses a sequential flat files to hold the guestbook data.

> **Note:** This book's companion CD-ROM includes SGB1. On the CD you'll find listing 4.5 in its entirety (SGB1.C), along with an appropriate make file for Visual C 2.x (SGB1.MAK). You'll also find a ready-to-run compiled version suitable for Windows NT (SGB1.EXE).

Listing 4.5   SGB1.C—the Complete C Source Code for SGB1

```
#include <windows.h>
#include <stdio.h>
#include <stdlib.h>
```

continues

Listing 4.5 Continued

```c
// Global storage

char    szBuffer[2048];              // generic input buffer
char    *szFileName={"sbg1.dat"};    // name of gb file
char    szEmail[80];                 // user's e-mail address
char    szComments[1024];            // user's comments
char    szName[80];                  // user's name

// SwapChar:  This routine swaps one character for another

void SwapChar(char * pOriginal, char cBad, char cGood) {
    int i;     // generic counter variable

    // Loop through the input string (cOriginal), character by
    // character, replacing each instance of cBad with cGood

    i = 0;
    while (pOriginal[i]) {
        if (pOriginal[i] == cBad) pOriginal[i] = cGood;
        i++;
    }
}

// IntFromHex:  A subroutine to unescape escaped characters.

static int IntFromHex(char *pChars) {
    int Hi;        // holds high byte
    int Lo;        // holds low byte
    int Result;    // holds result

    // Get the value of the first byte to Hi

    Hi = pChars[0];
    if ('0' <= Hi && Hi <= '9') {
        Hi -= '0';
    } else
    if ('a' <= Hi && Hi <= 'f') {
        Hi -= ('a'-10);
    } else
    if ('A' <= Hi && Hi <= 'F') {
        Hi -= ('A'-10);
    }

    // Get the value of the second byte to Lo

    Lo = pChars[1];
    if ('0' <= Lo && Lo <= '9') {
        Lo -= '0';
    } else
    if ('a' <= Lo && Lo <= 'f') {
        Lo -= ('a'-10);
```

```
      } else
      if ('A' <= Lo && Lo <= 'F') {
          Lo -= ('A'-10);
      }
      Result = Lo + (16 * Hi);
      return (Result);
}

// URLDecode -- un-URL-Encode a string.  This routine loops
// through the string pEncoded, and decodes it in place.  It
// checks for escaped values, and changes all plus signs to
// spaces. The result is a normalized string.  It calls the
// two subroutines directly above in this listing.

void URLDecode(unsigned char *pEncoded) {
    char *pDecoded;              // generic pointer

    // First, change those pesky plus signs to spaces

    SwapChar (pEncoded, '+', ' ');

    // Now, loop through, looking for escapes

    pDecoded = pEncoded;
    while (*pEncoded) {
        if (*pEncoded=='%')
        {
            // A percent sign followed by two hex digits means
            // that the digits represent an escaped character.  We
            // must decode it.

            pEncoded++;
            if (isxdigit(pEncoded[0]) && isxdigit(pEncoded[1]))
            {
                *pDecoded++ = (char) IntFromHex(pEncoded);
                pEncoded += 2;
            }
        }
        else
        {
            *pDecoded ++ = *pEncoded++;
        }
    }
    *pDecoded = '\0';
}

// GetPOSTData:  Read in data from POST operation

void GetPOSTData() {
    char * pContentLength;  // pointer to CONTENT_LENGTH
    int  ContentLength;     // value of CONTENT_LENGTH string
    int  i;                 // local counter
```

continues

73

Listing 4.5 Continued

```c
    int  x;                  // generic char holder

    // Retrieve a pointer to the CONTENT_LENGTH variable

    pContentLength = getenv("CONTENT_LENGTH");

    // If the variable exists, convert its value to an integer
    // with atoi()

    if (pContentLength != NULL)
    {
      ContentLength = atoi(pContentLength);
    }
    else
    {
      ContentLength = 0;
    }

    // Make sure specified length isn't greater than the size
    // of our statically allocated buffer

    if (ContentLength > sizeof(szBuffer)-1)
    {
      ContentLength = sizeof(szBuffer)-1;
    }

    // Now read ContentLength bytes from STDIN

    i = 0;
    while (i < ContentLength)
    {
      x = fgetc(stdin);
      if (x==EOF) break;
      szBuffer[i++] = x;
    }

    // Terminate the string with a zero

    szBuffer[i] = '\0';

    // And update ContentLength

    ContentLength = i;
}

// PrintMIMEHeader:  Prints content-type header

void PrintMIMEHeader() {
    // This is the basic MIME header for the
    // CGI.  Note that it is a 2-line header,
    // including a "pragma: no-cache" directive.
    // This keeps the page from being cached,
```

```
        // and reduces the number of duplicate
        // entries from users who keep hitting the
        // submit button over and over
        printf("Content-type: text/html\n");
        printf("Pragma: no-cache\n");
        printf("\n");

}

// PrintHTMLHeader:  Prints HTML page header

void PrintHTMLHeader() {
    printf(
        "<html>\n"
        "<head><title>SGB1.c</title></head>\n"
        "<body "
            "bgcolor=#FEFEFE "
            "text=#000000 "
            "link=#000040 "
            "alink=FF0040 "
            "vlink=#7F7F7F"
            ">\n"
        "<h1><i>CGI by Example</i></h1>\n"
        "<b>SGB1.c</b> -- demonstration CGI written "
        "in C to make a simple guestbook <p>\n"
        );
}

// PrintHTMLTrailer:  Prints closing HTML info

void PrintHTMLTrailer() {
    printf(
        "</body>\n"
        "</html>\n"
        );
}

// ProcessPair:  Processes a var=val pair

void ProcessPair (char * VarVal) {
    char * pEquals;                    // pointer to equal sign

    // Find the equal sign separating Var from Val
    pEquals = strchr(VarVal, '=');

    // If equal sign is found....
    if (pEquals != NULL)
    {
        // terminate the Var name
        *pEquals++ = '\0';

        // decode the Varname (*VarVal)
```

continues

Listing 4.5 Continued

```c
        URLDecode(VarVal);

        // and the value (*pEquals)
        URLDecode(pEquals);

        if (stricmp(VarVal,"email")==0)
        {
            // copy into szEmail global variable, being
            // careful not to overflow the variable

            strncpy(szEmail,pEquals,sizeof(szEmail)-1);
        }
        else if (stricmp(VarVal,"comments")==0)
        {
            // copy into szComments global variable, being
            // careful not to overflow the variable

            strncpy(szComments,pEquals,sizeof(szComments)-1);
        }
        else if (stricmp(VarVal,"name")==0)
        {
            // copy into szName global variable, being
            // careful not to overflow the variable

            strncpy(szName,pEquals,sizeof(szName)-1);
        }
    }
}

// FilterHTML -- removes any HTML tags from data.
// This routine removes any <> tags found in the
// szData string.  If we didn't remove these tags,
// malicious (or silly) visitors could wreak havoc
// with our guestbook data, or possibly execute an
// SSI or CGI command to get at private data

void FilterHTML (char *szData) {
    char    *pOpenAngle;
    char    *pCloseAngle;
    while (TRUE)
    {

        // Find an opening angle bracket
        pOpenAngle = strchr(szData,'<');

        // If none, all done here
        if (pOpenAngle==NULL) break;
```

```
        // Otherwise, look for the closing angle bracket
        pCloseAngle = strchr(pOpenAngle,'>');

        // If we found a closing angle bracket, snug
        // up all the characters after it, thus removing
        // the tag entirely from the string

        if (pCloseAngle)
        {
            strcpy(pOpenAngle,pCloseAngle+1);
        }

        // If no closing angle bracket, then the visitor
        // has provided invalid HTML, so truncate at the
        // opening bracket
        else
        {
            *pOpenAngle = '\0';
        }
    }
}


// FormatGBEntry -- formats GB entry

void FormatGBEntry() {
    char        szTmp[128];
    SYSTEMTIME  st;

    // start each entry with an <hr> tag
    strcpy(szBuffer,"<hr>\r\n");

    // fill in default if visitor left
    // the name field blank

    if (*szName == '\0') strcpy(szName, szEmail);

    // Remove any unwanted characters from the visitor parms

    FilterHTML(szName);
    FilterHTML(szEmail);
    FilterHTML(szComments);

    // replace any CRs or LFs in the comments
    // from the visitor with spaces
    SwapChar(szComments,'\r',' ');
    SwapChar(szComments,'\n',' ');

    // add the visitor's comments, if any
    if (*szComments != '\0')
    {
```

continues

77

Listing 4.5 Continued

```
        // make the visitor comments bold italic
        strcat(szBuffer,"<b><i>");
        strcat(szBuffer,szComments);
        strcat(szBuffer,"</i></b><br>");
    }


    // if e-mail is blank, but name isn't, use name

    if ((*szEmail=='\0') && (*szName !='\0'))
    {
        sprintf(szTmp,"%s",szName);
        strcat(szBuffer,szTmp);
    }

    // if e-mail and name are blank, say "anonymous"

    else if ((*szEmail=='\0') && (*szName =='\0'))
    {
        strcat(szBuffer,"Anonymous Visitor");
    }

    // else use e-mail address in a mailto tag

    else
    {
        strcat(szBuffer,"<a href=mailto:");
        sprintf(szTmp,"\"%s\">%s</a>",szEmail,szName);
        strcat(szBuffer,szTmp);
    }

    // whatever name we have so far, add " signed the
    // guestbook on " to it

    strcat(szBuffer," signed the guestbook on ");

    // now add the date and time

    GetLocalTime(&st);
    GetDateFormat(0,0,&st,"ddd dd MMM yyyy",szTmp,sizeof(szTmp));
    strcat(szBuffer,szTmp);
    sprintf(szTmp," at %02d:%02d:%02d.\r\n",
        st.wHour,st.wMinute,st.wSecond);
    strcat(szBuffer,szTmp);


    // always add a <br> tag and CRLF at the end

    strcat(szBuffer,"<br>\r\n");
}
```

```
// AppendToGB -- appends new entry to gb file

void AppendToGB() {
    int         iWaitForIt;         // generic counter
    HANDLE      hFile;              // file handle
    BOOL        bSuccess;           // success indicator
    DWORD       dwBytesWritten;     // num bytes written
    DWORD       dwNumBytes;         // generic counter

    // First, format the entry

    FormatGBEntry();

    // Now inform the user

    printf("<h1>Thank you for signing the guest book!</h1>\n");
    printf("Here is your entry:<p>\n");
    printf(szBuffer);

    // Set up a counter/loop.  We'll use the iWaitForIt
    // variable as our counter, and we'll go through the
    // loop up to 100 times.

    for (iWaitForIt = 0; iWaitForIt < 100; iWaitForIt++)
    {

        // Each time within the loop, we'll try to get
        // exclusive read-write access to the log file.

        hFile = CreateFile (
            szFileName,
            GENERIC_READ | GENERIC_WRITE,
            0,0,OPEN_ALWAYS,
            FILE_ATTRIBUTE_NORMAL | FILE_FLAG_WRITE_THROUGH,
            0
            );

        // If we were able to open the file, proceed with
        // the business of writing the log entry.

        if (hFile != INVALID_HANDLE_VALUE)
        {

            // This is an append operation, so we want to
            // position the file pointer to the end of the
            // file

            SetFilePointer (hFile,0L,0L,FILE_END);

            //Write out the entry now

            dwNumBytes = strlen(szBuffer);
```

continues

Listing 4.5 Continued

```c
            bSuccess = WriteFile (
                hFile,
                szBuffer,
                dwNumBytes,
                &dwBytesWritten,
                0
                );

            // And close the file, releasing the locks, so
            // another thread (or external process) can
            // access the file

            CloseHandle (hFile);

            // If the write operation was successful, and
            // the number of bytes written equals the number
            // of bytes we wanted to write, all done here

            if ( (bSuccess) && (dwNumBytes == dwBytesWritten))
            {
                return;
            }
            else
            {
                printf("Could not write to file.  "
                        "Error code %d\n",GetLastError());
                return;
            }
        }

        // Control comes here if the CreateFile call above
        // failed.  We don't care why it failed at the
        // moment.  Instead, we'll just sleep for 100 milliseconds
        // and try again (up to 100 times, or 10 seconds).  A
        // more robust routine would call GetLastError() to find
        // out WHY the open failed.  If it's anything other than
        // the file being busy right now, we should exit the loop
        // instead of trying again.

        else
        {
            Sleep(100);
        }
    }

    // If we never could get access to the file,
    // tell caller we failed

    printf("Couldn't open file.");
    return;
}
```

```
// ProcessPOSTData:  Processes data from POST buffer.
// This routine splits up the Var & Val pairs, calls
// ProcessPair() to handle the data, then calls
// AppendtoGB() to write the new record to disk.

void ProcessPOSTData() {
    char    * pToken;              // pointer to token separator

    // Find the first "&" token in the string
    pToken = strtok(szBuffer,"&");

    // If any tokens in the string
    while (pToken != NULL)
    {

        // Process the pair of tokens (var=val)
        ProcessPair (pToken);

        // And look for the next "&" token
        pToken = strtok(NULL,"&");
    }

    // Now append the data to the guestbook file
    AppendToGB();
}

// PrintGBEntries -- print out the contents of the guestbook

BOOL PrintGBEntries() {
    int        iWaitForIt;         // generic counter
    HANDLE     hFile;              // file handle
    BOOL       bSuccess;           // success indicator
    DWORD      dwBytesRead;        // num bytes written
    DWORD      dwNumBytes;         // generic counter
    DWORD      dwLastError;        // hold last err code
    char       szBuffer[1024];     // buffer for data

    // Set up a counter/loop.  We'll use the iWaitForIt
    // variable as our counter, and we'll go through the
    // loop up to 100 times.

    for (iWaitForIt = 0; iWaitForIt < 100; iWaitForIt++)
    {

        // Each time within the loop, we'll try to get
        // nonexclusive read access to the log file.

        hFile = CreateFile (
            szFileName,
            GENERIC_READ,
            FILE_SHARE_READ,0,OPEN_EXISTING,
```

continues

Listing 4.5 Continued

```
                    FILE_ATTRIBUTE_NORMAL,
            0
            );

        // If we were unable to open the file, find out
        // why

        if (hFile == INVALID_HANDLE_VALUE)
        {
            dwLastError = GetLastError();
            switch (dwLastError)
            {
                case ERROR_FILE_NOT_FOUND:

                    // file doesn't exist

                    return FALSE;

                case ERROR_SHARING_VIOLATION:
                case ERROR_LOCK_VIOLATION:

                    // file is busy
                    // so sleep for .1 second

                    Sleep(100);
                    break;

                default:

                    // some other fatal error
                    // we don't care what; just
                    // exit

                    return FALSE;
            }
        }
    }

    // At this point, the file is open for read.
    // Loop through the whole thing, reading as
    // much as possible at a time, printing whatever
    // we get.  When the file reaches the end,
    // close it and return

    while (TRUE)
    {
        dwNumBytes = sizeof(szBuffer);
        bSuccess = ReadFile (
            hFile,
            szBuffer,
            dwNumBytes,
```

```
            &dwBytesRead,
            0
            );
        if ( (bSuccess==FALSE) ¦¦ (dwBytesRead==0))
        {

            // file is done, or there was an error

            CloseHandle(hFile);
            return TRUE;
        }
        else
        {

            // print out what we got

            szBuffer[dwBytesRead]='\0';
            printf(szBuffer);
        }
    }
}

// PrintForm -- prints the fill-in form at the head of the
// guestbook display

void PrintForm() {

    // This is a self-referencing form.  That is, it takes the
    // name of the script from the SCRIPT_NAME environment
    // variable, and creates a form to reinvoke the script using
    // the POST method

    printf("<b>Won't you please sign the guestbook?</b><p>\n");
    printf("<ul>\n");
    printf("<form method=POST action=\"%s\">\n",getenv("SCRIPT_NAME"));
    printf("Your name:  ");
    printf("<input type=TEXT name=name  size=30 maxlength=80><br>\n");
    printf("Your email address:  ");
    printf("<input type=TEXT name=email size=30 maxlength=80><br>\n");
    printf("Your comments:<br>\n");
    printf("<textarea rows=3 cols=40 name=comments>\n");
    printf("</textarea><p>\n");
    printf("<input type=submit value=\" Submit \"><br>\n");
    printf("</form>\n<p>\n");
    printf("</ul>");
}

// The script's entry point

void main() {
```

continues

Listing 4.5 Continued

```c
char * pRequestMethod;  // pointer to REQUEST_METHOD

// First, set STDOUT to unbuffered

setvbuf(stdout,NULL,_IONBF,0);

// Zero out the global variables

ZeroMemory(szEmail,sizeof(szEmail));
ZeroMemory(szComments,sizeof(szComments));
ZeroMemory(szName,sizeof(szName));

// Figure out how we were invoked, and determine what
// to do based on that

pRequestMethod = getenv("REQUEST_METHOD");

if (pRequestMethod==NULL) {

    // No request method; must have been invoked from
    // the command line.  Print a message and terminate.

    printf("This program is designed to run as a CGI script, "
           "not from the command-line.\n");

}

else if (stricmp(pRequestMethod,"GET")==0) {

    // Request-method was GET; this means we should
    // print out the guestbook

    PrintMIMEHeader();      // Print MIME header
    PrintHTMLHeader();      // Print HTML header
    PrintForm();            // Print guestbook form
    PrintGBEntries();       // Print contents of guestbook
    PrintHTMLTrailer();     // Print HTML trailer
}

else if (stricmp(pRequestMethod,"POST")==0) {

    // Request-method was POST; this means we should
    // parse the input and create a new entry in
    // the guestbook

    PrintMIMEHeader();      // Print MIME header
    PrintHTMLHeader();      // Print HTML header
    GetPOSTData();          // Get POST data to szBuffer
    ProcessPOSTData();      // Process the POST data
    PrintHTMLTrailer();     // Print HTML trailer
```

```
    }

    else
    {

        // Request-method wasn't null, but wasn't GET or
        // POST either.  Output an error message and die

        PrintMIMEHeader();        // Print MIME header
        PrintHTMLHeader();        // Print HTML header
        printf("Only GET and POST methods supported.\n");
        PrintHTMLTrailer();       // Print HTML trailer
    }

    // Finally, flush the output & terminate

    fflush(stdout);
}
```

Summary

The SGB1 program provides a simple guestbook. It is not robust enough for long-term use on a busy site, but should provide you with enough information to start writing your own guestbook.

In this chapter, you learned practical methods of applying the principles discussed in earlier chapters, and had the opportunity to learn CGI by example.

Review Questions

1. How does SGB1 validate the e-mail address supplied by the user?

2. How does SGB1 prevent szBuffer from overflowing while reading STDIN on a POST operation?

3. How does SGB1 know whether to create and display the fill-in form for signing the guestbook?

4. Can a visitor use any tricks to override the name or location of the guestbook data file?

5. What is the name and location of the guestbook data file?

6. What environment variable does SGB1 use to create the URL necessary for reinvoking itself under the POST method?

7. What three variables does SGB1 create for the fill-in form during GET, then read back during POST?

Review Exercises

1. Expand SGB1 to include more information about each visitor. Add fields for the visitor's browser and IP address. Could you keep the same basic structure, or would you have to redesign the script?

2. Develop an alternative way of deciding the name of the guestbook data file and the directory in which the file should be located. Do you understand why hard-coding the file name is not an attractive option in a real-life situation? How can you improve this aspect of the script?

3. SGB1 hard-codes screen background and text colors. Redesign the script so that it can blend in with any given site's color and background scheme?

4. Modify the `FilterHTML()` routine so that it screens out only "harmful" HTML tags? What HTML tags would you consider appropriate for visitors to use in their comments?

## CHAPTER 5

An Online Order Form

One of the best uses for CGI is to enable a potential customer to visit your site and order a product online. Although such commercial enterprises aren't the most important facet of the Internet, the market is driving the development of the Internet and its standards. Enabling businesses to market products online is the Internet's next evolutionary step.

All of a sudden, just about every other television commercial is displaying the sponsor's Web address, because businesses believe that the Internet holds marketing potential. Originally, people thought that the Web would only be a medium for displaying information. CGI changes that.

This chapter discusses online order forms. Such forms enable a visitor to your site to order a product online. After the visitor submits the order, the request is sent by e-mail to someone who processes the request. Although this chapter's example application involves a fictitious car sales company, the same form can apply to anything—flowers, computers, candy, or anything else that you can imagine selling on the Web.

The Web Page

You first need to create the Web page. This page enables the visitor to enter information, select items from lists or check boxes, and submit the information that they entered, which is then sent to a script.

For the HTML document to be effective, it must be intuitive. Simply by looking at the page, the visitor should be able to understand what information needs to be entered where. The more intuitive your page, the more likely your script will work properly, and the less likely your page is to confuse and discourage the visitor.

The document's first section should tell the visitor the page's purpose. In this chapter's example page, a car dealership wants to sell its autos on the Web.

Next, you want to enable the visitor to enter personal information, such as his or her name, e-mail address, home address, and anything else that you need to process the order and send the product to the customer.

Finally, you give the visitor a list of order items from which to choose. In this chapter's example page, you enable the visitor to select an automobile and choose various options to customize the selected car.

The HTML Document's Introductory Section

You start by creating the HTML document's first section. In this section, as shown in listing 5.1, you simply open the HTML document, give it a title, and provide a little introductory information for your visitors.

Listing 5.1   BUYCAR.HTML—the First Portion of the HTML Document

```
<HTML>
<HEAD>
<TITLE>Supkay's New Cars </TITLE>
</HEAD>

<BODY>
<H1> Welcome to Supkay's New Cars! </H1>
Why it's nice to see you! We have here some <b>BIG</b> deals just
awaitin' for you to come by and drive off with them! With our
wide range of choices, I'm sure you'll just find somethin'
you'll <b>love</b>!

<HR>
<FORM ACTION="/cgi-bin/buycar.pl" METHOD="POST">

<PRE>
```

You name the HTML page BUYCAR.HTML, and the script BUYCAR.PL. You use the <PRE> tag to make formatting the page a little easier. You could use tables instead.

Determining the Information To Elicit from the Customer

You next need to decide what information you want or need from the customer. You definitely need to enable the visitor to choose specific items. You also need the visitor's name and address. You most likely need to determine a way for the visitor to pay for the item that he or she is purchasing—unless, of course, the item is free. You also must decide which NAME to assign to each entry. You should keep the NAME short, but at the same time, you want it to be clear. The following is a list of items that the visitor should fill out, with a name assigned to each:

First Name = `fname`

Last Name = `lname`

Email   = `email`

Now place this list in the document as follows:

```
Enter your first name:<INPUT TYPE="text" NAME="fname" SIZE=46>
 Enter your last name:<INPUT TYPE="text" NAME="lname" SIZE=46>
   Your email address:<INPUT TYPE="text" NAME="email"
➥    VALUE="you@your.domain.com" SIZE=46>
```

Separating the first and last name, instead of having one field contain both, is a good idea. Then you can more easily manipulate the first and last names separately when creating the script. The last line creates a text box in which the customer can enter an e-mail address. Notice the use of the VALUE attribute. This usage helps give the visitor an idea of the type of input that you want. Also, you use the SIZE attribute to limit the length of each field to 46. You do so only to manipulate the HTML document's appearance.

Now you need a mailing address so that you can send your product to the customer:

Street = `street`

City = `city`

State = `state`

Zip = `zip`

You can also ask for a telephone number—just in case you can't reach the customer by e-mail:

Home Phone = `hphone`

Work Phone = `wphone`

This should be enough information for this Web page. Of course, you can add any additional information specific to your requirements. Now place this information in the document:

```
Street Address:<INPUT TYPE="text" NAME="street" SIZE=46>
          City:<INPUT TYPE="text" NAME="city" SIZE=12>
         State:<INPUT TYPE="text" NAME="state" SIZE=14>
           ZIP:<INPUT TYPE="text" NAME="zip" SIZE=6>

    Home Phone:<INPUT TYPE="text" NAME="hphone" SIZE=13>
    Work Phone:<INPUT TYPE="text" NAME="wphone" SIZE=13>
<HR>
```

Presenting Product Options

Now you need to present visitors with a list of products that they can buy. Most likely, you will also need to list additional options. For example, a florist who is selling roses would want to give the customer a choice of a specific color, length, and so on.

In this chapter's example, you're selling cars, so you want to give the customer a choice of various models, colors, years, and some additional features.

For the model, you offer choices of the Tortoise, the Hyena, the Aphid, and the Diamond Back:

> model = Tortoise
>
> Hyena
>
> Aphid
>
> Diamond Back

In this example, model is the NAME, and Tortoise, Hyena, Aphid, and Diamond Back are the values. You can let the user select a model by using the <SELECT> tag, or you can use the radio input type. In this example, you use the <SELECT> tag.

For color options, you offer green, purple, brown, and teal:

> Color = green
>
> purple
>
> brown
>
> teal

Next you offer the customer the options of the 1995, 1996, or 1997 models:

> Year = 1995
>
> 1996
>
> 1997

To provide these options in the code, listing 5.2 uses <SELECT> for the model and year, and a radio input type for the color.

Listing 5.2   BUYCAR.HTML—Let the Visitor Pick a Car

```
Here's your chance to pick out some top quality cars from
Storlie Automotive!

Model/Year: <SELECT NAME="model">
<OPTION> Tortoise
<OPTION> Hyena
<OPTION> Aphid
<OPTION> Diamond Back
</SELECT><SELECT NAME="year">
```

```
<OPTION> 1995
<OPTION> 1996
<OPTION> 1997
</SELECT>

Color:</PRE>
<INPUT TYPE="radio" NAME="color" VALUE="purple">Purple
<INPUT TYPE="radio" NAME="color" VALUE="green">Green
<INPUT TYPE="radio" NAME="color" VALUE="brown">Brown
<INPUT TYPE="radio" NAME="color" VALUE="teal">Teal
```

Note: Notice that you remove the `<PRE>` tag temporarily so that the radio buttons display side-by-side. If you were to include the `<PRE>` tag, you would have to place all four colors on one line—and because this book's width is limited, you wouldn't get to see half the information. Without the `<PRE>` tag, the choices are placed side-by-side. (HTML doesn't recognize white spaces.)

Now you present additional options: a passenger-side airbag, rear window defroster, plastic hubcaps, and a spare tire.

Give each of these options its own value. Also use the `checkbox` input type so that if the customer doesn't choose an option, you don't have to worry about it within your script. The script simply checks whether the user selected the check box, and if so, reacts appropriately.

Passenger Side Airbag = `airbag`

Plastic Hub Caps   = `pcaps`

Rear Window Defrost = `rdefrost`

Spare Tire   = `stire`

The HTML page would look like the following:

```
<PRE>
<INPUT TYPE="checkbox" NAME="airbag">Passenger Side Airbag
<INPUT TYPE="checkbox" NAME="pcaps">Plastic Hub Caps
<INPUT TYPE="checkbox" NAME="rdefrost">Rear Window Defrost
<INPUT TYPE="checkbox" NAME="stire">Spare Tire
```

Notice that each name describes what the value actually is. When examining your code, you can easily determine what each value represents. The names are short, but self-explanatory.

Now enable the visitor to choose from a two-door, three-door, or a four-door model:

Doors = 2

        3

        4

You could use the <SELECT> tag, or the radio input type. Here you use another radio input type to let the visitor choose one of the three choices:

```
<INPUT TYPE="radio" NAME="doors" VALUE="2"> 2-door
<INPUT TYPE="radio" NAME="doors" VALUE="3"> 2-door with hatchback
<INPUT TYPE="radio" NAME="doors" VALUE="4"> 4-door
```

After getting the customer's personal information and choice of car, you need to find out how the customer is going to pay for it.

Using the name Billing, you give the customer two options: Bill Me and Credit Card:

Billing = bill

　　　　 ccard

(Of course, car dealers don't simply "bill" customers. The example uses these somewhat unrealistic options just to demonstrate how you can present different options for customers.) If the customer chooses the credit card option, you have to get the credit card information as well.

Next, you provide three fields normally associated with credit cards: the credit card name, the credit card number, and an expiration date for the card:

Credit card name　　　 = Cname

Credit card number　　 = cnum

Credit card expiration = cexpire

When you write the script, you check whether the customer selected the credit card option; if so, you include the credit card information when mailing the request.

Now you simply format the payment options with HTML, as shown in listing 5.3.

Listing 5.3   BUYCAR.HTML—Let the Visitor Choose How To Pay for the Car

```
<HR>
Payment:
<INPUT TYPE="radio" NAME="billing" VALUE="bill">Bill me!
<INPUT TYPE="radio" NAME="billing" VALUE="ccard">Credit Card
   Name on card:<INPUT TYPE="text" NAME="cname" SIZE=46>
   Credit card number:<INPUT TYPE="text" NAME="cnum" SIZE=14>
   Expiration date:<INPUT TYPE="text" NAME="cexpire" SIZE=8>
</PRE>
<HR>
```

Sending the Order

Finally, you want to enable the customer to send the information to you. To do so, you simply use the input type submit; you also include the input type reset just in case the customer wants to start reentering the order.

```
Now if this is what you want, press <INPUT TYPE="submit"
➥ VALUE="HERE"><br>
Or if you think you're making a mistake, <INPUT TYPE="reset"
➥ VALUE="Clear the form">

</FORM>
</BODY>
</HTML>
```

You don't want to add anything else to the form, so close the <FORM> tag, as well as the <BODY> and the <HTML> tags.

Now that you're finished, your order form should look much like the page shown in figure 5.1.

Figure 5.1

You now have a complete form in which customers can purchase a shiny new car.

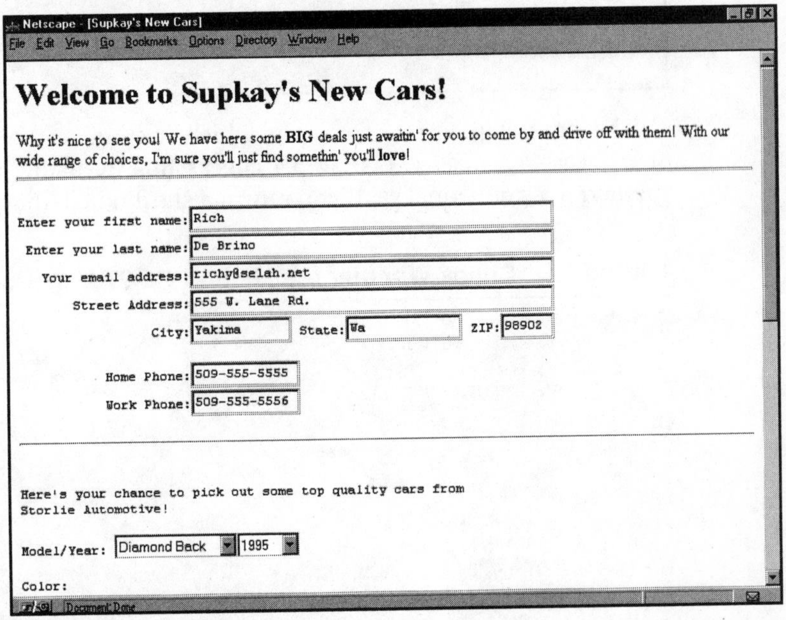

Of course, you can add any graphics, backgrounds, or links to other pages to give the order form a professional appearance. You could even change the HTML page's formatting to suit your particular taste. For the purposes of this particular example, however, the form is finished. Now it's time to work on the script.

The Script

Now all you have to do is take the information that the visitor painstakingly entered. Create a script that sends the information by e-mail to someone who can process it. Then let the visitor know that the order is successful.

Determining the Method

You first need to find out whether the script used the method POST to receive the information.

Was the information sent using the method POST?

If not, then let the visitor know.

If so, then continue.

First you tell the script which program you are using to interpret it. In this case, you are using Perl. You have to tell the script the interpreter's path and file name.

> **Note:** Using UNIX, the easiest way to find a file's path is by the use of the which and whereis commands. Many flavors of UNIX exist, so if one of these commands doesn't work, try the other.

The next step is to determine which method is being used by checking $ENV{'REQUEST_METHOD'}. Listing 5.4 checks this by using an if statement. If the method does not equal POST, you return a short note telling the visitor so.

Listing 5.4   Check Whether the Method *POST* Was Used

```perl
#! /usr/local/bin/perl

if ($ENV{'REQUEST_METHOD'} ne 'POST')
{
    print <<"HTML";
    <HTML>
    <HEAD>
    <TITLE>Sorry!</TITLE>
    </HEAD>
    <BODY>
    <H1>Sorry, wrong METHOD used!</H1>

    I'm sorry, but we only use the method POST here.
    </BODY>
    </HTML>

HTML

    exit;
}
```

Splitting the Information into Name/Value Pairs

You next need to split the information into the name/value pairs. Listing 5.5 shows how to do so.

Listing 5.5   Split the Incoming Stream into Name/Value Pairs

```
read(STDIN, $buffer, $ENV{'CONTENT_LENGTH'});
@pairs = split(/&/, $buffer);
foreach $pair (@pairs)
    {
    ($name, $value) = split(/=/, $pair);
    $value =~ tr/+/ /;
    $value =~ s/%([a-fA-F0-9][a-fA-F0-9])/pack("C", hex($1))/eg;
    $form{$name} = $value;

    }
```

You first read STDIN until the end of the stream as defined by the use of $ENV{'CONTENT_LENGTH'}. Next you separate the lines, dividing the line at the ampersand (&) into the @pairs array. At this point, you have a bunch of name/value pairs sitting in the array. For each pair, you need to split the name/value and replace any plus signs with the appropriate spaces. (Remember that when you send the data stream to the server, spaces are replaced with the plus sign.) Then you need to convert any escaped characters back into their ASCII form. You then place each name/value pair into the array $form. Then you can call up each name/value pair using $form{'name'}.

Handling Elements That the Form Doesn't Pass

Now that you have finished the hardest part of the script, you need to prepare the rest. The form has not passed four things that the script needs:

♦ The date.

♦ The e-mail address of the person who receives the request.

♦ The mail program's path and name.

♦ A subject line for the e-mail that tells the receiver that the order form is for a car purchase. This line helps the reader learn the nature of the request without having to look at the whole message.

Getting the Date

You can get the date automatically by using Perl's chop() function:

```
chop($date = 'date');
```

This command yields a result such as the following:

```
Thu May 23 15:02:15 PDT 1996
```

You can change the $date string's format. Check the man pages on date for information concerning the format.

Handling E-Mail

Now you set up the strings that define the e-mail's destination, the mail program, and the subject line:

```
$mailprog ="/usr/lib/sendmail";
$sendto = "rniles\@selah.net";
$subject = "Automobile purchase";
```

Next you want to send your e-mail. You first use the open() function to route your output to sendmail:

```
open(MAIL, "|$mailprog -t")
```

This command simply assigns the handle MAIL to pipe to the $mailprog string that you defined earlier. A pipe changes STDOUT. Without the pipe, all the information returns to the visitor within an HTML document. If you change the pipe's direction, you can send the information to the UNIX sendmail program instead.

The next three lines create your e-mail header. The $sendto string that you set earlier defines the To: line. The From: line is a mixture of three of the fields that the visitor entered. You use the visitor's e-mail address, first name, and last name. Finally, you add the subject.

Together the three lines are as follows:

```
print MAIL "To: $sendto\n";
print MAIL "From: $form{'email'} ($form{'fname'} $form{'lname'})\n";
print MAIL "Subject: $subject\n\n";
```

Notice the use of \n, which is a line feed. Without \n, everything would be on one line. After you print the Subject:, you provide two new lines that separate the message header from the message's body.

Next you tell the print statement to print out everything to the MAIL handle until it finds EOM. This condition enables you to use the print statement once to print multiple lines.

```
print MAIL <<"EOM";

On $date, $form{'fname'} $form{'lname'} decided to buy a car from us.

$form{'fname'} chose a $form{'color'} $form{'year'} $form{'model'}
➡ $form{'doors'}-door.

$form{'fname'} wanted the following options as well:
EOM
```

Notice how you use the strings from the form to create a sentence. You simply insert the strings into the text so that they help create your message. Depending on the customer's form entries, the message might look like the following:

```
On Thu May 23 15:02:15 PDT 1996, John Doe decided to buy a car
➡ from us.

John chose a green 1996 Hyena 4-door.

John wanted the following options as well:
```

Next you perform a few `if()` statements. The script essentially says

If `airbag` *exists, then print* Passenger Airbag.

If `pcaps` *exists, then print* Plastic Hubcaps.

If `rdefrost` *exists, then print* Rear Window Defrost.

If `stire` *exists, then print* Spare Tire.

With Perl, you code these `if()` statements as follows:

```
if ($form{'airbag'})
    {
     print MAIL "- Passenger Airbag\n";
    }
if ($form{'pcaps'})
    {
     print MAIL "- Plastic Hubcaps\n";
    }
if ($form{'rdefrost'})
    {
     print MAIL "- Rear Window Defrost\n";
    }
if ($form{'stire'})
    {
     print MAIL "- Spare Tire\n";
    }
```

Then, to save effort, you once again enter the following command:

```
print MAIL <<"EOM";
```

This command saves you from having to add the `print` statement for each line. See whether you can figure out what is going on in the following example:

```
Here's $form{'fname'}\'s personal information:
$form{'fname'} $form{'lname'}
$form{'email'}
$form{'street'}
$form{'city'}, $form{'state'} $form{'zip'}

Home phone: $form{'hphone'}
Work phone: $form{'wphone'}

$form{'fname'} asked that we:

EOM
```

Determining the Customer's Billing Choice

Next you need to determine which billing method the customer chose. Again, you use the `if()` statements as follows:

See whether the customer chose Bill Me.

If so, print Bill Me.

See whether the customer chose Credit Card.

If so, print credit card information.

Because the form uses the `radio` input type, the customer must select either Bill Me or Credit Card. You simply check which of these the customer chose.

```
if ($form{'billing'} eq "bill")
   {
    print MAIL "Bill them later.\n";
   }
if ($form{'billing'} eq "ccard")
   {
    print MAIL "Charge it to a credit card, which is in the name of ";
    print MAIL "$form{'cname'}.\n";
    print MAIL "CC\#$form{'cnum'}
    ➥ and expires on $form{'cexpire'}.\n\n";
   }
```

Now whenever you open a file handle, you must close it. You opened the MAIL file handle, so when you finish using the handle, you must use the close() function to close the file handle:

```
print MAIL "Please process the request as soon as possible";
close(MAIL);
```

After you close the file handle, you send the mail on its way. Figure 5.2 shows the e-mail message in its final form.

Figure 5.2

The script processes the form, creating an e-mail message.

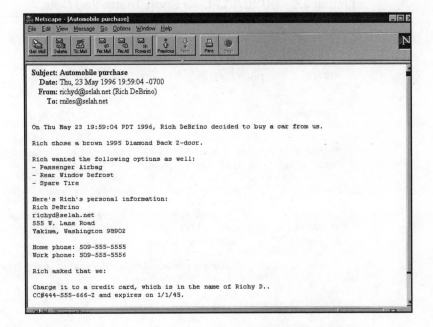

Returning a Message to the Customer

At this point, you could consider your script done. It receives the customer's information and sends out the request by e-mail. However, the main purpose of a CGI script is to return something new to the visitor. In this case, you might simply want to tell the customer that the program processed the order okay, and that he or she can move on.

In this section, you create a quick page that presents just such a message. You simply append to your script the code that generates this page. After sending the e-mail, the script returns a message to the customer.

You first must tell the server the script's MIME type. Although a script usually uses text/html, you can also use text/plain; if you are sending a .GIF file, you use image/gif. Other options are available, but these are the most commonly used ones.

Here is the `print` statement that reveals the script's MIME type:

```
print "Content-type: text/html\n\n";
```

As you might recall from Chapter 4, "A Simple Guestbook," you must follow the content type with two line feeds.

Now you use the shortcut shown in listing 5.6, which simply prints everything until reaching HTML.

Listing 5.6 BUYCAR.PL—a Short Thank-You Note

```
print <<"HTML";
<HTML>
<HEAD>
<TITLE>Thank you!</TITLE>
</HEAD>

<BODY>
<H1> Thank you for your order! </H1>

Thank you for your order <B>$form{'fname'}</B>! I assure you that this
message has been emailed to the proper department, and we'll be getting
your brand new $form{'color'} $form{'year'} $form{'model'}
$form{'doors'}-door to you as soon as we check your credit history
with a fine tooth comb.<P>
If you don't hear from us for over 8 months or so, please contact
<A HREF=\"mailto:$sendto\">$sendto</A>, and ask why your order hasn't
processed as <B>quickly</B> as you expected.<P>

In the meantime, enjoy yourself! It was sure nice having you along!!<P>

<I>Sincerely,</I><BR>
Mr. Supkay himself.
</BODY>
</HTML>

HTML
```

> **Note:** Notice the backslash in the `mailto:` line. To ensure that you don't confuse Perl, sometimes it is best to escape the quotation marks by using the backslash. Then the Perl interpreter knows that the quotation marks are part of the display text, not part of the Perl code.

Finally, you exit the program using the `exit()` function:

```
exit();
```

Believe it or not, your order form application is finished! Figure 5.3 shows the message that you return to the customer.

Figure 5.3

You return this page to customers, letting them know that you have processed their query.

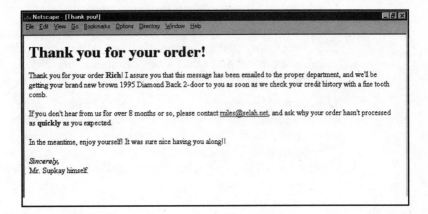

Summary

Although this chapter has presented one example of an order form, this example is by no means the extent of the script's possibilities. You can have the script save this information to a log file. You could even use a database to store information. The possibilities are endless.

In this chapter, you learned how to create an HTML document using forms. You have also learned how to create a script that enables this information to be sent to another user. Essentially, you have just created a Web interface to e-mail information to another person. With just a few changes, you could create a script that enables a visitor to use a form to leave you messages. You also learned the most important concept of CGI programming: how to return to the visitor a document that you created on the fly.

Review Questions

1. When using the POST method, what string do you use to find out the length of the data being sent?

2. When you use Perl, what does \n do?

3. Which character separates name/value pairs within a query?

4. Which character separates the name from the value within a query?

Review Exercises

1. Write a script that takes the name of a visitor, along with his or her e-mail address, and then enables the visitor to e-mail you a short comment.

2. Write a script that processes an order for your organization. If you don't belong to any particular organization, write a script that enables a visitor to order a camera and select accessory items such as lens, flash, and camera stand. E-mail the order to yourself or someone else in your organization.

3. Rewrite your script from Exercise 5-2 so that after the visitor enters ordering information, the script e-mails the order back to the visitor for confirmation. Alternatively, alter the script so that visitors can place an order by regular mail. This alternative might be attractive to customers unsure about sending payment or credit card information over the Internet.

Part III

User Interaction

## CHAPTER 6

Advanced Scripts

So far, you've learned how to create a form to interact with the visitors to your site. You have also learned how to create simple scripts that process input information in some way. Now you need to prepare for some of the problems that you might encounter when using these scripts.

This chapter covers some of these problems and discusses some solutions that you can use to ensure that any bad results don't get any worse. Although you cannot anticipate everything that could go wrong, you can take some precautions to reduce the likelihood of anything going wrong.

You also learn how to return information to visitors so that they can confirm the information that they previously entered. Finally, the chapter describes how to use CGI scripts to personalize your Web pages.

Error Detection

Humans are prone to error. Both the script creator and the script user can eventually do something that causes the script to fail to perform as intended. Your script could encounter a problem that you didn't anticipate, or a user could enter information that your script didn't expect.

In this section, you create a script in which the visitor enters a name and e-mail address (see fig. 6.1). The script then adds the visitor to a text file used for a mailing list. Listing 6.1 shows this basic script, which simply prompts for a name and an e-mail address and then stores the information in a text file.

Figure 6.1

This simple form enables visitors to add themselves to a mailing list.

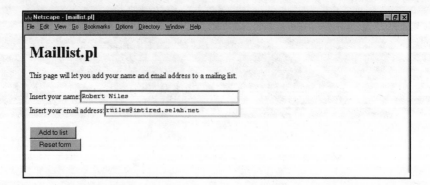

Listing 6.1 MAILLIST.PL—a Simple Script To Add a Visitor to a Mailing List

```perl
#! /usr//bin/perl
print "Content-type: text/html\n\n";

if ($ENV{'REQUEST_METHOD'} ne 'POST')
{
    print <<"HTML";
    <HTML>
    <HEAD>
    <TITLE>Sorry!</TITLE>
    </HEAD>
    <BODY>
    <H1>Sorry, wrong METHOD used!</H1>

    I'm sorry, but we only use the method POST here.
    </BODY>
    </HTML>

HTML

    exit;
}

read(STDIN, $buffer, $ENV{'CONTENT_LENGTH'});
@pairs = split(/&/, $buffer);
foreach $pair (@pairs)
    {
    ($name, $value) = split(/=/, $pair);
    $value =~ tr/+/ /;
    $value =~ s/%([a-fA-F0-9][a-fA-F0-9])/pack("C", hex($1))/eg;
    $form{$name} = $value;

    }
open(LIST, ">>weblist.txt");
print LIST "$form{'name'}\:$form{'email'}\n";
close(LIST);
print <<"HTML";
```

```
<HTML>
<HEAD><TITLE>Thank you</TITLE></HEAD>
<BODY>
<H1>Thank you</H1>
Your name has been added to the mailing list. If you would like
➥ to be removed from the mailing list, please let
<A HREF="mailto:rniles\@selah.net">Robert Niles</A> know.
</BODY>
</HTML>
```

The script takes the visitor's name and e-mail address and stores that information in a file called WEBLIST.TXT. Then the script sends the visitor a small note explaining that he or she has been added to the list (see fig. 6.2).

Figure 6.2

When you return a small message, you give the visitor a sign that the script is successful.

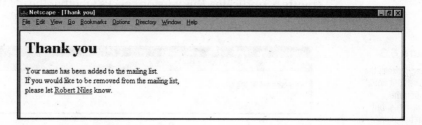

The script seems simple enough, but anyone who works with computers knows that anything can go wrong. You need to reduce the chances of such mishaps. Doing so can only make your script more stable.

Examine the following code line:

```
open(LIST, ">>weblist.txt");
```

You can see that a file handle has been opened to write information to WEBLIST.TXT. What would happen if you moved WEBLIST.TXT to some other location, or if the server can't write the file? In this example, the script would simply continue as if nothing happened. Of course, the script wouldn't add visitors to the mailing list, so when they return to the mailing list, they will wonder why their name isn't included. Meanwhile, you will begin to wonder why no one is interested in your mailing list.

You need to find out whether your script can open the file as you requested. If it can't, you must ensure that your script informs the visitor.

Open the file.

Is there a problem?

If so, let the visitor know.

If not, continue with the script.

If your script cannot open the file, you can have your script simply exit by using the die function. For example, the following line evaluates the open() function; if the script cannot open the file, the expression on the right executes:

```
open(LIST, ">>weblist.txt") || do {print "Can't open weblist.txt"; die;};
```

Note the pseudocode version of the preceding line:

Open WEBLIST.TXT.

If the open fails,

   tell the visitor Can't open WEBLIST.TXT

   exit the script.

As figure 6.3 indicates, this version checks whether the file WEBLIST.TXT exists. However, the version doesn't explain why the script failed.

Figure 6.3

This script tells the visitor that it could not open the database file, but doesn't explain why.

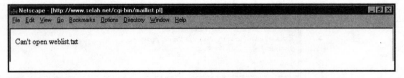

The following line returns a bit more information to the user:

```
open(LIST, ">>weblist.txt") || do {print
➥ "Can't open weblist.txt: $!"; die;};
```

The $! variable tells you why the statement on the left failed. Using the $! variable not only tells visitors that something went wrong, it gives them an idea of why the failure occurred (see fig. 6.4).

Figure 6.4

You can use Perl's $! variable to tell your visitor why the script failed.

At this point, your visitor knows that the script failed and has a general idea why. Unless you are constantly ensuring the integrity of your scripts, you might want to give the visitor a way to contact you and tell you that an error exists. By giving visitors a way to help correct problems, you make your life a little easier, and make your page less annoying for visitors.

To enable visitors to inform you about problems, you have the script call a subroutine if it encounters an error when writing to the WEBLIST.TXT file:

```
open(LIST, ">>weblist.txt") || &error;
```

In pseudocode, this subroutine is as follows:

Open WEBLIST.TXT.

If you cannot open the file, then go to the subroutine &error.

Listing 6.2 shows the code that informs the visitor about errors. Note that along with the information explaining why the script can't open the file, you give the visitors a chance to tell you about the error, by providing them with a hyperlink that enables them to e-mail you. This user-friendly feature might make visitors more inclined to let you know about the problem.

Listing 6.2 MAILLIST.PL—Let Visitors Know about Any Error and Give Them A Chance to Let You Know About It

```
sub error {

print <<"HTML";
<HTML>
<HEAD><TITLE>Error!</TITLE></HEAD>
<BODY>
<H1>Error!</H1>
I'm sorry but there has been an error while opening the
mailing list: <B>$!</B>.
<P>
Please let the <A HREF="mailto:webmaster.selah.net">
➥ webmaster</A> know.<P>
Thank you.
</BODY>
</HTML>
HTML
exit();

}
```

This subroutine returns to the visitor a message similar to that shown in figure 6.5. This time, however, the subroutine provides a `mailto:` link.

Figure 6.5

Providing a little more information and a means by which the visitor can inform you of a problem can help immensely when an error occurs that you need to correct.

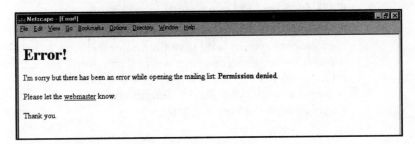

> **Note:** When you create a script, there is great potential for problems to arise. You should always test the script thoroughly before unleashing it on the public. Of course, whenever you can enable the script to check itself for errors, you should always do so.

Visitor Errors

When entering information into a database, a visitor can easily make a mistake such as placing an e-mail address where the name belongs. If such a mistake occurs, it can invalidate the database's contents. If a user needs your name but instead receives an e-mail address, the database isn't functioning as intended.

User errors are one of the biggest problems with creating scripts. In the preceding example, the mailing list doesn't function correctly if the visitor mistakenly reverses the name and the e-mail address. When you write CGI scripts, you have to consider such possible errors and, where possible, check to ensure that visitors have entered information as intended.

In the database example, the visitor might commit five errors:

♦ Failing to fill out the form completely

♦ Entering an e-mail address where the name belongs

♦ Placing something other than the e-mail address where it belongs (for example, many people mistakenly try to add their HTTP URL)

♦ Adding their entry when they already have an entry in your mailing list

♦ Entering someone else's name and e-mail address

This section discusses corrective actions for each error, so that you can limit the potential problems that might occur as visitors use your script.

Fill It Up, Please

You should first check whether the visitor filled out the form completely. If the form is incomplete, you should give the visitor a chance to try again. Although you're unlikely to encounter this error with a short, simple form, the error is quite common on larger forms.

In your script, you simply determine whether the values for each name and e-mail address contain any data.

Check whether the name and e-mail values contain any data.

If the name lacks a value, then tell the visitor that the form is incomplete.

If the e-mail address lacks a value, then tell the visitor that the form is incomplete.

You can easily accomplish these objectives with the following two lines:

```
&not_complete unless $form{'name'};
&not_complete unless $form{'email'};
```

You add these lines right after you finish breaking up STDIN, so the script checks these conditions before doing anything else. These lines tell the script to go to the subroutine not_complete (shown in listing 6.3) unless the strings contain a value.

Listing 6.3   A Subroutine That Informs the Visitor That the Information Is Complete

```
sub not_complete {
print <<"HTML";
<HTML>
<HEAD><TITLE>Form incomplete</TITLE></HEAD>

<BODY>
<H1> Form Incomplete</H1>
I'm sorry, but the form was not completely filled out.<P>
If you wish to be added to the mailing list, please enter your
name and email address.<BR>
Thank you<P>
<HR>

<FORM ACTION="/cgi-bin/maillist.pl" METHOD="POST">
Insert your name:<INPUT TYPE="text" NAME="name" VALUE="$form{'name'}
➥ " SIZE=40><br>
Insert your email address:<INPUT TYPE="text" NAME="email"
➥ VALUE="$form{'email'}" SIZE=34><br>

<p>
<INPUT TYPE="submit" VALUE="Add to list"><br>
<INPUT TYPE="reset" VALUE="Reset form">

</FORM>
</BODY>
</HTML>
HTML
exit();
}
```

This subroutine creates a form that the script returns to the visitor. Any information that the visitor entered passes along with the form. Figure 6.6 shows the form.

Figure 6.6

If the visitor didn't complete the form, your script creates another form that alerts the visitor and provides another opportunity to complete the form.

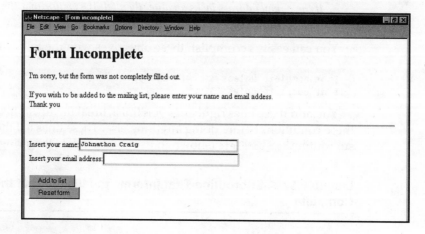

What's in a Name?

Although ensuring that a name is correctly entered is quite difficult, you can take a few steps to ensure that the visitor hasn't entered something else where the name belongs. You can at least ensure that the information entered isn't a URL, an e-mail address, or something else off the wall. To do so, you check whether the visitor entered symbols not normally associated with names. The following statement checks whether the visitor's name includes any strange characters:

```
if ($form{'name'} =~ /[!@#\$%^&*()+=:\/]/) {
&not_name;
   }
```

Here's the same statement as represented in pseudocode:

*If the name includes !, @, #, $, %, ^, &, *, (,), =, +, or /*

Go to subroutine not_name

This statement is by no means perfect; anyone determined to find a way to enter an unusual character most likely will find a way to do so. However, the statement does check for the common characters that might find their way into the name field.

After finding one of these characters, the statement calls the subroutine not_name (see listing 6.4).

Listing 6.4   A Subroutine That Tells the Visitor That the Entered Name Is Invalid

```
sub not_name {
print <<"HTML";
<HTML>
<HEAD><TITLE>Name Incorrect</TITLE></HEAD>

<BODY>
<H1> Name Incorrect</H1>
I'm sorry, but the name you entered is not correct. Please try
entering a proper name, first and last.

Thank you<P>
<HR>

<FORM ACTION="/cgi-bin/maillist.pl" METHOD="POST">
Insert your name:<INPUT TYPE="text" NAME="name" VALUE="$form{'name'}"
➥ SIZE=40><BR>
Insert your email address:<INPUT TYPE="text" NAME="email"
➥ VALUE="$form{'email'}" SIZE=34><BR>

<P>
<INPUT TYPE="submit" VALUE="Add to list"><br>
<INPUT TYPE="reset" VALUE="Reset form">

</FORM>
</BODY>
</HTML>
HTML
exit();
}
```

Figure 6.7 shows the resulting form. Notice that this subroutine keeps the value for the name and e-mail address intact, so that the visitor can see the error. By maintaining this value, you help clarify what the visitor did incorrectly. The visitor then simply reenters his or her name and clicks the submit button.

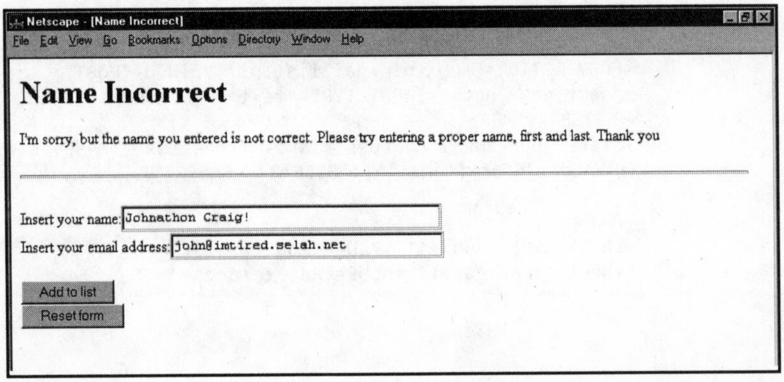

Figure 6.7

If the name entered contains characters not normally associated with a name, you give the visitor a chance to try again.

Netscape - [Name Incorrect]

File Edit View Go Bookmarks Options Directory Window Help

Name Incorrect

I'm sorry, but the name you entered is not correct. Please try entering a proper name, first and last. Thank you

Insert your name: Johnathon Craig!
Insert your email address: john@imtired.selah.net

Add to list
Reset form

E-Mail Only

To check the e-mail address, you simply check whether the entered value includes the *at* sign (@). Although checking for every conceivable problem is virtually impossible, you know for certain that every e-mail address must include this particular symbol. The following statement shows how you check for the character:

```
if ($form{'email'} !~ /@/) {
&not_email;
    }
```

This script requires the visitor to enter a full e-mail address. If a visitor belongs to the same domain as the host in which this script resides, that visitor cannot enter only a username. He or she must enter a full e-mail address, as would any other visitor.

Here's the same statement as represented in pseudocode:

If the e-mail address lacks an at *sign* (@)

Then go to the subroutine not_email.

If the value lacks this character, you enter a subroutine that creates a form informing the visitor of this omission (see listing 6.5).

Listing 6.5 Give the Visitor Another Chance To Enter an E-Mail Address

```
sub not_email {
print <<"HTML";
<HTML>
<HEAD><TITLE>Email Incorrect</TITLE></HEAD>

<BODY>
<H1> Email Address Incorrect</H1>
I'm sorry, but the email address you entered is not correct. Please try
entering a proper email address like so: user\@somewhere.com.

Thank you<P>
<HR>

<FORM ACTION="/cgi-bin/maillist.pl" METHOD="POST">
Insert your name:<INPUT TYPE="text" NAME="name" VALUE="$form{'name'}"
➥ SIZE=40><BR>
Insert your email address:<INPUT TYPE="text" NAME="email"
➥ VALUE="$form{'email'}" SIZE=34><BR>

<P>
<INPUT TYPE="submit" VALUE="Add to list"><br>
<INPUT TYPE="reset" VALUE="Reset form">
```

```
</FORM>
</BODY>
</HTML>
HTML
exit();
}
```

One Per Customer

Another problem that you might encounter is a visitor entering information that already exists. To detect this problem, you should check the e-mail address. Several people might have the same name (check the telephone book to see how many people have the last name Smith or Brown), but a person's e-mail address is always unique.

Therefore, you need to check whether someone else previously entered the same e-mail address. To do so, you include a few lines of code that do something like the following:

Open the WEBLIST.TXT file.

Check whether the visitor has entered an e-mail address that already exists in the database.

If so, then inform the visitor and let him or her try again.

If not, then continue with the script.

Listing 6.6 shows the actual code.

Listing 6.6   Open the WEBLIST.TXT File and Check Whether the E-Mail Address Was Previously Entered

```
open (CHECK, "weblist.txt");
  until (eof (CHECK))
  {
      $line =<CHECK>;
      chop ($line);
      if ($line =~ /$form{'email'}/)
      {
      &exists;
    }
  }
close(CHECK);
```

First you open WEBLIST.TXT using the file handle CHECK. Then you load the file's contents into the string $line. You next check whether the file already holds the e-mail address that the visitor has just entered. If so, you enter the subroutine exists. This subroutine informs the visitor of the mistake and provides another chance to enter the address correctly. Listing 6.7 shows the subroutine exists.

Listing 6.7   If the E-Mail Address Already Exists, Let the Visitor Try Again To Enter the Address Correctly

```
sub exists {
print <<"HTML";
<HTML>
<HEAD><TITLE>User Exists</TITLE></HEAD>

<BODY>
<H1> User Exists!</H1>
I'm sorry, but the email address you entered already exists.
If you wish to enter another name and email address, do so below.<BR>
Thank you<P>
<HR>

<FORM ACTION="/cgi-bin/maillist.pl" METHOD="POST">
Insert your name:<INPUT TYPE="text" NAME="name" VALUE="$form{'name'}"
➥ SIZE=40><BR>
Insert your email address:<INPUT TYPE="text" NAME="email"
➥ VALUE="$form{'email'}" SIZE=34><BR>

<P>
<INPUT TYPE="submit" VALUE="Add to list"><br>
<INPUT TYPE="reset" VALUE="Reset form">

</FORM>
</BODY>
</HTML>
HTML

close(CHECK);
exit();
}
```

Is It Really You?

Some visitors might purposely try to enter incorrect information on the form. You can't really protect your form from such chicanery, but you might be able to prevent a visitor from including someone on an undesired mailing list. You could have your script e-mail the entered address and inform the people at that address that they have been placed on your mailing list. If the recipients return a message stating that they never requested your list, you can simply delete the address from the WEBLIST.TXT file. Listing 6.8 shows how to do so.

Listing 6.8   Send Visitors E-Mail Thanking Them for Getting on Your Mailing List

```
open(MAIL, "¦/usr/lib/sendmail -t");
print MAIL "To: $form{'email'} ($form{'name'})\n";
print MAIL "From: listserv\@selah.net\n";
print MAIL "Subject: Maillist subscription\n\n";
print MAIL "Dear $form{'name'},\n\n";
print MAIL "Thank you for subscribing to our mailing list!\n";
print MAIL "As of $date, your name and email ";
print MAIL "address have been added to our list. If you wish\n";
print MAIL "to unsubscribe, please let Robert Niles at
➥ rniles\@selah.net\n";
print MAIL "know, and you will be removed from our list.\n\n";
print MAIL "Thank you,\n";
print MAIL "listserv\@selah.net\n";
close(MAIL);
```

You've now seen how to check for several possible entry errors. However, because every script is different, you'll have to decide which items in your script need to be verified. A simple e-mail script might need either more or less checking, depending on what you are asking for within your form. As you learn more about CGI, you will also be able to figure out ways to reduce the amount of code that you have to generate to double-check information.

Returning Information to the User

In the mailing list example, you pass information that the user previously entered by using variables that the script creates. By doing so, you can return information to the user. You might want to return information to the user so that you can personalize your pages to fit that particular user. Receiving a page that seems to have been created just for you gives your application a nice touch. You might also want to return information to visitors so that they can verify it.

As was previously mentioned, humans are prone to errors. Many Web surfers stay up through the middle of the night exploring the Web, and might possibly end up stumbling across your form. When your eyes are barely open and bloodshot, and your brain is functioning at half power, you might fill out a form completely wrong. So you might just want to give that poor visitor a second chance.

As you have seen in previous scripts, you can return to the visitor the variables that your scripts create, so that the visitor can confirm the entered information. This technique can save you many headaches if you end up having to remove something from a database or file because a visitor entered the information incorrectly.

Listing 6.9 shows a script that receives information that visitors enter about themselves and, using the hidden input types, creates a Web page that enables visitors to confirm their previous input. You use this script with the WAKE-UP.HTML document, which is on this book's companion CD-ROM.

Listing 6.9   WAKE-UP.PL—a Small Script That Enables Visitors To Enter a Little Information about Themselves

```
#! /usr/bin/perl

# wake-up.pl

print "Content-type: text/html\n\n";

if ($ENV{'REQUEST_METHOD'} ne 'POST')
{
    print <<"HTML";
    <HTML>
    <HEAD>
    <TITLE>Sorry!</TITLE>
    </HEAD>
    <BODY>
    <H1>Sorry, wrong METHOD used!</H1>

    I'm sorry, but we only use the method POST here.
    </BODY>
    </HTML>

HTML

    exit;
}

read(STDIN, $buffer, $ENV{'CONTENT_LENGTH'});
@pairs = split(/&/, $buffer);
foreach $pair (@pairs)
    {
    ($name, $value) = split(/=/, $pair);
    $value =~ tr/+/ /;
    $value =~ s/%([a-fA-F0-9][a-fA-F0-9])/pack("C", hex($1))/eg;
    $form{$name} = $value;

    }

print <<"HTML";
<HTML>
<HEAD><TITLE>Wake up call</TITLE></HEAD>
<BODY>
<H1>Did you get it right!??</H1>
Ok, this is what you entered:<p>
Your name is: <B>$form{'fname'} $form{'lname'}</B><BR>
```

```
You are $form{'age'} years old and were born in $form{'born'},<BR>
HTML
if ($form{'dog'} eq "yes") {
    print "and you have the best friend a person could ever have.<P>";
    }

if ($form{'dog'} eq "no") {
    print "and you really need to get a dog!<P>";
    }

print "If this is correct, click on the submit button below.<P>";

print <<"HTML";
<FORM ACTION="/cgi-bin/wake-up.pl" METHOD="POST">
<INPUT TYPE="hidden" NAME="fname" VALUE="$form{'fname'}">
<INPUT TYPE="hidden" NAME="lname" VALUE="$form{'lname'}">
<INPUT TYPE="hidden" NAME="age" VALUE="$form{'age'}">
<INPUT TYPE="hidden" NAME="born" VALUE="$form{'born'}">
<INPUT TYPE="hidden" NAME="dog" VALUE="$form{'dog'}">

<HR>
<P>
<INPUT TYPE="submit">
</FORM>
</BODY>
</HTML>

HTML

exit;
```

First the form accepts information from the visitor (see fig. 6.8).

Figure 6.8

This form asks the visitor for a little information so that your script can manipulate the data and return it.

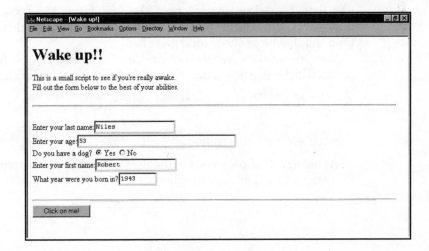

Your script then uses that information to create a form that displays the information that the user entered. The secret to passing information is to include it in a `hidden` input type along with each field's value. Examine the following example:

```
<INPUT TYPE="hidden" NAME="fname" VALUE="$form{'fname'}">
```

Notice that this example adds the variable `$form{'fname'}` into the value of the input type. When the script returns this information to the visitor as an HTML page, it looks something like the following:

```
<INPUT TYPE="hidden" NAME="fname" VALUE="Robert">
```

The script simply creates another form and returns it to the user with the information already filled out. If the information is correct, the user clicks the submit button. The information then returns to the script. You can then have the script do something else, or you can pass the information to a completely different script. As Chapter 2, "The Common Gateway Interface (CGI)," mentioned, the `hidden` input types *aren't* really hidden. Anyone can view them with a Web browser's View Source command. The `hidden` input type just doesn't appear on the HTML document itself.

Creating Customized Pages

To create customized pages, you first get some information from the visitor, personalize it for the visitor, and then return that information to the visitor. If you keep passing that information to various scripts, you can create the impression that all your pages were created specifically for that particular visitor.

For example, try expanding the wake-up script. You can use the form that your script created to send the visitor to yet another script while retaining the information that the visitor entered from the first form. The second script takes the information from the form that the first script created, and then tells the visitor the time and that he or she should go to bed.

You first must change the WAKE-UP.PL script so that the form calls your new script, which you should name BED.PL. Therefore, you change the line

```
<FORM ACTION="/cgi-bin/wake-up.pl" METHOD="POST">
```

to

```
<FORM ACTION="/cgi-bin/bed.pl" METHOD="POST">
```

As listing 6.10 shows, you can use the same information from the previous script to create yet another page for the visitor.

Listing 6.10 BED.PL—Return the Information to the User

```perl
#! /usr/bin/perl

# bed.pl

print "Content-type: text/html\n\n";

if ($ENV{'REQUEST_METHOD'} ne 'POST')
{
    print <<"HTML";
    <HTML>
    <HEAD>
    <TITLE>Sorry!</TITLE>
    </HEAD>
    <BODY>
    <H1>Sorry, wrong METHOD used!</H1>

    I'm sorry, but we only use the method POST here.
    </BODY>
    </HTML>

HTML

    exit;
}

read(STDIN, $buffer, $ENV{'CONTENT_LENGTH'});
@pairs = split(/&/, $buffer);
foreach $pair (@pairs)
    {
    ($name, $value) = split(/=/, $pair);
    $value =~ tr/+/ /;
    $value =~ s/%([a-fA-F0-9][a-fA-F0-9])/pack("C", hex($1))/eg;
    $form{$name} = $value;

    }

chop($time = 'date +%H:%M');

print <<"HTML";
<HTML>
<HEAD><TITLE>Time to go nite-nite</TITLE></HEAD>
<BODY>
<H1>Time to say good night</H1>
Well $form{'fname'} it's $time, and I really think that you should
go to bed.<BR>
Before the other $form{'lname'}\'s wake up and see your
bloodshot eyes and give you that awful look.
<BR>I think you know what I mean.
<BR>
```

continues

121

Listing 6.10 Continued

```
You know, being $form{'age'}, you're not as young as you once were.<P>
So, it's time to turn off the computer and go to bed.<P>
Thanks for visiting!

HTML

if ($form{'dog'} eq "yes") {
 print "<P>Oh! ...don't forget to take out your dog!";
 }

print "</BODY>";
print "</HTML>";

exit;
```

As shown in figure 6.9, the page seems to "speak" to the current visitor personally.

Figure 6.9

There's nothing like a page that talks directly to you.

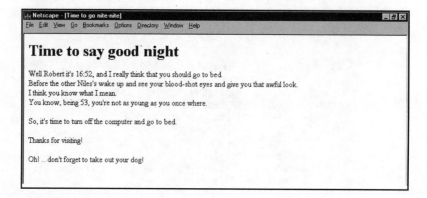

These scripts are simple, and only hint at all that you can accomplish. By having scripts create your Web pages, you can more easily manipulate and personalize them. With a little imagination, you can create wonderful interactive scripts.

Summary

In this chapter, you learned how to check for errors, both to ensure that the script is behaving properly and that the information entered by the user is valid. You also learned how to enable visitors to verify information that they previously entered. The chapter explained how to return information to the visitor, and how you can use that process to customize your pages so that your documents create the impression that you created each one specifically for the current visitor.

Review Questions

1. For what types of problems should you have your scripts check?

2. For what purpose do you use Perl's $! variable?

3. How do you return to the visitor information that the visitor previously entered?

4. Do you always need to use the hidden input type when returning information to the visitor?

Review Exercises

1. Create a form that enables the visitor to enter a name and phone number, and then create a script that returns the information entered by the visitor for confirmation.

2. Using the same form, revise the script to send the visitor a confirmation page in which the information entered by the visitor is redisplayed into a form that looks like the first form that the visitor used to enter information.

3. Create a script that checks the information that a visitor entered to determine whether the visitor entered appropriate text. For example, if you ask the visitor to enter a URL to a Web page, ensure that the visitor doesn't enter a mailto: or ftp: site.

## CHAPTER 7

A More Complex Guestbook

In Chapter 4, "A Simple Guestbook," you learned how to build SGB1, a simple guestbook application. In this chapter, you use SGB1's framework to build SGB2, a more complex guestbook.

Your goal is to retain as much of SGB1's code as possible while making SGB2 more robust. (This development will be a good test of SGB1's design.) In particular, you do the following:

♦ Analyze SGB1's strengths and weaknesses

♦ Create a separate entry form

♦ Collect more information from each visitor

♦ Display the guestbook in reverse order

♦ Display the guestbook page by page, using navigational aids

♦ Add configuration options

> **Tip:** Like SGB1, SGB2 is a C program with Windows NT-centric code. To implement SGB2 on a UNIX machine, you must change path name references to use forward slashes rather than backslashes, and replace the Win32 file input/output (I/O) calls with standard C file handlers.

Analyzing SGB1's Strengths and Weaknesses

To start, you need to analyze briefly SGB1's strengths and weaknesses, so that you can identify changes that will make SGB2 better.

SGB1's strengths include the following:

♦ Reacts differently to GET than to POST.

♦ Doesn't require any HTML other than a simple `<a href...>` link to start the guestbook.

♦ Creates the "Sign the Guestbook" form on the fly.

♦ Filters the visitor's input to remove HTML tags.

♦ Creates a "Thank you" screen and shows visitors their entry immediately after they sign.

Weaknesses include the following:

♦ Displays the "Sign the Guestbook" form on the same page as the existing entries in the guestbook.

♦ Collects little information from each visitor.

♦ Displays the entire contents of the guestbook every time.

♦ Lacks navigational aids (links for going back, going forward, leaving the guestbook, and so forth).

♦ Displays the guestbook entries in the order in which they were added, which makes the most recent entry the last entry.

♦ Lacks configuration options, so you cannot change its appearance to match that of the rest of the Web site. Has hard-coded defaults only.

You want to address the weaknesses of SGB1 without eliminating the strengths and without rewriting most of the code. Fortunately, SGB1 is quite modular, so you should find it easy to swap out or revise bits here and there without affecting the program structure.

> **Note:** This book's companion CD-ROM includes SGB2. You can find the complete source code (SGB2.C), along with an appropriate make file for Visual C 2.x (SGB2.MAK). The CD also includes a ready-to-run compiled version suitable for Windows NT (SGB2.EXE).

> **Note:** See listing 4.5 for SGB1's complete code. See listing 4.2 for just the `main()` routine.

Creating a Separate Entry Form

During the normal GET processing of SGB1, the application displays the entry form for signing the guestbook.

You want SGB2 to have an entry form separate from the guestbook display. The portion of SGB1's `main()` routine that handles the GET request is as follows:

```
else if (stricmp(pRequestMethod,"GET")==0) {

        // Request-method was GET; this means we should
        // print out the guestbook

        PrintMIMEHeader();      // Print MIME header
        PrintHTMLHeader();      // Print HTML header
        PrintForm();            // Print guestbook form
        PrintGBEntries();       // Print contents of guestbook
        PrintHTMLTrailer();     // Print HTML trailer
    }
```

This part of the routine must change. You don't want SGB2 to print both the entry form and the guestbook entries every time. Instead, you want the application to do one or the other.

Use the QUERY_STRING environment variable to distinguish between requests to sign the form and requests to display the form. Signing and viewing are distinct operations, so you create a global variable, `iOperation`, and define a couple of constants to give the variable meaning:

```
#define Op_SignBook    1        // op is "sign"
#define Op_ViewBook    2        // op is "view"
int     iOperation;             // sign or view?
```

These declarations belong at the top of the source code file, with the other global variables and constants.

Next, add a routine to find and parse the QUERY_STRING environment variable:

```
void DecodeQueryString() {
    char    *pQueryString;      // pointer to QUERY_STRING
    char    *p;                 // generic pointer

    iOperation = 0;             // undefined value
```

```
pQueryString = getenv("QUERY_STRING");

// If query string absent, or op = view, set
// the operation to view

if ( (pQueryString==NULL) ||      // no query string
     (*pQueryString=='\0'))       // query string blank
{
    iOperation = Op_ViewBook;
    return;
}

_strlwr(pQueryString);

if (strstr(pQueryString,"op=view"))
{
    iOperation = Op_ViewBook;
}

// else if op = sign, set operation to sign

else if (strstr(pQueryString,"op=sign"))
{
    iOperation = Op_SignBook;
}
}
```

This routine uses the word op to refer to the operation, and the words view and sign to denote viewing and signing. Notice also that by using an integer with defines for iOperation, you leave room for future expansion. You can add new operations simply by adding new defines and testing the QUERY_STRING.

Later in this chapter, listing 7.3 shows the complete code for the DecodeQueryString() routine. You use the QUERY_STRING variable for more than just setting the iOperation code.

Now modify the main() routine to call the DecodeQueryString() routine and take action based on the value of iOperation:

```
else if (stricmp(pRequestMethod,"GET")==0) {

    // Request-method was GET; this means we should
    // print out the guestbook

    PrintMIMEHeader();      // Print MIME header
    PrintHTMLHeader();      // Print HTML header

    // We can do two things on a GET -- either
    // print out the form (a "sign" operation),
    // or print out the guestbook's entries (a
    // "view" operation).  We figure out which
    // by looking at the QUERY_STRING environment
    // variable.
```

```
        DecodeQueryString();      // decode QUERY_STRING

    if (iOperation==Op_SignBook)
        PrintForm();

    else if (iOperation==Op_ViewBook)
        PrintGBEntries();

    else
        printf("Unknown operation specified.");

    PrintHTMLTrailer();       // Print HTML trailer
}
```

After you determine that the method is GET, the QUERY_STRING contents (and therefore the iOperation variable) become important. You could have the DecodeQueryString() routine return the iOperation variable as its result code. However, you don't do so, for two reasons. First, iOperation is properly defined as a global variable. Although the only use of the variable (so far) is within the main() routine, future uses of the variable might be global in scope. Second, you might want the DecodeQueryString() routine to look at more than just the operation. In fact, in the section "Adding Navigational Aids," you have the routine do just that.

Note: Refer to Chapter 2, "The Common Gateway Interface (CGI)," for details on the QUERY_STRING environment variable.

Collecting More Information

Another goal for SGB2 is to collect more information about the visitor. SGB1 already collects the visitor's name, e-mail address, and comments (all three fields being optional). For SGB2, add the visitor's browser, IP number, and host name.

A typical entry from SGB1 might end with the following message:

Karla Borden signed the guestbook on Sun 23 Jun 1996 at 19:53:10.

For SGB2, the message should look similar to the following:

Karla Borden signed the guestbook on Sun 23 Jun 1996 at 19:53:10, using Mozilla/3.0B2 (WinNT; I) from 38.247.88.31 (twilight.greyware.com)

You format the guestbook entry using the FormatGBEntry() routine, so you need to modify that routine. First, you must change the period and <br> following the date and time to a comma and space character. Making this change is a simple matter of editing the sprintf() call that formats the string:

```
sprintf(szTmp," at %02d:%02d:%02d, ",
        st.wHour,st.wMinute,st.wSecond);
strcat(szBuffer,szTmp);
```

Now you can add the browser identification, the IP number, and the host name. Note that any of these three strings might be missing, depending on the browser and the server. It is unlikely that all three will be missing, however, so leaving the dangling comma is fairly safe.

To retrieve the new information, you obtain the contents of the relevant CGI environment variables and append the information to the guestbook entry. Listing 7.1 shows the relevant code.

Listing 7.1   Adding Browser, IP, and Host Information to the Guestbook Entry

```
// now add the visitor's IP address and browser, if
// available

p = getenv("HTTP_USER_AGENT");
if (p)
{
    sprintf(szTmp,"using %s",p);
    strcat(szBuffer,szTmp);
}

p = getenv("REMOTE_ADDR");
if (p)
{
    sprintf(szTmp," from %s",p);
    strcat(szBuffer,szTmp);
}

p = getenv("REMOTE_HOST");
if (p)
{
    sprintf(szTmp," (%s)",p);
    strcat(szBuffer,szTmp);
}
```

Like SGB1, SGB2 ends the guestbook entry by adding a <br> tag and a CRLF to mark the entry's ending:

```
// always add a <br> tag and CRLF at the end
strcat(szBuffer,"<br>\r\n");
```

Because SGB1's code modules are nicely insulated from each other, no other routines know anything about the format of a guestbook entry. Therefore, you need not make any other changes elsewhere.

Reversing the Display Order

Real-life guestbooks (those kept on paper) start at the beginning, and each visitor adds his or her entry at the end of the book. Readers of paper guestbooks usually start at the last page and read backward, because the most recent visitors are usually of the most interest. SGB1 keeps and displays its records the same way that a real-life guestbook does. The records are variable-length, stored all together as one big text file without record separators.

Because it operates in cyberspace, SGB2 can accommodate readers by reversing the order in which it displays the entries. To handle this sort of task, two primary solutions are available:

♦ Keep the format of the guestbook data file intact and scan through it (from back to front) to reverse the display. This solution works because all guestbook entries start with an <hr> tag, which you can use as a unique identifier.

Advantages: Keeps the data file format intact. Leaves no slack space between records.

Disadvantages: Makes further changes to the guestbook entry format difficult, because you must maintain a unique identifier. Requires parsing of the guestbook data file to find each entry, count total entries, and navigate forward and backward.

♦ Change the format of the guestbook data file to use fixed-length records. This solution enables users to access individual records in any order.

Advantages: Makes it easy to calculate the position of any particular record or obtain a count of the records. Doesn't require any parsing.

Disadvantages: Introduces a new format that might be incompatible with old data files. Wastes some disk space by adding slack between records.

The amount of time and effort required to parse records in a file of variable-length records (with no official record-separator marks) is prohibitive for files of any measurable length. The first solution, therefore, isn't much of an option. You want the guestbook to grow, and you want to access it quickly. SGB2, therefore, uses the second solution.

Note: In Chapter 10, "Storing Information in Flat Files," you learn all about flat file organization and access methods. SGB2 uses a random-access flat file with fixed-length records to hold the guestbook data.

To change SGB1's variable-length records to SGB2's fixed-length records when writing records, you need only make one change. Again, you don't need to make more changes elsewhere because you have encapsulated the logic of record handling. Only two routines, `AppendToGB()` and `PrintGBEntries()`, know anything about the data file's organization.

Writing Records

After you format the record with `FormatGBEntry()`, `AppendToGB()` opens the data file, positions the pointer to the end of the file, and writes a new variable-length record:

```
// This is an append operation, so we want to
// position the file pointer to the end of the
// file.

SetFilePointer (hFile,0L,0L,FILE_END);

//Write out the entry now

dwNumBytes = strlen(szBuffer);
bSuccess = WriteFile (
    hFile,
    szBuffer,
    dwNumBytes,
    &dwBytesWritten,
    0
    );
```

The variable `dwNumBytes` holds the number of bytes appended to the data file. In the preceding snippet from SGB1, the variable is set to the length of valid data in `szBuffer`. If `szBuffer` contains 10 bytes of data, 10 bytes get appended to the disk file; if `szBuffer` contains 100 bytes, 100 bytes get appended; and so forth.

To change this behavior, you write the entire contents of `szBuffer`, even though only the first 10, 100, or 1,000 bytes can contain valid entry data.

`szBuffer` is a global buffer area, defined as 1,024 bytes long. Each record, therefore, is exactly 1,024 bytes long, no matter how long the actual record data might be. To change how many bytes get written, find the following line:

```
dwNumBytes = strlen(szBuffer);
```

Change this line to the following:

```
dwNumBytes = sizeof(szBuffer);
```

The C `sizeof()` operator returns the defined length, in bytes, of a declared variable.

The `AppendToGB()` routine has one other minor change: You change the reference to the name of the data file to `szDataFile`. In SGB1, this reference is `szFileName`. As the section "Making the Guestbook Configurable" explains, SGB2 uses more than one

CGI *By*
EXAMPLE

file. Having one of them named `szFileName` would be confusing—*which* file is `szFileName`? The variable holding the file name should have been named better in SGB1, to allow for this sort of change. In SGB2, you correct this flaw in the design of SGB1.

Reading Records

If you want to keep the display order the same in SGB2 as in SGB1, you don't have to make any changes to the `PrintGBEntries()` routine. (Refer to listing 4.5 for the SGB1 code.) `PrintGBEntries()` already uses `szBuffer` to transfer data from the disk file to the output, and already reads the data in chunks the size of `szBuffer`. This technique works because the data file of SGB1 is just one long text file, and all SGB1 wants to do is display the entire guestbook. SGB1 therefore starts at the beginning of the file, reading and printing in `szBuffer`-size chunks, until reaching the end of the file.

Although SGB2 writes each record in `szBuffer`-size chunks, a byte of zero terminates the actual data internally within each chunk. When reading a record, `PrintGBEntries()` reads the entire `szBuffer`-size chunk. But when printing a record, the routine prints only the valid portion, thanks to `printf()`'s definition. Each chunk read from the data file contains exactly one record in the SGB2 format. The SGB1 format splits records across the `szBuffer` boundary, but doesn't terminate the records internally.

SGB2 does not read sequentially, however. Instead, for each record number to be read, SGB2 calculates the offset into the file for the beginning of that record, and reads only that record. This approach enables SGB2 to read records in any order.

In the section "Adding Navigational Aids," you modify SGB2's behavior so that the application displays only a pageful of records at any one time. `PrintGBEntries()` knows how to retrieve records from the data file in reverse order, but needs to know which record to retrieve first, and how many records to retrieve. You add these two variables, both long integers, to the list of global variables:

```
long    liFirstRecord;          // first entry to view
long    liHowMany;              // how many to show
```

These variables are global rather than parameters passed to the `PrintGBEntries()` routine, because they are accessed and modified elsewhere. One other change to `PrintGBEntries()` is the reference to the data file name. The reference is now `szDataFile`, just as in the new `AppendToGB()` routine, and for the same reason.

The basic flow and structure of `PrintGBEntries()` doesn't change from SGB1 to SGB2. However, SGB2 adds much code to calculate the record numbers and positions. Also, because you want to encapsulate knowledge about the data file within `PrintGBEntries()`, that routine produces the navigational links for scrolling through the guestbook.

Listing 7.2 shows the entire `PrintGBEntries()` routine. The code is commented extensively. You have to add several local variables to hold the file size, the current record number, and the total number of records. Also, to comply with the `liHowMany` setting, you need a dynamic counter variable to keep track of how many records you have displayed.

Listing 7.2   The *PrintGBEntries()* Routine

```
// PrintGBEntries -- print out the contents of the guestbook

BOOL PrintGBEntries() {
    int        iWaitForIt;        // generic counter
    HANDLE     hFile;             // file handle
    BOOL       bSuccess;          // success indicator
    DWORD      dwBytesRead;       // num bytes written
    DWORD      dwNumBytes;        // generic counter
    DWORD      dwLastError;       // hold last err code
    DWORD      dwLoWord;          // file size lo word
    DWORD      dwHiWord;          // file size hi word
    long       liRecordNumber;    // record number
    long       liTotalRecords;    // tot recs in file
    long       dwNumPrinted = 0;  // num printed so far

    // First, print a link to allow the visitor to sign
    // the guestbook.  A sign operation is accomplished
    // by invoking the script with the GET method (an
    // <a href...> link, with a query string of "op=sign")

    printf("<a href=\"%s"
        "?op=sign\">"
        "Sign the Guestbook"
        "</a><p>\n",
        getenv("SCRIPT_NAME")
        );

    // Set up a counter/loop.  We'll use the iWaitForIt
    // variable as our counter, and we'll go through the
    // loop up to 100 times.

    for (iWaitForIt = 0; iWaitForIt < 100; iWaitForIt++)
    {

        // Each time within the loop, we'll try to get
        // nonexclusive read access to the log file.

        hFile = CreateFile (
            szDataFile,
            GENERIC_READ,         // read-only
            FILE_SHARE_READ,      // let others read, too
            0,                    // no special security
```

```
        OPEN_EXISTING,        // fail if not there
        FILE_ATTRIBUTE_NORMAL,
        0
        );

    // If we were unable to open the file, find out why

    if (hFile == INVALID_HANDLE_VALUE)
    {
        dwLastError = GetLastError();
        switch (dwLastError)
        {
            case ERROR_FILE_NOT_FOUND:

                // file doesn't exist

                return FALSE;

            case ERROR_SHARING_VIOLATION:
            case ERROR_LOCK_VIOLATION:

                // file is busy
                // so sleep for .1 second

                Sleep(100);
                break;

            default:

                // some other fatal error
                // we don't care what; just
                // exit

                return FALSE;
        }
    }
    else
    {
        // At this point, the file is open for read.
        // Loop through backward, starting with
        // liFirstRecord, for liHowMany records

        dwLoWord = GetFileSize(hFile,&dwHiWord);
        liTotalRecords = dwLoWord / sizeof(szBuffer);


        // If liFirstRecord is zero, we want to start
        // at the end of the file.  If liFirstRecord
        // is invalid (points beyond the end of the
        // file), adjust it backward
```

continues

135

Listing 7.2 Continued

```
            if ( (liFirstRecord==0) ||
                 (liFirstRecord > liTotalRecords)
               )
              liFirstRecord = liTotalRecords;

         liRecordNumber = liFirstRecord;

         if (liTotalRecords==0)        // if no records at all
         {
             CloseHandle(hFile);
             return TRUE;
         }

         if ((liRecordNumber - liHowMany) > 0)
         {
             // not starting at beginning of
             // file, so print a link for "View
             // Earlier Records"

             liFirstRecord = liRecordNumber - liHowMany;
             if (liFirstRecord < 1) liFirstRecord = 1;

             printf("<a href=\"%s"
                 "?op=view&first=%li&howmany=%li\">"
                 "Earlier Records"
                 "</a>  ",
                 getenv("SCRIPT_NAME"),
                 liFirstRecord,
                 liHowMany
                 );
         }

         if (liRecordNumber!=liTotalRecords)
         {
             // not starting at end of file,
             // so print a link for "View Later
             // "Records"

             liFirstRecord = liRecordNumber + liHowMany;

             if (liFirstRecord > liTotalRecords)
                 liFirstRecord = liTotalRecords;

             printf("<a href=\"%s"
                 "?op=view&first=%li&howmany=%li\">"
                 "Later Records"
                 "</a>  ",
                 getenv("SCRIPT_NAME"),
                 liFirstRecord,
                 liHowMany
                 );
```

```
        }

printf("<p>\n");

while (dwNumPrinted < liHowMany)
{

    liRecordNumber--;        // record numbers are zero-based

    // Position the file pointer to the
    // beginning of the desired record.
    // This offset is liRecordNumber times
    // the length in bytes of each record

    SetFilePointer (
        hFile,
        liRecordNumber * sizeof(szBuffer),
        0L,
        FILE_BEGIN
        );

    // Read in exactly one record

    dwNumBytes = sizeof(szBuffer);
    bSuccess = ReadFile (
        hFile,
        szBuffer,
        dwNumBytes,
        &dwBytesRead,
        0
        );

    if ( (bSuccess==FALSE) || (dwBytesRead==0))
    {

        // file is done, or there was an error

        break;
    }
    else
    {

        // print out what we got


        // bump number of recs printed
        dwNumPrinted++;

        // terminate the record, in case
        // it is exactly sizeof(szBuffer)
        // in length
```

continues

137

Listing 7.2   Continued

```
                    szBuffer[dwBytesRead]='\0';

                    // print out the record
                    printf(szBuffer);

                    // print out the record number,
                    // just for fun

                    printf("(Record #%d of %d)<br>",
                        liRecordNumber+1,
                        liTotalRecords
                        );

                    // if that was the first record
                    // in the file, exit this loop
                    // immediately!

                    if (liRecordNumber==0) break;
                }

            } // end of while loop

            CloseHandle(hFile);
            return TRUE;

        } // end of if hFILE test

    } // end of for loop

    return FALSE;
}
```

Adding Navigational Aids

The section "Reading Records" showed how the `PrintGBEntries()` routine adds navigational aids for browsing forward and backward through the guestbook. These navigational aids take the form of `<a href...>` links included at the top of the guestbook display. Each link takes this form:

`<a href="/path/scriptname?op=view&first=nn&howmany=nn">`

You then add appropriate text to indicate whether the link goes forward or backward in the guestbook.

So far, this chapter has discussed only one `QUERY_STRING` variable, the `op` parameter, which can be either `view` or `sign`. If you don't specify the setting, the default is `view`.

The links printed by PrintGBEntries() use two more QUERY_STRING variables: first and howmany. first is a number representing the record number of the first entry to display. howmany is a number representing how many entries to display on each page.

If no QUERY_STRING is present, first defaults to zero, and howmany defaults to 10 (or whatever the Webmaster has set the default to be; see the section "Making the Guestbook Configurable").

If the QUERY_STRING is present, however, and the op setting is view, the QUERY_STRING is interrogated for the presence of first=*nn* and howmany=*nn* (where *nn* is a string of digits).

If first is zero or not present, PrintGBEntries() starts at the end of the data file and works backward toward the beginning. If first is any other number, PrintGBEntries() starts with that record number. This technique lets PrintGBEntries() create links that "remember" the correct position for the next viewing. Because the routine always knows where it started and how many entries it has displayed, it also knows where to start next time to continue browsing forward or backward in the file.

Listing 7.3 shows the complete code for the DecodeQueryString() routine. main() calls this routine when the method is GET.

Listing 7.3   The Complete *DecodeQueryString()* Routine

```
void DecodeQueryString() {
    char    *pQueryString;      // pointer to QUERY_STRING
    char    *p;                 // generic pointer

    iOperation = 0;             // undefined value
    liFirstRecord = 0;          // first entry to view

    pQueryString = getenv("QUERY_STRING");

    // If query string absent, or op = view, set
    // the operation to view

    if ( (pQueryString==NULL) ||    // no query string
        (*pQueryString=='\0'))      // query string blank
    {
        iOperation = Op_ViewBook;
        return;
    }

    _strlwr(pQueryString);
```

continues

Listing 7.3 Continued

```
    if (strstr(pQueryString,"op=view"))
    {
        iOperation = Op_ViewBook;
    }

    // else if op = sign, set operation to sign

    else if (strstr(pQueryString,"op=sign"))
    {
        iOperation = Op_SignBook;
    }

    // Look for first=xx in the query string

    p = strstr(pQueryString,"first=");
    if (p)
    {
        strcpy(szBuffer,p+6);
        p = strchr(szBuffer,'&');
        if (p) *p = '\0';
        liFirstRecord = atol(szBuffer);
        if (liFirstRecord < 0) liFirstRecord = 0;
    }

    // Look for howmany=xx in the query string

    p = strstr(pQueryString,"howmany=");
    if (p)
    {
        strcpy(szBuffer,p+8);
        p = strchr(szBuffer,'&');
        if (p) *p = '\0';
        liHowMany = atol(szBuffer);
        if (liHowMany < 1) liHowMany = 1;
        if (liHowMany > 999) liHowMany = 999;
    }
}
```

As you can see in listing 7.3, DecodeQueryString() cheats a bit in decoding the QUERY_STRING. In fact, the routine doesn't decode this environmental variable at all. Because this program defines only three variables as having meaning, and none of them can contain spaces or other special characters, you skip the URL-decoding step entirely and simply scan for the parameters that you want. You ignore any other text added to the QUERY_STRING and correct any invalid entries for op, first, or howmany. A more robust program would fully decode the QUERY_STRING and parse each parameter separately before examining any of the values.

The PrintGBEntries() routine uses the values obtained from DecodeQueryString() to determine where to start printing and how many entries to print. PrintGBEntries() creates navigational aids to facilitate browsing forward and backward through the guestbook.

Now you add a few more navigational aids:

♦ *A link for signing the book on the view page.* One of SGB2's goals is to save the Webmaster from writing HTML, but you can't expect a visitor to know to enter **?op=sign**. Therefore, SGB2 itself must offer the option to sign the book. The `PrintGBEntries()` routine does so (refer to listing 7.2).

♦ *A link for viewing the book from the sign form.* To provide this navigational aid, you simply add an `<a href="...?op=view">` link to the fill-in form. This link enables a visitor to change his or her mind about signing without having to use the browser's back button. The link also helps the visitor avoid signing the book several times in a row by error. Listing 7.4 shows the code to modify the sign form.

♦ *A link for viewing the book from the thank-you page.* This link is the same as the one added on the sign page, and lets the visitor go straight from signing to viewing the guestbook. If you don't provide this link, your guestbook might tempt the visitor to press the browser's back button, and the visitor might then get confused about where to go next. Listing 7.5 shows the code for modifying the thank-you page.

Listing 7.4 Adding a Link to the Sign Form

```
printf("<a href=\"%s"
       "?op=view&first=0&howmany=%li\">"
       "View the Guestbook"
       "</a><p>\n",
       getenv("SCRIPT_NAME"),
       liHowMany
       );
```

Listing 7.5 Adding a Link to the Thank-You Page

```
printf("<hr>\n");
printf(
    "<a href=\"%s"
    "?op=view&first=0&howmany=%li\">"
    "View the Complete Guestbook"
    "</a>\n",
    getenv("SCRIPT_NAME"),
    liHowMany
    );
```

Making the Guestbook Configurable

You want SGB2 to be configurable in two ways. First, it should handle the hard-coded data file name from SGB1 more elegantly, by creating the file name on the fly and making it appropriate to the server environment and script name. Second, SGB2 should enable the Webmaster to set the appearance, title, and other defaults controlling how the guestbook displays.

To accomplish these tasks, SGB2 uses the configuration file in the Windows .INI format. SGB2's .INI file looks something like the following:

```
[Info]
DataFile=i:\www\cgi\sgb2.dat
First Access=Fri 28 Jun 1996 at 07:49:20
Last Access=Sat 29 Jun 1996 at 12:27:36

[Settings]
BodyTag=bgcolor=#FEFEFE text=#000000 link=#000040
➥ alink=FF0040 vlink=#7F7F7F
Header=<h1><i>CGI by Example</i></h1><b>sgb2.c</b> —
➥ demonstration CGI written in C to make a simple
➥ guestbook<p>
HowMany=10
```

This .INI file has two sections: `[Info]` and `[Settings]`. SGB2 fills out the `[Info]` section by itself. The program doesn't use the information in this section.

Tip: If SGB2 used the `DataFile` setting in the `[Info]` section to learn the location of the data file, clever hackers might modify this setting to access other files on your server. SGB2 uses this section only to provide information to the Webmaster.

SGB2 fills out the `[Settings]` section the first time that the script runs, using the default values shown in the preceding code. The Webmaster can change the following settings at any time:

◆ `BodyTag`. The guestbook's `<body...>` tag uses the contents of this variable. If, for instance, you want to load a background graphic instead of setting colors, you can edit this line to read `BodyTag=background=/graphics/mybackground.gif`. From `background=/graphics/mybackground.gif`, SGB2 creates `<body background=/graphics/mybackgroung.gif>`.

◆ `Header`. This value's setting becomes the header displayed on every guestbook page. The value is plain text or HTML. SGB2 doesn't put the value inside any tags or do any formatting. If you want to change the name of the guestbook to *Martha's Guestbook*, just edit the .INI file to read `Header=Martha's Guestbook`.

♦ `HowMany`. This setting specifies the default number of entries to display per page when the visitor views the guestbook.

SGB2 finds its configuration file and its data file by examining its environment at startup. Using its own path and file name as the base entries, SGB2 constructs two variables: `szINIFile` and `szDataFile`. Suppose that the script resides in the directory C:\WEBFILES\CGI-BIN, and is called SGB2.EXE. `szINIFile` then has the value C:\WEBFILES\CGI-BIN\SGB2.INI, and `szDataFile` has the value C:\WEBFILES\CGI-BIN\SGB2.DAT.

By using this approach, you can have multiple guestbooks on the same server. Simply copy SGB2.EXE to another directory, or to another name in the same directory. Each copy will have its own configuration file and data file, based on its location and name.

The code to read and write the configuration file uses the Win32 calls `GetPrivateProfileString()` and `WritePrivateProfileString()`. If you are adapting this script for UNIX, you must change the `GetINIValues()` routine to use a different form of file access and parsing.

Summary

In this chapter, you learned how to modify an existing script to add enhancements and new functionality. You also learned how to use random access with fixed-length records in a flat file, and how to store configuration values in a configuration file.

The result, SGB2, is a much more complex guestbook than its forebear SGB1, although SGB2 is easier for the visitor to use.

Review Questions

1. Why does SGB2 use fixed-length records?

2. What does SGB2 do if a visitor changes the `howmany` portion of the `QUERY_STRING` while scrolling through the guestbook? (Refer to the complete listing on the CD-ROM to verify your answer.)

3. What is the current limit on the number of records in the guestbook, based on how SGB2's code is written?

4. What are the three valid parameter names that can appear in the `QUERY_STRING`?

5. What does SGB2 do if you enter an operation code other than **view** or **sign**?

6. If you rename SGB2.EXE to **MYGUESTBOOK.EXE**, what will the configuration file name be?

7. What kind of access does SGB2 need in its own directory?

8. What kind of access does SGB2 need in the Web root directory?

9. What happens if a visitor supplies more than 512 bytes in the comments field?

Review Exercises

1. Modify SGB2 to provide more meaningful error messages when it cannot access the data file.

2. Define a new operation called `mail`, which mails the guestbook to the visitor. What new defines do you need? What new links? What restrictions? Would you mail the data file as raw data, or as formatted text?

3. Modify SGB2's configuration file and internal processing to allow a Webmaster-specified graphical rule rather than the built-in HTML `<hr>` tag. How do you handle the rule's `ALT` portion?

4. Modify the code in the `PrintGBEntries()` routine to handle very large guestbook files (where `dwHiWord` becomes significant).

5. If you wrote a program to imitate a browser, but with a browser identification string 512 bytes long, then signed the guestbook, how would this affect SGB2? Modify SGB2 to protect against this kind of attack.

## CHAPTER 8

A Shopping Cart Script

A *shopping cart script* enables visitors to browse through a virtual store, pick items, and then eventually go to the virtual checkout counter to pay for the selected items in the virtual shopping cart.

This deceptively simple explanation might lead you to believe that such a script is easy to write. Unfortunately, a shopping cart script is one of the hardest to create. To understand why a shopping cart script is so difficult, you need to consider for a moment the mechanism behind a basic browsing transaction.

When you start your browser and ask for a URL (either an HTML page or a CGI script), the browser searches for the server, opens a connection, and asks for the URL. The server gives you the requested information and then disconnects, forgetting that you've ever been there.

If the document that you receive has links to other documents (for example, inline graphics or a fill-in form), your browser must search for the server again, establish a new connection, and either ask for the next document or submit the form. The server satisfies this request and then disconnects, forgetting all about you *again*.

Each time that you contact the server, it behaves as if you had never been there before, and each request yields a single response. This contact is a *stateless connection*. The server doesn't remember you, and can't tell whether this visit is your first or your thousandth.

The State of HTTP

Because the server doesn't remember you between visits, the HTTP 1.0 protocol is *stateless*. The server doesn't know the *state* of your browser—whether you are making your first or your hundredth request for information composing the same visual page. Each GET or POST in HTTP 1.0 must carry all the information necessary to service the request. This makes distributing resources easy, but places the burden of maintaining state information on the CGI application.

The Web has used HTTP 1.0 since 1990, but since then many proposals for revisions and extensions have been discussed. If you're interested in the technical specifications, stop by **http://www.w3.org/hypertext/WWW/Protocols/** and read about what's coming down the road in the near future. Of particular interest to CGI programmers is the proposal for maintaining state information at the server. You can retrieve a text version of the proposal from the following site:

http://www.ics.uci.edu/pub/ietf/http/draft-kristol-http-state-info-01.txt

HTTP 1.1, when approved and in widespread use, will provide many improvements in the state of the art. In the meantime, however, the art is stateless, and you have to keep that in mind as you develop your programs.

Statelessness raises many thorny problems for certain types of scripts—the shopping cart script being the prime example. When the visitor picks an item and places it in a virtual shopping cart, the script must remember that the item is in the cart. Then, when the visitor gets to the virtual checkout counter, the script is aware of all the items that the visitor is purchasing.

The server can't remember all the visitor's items for you, and you certainly don't want the visitor to have to retype the information each time that he or she sees a new page. Your script must track all the variables itself and determine, each time that it is called, whether it's been called before, whether this call is part of an ongoing transaction, and what to do next.

Most scripts similar to shopping cart scripts handle this problem by shoveling hidden fields into their output so that when your browser calls again, the hidden information from the last call is available. In this way, the script determines the proper state and thus whether the visitor is continuing a shopping spree. The script handles this problem behind the scenes, out of the visitor's view.

Other scripts use browser-side *magic cookies*—text strings that the browser can save in a file on the local machine. Cookies are a way around the problem of statelessness, but they pose security risks and aren't supported by all browsers.

In this chapter, you learn how to maintain state information by using hidden fields.

All That Baggage

Can you imagine what life would be like if, every time that you moved from one room to another in your house, you had to pack up everything you own and carry it with you?

That's pretty much how shopping cart scripts work. From invocation to invocation, they carry their baggage along with them—because otherwise, they lose it forever.

This chapter presents a script called ShopCart. Consider the goals of ShopCart, and figure out what kind of baggage it will have to carry. Don't worry if this discussion seems overly detailed right now; when you examine the code later in this chapter, it will all make sense.

Who Will Buy?

ShopCart enables visitors to buy fresh fruit. A visitor can wander the virtual store, fondling the oranges, shining the apples, pinching the mangos, and deciding what to buy. At any time, the visitor can put any number of fruits into the shopping cart, or remove fruits from the cart. For example, when the visitor goes to the checkout counter to pay for the purchases, he or she may decide to trade three of the apples for seven kiwi fruits. Each kind of fruit has its own price. In addition, your virtual store will give away plastic bags for free.

The list of items in the shopping cart has three properties: quantity, price, and description. The cart can hold any number of items, each with its own quantity, price, and description. Figure 8.1 shows ShopCart's first screen, before any shopping has taken place.

Figure 8.1

ShopCart in action, before the visitor has selected any items. The table at the top of the screen displays the cart's contents, and the fields at the bottom enable the visitor to select items to put into the cart.

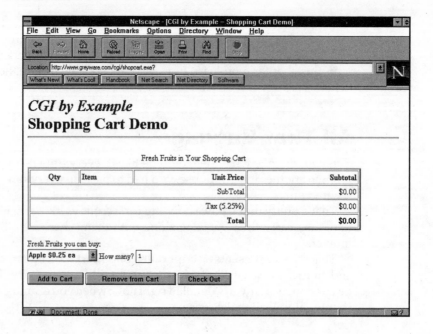

The State of *Main()*

Almost all the functions within ShopCart rely on maintaining a list of items inside the cart. Because the cart's contents are fixed when the script is invoked (empty the first time, of course, then almost any state thereafter), the main() routine decodes this information and makes it available to all the subfunctions.

The main() routine also determines how the visitor invoked the script. Did a GET operation invoke the script the first time? Did a POST operation invoke the script? If so, which button did the visitor click?

Each time that a visitor invokes ShopCart, the script must examine its input for the previously saved cart information and for previously saved invocation information (which button the visitor clicked). Each time that the script outputs another form or status screen, ShopCart must also output the cart information and the button information. Figure 8.2 shows the screen after the visitor has selected several fruits, but hasn't checked out yet.

ShopCart relegates the bother of storing and retrieving state information to two routines. BaggageToArray() parses the baggage from the hidden form fields and stuffs it into an array. PrintArray() does the opposite, printing the array's information into a hidden form field.

The rest of the program doesn't worry about how the baggage is carried along. The various functions simply manipulate the array and trust that it will be around again next time that the visitor invokes the script.

Figure 8.2

ShopCart after the visitor has selected several items and placed them in the shopping cart. Notice that ShopCart calculates the line subtotal, the tax, and the grand total (so far).

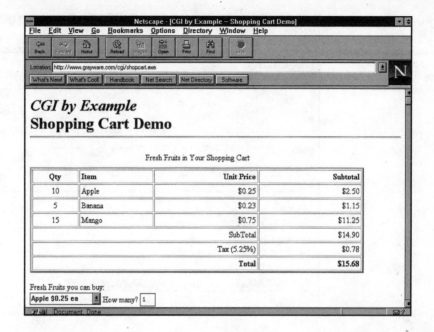

The hidden field's format isn't relevant to the rest of the program, so this chapter doesn't discuss it in depth. However, you should take a moment now to study the format, so that you can incorporate this mechanism into your own scripts.

A record in the array consists of three fields: quantity, price, and description. For a record specifying two oranges at 24 cents each, ShopCart writes the following to the hidden field:

```
2/0.24/Orange;
```

The semicolon marks the end of the record, and slashes separate the fields within the record. By using this format, ShopCart can concatenate any number of records together into one long string, and still be capable of separating the records from their fields later.

To decode this information, ShopCart simply searches for a semicolon and then the slashes within each substring.

Check It Out!

When the visitor is ready to check out (that is, when the visitor is ready to stop shopping and start paying), many other variables come into play. To process an order, ShopCart must collect the visitor's name, address, credit card type, credit card number, and credit card expiration date. The script must maintain all this information *in addition to* the list of whatever the visitor has put in the shopping cart. Figure 8.3 shows ShopCart's display after the visitor has finished shopping and is ready to check out.

Figure 8.3

ShopCart's display
after the visitor
has finished
shopping and is
ready to check out.

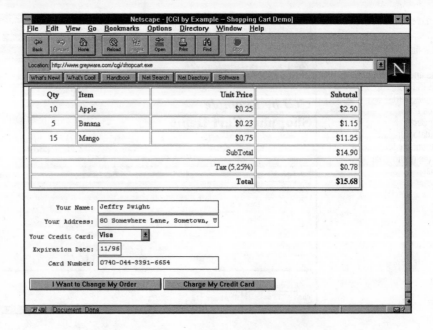

Because the quantity and type of information required for the checkout process is static, ShopCart doesn't make another special hidden field. Instead, the script lets each field on the fill-out form function the usual way and retrieves the variables separately.

One of your goals, however, is to enable visitors to change their minds at the checkout counter and return to shopping. For this reason, the checkout routine must continue preserving the cart information.

Validation

For the last step in the process, you also have to worry about state variables. After the visitor fills in the checkout form, you must validate the form's information. You can't simply force visitors to go through the whole shopping process again simply because they omitted their name from the form by mistake.

If ShopCart discovers an error during validation, the script prints an error message and redisplays the checkout form, with all the information still present in the form's fields. In addition, the checkout form enables the visitor to go back and shop some more, so you must preserve all the cart's state information, too. Figure 8.4 shows ShopCart accepting the visitor's credit card information and saying "Thank you."

Figure 8.4

ShopCart
accepting the
visitor's credit
card information
and thanking the
visitor.

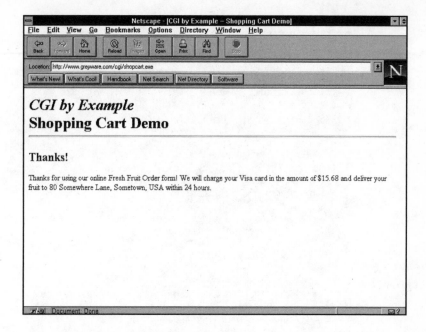

How ShopCart Works

ShopCart is a VB4-32 program (that is, the script is written for the 32-bit edition of Visual Basic version 4). You use VB4-32 for this script for two reasons. First, ShopCart requires much string manipulation, a task for which Visual Basic 4 is well suited. String manipulation tasks that are difficult or unwieldy in Perl or C are a snap with Visual Basic.

Second, ShopCart is a full-blown application that uses the VB4CGI.BAS routines discussed in Chapter 20, "Using Visual Basic." That chapter covers only the theoretical and technical aspects of using Visual Basic for CGI scripting; for the full flavor of VB4CGI.BAS's power, you need to see it in action. (See Chapter 20 for an in-depth look at how to use VB4-32 for CGI scripting, and for an explanation of the routines in VB4CGI.BAS.)

Listing 8.1 shows ShopCart's declaration section and the entire Sub Main() routine. Although this section uses subroutines that you haven't explored yet, this listing presents the main logic flow of the entire script.

Listing 8.1   ShopCart's *Sub Main()* Routine

```
'
' Declarations section
'
Option Explicit
DefInt A-Z


' ----- Some constants used throughout the script

Const txtTitle = "CGI by Example -- Shopping Cart Demo"
Const txtHeader = "<i>CGI by Example</i><br>Shopping
➥ Cart Demo<hr>"

' ----- A global variable, holding the choice made when
'       the user last clicked a button

Dim Choice As String


' ----- The type-declaration for our purchase array.
'       This array holds the purchase info while the
'       user is browsing around

Type PurchaseLine
    Item       As String
    Quantity   As Integer
    Price      As Currency
End Type

' ----- Declare a dynamic array of type PurchaseLine

Dim Purchases() As PurchaseLine

'
' This is the entry point for the script
'
Sub Main()
    Dim x As Integer

    ' Standard startup stuff

    cgiStartup

    ' Output the title

    cgiTitle txtTitle

    ' Output the body tag

    Out "<body>" + vbCrLf
```

```
    ' Output the level 1 header

    cgiHeader txtHeader


    ' If this is a POST operation, then
    ' the CGI variable 'Choice' will reflect
    ' the caption of the button last clicked.
    ' Retrieve that variable now, and trim
    ' all but the first word

    Choice = Trim(cgiGetEnv("Choice"))
    x = InStr(Choice, " ")
    If x Then Choice = Left(Choice, x - 1)
    Choice = UCase(Choice)

    ' If this is a repeat operation of any
    ' sort, then we'll have all sorts of state
    ' information baggage tucked up inside the
    ' form.  Get it out of the CGI variable and
    ' into an array where we can deal with it
    ' decently and in order.

    BaggageToArray

    ' Now, depending on how the script was
    ' invoked, go do something with all this
    ' information!

    Select Case UCase(cgiGetEnv("REQUEST_METHOD"))
        Case "GET"
            CreateForm
        Case "POST"
            ProcessForm
    End Select

    ' Do the standard shutdown stuff

    cgiShutdown
End Sub
```

As you can see from examining listing 8.1, the `Sub Main()` routine handles some basic housekeeping and controls the script's overall flow. Listings 8.2 and 8.3 show the two primary subroutines that `Sub Main()` calls: `CreateForm()` and `ProcessForm()`. Good code is largely self-documenting; whatever the code itself cannot document, you should document with comments. These two listings demonstrate good documentation—good enough that simply by reading the comments, you should be able to figure out what the code does.

Listing 8.2 The *CreateForm()* Routine

```
'
' Control comes here on a GET operation (the first
' time the script is invoked).  Control also comes
' here every time a POST operation decides to print
' the order form again.
'
Sub CreateForm()

    ' First, show the current orders
    ShowOrders

    ' Now print the order form, so the visitor
    ' can pick items to order

    ' First the <form...> line
    Out "<form method=POST action="
    Out Q(cgiGetScript()) + ">" + vbCrLf

    ' Now the state information, if any
    Out "<input type=hidden name=baggage value="
    PrintArray
    Out ">" + vbCrLf

    Out "Fresh Fruits you can buy:<br>"
    ' Now the Fruit options
    Out "<select name=Item>"
    Out "<option>Apple $0.25 ea"
    Out "<option>Orange $0.24 ea"
    Out "<option>Mango $0.75 ea"
    Out "<option>Banana $0.23 ea"
    Out "<option>Kiwi $1.19 ea"
    Out "<option>Plastic Bag (free)"
    Out "</select>"

    ' Now the quantity
    Out "  How many? "
    Out "<input type=text name=Quantity "
    Out "size=3 value=1 maxlength=3>"
    Out "<p>"

    ' Now the submit buttons
    Out "<input type=submit name=Choice value="
    Out Q(" Add to Cart ") + ">" + vbCrLf

    Out "<input type=submit name=Choice value="
    Out Q(" Remove from Cart ") + ">" + vbCrLf

    Out "<input type=submit name=Choice value="
    Out Q(" Check Out ") + ">" + vbCrLf

    ' End the form
    Out "</form>"

End Sub
```

Listing 8.3   The *ProcessForm()* Routine

```
'
' Control comes here any time the script is invoked
' with the POST method.  Depending on what button was
' clicked to cause the POST, this routine does
' different things
'
Sub ProcessForm()

    ' Some local variables used for handling
    ' the input and manipulating the Purchases()
    ' array

    Dim Items As Integer
    Dim Thing As String
    Dim Bucks As Currency
    Dim x As Integer
    Dim FoundInCart As Integer
    Dim Qty As Integer


    ' Examine the CGI environment variable 'choice'
    ' and take appropriate action.  This variable is
    ' set by clicking on a button, and the Main()
    ' routine cleans it up for us.

    If Choice = "ADD" Then

        ' Visitor selected something and clicked on
        ' Add to Cart, so do that thing

        Items = UBound(Purchases, 1)

        ' What thing does the visitor want to buy?

        Thing = cgiGetEnv("Item")

        ' How many of 'em?

        Qty = Val(cgiGetEnv("Quantity"))

        ' Did tricksy visitor say zero or negative?
        ' If not, go ahead; otherwise ignore

        If Qty > 0 Then
            ' Item descriptions contain the price
            ' (if there is a price) and indicate it
            ' with a dollar sign

            x = InStr(Thing, "$")    ' Free item?
```

continues

Listing 8.3 Continued

```
            ' Item is not free if $ is present
            If x Then
                Bucks = Val(Mid(Thing, x + 1))
                Thing = Trim(Left(Thing, x - 1))
            Else
                Bucks = 0
            End If

            ' See if visitor already has some of
            ' this thing; if so, just adjust the
            ' quantity

            FoundInCart = False
            For x = 1 To Items
                If Purchases(x).Item = Thing Then
                    Purchases(x).Quantity _
                        = Purchases(x).Quantity + Qty
                    FoundInCart = True
                    Exit For
                End If
            Next x

            ' If not found in cart, then add a new
            ' item to the Purchases() array

            If Not FoundInCart Then
                Items = Items + 1
                ReDim Preserve Purchases(Items)
                Purchases(Items).Item = Thing
                Purchases(Items).Price = Bucks
                Purchases(Items).Quantity = Qty
            End If

        End If
        CreateForm  ' back for more

    ElseIf Choice = "REMOVE" Then

        ' Visitor selected some item and clicked
        ' Remove from Cart, so let's do that

        Items = UBound(Purchases, 1)

        ' What thing shall we remove?

        Thing = cgiGetEnv("Item")

        ' How many must go away?

        Qty = Val(cgiGetEnv("Quantity"))
```

```
            ' Say, is that a positive number > zero?

        If Qty > 0 Then
            ' If so, see if the thing is in the
            ' cart already; otherwise ignore

            x = InStr(Thing, "$")
            If x Then Thing = Trim(Left(Thing, x - 1))

            For x = 1 To Items
                If Purchases(x).Item = Thing Then
                    Purchases(x).Quantity _
                        = Purchases(x).Quantity - Qty
                    If Purchases(x).Quantity < 1 _
                        Then Purchases(x).Item = ""
                    Exit For
                End If
            Next x
        End If
        CreateForm  ' back for more

    ElseIf Choice = "CHECK" Then
        ' Visitor is done shopping and wants to
        ' check out.  Go do that thing.
        CheckOut

    ElseIf Choice = "CHARGE" Then
        ' Visitor filled in the checkout form
        ' and said "Charge me, Momma!"
        ' Go validate the input and take his
        ' money away from him!
        Finishup

    Else
        ' ignore unknown choices
        ' just reprint the form
        CreateForm
    End If
End Sub
```

The Webmaster needn't do much to make ShopCart work. To install the script, copy it to the Web server's CGI-BIN directory (whatever you call the directory on your system); then, to link to the script from any page, create an `<a href...>` link to the script that looks like the following:

```
<a href="/cgi-bin/shopcart.exe">ShopCart</a>
```

Thereafter, ShopCart itself handles all HTML.

Compiling and Modifying ShopCart

As is, ShopCart is a good demonstration of a shopping cart script, but not terribly useful in the real world.

To recompile or modify it, you need a full copy of the VB4 32-bit development environment. After you've made your changes and come up with a script that suits your needs, you can transfer the executable to your Web server. The Web server must have the run-time DLL living in its system directory (%SYSTEMROOT%\SYSTEM32 on Windows NT; C:\WINDOWS\SYSTEM on Windows 95) and be running either Windows NT or Windows 95.

> **Tip:** If you want to experiment with ShopCart some more but can't compile it yourself, stop by Greyware Automation Products, where it is installed and running. The URL is **http://www.greyware.com/cgi/shopcart.exe**.

This book's companion CD-ROM includes the full source code for ShopCart, SHOPCART.BAS. The CD also includes VB4CGI.BAS, the include file discussed in Chapter 20, and VB40032.DLL, the run-time DLL required by VB4-32. SHOPCART.BAS is *extensively* documented, and designed to be easily modified for incorporation into your own scripts.

Adding a Configuration File

A demo can get away with using hard-coded values for variables, but a useful program must be configurable. ShopCart hard-codes several things that really belong in a configuration file:

◆ *The tax rate.* This varies from area to area, and in some cases is inapplicable altogether. ShopCart's logic allows for any tax rate (including zero), but provides no way for the Webmaster to adjust it.

◆ *The items for sale.* Selling fresh fruit probably isn't a good purpose for a shopping cart script. You should move the list of items for sale, and their associated prices, to a configuration file.

◆ *The script's headers and messages.* Throughout the script, headers and messages refer to fresh fruits.

Listing 8.4 shows a suggested organization for your configuration file. You should modify the values supplied in listing 8.4 as necessary. Try using the Win32 API call GetPrivateProfileString to read this kind of file.

Listing 8.4   SHOPCART.INI—a Likely Configuration File for ShopCart

```
[General]
ScriptTitle=Fresh Fruit Farm
ScriptHeader=Fresh Fruit Online Ordering System
TaxRate=0.0525

[Items]
Item1=Apple $0.25 each
Item2=Orange $0.24 each
Item3=Mango $1.25 each
...
```

Saving the Output

As written, ShopCart simply thanks the visitor and then discards the visitor's order. To become more than a curiosity, ShopCart must save the visitor's order—either in a flat file or a database—and perhaps send an e-mail confirmation to the visitor.

> **Note:** See Chapter 10, "Storing Information in Flat Files," for theory and examples of how to use flat files. See Chapter 11, "Storing Information in Databases," for theory and examples of keeping information in databases.

Summary

In this chapter, you learned about the importance of state information, why such information is hard to get, and how to make it available to your script. You also learned about the program flow of a shopping cart script, and saw how to convert information from a usable array to a string suitable for inclusion in a hidden field on a form.

Review Questions

1. Between visits, what does a Web server remember about the visitor?

2. How many requests for information can a Web server fulfill during any one connection to a browser?

3. What two methods for storing state information does this chapter discuss?

4. How does ShopCart know what to do each time that it gets invoked? That is, how does the script know whether to add an item to the cart, remove an item from the cart, or do something else?

Review Exercises

1. What are the theoretical limits to the amount of information that you can store in a hidden text field? What are the practical limits? Devise an alternate method for handling state information using multiple hidden fields.

2. Write a routine to validate the expiration date and credit card number provided by the visitor. What can you do besides check the data's format? What would an online merchant have to do before accepting this kind of order?

3. Add functionality to ShopCart for back-ordered items. What do you need to change?

4. Create the configuration file suggested in listing 8.4, and add code within ShopCart to find and read the file. For ideas, refer to the section "Making the Guestbook Configurable" in Chapter 7, "A More Complex Guestbook."

5. Referring to Chapter 18, "JavaScript," write a JavaScript program that duplicates ShopCart's fill-the-cart functions. Is this a better approach to the problem? Name several advantages and disadvantages of using JavaScript rather than standard CGI for a shopping cart.

Part IV

Database Connectivity

## CHAPTER 9

Collecting Information

As Chapter 2, "The Common Gateway Interface (CGI)," briefly touched on, both the client and server provide information about themselves. They do so by creating environmental variables that you can use within your scripts.

You can use this information to create logs of the pages that are getting hit, which sites have links to your pages, which browser is the most popular, and so on. You can also use this information within your scripts to tell visitors what server and version of the CGI protocol you are using, and more.

Providing this information is quite simple, and can help you use CGI scripts to create Web pages that are more informative and personal.

Using Information from the Visitor

Whenever a client connects to your server, the client passes information that you usually don't see while simply browsing around the Web. You can create a script that generates a Web page that supplies this information to the visitor. You can also create a log that records this information to a file. The server's log files store most of this information, but if you don't have access to the server's logs, you can create your own. First, you should create a script that creates an HTML document in which visitors to your site can see a little information about themselves.

As you learned in Chapter 2, the client sends quite a bit of information to the server about itself and about the person using it. The information doesn't include anything extremely personal, but can show the domain name and IP address of the host that the visitor is using, the Web browser that the visitor is using, and which document the visitor requested. The information can also specify the URL of the document that referred the visitor to your site.

Most servers can recognize certain document extensions as scripts. In particular, servers usually recognize documents with .CGI or .PL extensions as scripts. Normally such documents reside in the CGI-BIN directory. Sometimes a server administrator might have the server recognize any document with the extension .SHTML as a script. By doing so, the administrator enables you to place scripts somewhere other than the CGI-BIN directory.

The script that you are going to create must be in the CGI-BIN directory. You could also set up the server to recognize the script by its extension outside of the CGI-BIN directory. To set up the server to do so, you must check the server's documentation. For this example, however, you simply keep the script in the CGI-BIN directory.

Most scripts usually check which REQUEST_METHOD was used, and then split the name/value pairs into variables that the scripts can use. The script that you are creating doesn't need to perform this checking and splitting, however, because it doesn't grab anything from a form. If the client requests your script, the script uses existing information to create a document that you then return to the visitor.

Your script retrieves the information stored in the environmental variables and displays that information to the visitor. You can find this script on the CD-ROM accompanying this book. First, you must tell the script where to find Perl:

```
#! /usr/bin/perl
# hello.pl
```

Whenever you return information to the server, you must define the Content-type. You're creating a Web page, so you use the MIME type text/html:

```
print "Content-type: text/html\n\n";
```

When you retrieve the HTTP_USER_AGENT variable, it contains one line with the name of the agent and a version. For example, if you are using Netscape, you get a line such as the following:

```
Mozilla/2.01 (Win95;I)
```

To split the browser name from the version and place both the browser name and the version in their own variables, you use Perl's split() function:

```
($browser, $version) = split(/\//, $ENV{'HTTP_USER_AGENT');
```

You next replace the word Mozilla with the word Netscape. Essentially, you instruct the script to do the following:

If the agent is Mozilla,

Then browser equals Netscape.

Next you change the browser's name from Mozilla to Netscape. This name change isn't absolutely necessary, but more people are familiar with the name Netscape than Mozilla.

```
# Change Mozilla to something more recognized
if ($browser eq "Mozilla") {
$browser = "Netscape";
    }
```

Some older versions of Microsoft's Internet Explorer reported themselves as the agent Mozilla. To be fair, the version sections did state that the versions were "compatible" and added the notation "MSIE." This information reveals that the agent is actually Microsoft's Internet Explorer, not the Mozilla agent as you might suspect. Because some of these older Internet Explorer versions are still in use, you want to ensure that your script reports the correct browser. Therefore, you tell your script to perform the following check:

If the variable version includes the string MSIE,

Then change the value for the browser to Microsoft Internet Explorer.

The script's actual code is as follows:

```
if ($version =~ /MSIE/) {
$browser = "Microsoft Internet Explorer";
    }
```

You begin building your page by creating the script's main section:

```
print "<HTML>";
print "<HEAD><TITLE>Hello!</TITLE></HEAD>";
print "<BODY><H1>Hello!</H1>";
```

You then have the script check whether the REMOTE_HOST environmental variable has a value. If so, you print the REMOTE_HOST and the REMOTE_ADDR, which displays the domain address that the client is on, and the IP address.

Note: The REMOTE_HOST and REMOTE_ADDR environment variables only report the host that the client is using. Many Internet service providers (ISPs) provide a dynamic IP address to a user making a Serial Line Internet Protocol (SLIP) or Point-to-Point Protocol (PPP) connection. This address changes each time that a user connects, so it doesn't reflect the actual site to which the visitor belongs.

If the REMOTE_HOST environmental variable is absent, you have the script display only the IP address:

```
if ($ENV{'REMOTE_HOST'}) {
print "Hello user from $ENV{'REMOTE_HOST'} ($ENV{'REMOTE_ADDR'})!<BR>";
   }
else {
print "Hello user from $ENV{'REMOTE_ADDR'}!<BR>";
    }
```

Next you display a small line that tells the visitor which browser he or she is using and the browser's version:

```
print "I see you're using $browser, version $version. Do you like it?";
```

Finally, the script displays the HTTP_REFERER variable (see listing 9.1). This variable holds the site from which the visitor linked to your site. Then the script displays the DOCUMENT_URI variable, which is the path and file name of the document that the visitor requested.

Listing 9.1   HELLO.PL—Checking *HTTP_REFERER*

```
print "<BR>";
if ($ENV{'HTTP_REFERER'}) {
print "You have requested the document $ENV{'DOCUMENT_URI'} from ";
print "<A HREF=\"$ENV{'HTTP_REFERER'}\">$ENV{'HTTP_REFERER'}</A>.<BR>";
print "I hope you enjoy it!";
   }
print "</BODY>";
print "</HTML>";
exit;
```

Figure 9.1 provides an example of the resulting screen's appearance. This script is relatively simple, but demonstrates the kinds of information that you can provide to your visitors. Depending on how you have set up this script and how the script is being accessed, your results will vary. Change the script yourself to see what happens under various circumstances.

Some browsers can do things that others cannot. If you want to ensure that your site uses every browser to its full potential, you can create a script that checks which browser the visitor is using. Then the script can either display only information which that particular browser can use, or refer the browser to a page that includes only information that the browser can use. The following pseudocode shows how you might implement this strategy:

Figure 9.1

You can surprise your visitors with your magically acquired knowledge by adding client information to your scripts.

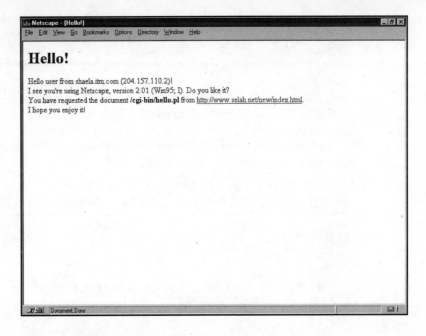

Are you using Netscape?

If so, go to NETSCAPE.HTML.

Are you using MSIE?

If so, go to MSIE.HTML.

Are you using Lynx?

If so, go to LYNX.HTML.

Are you using something else?

If so, go to ELSE.HTML.

The following script fragment shows how you code this scheme. You can find the complete script on the companion CD-ROM under the name RELOCATE.PL.

```
#! /usr/bin/perl
# relocate.pl
```

Now check whether the visitor is using the Mozilla client. Remember that you have to check whether the line contains *MSIE*.

```
if ($ENV{'HTTP_USER_AGENT'} =~ /Mozilla/) {
if ($ENV{'HTTP_USER_AGENT'} !~ /MSIE/) {
print "Location: netscape.html\n\n";
exit;
 }
}
```

Notice the use of double line feeds, which are required at the end of the header information.

In listing 9.2, you check whether HTTP_USER_AGENT includes either MSIE or the word Microsoft.

Listing 9.2   Find Both the Old and New Versions

```
if ($ENV{'HTTP_USER_AGENT'} =~ /MSIE/) {
print "Location: msie.html\n\n";
exit;
 }
if ($ENV{'HTTP_USER_AGENT'} =~ /Microsoft/) {
print "Location: msie.html\n\n";
exit;
}
```

Next check whether the visitor is using Lynx. If so, you send the visitor to view LYNX.HTML:

```
if ($ENV{'HTTP_USER_AGENT'} =~ /Lynx/) {
print "Location: lynx.html\n\n";
exit;
  }
```

The Location: line tells the server to send the file (in this example, LYNX.HTML) to the visitor. Using Location: is beneficial when a file that you can use already exists. Otherwise, you would have to expand your script to create a document.

Last, you need to cover all your bases. If the visitor isn't using any of the previously handled browsers, you need to give the visitor somewhere else to go:

```
print "Location: else.html\n\n";
exit;
```

When you use the information that clients provide, you can make your Web server do many things. If the client is from a certain IP address, you can send it to a specific page; otherwise, you can send the client to another page. Using client information can give you a little more control over your pages, even if you lack access to the server's configuration files. You must, however, have the ability to run scripts, no matter where you decide to place them. If you're not the server administrator, the administrator's restrictions might limit your options. If you're not sure what you can do, contact your administrator. Most administrators should be willing to work with you.

Using Information from the Server

The server, like the client, places information into environmental variables. Unfortunately, the server doesn't provide much information that you would want to place into your scripts. Other than creating scripts that give the visitor information about your server, the only real purpose is to create a script that you can use to test your forms.

The National Center for Supercomputing Applications (NCSA) Web server comes with a couple programs that can help you check your HTML forms to ensure that your forms are doing exactly what you expected. You can find these scripts at the following address:

> **http://hoohoo.ncsa.uiuc.edu**

TEST-CGI is a shell script that displays the information in the environmental variables (see listing 9.3).

Listing 9.3   TEST-CGI—an NCSA Script That Helps You Test Your Forms

```
#!/bin/sh
echo Content-type: text/plain
echo

echo CGI/1.0 test script report:
echo
echo argc is $#. argv is "$*".
echo

echo SERVER_SOFTWARE = $SERVER_SOFTWARE
echo SERVER_NAME = $SERVER_NAME
echo GATEWAY_INTERFACE = $GATEWAY_INTERFACE
echo SERVER_PROTOCOL = $SERVER_PROTOCOL
echo SERVER_PORT = $SERVER_PORT
echo REQUEST_METHOD = $REQUEST_METHOD
echo HTTP_ACCEPT = "$HTTP_ACCEPT"
echo PATH_INFO = "$PATH_INFO"
echo PATH_TRANSLATED = "$PATH_TRANSLATED"
echo SCRIPT_NAME = "$SCRIPT_NAME"
echo QUERY_STRING = "$QUERY_STRING"
echo REMOTE_HOST = $REMOTE_HOST
echo REMOTE_ADDR = $REMOTE_ADDR
echo REMOTE_USER = $REMOTE_USER
echo AUTH_TYPE = $AUTH_TYPE
echo CONTENT_TYPE = $CONTENT_TYPE
echo CONTENT_LENGTH = $CONTENT_LENGTH
```

To use the TEST-CGI script, create your HTML form and have the ACTION attribute point to the location at which you have placed the TEST-CGI script (normally in CGI-BIN), as in the following example:

```
<FORM ACTION="/cgi-bin/test-cgi">
```

Use whichever method you prefer. The script then reports information about your client, the server, and any information passed from a form. Figure 9.2 shows an example of the TEST-CGI script, using the method GET.

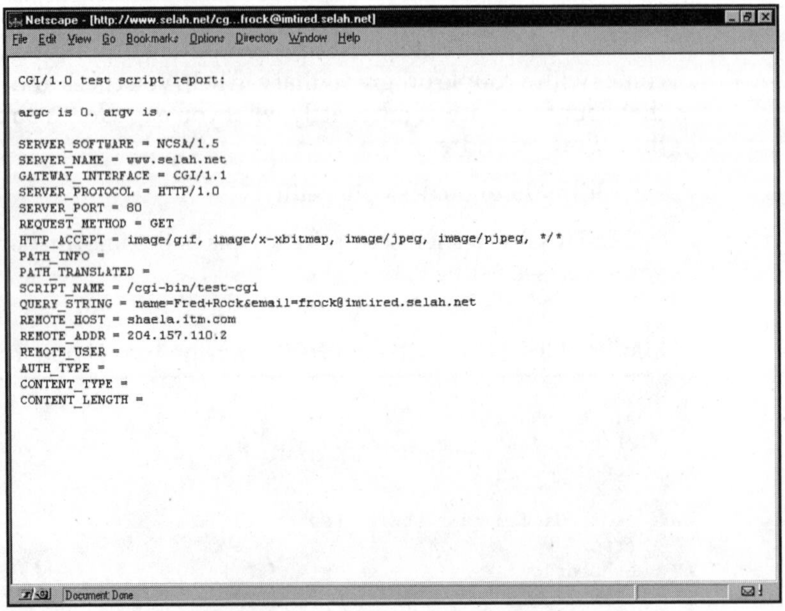
Netscape - [http://www.selah.net/cg...frock@imtired.selah.net]
File Edit View Go Bookmarks Options Directory Window Help
CGI/1.0 test script report:
argc is 0. argv is .
SERVER_SOFTWARE = NCSA/1.5
SERVER_NAME = www.selah.net
GATEWAY_INTERFACE = CGI/1.1
SERVER_PROTOCOL = HTTP/1.0
SERVER_PORT = 80
REQUEST_METHOD = GET
HTTP_ACCEPT = image/gif, image/x-xbitmap, image/jpeg, image/pjpeg, */*
PATH_INFO =
PATH_TRANSLATED =
SCRIPT_NAME = /cgi-bin/test-cgi
QUERY_STRING = name=Fred+Rock&email=frock@imtired.selah.net
REMOTE_HOST = shaela.itm.com
REMOTE_ADDR = 204.157.110.2
REMOTE_USER =
AUTH_TYPE =
CONTENT_TYPE =
CONTENT_LENGTH =
Document: Done

Figure 9.2
The NCSA server's TEST-CGI script can help you check your HTML forms.

Creating Your Own Log Files

If you don't have access to the server logs, you can create your own log file. You can use this file for informational purposes. Perhaps your curiosity—about your site's visitors, which browser they're using, or even which pages on the vast Web have a link to your page—is as great as mine. In any event, creating log files is simple, although you must be able to use Server-Side Includes (SSI) within the directory that contains the script. For more information on SSI, see Chapter 16, "Server-Side Includes." To activate the script, simply call an <!--#exec cgi=""--> command in the HTML pages that you want to log.

First you must decide what information you want to log. The following are a few good choices:

- REMOTE_HOST
- HTTP_USER_AGENT
- DOCUMENT_URI
- HTTP_REFERER

To create the script, you need only open a file and dump the contents of the environmental variables to the file, as shown in listing 9.4. To call this script, you need to add `<!--#exec cgi="/cgi-bin/log.pl"-->` within your HTML document.

> **Caution:** Whenever you use SSI, you need to be a bit cautious. Sometimes server administrators do not allow the use of SSI. Again, see Chapter 16 for more details on SSI.

Listing 9.4   LOG.PL—a Small Log Script

```
#! /usr/local/bin/perl

# log.pl - Log file generator.
print "Content-type: text/plain\n\n";
$logfile = "log.txt";
chop($shortdate = 'date +%m%d');
open (LOG, ">>$logfile");
print LOG "$shortdate¦";
print LOG "$ENV{'REMOTE_HOST'}¦";
print LOG "$ENV{'HTTP_USER_AGENT'}¦";
print LOG "$ENV{'DOCUMENT_URI'}¦";
print LOG "$ENV{'HTTP_REFERER'}\n";
close (LOG);
exit;
```

A pipe character (¦) separates each field. You can use this character within a script to separate each line's contents. When your page starts to get a few hits, your log will start to look like the following:

```
0528¦yak-ts1-p35.wolfenet.com¦Mozilla/2.01 (Win95; I)¦/cgi.html¦
0528¦max80ppp245.pacific.net.sg¦Mozilla/1.2 (Windows; I; 16bit)¦
➥ /cgi.html¦
0528¦dp1-015.ppp.iglou.com¦Mozilla/1.22 (Windows; I;
➥ 16bit)¦/cgi.html¦http://www.somewhere.org/
0528¦yak-ts1-p35.wolfenet.com¦Mozilla/2.01 (Win95; I)¦/cgi.html¦
```

The log shows the month and date that a visitor requested the document, the visitor's domain address, the user agent, the page requested, and if passed, the referrer.

Building Statistics

Your server keeps a log or set of logs that record information. The log keeps track of which browsers (agents) are being used as well as information about which files were requested, and information about the referrer.

You could use the logs to provide a page containing statistical information about your server. Much of this information is completely FYI (for your information) only.

Determining which browser is the most popular is always interesting, so in this section you create a script that does just that.

The first script provides the path to Perl, then prints the Content-type. Next you set the path to the server's agent log file.

```
#! /usr/bin/perl
print "Content-type: text/html\n\n";
$agent = "/httpd/logs/agent_log";
```

Now you need to open the log file and assign it the file handle AGENT:

```
open(AGENT, $agent) || die "Can't open log\n";
```

While reading the agent log file, the script creates a count of the amount of hits that your server has received since the last time that you reset the logs (see listing 9.5). The script also increments the count for each agent for which you are recording statistics.

Listing 9.5   AGENT.PL—Start the Count!

```
while(<AGENT>) {
$count++;
$mozilla++ if /^Mozilla/;
$ibmex++ if /^IBM/;
$lynx++ if /^Lynx/;
$msie++ if /MSIE/;
$msie2++ if /Microsoft/;
$harvest++ if /^Harvest/;
$bot++ if /bot/;
$ibot++ if /Infoseek/;
 }

close(AGENT);
```

After closing the file, you subtract the amount of $msie from the $mozilla variable. Remember that older versions of the Microsoft Internet Explorer specify Mozilla as their agent name.

```
$mozilla = $mozilla-$msie;
```

Next, because $bot counts any line that contains the string bot, you must subtract the Infoseek $ibot, because it also contains the the string bot:

```
$bot=$bot-$ibot;
$msie=$msie+$msie2;
$they=$mozilla+$ibmex+$lynx+$bot+$msie+$ibot+$harvest;
$other=$count-$they;
```

Now you subtract the various counts from the main count to find out how many agents were used other than the main ones for which you previously searched. Add each browser type together and assign the amount to $they. Then subtract $they from the main count, which provides the $other variable.

Next you create the HTML document. In listing 9.6, you use a table to format the page. By doing so, you create a page with the agent type and the counts properly aligned.

Listing 9.6 AGENT.PL—Creating the Agent Page

```
print <<"HTML";
<HTML>
<HEAD><TITLE>User agent stats</TITLE></HEAD>
<BODY>
<H1>User Agent Statistics</H1>
<TABLE BORDER=1>
<TR><TD COLSPAN=2>There has been a total of <B>$count</B> hits
➥ on this website</TD></TR>
<TR><TD>Netscape</TD><TD>$mozilla</TD></TR>
<TR><TD>IBM Explorer</TD><TD>$ibmex</TD></TR>
<TR><TD>MS Internet Explorer</TD><TD>$msie</TD></TR>
<TR><TD>Lynx</TD><TD>$lynx</TD></TR>
<TR><TD>The Infoseek Bot</TD><TD>$ibot</TD></TR>
<TR><TD>A Harvest Bot</TD><TD>$harvest</TD></TR>
<TR><TD>Other Bot</TD><TD>$bot</TD></TR>
<TR><TD>Other</TD><TD>$other</TD></TR>
</TABLE>
</BODY>
</HTML>

HTML
exit;
```

This code results in a page that looks like figure 9.3.

Without creating another page hit counter, you might want to create a script that indicates how often different types of files are requested. The next script that you create checks the access log and counts how many HTML files visitors requested, along with .GIFs, JPEGs, and your scripts.

As shown in listing 9.7, the script ACCESS.PL sets all the counters equal to zero just in case the script doesn't find anything. The value zero is better than NULL. You can check for a value if the string has been assigned the value of zero. If the value were NULL, you couldn't do so.

Figure 9.3

You can see which browser is the most popular and compare the popularity of other browsers.

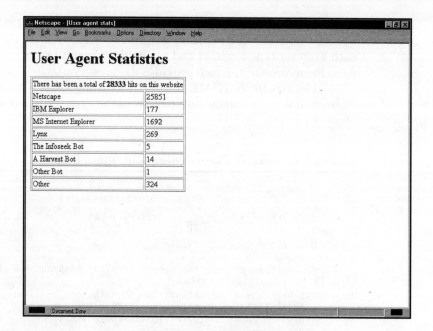

Listing 9.7   ACCESS.PL—Set the Counters to Zero

```perl
#! /usr/bin/perl

print "Content-type: text/html\n\n";

$access = "/httpd/logs/access_log";

$count=0;
$html=0;
$gif=0;
$pl=0;
$jpeg=0;
$cgi=0;
```

Next open the access log and begin counting anything that matches the search patterns. As you can see in listing 9.8, you need to add the backslash (\) before the period because it is considered a metacharacter within the search parameter. For example, suppose that you want to search for anything that includes *.html*. Normally the period (.) is considered a wild card (it matches any character except a newline).

Listing 9.8   ACCESS.PL—Open the Access Log File and Count Each Item

```
open(ACCESS, $access) || die "Can't open log\n";

while(<ACCESS>) {
$count++;
$html++ if /\.html/;
$gif++ if /\.gif/;
$pl++ if /\.pl/;
$jpeg++ if /\.jpeg/;
$cgi++ if /\.cgi/;
  }
```

To find out how many visitors hit documents other than those specified, you need to add the count of each file type together and subtract the total from the main count:

```
$total=$html+$gif+$pl+$jpeg+$cgi;
$other=$count-$total;
```

Finally, you create a document that displays statistics, as shown in listing 9.9.

Listing 9.9   ACCESS.PL—Create the Page That Displays the Statistics

```
print "<HTML>\n";
print "<HEAD><TITLE>Page hits</TITLE></HEAD>\n";
print "<BODY>\n";
print "<H1>More stats</H1>\n";
print "<PRE>\n";
print "Out of a total of $count, I have had... \n\n";
print "$html hits on the HTML pages,\n";
print "$gif hits on the GIF files,\n";
print "$jpeg hits on the JPEG images,\n";
print "$pl hits on the Perl scripts,\n";
print "$cgi hits on the CGI scripts,\n";
print "and $other hits on everything else.\n";
print "</PRE>\n";
print "</BODY>\n";
print "</HTML>\n";

close(ACCESS);
exit;
```

This script creates a page that looks like figure 9.4. Although these statistics are not completely meaningful, they give you an idea of what is happening with your pages.

Figure 9.4

ACCESS.PL shows a listing of how many hits each type of document received.

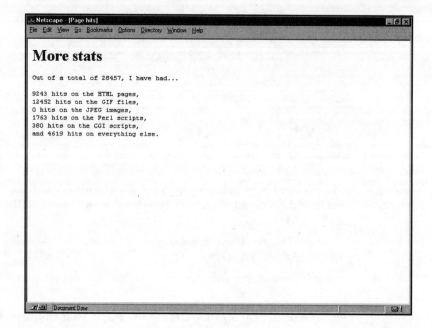

Summary

Servers and clients provide a small treasure of information. You don't even have to wait for input from a visitor. By using the information that the server and the client have already provided, you can create pages that are informational, can help you control access to documents, and even redirect a visitor to other pages based solely on the type of browser that the visitor is using.

Review Questions

1. What kind of information does the client pass to the server?

2. What kind of information does the server create?

3. Is the information that the client sends always accurate?

4. What logs does the server create?

Review Exercises

1. Create a script that gathers statistical information from the results of the LOG.PL file.

2. Create a script that redirects a user to different pages depending on whether the visitor is from an education, government, or commercial domain.

3. Create a script that displays all the environmental variables from the server and the client.

## CHAPTER 10

Storing Information in Flat Files

Relational databases are all the rage these days. Some back-end servers can handle hundreds of gigabytes of data without breaking into a sweat. Databases that provide a Structured Query Language (*SQL,* pronounced "sequel") interface are particularly popular.

Yet there is still a place for the workaday flat file, especially for handling small amounts of information, or for which you prefer the efficiency of a local file and don't need the power of a full-fledged back-end database.

In this chapter, you learn how to roll your own flat-file databases. You start by reviewing fields and records, and then explore how to manage your files. This discussion is primarily theoretical, because the theories covered apply to any kind of flat-file database, in any environment. Specifically, you'll look at the following:

♦ Fields and records

♦ Text fields

♦ Other types of fields

♦ Sequential and random access

♦ The use of flat files

♦ Concurrency management

> **Note:** See Chapter 11, "Storing Information in Databases," and Chapter 12, "Common Database Solutions," for more information about SQL database engines.

Fields and Records

Information stored in files is organized into fields and records. A *field* is any individual bit of information, and a *record* is a collection of fields. Listing 10.1 shows the first three entries in an organized address book.

Listing 10.1   An Organized Address Book

```
Doe, John, 1122 Pine Street, PA
Hammer, Jane, 4003 Elm Street, OR
Volue, Douglass, 1001 Milliways, IL
```

Each line of listing 10.1 is a record consisting of four fields, named `LastName`, `FirstName`, `StreetAddress`, and `State`. Note that each record has the same number of fields, and how the fields are in the same order.

Humans don't always organize their information this way. Many people compile address books (often on paper) that look more like listing 10.2.

Listing 10.2   An Unorganized Address Book

```
John Doe, 1122 Pine Street, Penn.  3 kids - hates pizza
Hammer, Jane, moved to Oregon.  Staying with Fred at 4003 Elm.
Doug (Douglass or Doug, never Douglas), 1001 Milliways, IL
```

A computer would have a tough time dealing with the address book in listing 10.2. Not only does the information differ in each record, but the order of the fields is haphazard. About the only way for a computer to handle this kind of information is to treat the entire line as a free-form field, so that each record consists of one field called, perhaps, `Entry`.

In listing 10.1, the computer can treat each line—that is, each record—as an entity with replaceable parts. Each record always contains the fields `LastName`, `FirstName`, `StreetAddress`, and `State`, even though the contents of those fields change from record to record. For record number 1, the `LastName` field contains `Doe`; for record number 2, the `LastName` field contains `Hammer`.

Text Fields

The fields in listing 10.1 are all *text fields*. That is, the information in the fields consists of alphanumeric characters. If you were to write a computer program to handle these fields, you would assign a couple of attributes to the fields:

♦ The fields consist of text.

♦ Each field has a maximum length appropriate for the field.

For example, if you were using C as your development language, you might declare the record (and its fields) using syntax similar to listing 10.3. Listing 10.4 shows the same procedure, but using Visual Basic's syntax.

Listing 10.3   Declaring Records in C

```
// Define a record for our address book
typedef struct _bookentry
{
    char      LastName[30];
    char      FirstName[20];
    char      StreetAddress[50];
    char      State[2];
} BOOKENTRY;

// Now allocate storage for 10 records
BOOKENTRY BookEntry[10];
```

Listing 10.4   Declaring Records with Visual Basic

```
; Create a user-defined type for our record

Type _BookEntry
    LastName       As String * 30
    FirstName      As String * 20
    StreetAddress  As String * 50
    State          As String * 2
End Type

; Now allocate storage for 10 records

Dim BookEntry(0 to 9) as _BookEntry
```

Listings 10.3 and 10.4 both create storage for 10 records named BookEntry[0] through BookEntry[9], with each record having identical fields: LastName, a character field of up to 30 characters; FirstName, a character field of up to 20 characters; StreetAddress, a character field with up to 50 characters; and State, a character field with up to 2 characters.

Fixed-Length versus Variable-Length

An interesting aspect about the declarations in listings 10.3 and 10.4 is that the text is stored as *fixed-length fields*. Therefore, the length of the field never changes, even though the length of the information stored in the field might vary from record to record.

For example, examine the `LastName` field of the first two records from listing 10.1. You have declared the length of the `LastName` field to be 30 characters. Each text character occupies a byte of memory, so inside the computer the fields might look like the following:

```
D o e _ _ _ _ _ _ _ _ _ _ _ _ _ _ _ _ _ _ _ _ _ _ _ _ _ _
0 . . . . . . . .10 . . . . . . . . .20 . . . . . . . .29

H a m m e r _ _ _ _ _ _ _ _ _ _ _ _ _ _ _ _ _ _ _ _ _ _
0 . . . . . . . .10 . . . . . . . . .20 . . . . . . . .29
```

As Easy as Zero, One, Two!

You might have noticed that you count to 30 by starting with 0 and ending with 29, instead of using the more common way of starting with 1 and ending with 30.

This convention isn't simply to confuse you. Computer programmers usually count this way, although the reason for doing so is somewhat obscure unless you are used to handling computer arrays or strings.

The simplest example that helps to explain why starting with zero is useful is a string of characters in memory. The characters are stored as contiguous bytes, one right after the other. You refer to the string by its starting address. For example, suppose that the string "For the sake of the country" (27 bytes long) is stored starting at address 1000 in memory.

The first byte, *F,* is at address 1000. The second byte, *o,* is at address 1001, and so on, until you reach the last byte, *y,* at address 1026. Notice that the first character is at 1000, not 1001, and the last character is at 1026, not 1027, even though the string is 27 bytes long.

If you were looping through this string, doing something with each byte on the way, you would set an anchor of some sort (a pointer in C, an index register in assembler, and so forth) to the starting address of 1000. Then, to retrieve the first character, you add zero to the starting address. To retrieve the second character, you add one to the starting address, and so on.

This process seems confusing only until you remember that the starting address stays constant during your calculations, although the offset—the number of bytes into the string—changes as you loop through the string. The first character is how many bytes away from the starting address? (That is, 1000 plus how many is 1000?)

Each field has room for 30 characters, numbered 0 through 29. In the first record, only the first three bytes are used, and the rest are blank. In the second record, the first six bytes are used, and the rest are blank. In either case, all 30 bytes in each record are dedicated to the `LastName` field, no matter how many of the bytes are actually used for the last name.

This is obviously not the most efficient way to store text information. The first record wastes 27 bytes, and the second record wastes 24 bytes. You could pack this information down to far fewer bytes if you reserved only as much memory as needed for each field. But how can you know that in advance?

You can't know, but you can make an educated guess. Few last names are longer than 30 characters, so that's a reasonable number to pick.

You could avoid the problem altogether by storing a length byte followed by the data. That is, for the first record, you would have a length byte of 3, followed by "Doe." For the second record, you'd have a length byte of 6, followed by "Hammer." This wastes one byte keeping track of the field length, but reduces the size of the field itself. Another method is to *delimit* the fields with some special character—for example, terminating the field with a comma, or enclosing the field in quotation marks. Delimiting fields requires extra work when you *parse* (scan and interpret) the record to find the start and end of each field.

Sometimes using variable-length fields makes sense, but fixed-length fields have certain advantages, as you'll soon see.

Other Types of Fields

Because you are using computers, however, you don't need (or want) to store everything as text. Text (that is, a string of characters) is the only way to store such things as names and addresses, but computers can handle numbers much more efficiently if you store them as machine-readable numbers rather than as textual representations of numbers.

Suppose that you are using a name and address book to keep track not only of names and addresses, but how many copies of this book each person has purchased. Listing 10.5 shows the record definition expanded (for both C and Visual Basic) to include a new field called Copies.

Listing 10.5   Defining a Numeric Field

```
In C, use the following declaration:

// Define a record for our address book
typedef struct _bookentry
{
    char      LastName[30];
    char      FirstName[20];
    char      StreetAddress[50];
    char      State[2];
    int       Copies;
} BOOKENTRY;
```

continues

183

Listing 10.5 Continued

```
// Now allocate storage for 10 records
BOOKENTRY BookEntry[10];

In Visual Basic, use this declaration:

; Create a user-defined type for our record

Type _BookEntry
    LastName        As String * 30
    FirstName       As String * 20
    StreetAddress   As String * 50
    State           As String * 2
    Copies          As Integer
End Type

; Now allocate storage for 10 records

Dim BookEntry(0 to 9) as _BookEntry
```

Notice that the new field isn't a text field like the others. It is a *numeric* field, of the type integer. An *integer* is a signed whole number. The range of an integer depends on your computer, your operating system, and your development environment. More specifically, the range depends on the number of bytes defined as an integer. A single-byte integer (eight bits) has a range of −128 to +127. A two-byte integer has a range of −32768 to +32767. A four-byte integer has a range of −2147483648 to +2147483647.

Suppose that these integers are two-byte integers (the most common size). Instead of needing up to six bytes to store the maximum possible value as a string of text digits, the computer simply stores the value in the two-byte integer. When adding, subtracting, multiplying, or otherwise manipulating the value of the integer, the computer can use its built-in functions for handling numbers. If you store the value as a string of text digits, the computer has to translate the digits to a numeric value, do the manipulation, and then translate the result back to a string.

Using a numeric field for numbers makes life easier for the computer, but how does it affect the programmer? The binary representation that the computer uses is almost useless to a programmer who wants to print the number, or just find out what the number is.

Fortunately, almost every development environment includes a wide variety of *functions*—routines that you can call—to convert numbers from bits and bytes to human-readable text strings. In Visual Basic, you don't even have to worry about how the value is stored. If you want to print the value, you simply refer to the variable name, and Visual Basic then converts the name for you. In C, the process is almost as easy. Listing 10.6 shows how to print a mixture of strings and numbers from within each language.

Listing 10.6   Mixing Strings and Numbers

```
In C, use the following declaration:

// Define a record for our address book
typedef struct _bookentry
{
    char      LastName[30];
    char      FirstName[20];
    char      StreetAddress[50];
    char      State[2];
    int       Copies;
} BOOKENTRY;

// Now allocate storage for 10 records
BOOKENTRY BookEntry[10];

// print out record x

void PrintRecord(int x) {
 printf("%s %s: %i copies\r\n",
            BookEntry[x].FirstName,
            BookEntry[x].LastName,
            BookEntry[x].Copies);
}

In Visual Basic, use this declaration:

; Create a user-defined type for our record

Type _BookEntry
    LastName        As String * 30
    FirstName       As String * 20
    StreetAddress   As String * 50
    State           As String * 2
    Copies          As Integer
End Type

; Now allocate storage for 10 records

Dim BookEntry(0 to 9) as _BookEntry

; print out record x

Sub PrintRecord (x as Integer)
    Debug.Print BookEntry(x).LastName; " ";
    Debug.Print BookEntry(x).FirstName; ": ";
    Debug.Print BookEntry(x).Copies;
    Debug.Print " copies"
End Sub
```

Numeric fields are always fixed-length, and the length depends on the definition of the field type. For this reason, you need not specify how many bytes to reserve in the record definition.

You can use many other types of fields—whatever your development environment supports. Table 10.1 shows some of the most common field types for Visual Basic and C.

Table 10.1 Common field types

Visual Basic Field Type	Description	C Field Type	Description
integer	2 bytes, −32768 to +32767; long integer, 4 bytes, −2147483648 to 2147483647	int signed by default	1 or 2 bytes, −128 to +127, or −32768 to +32767; long int, 4 bytes, −2147483648 to +2147483647
string	10 bytes plus the actual length of string (up to 64K in Windows 3.1, or 2 million in NT)	char or unsigned char	Signed byte, −128 to +127, or unsigned byte, 0 to 255
single	4 bytes, −3.402823E38 to −1.401298E-45 for negative values; 3.402823E38 to 1.401298E-45 to for positive values	float	4 bytes, 3.4E +/−38 (7 digits)
double	8 bytes, −1.79769313486232E308 to −4.94065645841247E-324 for negative values; 4.94065645841247E-324 to 1.79769313486232E308 for positive values	double	8 bytes, 1.7E +/−308 (15 digits)
currency	Scaled integer, 8 bytes, −922,337,203,685,477.5808 to +922,337,203,685,477.5807	long double	10 bytes, 1.2E +/−4932 (19 digits)
date	8 bytes, 1 Jan 100 to 31 Dec 9999		

Sequential versus Random Access

In the section "Fixed-Length versus Variable-Length," you learned that using fixed-length fields has some advantages, even though fixed-length fields inherently waste more space. In this section, you explore ways to store records on disk, and you learn why fixed-length fields are so useful.

A record that consists of fixed-length fields is itself fixed-length, whereas a record consisting of variable-length fields must, by definition, be of variable-length itself.

To store and retrieve records from disk, two primary methods are available: sequential and random access.

Sequential Access

Sequential means one after another, or used in sequence. Sequential files are written to disk starting at the beginning and continuing, record after record, until the end. They are read back the same way.

Listing 10.7 shows a typical DOS AUTOEXEC.BAT file. Each record in this file consists of one field, an entire line. A CRLF, or end-of-line marker, terminates each record. Don't worry about what each line means; just notice the file structure.

Listing 10.7   A Typical DOS AUTOEXEC.BAT File

```
@echo off
set path=c:\dos;c:\bat;c:\utl;c:\windows
lh doskey
cls
prompt $p$g
win
```

The records in this file are variable-length. That is, each line can be anything from one character long to any desired length. To read this file, your program must read byte by byte until it encounters a CRLF. That character tells your program that it has reached the end of the record. The next record starts with the byte following the CRLF.

Fortunately, most development environments provide a function to read a line of input from a file, so you don't have to parse for the CRLF yourself. But even so, to get to the third line, you must first read the first two lines.

You have to do so because the lines vary in length, and the only way to find out where the third line starts is to find out where the first line ends (so that you know where the second line starts), then where the second line ends (so you know where the third line starts).

This technique is fine for files such as DOS's AUTOEXEC.BAT, which is designed so that you can access it sequentially. But suppose that you want to edit the file, removing the lh from lh doskey? You can't simply overwrite the third line with the new information, because doing so would leave the fourth, fifth, and sixth lines misaligned. (Remember, the records are stored sequentially, with each one snuggled right up against the last.)

To edit a line in a sequential file, you must read the entire file first, either storing it in memory or in a temporary file on disk. Then you must write it back out, record by record, but substituting your new information for the one record that you want to change, leaving everything else unchanged.

This process is awkward at best. It becomes even more awkward when you want to read just the last record from a sequential file. To do so, you must read the entire file, ignoring everything but the last record retrieved. If the file is several megabytes long, the time wasted can be prohibitive.

Most development environments offer some techniques to decrease the overhead of moving around in a sequential file. For instance, you can often manually set the file pointer (a byte offset maintained by the operating system to let it know where to read or write next). If you know that the record you want is near the end of the file, and not more than 128 bytes long, you can *seek* (move the file pointer) to the end of the file, then back up a couple of hundred bytes, and let the operating system read from that point.

In fact, most development environments have an "Open for Append" option that does something similar. When you open a file for append, the operating system automatically determines the file's length and positions the file pointer at the end of the file for you. Then you can write to the file, *appending* new records without having to seek through all the earlier records. Appending is used to write log files, guestbooks, and similar files.

These techniques are seldom useful, though, for making sequential files behave like nonsequential files. If you need to access the records in an order other than sequential, you should use a nonsequential file organization.

Random Access

Random means in any order. Files designed for random access have fixed-length records. If each record is 128 bytes, you know that the first record starts at byte zero, the second record at byte 128, the third record at byte 256, and so on. Random access makes positioning the file pointer quite simple, and enables you to get to any record in the file very quickly. It also enables you to update the file in place, simply by replacing a record. Because the records are of uniform length, swapping out a record doesn't change the file's structure. The subsequent records still start at the same place and remain unaffected.

Random-access files have yet another advantage. Because fixed-length records consist of fixed-length fields, your development environment can quickly and easily separate the fields for you simply by copying the entire record to a template in memory. Thus, with one instruction, you can retrieve a record from anywhere in the file, and have the record's fields instantly available to you.

Deleting records is difficult, however. To delete a record from a random-access file permanently, you must temporarily treat it as if it were sequential—that is, you must snug up the subsequent records and then shorten the file by one record. This process can be laborious, especially if your file has hundreds or thousands of records, and you want to delete a record near the beginning. For example, to delete the first record from a 2,000-record file, you must copy the second record to the first record, then the third record to the second record, then the fourth record to the third record, and so on, until you reach the end.

Fortunately, there is a workaround for this problem. You can define a field called Deleted. To delete a record, you read it in, mark the Deleted field, and write the record back out. Then, on subsequent uses of the file, you know to ignore the record. Occasionally you can physically delete the records marked for deletion. This process, called *compaction*, is quite important. If you don't compact your file, it never shrinks when you delete records.

Most databases use random access—and therefore fixed-length fields and records—to retrieve and store information on disk.

Comparing Access Methods

Each method of accessing a file has advantages and disadvantages. The type of method that you use (matching, of course, the overall design of the file) depends on how you are using the file.

Simple, short files, and log-type files benefit from sequential access. Database-type files, or files that need to be read out of order, benefit from random access.

Here are the advantages of sequential access:

♦ Stores information on disk compactly

♦ Allows quick appending

♦ Enables you to make fields as long or short as necessary

The disadvantages of sequential access include the following:

♦ Makes updating individual records difficult

♦ Makes separating multiple fields within records difficult

♦ Makes searches slow

♦ Enables you to open a file either for reading or writing, but not both

Random access has the following advantages:

♦ Allows quick access to any record

♦ Allows updating in place

◆ Enables you to pull fields from within records by using a template instead of by parsing

◆ Lets you open a file for reading and writing at the same time

The disadvantages of random access include the following:

◆ Requires more disk space for fields and records, because they are fixed-length

◆ Makes deleting records difficult; if you do not compact records occasionally, they continue to grow

Rolling Your Own Flat Files

Flat files can be either sequential or random, although flat-file databases are almost always random with fixed-length fields and records.

The term *flat file* is easiest to understand in contrast to relational databases. A brief comparison to geometry should help clarify the distinction:

All the file types that this chapter has discussed so far consist of records, with each record written on disk right after the previous one. Sequential files have records of varying length plus a record terminator, whereas random files have records of identical length and with no record terminator. In either case, however, the second record immediately follows the first record on disk.

You can view this type of file as one long line of bytes. Even though the line divides logically into fields and records, it starts in one place and continues, byte by byte, until done. Such a line is called *one-dimensional*, just as in geometry. A one-dimensional line has a single dimension and a single measurement (length).

A more useful way to understand this type of file is in two dimensions. Instead of concentrating on the physical layout (a long, one-dimensional line of bytes), you can think of the logical layout (a series of one-dimensional lines). The logical layout of a file is *two-dimensional*—in geometry, a square. Squares have two measurements: height and width. The height of a database file is the number of records. The width is the length of each record. Only files using fixed-length records can form a true square, because variable-length records each have a different length. But the concept still holds, even if your square ends up being an irregular polyhedron.

In geometry, squares and lines inhabit a single plane—they are flat figures.

Suppose that you have several files, each one like a square. Within each record in the first file is a *key field*, one that corresponds exactly to one or more records in the next file. Imagine that you stack your squares and then draw a vertical line down through the intersections of these key fields. A third dimension emerges, yielding a relationship among the individual files. This kind of *three-dimensional* arrangement describes how relational databases are constructed, although this simple little example doesn't begin to touch on the complexity and power available in relationships.

When would you use a relational database rather than a flat file? A common example is a customer information database. For each customer, you have a customer-definition record, containing a unique customer-identification key. Then, in another file (or *table*, in database terminology), you have individual transaction records: the customer purchased product A; the customer paid $25; the customer purchased product B; the customer paid $50; and so forth. You store all the transaction records, for all your customers, in a single table. But each record includes the unique customer-identification key.

To extract just the records for a particular customer, you first search for the customer-definition record. Then, using that record's customer-identification key, you select all the records in the transaction table that share that key.

This kind of setup is overkill for a simple guestbook or log file. For such applications, you don't need the flexibility of the relational database, and don't want the overhead associated with it.

Using Flat Files

Now that you have a good understanding of what flat files are, and how they are arranged internally, you are ready to start using them.

In earlier chapters, you learned how to collect information using a fill-out form and CGI. Now use some of that information with a flat file.

Reading Sequential Files

To read a sequential file, your program must take the following steps:

1. Determine the file name and location. You can hard-code them into your program (usually a bad idea), take them from the form's data (sometimes a good idea, as long as you validate the path, as explained in Chapter 17, "Security Issues"), or set them as a system-level variable (almost always a good idea).

2. Attempt to open the file for read access. If successful, this action sets the file pointer to the beginning of the file, ready to read the file. If the attempt fails, you need to determine why. Did the attempt fail because another process locked the file? If so, try again a bit later. Did the attempt fail because no such file exists? If so, do you want your program to create it now, or to ignore the error and continue?

3. Read each successive record. Because you cannot know how many records are in the file, you must test for end-of-file (EOF). When you reach EOF, the file has no more records.

4. Do something with each record after reading it. For example, if you are reading C:\AUTOEXEC.BAT as your input file, you might want to print each line so that at the end of the process, you display the file's contents on the browser. (This example might not be good for security.)

5. Close the file when you are done.

Writing Sequential Files

To write to a sequential file, your program needs to take these steps:

1. Determine the file name and location. You can hard-code them into your program (usually a bad idea), take them from the form's data (sometimes a good idea, as long as you validate the path, as explained in Chapter 17), or set them as a system-level variable (almost always a good idea).

2. Attempt to open the file for write or append access. Use write access (sometimes called *output*) if you want to create a new file, or overwrite an existing file. Use append access if you want to tack a new record to the end of an existing file.

If successful, this action sets the file pointer either at the beginning of the file (if you used write access) or at the end of the file (if you used append access). If the attempt fails, you need to determine why. If the attempt failed because another process locked the file, try again a bit later.

3. Write as many new records as you want. The operating system or development environment automatically advances the file pointer after each write, so that the pointer is always ready for the next sequential record. Remember that unless you open the file for append access, you overwrite any existing records. If you want to write something in the middle of the file, first copy the file's contents somewhere else (either in memory or a temporary file); then, as you write the file, copy the parts that you want to keep.

4. Close the file when you are done.

Reading and Writing Random-Access Files

To read and write records from a random-access file, your program needs to take these steps:

1. Determine the file name and location. You can hard-code them into your program (usually a bad idea), take them from the form's data (sometimes a good idea, as long as you validate the path, as explained in Chapter 17), or set them as a system-level variable (almost always a good idea).

2. Attempt to open the file for read/write access. Typically, you tell the operating system the record length during the open process, so that the system can calculate record pointers for you afterward. If the open fails, determine what went wrong. Did the attempt fail because another process locked the file? If so, try again a bit later. Did the attempt fail because no such file exists? If so, does your program want to create it now, or just ignore the error and continue?

3. Decide which record you want to read or write. If you are searching for something already in the file, you might have to go through the records one by one, starting at the beginning. If you are planning to add a record, you need to know how many records are already in the file.

> **Tip:** You can calculate how many records are in the file by dividing the file size (in bytes) by each record's length. For example, if each record is 20 bytes long and the file is 200 bytes long, the file must consist of 10 records. (In computerese, the formula is `NumRecs = FileLen/RecLen`.)
>
> When appending, just use `NumRecs+1` as your record number. The operating system automatically extends the file to accommodate the new record.
>
> Some development environments handle this complexity by using functions that determine the number of records for you based on the record definition.

4. To read a record, call `Get`, `readrec`, or whatever operation is appropriate to call in your development environment. Typically, you need to pass a couple of parameters to this call: the desired record number and the address of a buffer or template into which the information is read. You don't have to specify the kind of information that you are retrieving or its length. You already told the operating system the length during the open process, and that length, plus the record number, is all the operating system needs to determine where the record resides inside the file. You don't have to specify the type of information because the operating system doesn't care. It reads a string of bytes equal in length to the record length and places the string into the buffer or template that you specified. You then have to inform your program of the fields within the record.

5. Write a record. Writing a record is the same as reading one, except that you must fill in the buffer or template first. A write operation stores the buffer's or template's information in the disk file, at the proper location for the given record number.

6. Close the file when you are done.

Managing Concurrency

If your script accesses external files, you must plan how to handle concurrency. *Concurrency* means happening at the same time. In programming, the term usually refers to one or more programs running at the same time that want to access the same data file.

You might think that because no other program will read your CGI data file, you don't have to worry about concurrency. However, you do have to worry about your own CGI script. Nothing prevents the HTTP server from launching 2, 3, 5, or even 100 copies of your script all at once. If each of these copies doesn't handle concurrency, your data file more closely resembles alphabet soup than meaningful information.

There are a couple of ways to manage concurrency. First, you can ensure that only one program will touch the data file at any one time. You can do so either by using the operating system's file-locking routines, or by establishing and using a private semaphore.

My Own Private Semaphore

A *semaphore* is just a flag that indicates that something is in use. For example, if you want to use the restroom on an airplane, you first check the little sign that indicates whether it is "occupied" or "unoccupied." If the restroom is occupied, you know not to open the door and enter, but to wait until the occupant leaves. Even if you don't see the occupant leave, you can tell when the room is free because the sign then says "unoccupied." Setting the sign to "occupied" is *setting the semaphore*; setting the sign to "unoccupied" is *clearing the semaphore*.

When you use semaphores to manage concurrency, your program should first check for some indication that the file is in use (another process has locked the file with an exclusive lock, or a predefined semaphore file exists). If the semaphore is set, wait until it clears. Be prepared to wait a reasonable amount of time before giving up. Don't make the mistake of waiting forever or not waiting at all.

Some programming languages support semaphores directly. Others require you to develop your own semaphore strategy. Creating an empty file and checking for its existence is one common strategy.

If possible, using the operating system for your semaphores is usually best. For example, if you use the file-locking capabilities of Windows NT or UNIX as your semaphore (when the file is locked, the semaphore is set; when the file is unlocked, the semaphore is clear), then your program, as well as every other program on the system, knows to keep hands off while the semaphore is set.

A second way to handle concurrency, especially if the file consists of fixed-length records, is to lock only those parts that you need to lock, and only for the types of access that you need.

For example, if 9 times out of 10 your script reads only the data in the file, you probably need to lock it only on the 10th time—while you are actually updating the file's contents.

Ask only for the permissions that you need. If your program needs only to read the file this time, ask only for read permission, not read/write permission. If it doesn't matter that other programs read the file at the same time, ask only for nonexclusive read permission.

When you are going to update the file or a part of it, ask for an exclusive lock on the file (or just the portion of it, if possible). This request fails unless no one else has the file open. You can then try again periodically until the request is granted. Once you have an exclusive lock, no other process can read or write to the file. In this way, you prevent your updates from corrupting other processes that might just be reading the file, and you synchronize those processes that are trying to write to the file.

Listing 10.8 shows a fragment of C code that you can use to ensure that you can safely append a log entry to a log file. Although the code is written for the 32-bit Windows NT environment, the concepts are the same in any language.

Listing 10.8   Example of Waiting for Access

```
//Routine to append a variable-length string to a log file
BOOL AppendToLog (char *szFileName, char *szLogEntry)
{
    int       iWaitForIt;          // generic counter
    HANDLE    hFile;               // file handle
    BOOL      bSuccess;            // success indicator
    DWORD     dwBytesWritten;      // num bytes written
    DWORD     dwNumBytes;          // generic counter

    // Set up a counter/loop.  We'll use the iWaitForIt
    // variable as our counter, and we'll go through the
    // loop up to 100 times.
    for (iWaitForIt = 0; iWaitForIt < 100; iWaitForIt++)
    {

        // Each time within the loop, we'll try to get
        // exclusive read-write access to the log file.
        hFile = CreateFile (
            szFileName,
            GENERIC_READ ¦ GENERIC_WRITE,
            0,0,OPEN_ALWAYS,
            FILE_ATTRIBUTE_NORMAL ¦ FILE_FLAG_WRITE_THROUGH,
            0
            );
```

continues

Listing 10.8 Continued

```
        // If we were able to open the file, proceed with
        // the business of writing the log entry
        if (hFile != INVALID_HANDLE_VALUE)
        {

            // This is an append operation, so we want to
            // position the file pointer to the end of the
            // file.
            SetFilePointer (hFile,0L,0L,FILE_END);

            //Write out the entry now
            dwNumBytes = strlen(szLogEntry);
            bSuccess = WriteFile (
                hFile,
                szLogEntry,
                dwNumBytes,
                &dwBytesWritten,
                0
                );

            // And close the file, releasing the locks, so
            // another thread (or external process) can
            // access the file
            CloseHandle (hFile);

            // If the write operation was successful, and
            // the number of bytes written equals the number
            // of bytes we wanted to write, return TRUE
            if (bSuccess) return (dwBytesWritten == dwNumBytes);

            // Otherwise return FALSE (we don't care why it
            // failed)
            else return FALSE;
        }

        // Control comes here if the CreateFile call above
        // failed.  We don't care why it failed at the
        // moment.  Instead, we'll just sleep for 100 milliseconds
        // and try again (up to 100 times, or 10 seconds).  A
        // more robust routine would call GetLastError() to find
        // out WHY the open failed.  If it's anything other than
        // file is busy right now, we should exit the loop instead
        // of trying again.
        else
        {
            Sleep(100);
        }
    }
    // If we never could get access to the file,
    // tell caller we failed
    return FALSE;
}
```

The routine `AppendToLog()` takes two parameters: a pointer to the log file's name, and a pointer to the log entry to append. The routine returns a Boolean value (True or False) indicating whether the entry was written successfully. The routine is concurrency-aware in that it automatically waits for up to 10 seconds if the file is already locked.

You can use `AppendToLog()` as a common routine in multithreaded applications, in which case one thread writes to the log while another is trying to write to the log. By making the routine itself concurrency-aware, and giving ample time for conflicts to resolve themselves, the individual threads of the program can each pretend that they own the log file exclusively.

Summary

Operating systems and simple utilities still use flat files quite often. For example, the UNIX files `inetd.conf`, `hosts`, and `passwd` are flat sequential files with variable-length records, as are DOS's AUTOEXEC.BAT and CONFIG.SYS. All Windows' .INI files are flat sequential files. Most log files are flat sequential files. Most simple databases, like the ones you often use for CGI, are flat random-access files.

If you need relational operations, lookup tables, stored triggers, cascading updates, rollback facilities, and other advanced database features, you need a back-end relational database. But if all you need to do is store simple text and numbers, to be accessed either sequentially or randomly, then flat files are your best bet.

Review Questions

1. What is a record?

2. If a record consists of variable-length fields, is it variable-length itself?

3. Text fields are strings of sequential _____.

4. Is an integer always exactly two bytes long?

5. Would the name *Rumplestiltskin* fit into a field defined as `char[10]` or `String * 10`?

6. If an unsigned integer can hold any value from 0 to 65535, does it take anywhere from 1 to 5 bytes to store it?

7. Which field type stores string information on disk more compactly: variable-length or fixed-length?

8. Can you open a file in sequential mode for both read and write access simultaneously?

9. What is the process of physically deleting records from a random-access file called?

10. Name two methods of handling concurrent file access.

Review Exercises

1. Expand listing 10.5 to include three more fields: Phone number, birthday, and postal code. What kind of fields would you use? How long would you make the fields?

2. Create a record structure to keep track of your bank account. What kind of database is most appropriate for this type of information? Why?

3. Create a flat file with fixed-length fields and records, and then try to increase the length of a particular record. How can you change the record definition without destroying the existing information in the file?

4. Write a routine to lock only a range of records in a file with fixed-length records. Write the routine in such a way that other programs can still open and read unlocked records.

CHAPTER *11*

Storing Information in Databases

Although flat files are good for storing small amounts of information, once they start getting larger, it takes longer for your CGI scripts to query them. Therefore, the browsers used to visit your site might time out and thus frustrate the visitor.

There are many alternatives to flat file databases. Most UNIX systems have dbm or a dbm work-alike, such as ndbm, gdbm, and the Berkeley db database system. Another alternative is to use the more powerful SQL servers. This chapter discusses these different kinds of databases—how you can use them to better manage information, and how they can help you provide this information to visitors to your site.

Storing Information in a Dbm Database

Most UNIX systems have some sort of dbm database—in fact, I have yet to find a system that runs without one. Dbm is a set of library routines that manage data files consisting of key and value pairs. The dbm routines control how users enter and retrieve information from the database. Although not the most powerful mechanism for storing information, using dbm is a faster method of retrieving information than using a flat file. Because most UNIX sites use one of the dbm libraries, the tools that you need to store your information to a dbm database are readily available.

There are almost as many flavors of the dbm libraries as there are UNIX systems. Although most of these libraries are not compatible with each other, all basically work the same way. This section explores each of the dbm flavors to give you a good understanding of their differences. Afterward, you create an address book script, which should give you an idea of how dbm databases work.

Dbm

The library routines for dbm are simple, but can handle most jobs without problem. The library contains functions that enable you to create a database, and store, retrieve, and delete information, as well as a few functions that help you move around within the database.

Dbm stores the database in two files. The first has the extension .PAG and contains the bitmap. The second, which has the extension .DIR, contains the data. The database's creator specifies the database's name. The database doesn't lock files, so your scripts must do so to ensure that two or more users aren't writing to the database at the same time. See the section "More on Database Locking" for more information on database locking.

Ndbm

Ndbm is much like dbm with a few additional features. The ndbm command set includes the same basic functions as dbm does, but it was written to provide better, and hence, faster storage and retrieval methods. Ndbm also has better error reporting and an additional function for clearing an error. Last, within a script, dbm can only have one database open, whereas ndbm enables you to open many databases. Like dbm, ndbm stores its information in two files, using the extensions .PAG and .DIR. When using ndbm, you also must ensure that you lock the database files so that multiple users aren't writing to a file simultaneously. The section "More on Database Locking" discusses this in greater depth.

Sdbm

If you have installed Perl, you most likely have sdbm installed. Sdbm comes with the Perl archive, which has been ported to many platforms. Therefore, you can use dbm databases as long as there is a version of Perl for your computer. Sdbm was written to match the functions provided with ndbm, so portability of code shouldn't be a problem. For more information on sdbm and Perl, see the Perl language home page:

http://www.perl.com/perl/

Gdbm Version 1.7.1

Gdbm is the GNU version of the dbm family of database routines. (GNU stands for Gnu's Not UNIX.) GNU is a collection of programs developed by volunteers to help provide UNIX system commands and programs free to the public. Along with gdbm, you can find quite a few additional GNU programs like emacs (a powerful editor).

This library does its own file locking to ensure that two or more users cannot write to the database simultaneously. Gdbm has the same functions as ndbm, as well as the capability to reorganize the database.

> **Note:** You might notice that when you delete an item from a dbm database, you remove the information, but the file space remains the same. Don't be alarmed— the library reuses that space the next time that a user enters information into the database.

Gdbm also enables you to cache data, reducing the time that it takes to write to the database. Also, the database has no size limit. The database's size depends completely on your system's resources. Gdbm database files have the extension .DB. Unlike dbm and ndbm, which both use two files, gdbm uses only one file.

Berkeley Db Version 1.85

The Berkeley db expands on the original dbm routines significantly. Dbm, ndbm, and gdbm create hashed databases. Although the Berkeley db also creates these databases, the library also can create databases based on a sorted balanced binary tree (BTREE) and store information with a record line number (RECNO). The method that you use depends completely on how you want to store and retrieve the information from a database. Berkeley's db creates only one file, which has no extension.

If you can't find a particular dbm database on your system, search the Web for dbm databases. All the dbm-related interfaces, except for dbm itself, are freely available. Most likely, you will find at least one of the dbm interfaces on your favorite FTP site.

Inserting Information into a Dbm Database

Now that the preceding sections have briefly introduced the various dbm interfaces, this section demonstrates how you can use them. As mentioned earlier, dbm databases can decrease the amount of time that it takes to insert and retrieve information to and from a database. When your database starts growing, and using one of the larger database engines is overkill (especially on your pocketbook), you might want to look into using dbm.

Dbm databases have two fields: a key and the data (sometimes called the *value*). The *key* is a string that points to the data. The string within the key must be unique within a database. Note the following example:

Key	Data
Robert Niles	**rniles@selah.net**
Jason Lenny	**jason@yakima.net**
Ken Davis	**kdavis@wolfenet.com**

continues

continued

Key	Data
John Doe	**jdoe@imtired.selah.net**
Santa Claus	**sclaus@north.pole.com**
Bert	**rniles@selah.net**

The data, on the other hand, can contain any type of information. The data might contain a URL, an e-mail address, or even a binary file. Examine the following script, DBBOOKADD.PL, which adds information to a dbm database. This script is available on this book's companion CD-ROM.

First, you set the path to Perl. You then call the Perl module, DB_FILE.PM, and the file control module, FCNTL.PM. DB_FILE.PM acts as an interface to the dbm routines. The FCNTL.PM module provides you with functions that enable you to control access to the database so that two or more people cannot write to the database at the same time. Although the Berkeley db libraries lock the database whenever it is accessed for writing, you must use the FCNTL.PM module for the `tie()` function.

```
#!/usr/bin/perl

use DB_File;
use Fcntl;
```

You then must break up the information:

```
if ($ENV{'REQUEST_METHOD'} eq 'POST')
{
        read(STDIN, $buffer, $ENV{'CONTENT_LENGTH'});
        @pairs = split(/&/, $buffer);
        foreach $pair (@pairs)
        {
                ($name, $value) = split(/=/, $pair);
                $value =~ tr/+/ /;
                $value =~ s/%([a-fA-F0-9][a-fA-F0-9])/pack("C",
                hex($1))/eg;
                $form{$name} = $value;


        }
}
```

You assign the database's name to the variable `$file`:

```
$file="addresses";
```

This assignment enables you to change the database's name if necessary by editing one line rather than several. Changing the name isn't entirely necessary now, but will be as you expand this script.

To connect to the database, you use the `tie()` function. The syntax for `tie()` is as follows:

```
tie(%hashname, DB_File, filename, flags, mode)
```

You can assign any *hashname*, although the name must start with the percent sign (%). Because you are using the DB_FILE.PM module, you must specify that file name. The *filename* identifies the file in which you are storing the data. You next specify the *flags*, which vary depending on which dbm routines you are using. In this example, you use the flags that enable you to read from and write to files (`O_RDWR`) or, if the file doesn't exist, to create files (`O_CREAT`). The *mode* sets the database file's permissions. The mode 0660 specifies that the owner can read from and write to the database file, and that the group can only read from the file.

```
$database=tie(%db, 'DB_File', $file, O_RDWR¦O_CREAT, 0660);
```

This next line magically adds the information to the database. You use the hash variable to enter the information into the database. The syntax for this line is as follows:

```
$hashname{key}=value
```

The following line places `$form{'name'}` into the database as the key, and assigns `$form{'email'}` to that key as its value:

```
$db{$form{'name'}}=$form{'email'};
```

Now you use the `untie()` function, which releases control of the database, and then `undef()`, which undefines the variable `$database`:

```
untie(%db);
undef($database);
```

Although a dbm database can contain only the key and a pair, you can trick the database into adding more fields. For example, if you want to include a telephone number, you have to add it to the value; by inserting some sort of separator, you can later identify the two separate entries. The following example uses the `join()` function, which joins separate strings together with a colon:

```
$db{$form{'name'}}=join(":",$form{'email'},$form{'phone'});
```

For example, if `$form{'email'}` contains the string jdoe@selah.net and `$form{'phone'}` contains the string 555-5555, the `join()` function produces the following string:

```
jdoe@selah.net:555-5555
```

Because e-mail addresses and telephone numbers do not include colons, the colon is probably the best choice for separating each entry.

What happens if a user tries to enter a name already stored in a key? As your script currently stands, it would simply continue on as if nothing happened; however, because each key must be unique, the script will not add the information to the database. To tell the visitor that the entry failed, you have to add a line that checks whether the name entered matches an existing key. You can do so with one simple line that essentially says the following:

If the database has the same name as entered within the form,

Then go to the subroutine error.

If the database has the same name as entered within the form, the script goes to the subroutine &error:

```
&error if $db{"$form{'name'}:};
```

Your error subroutine tells the visitor what happened, and gives the visitor a chance to try again:

```
sub error {
print <<"HTML";
<HTML>
<HEAD><TITLE>Error!</TITLE></HEAD>
<BODY>
<H1>Error! -Name exists</H1>
I'm sorry, but the name you entered already exists.
➥ If you wish to try again, click
<A HREF="/dbbook.html">here</A>.
</BODY>
</HTML>
HTML

exit;
}
```

Retrieving Information from a Dbm Database

Now that you have entered information into the database, you want to enable your site's visitors to retrieve the information. This script, DBBOOK.PL, is on this book's companion CD-ROM.

You first specify the path to Perl:

```
#!/usr/bin/perl
# dbbook.pl
```

You then use the DB_FILE and FCNTL module just as you did when entering the information to the database:

```
use DB_File;
use Fcntl;
```

Next, you print the Content-type; otherwise, you get a server 500 error:

```
print "Content-type: text/html\n\n";
```

You then assign the database name to the $file variable and use Perl's tie() function to open the database. This time, you set the function to read-only, because you're not adding information to the database.

```
$file="addresses";
$database=tie(%db, 'DB_File', $file, O_READ, 0660) ¦¦ die "can't";
```

Then you print the HTML file's top portion, which goes to the visitor. To ensure that your output looks nice, you start a table:

```
print <<"HTML";
<HTML>
<HEAD><TITLE>Simple dbm address book</TITLE></HEAD>
<BODY>
<CENTER>
<H1>A Simple Address Book</H1>
<TABLE BORDER=1>
HTML
```

Because you've entered the phone number and e-mail address into the value separated by a colon, you now must separate the phone number and e-mail address. The easiest way to do so is with the split() function. After you split this information, you pass the contents to the array @part:

```
while (($key,$value)= each(%db)) {
 @part = split(/:/,$value);
```

You can use an if statement to check whether the visitor entered any e-mail address. If the visitor did so, you print a link, using the HREF anchor. Otherwise, you simply print the key. In pseudocode, the process looks like the following:

If an e-mail address exists, print the name as an HTML mailto: *link.*

Otherwise, just print the name.

The actual code is as follows:

```
if ($part[0]) {
  print "<TR><TD><A HREF=\"mailto:$part[0]\">$key</A></TD>";
  }
 else {
print "<TR><TD>$key</TD>";
  }
```

You then use the array to print the e-mail address and phone number:

```
print "<TD>$part[0]</TD><TD>$part[1]</TD></TR>\n";
}
```

Whether you choose to add the following lines of code depends on how you intend to use the phone book (or whatever other application for which you might adapt this script). You might not want to grant access to write to the address book if you want to display this information to all visitors. In a closed service (such as an intranet), where you should be able to trust all visitors, the link might not be a bad idea. You could even use a password-protected area as the location for the Web page that enables the visitor to add information to the address book database. In any event, the following lines close the table, create a link that the visitor can click to add another entry into the database, and close the remaining tags:

```
print <<"HTML";
</TABLE>
<P>
<A HREF="/dbbook.html">[Add to address book]</A>
<CENTER>
</BODY>
</HTML>
HTML
```

After closing the HTML tags, use untie() to release control of the database, undefine the $database variable, and exit the script.

```
untie(%db);
undef($database);

exit;
```

Your script then displays an address book that looks like that shown in figure 11.1.

Figure 11.1

You can use dbm to store an address book's information easily.

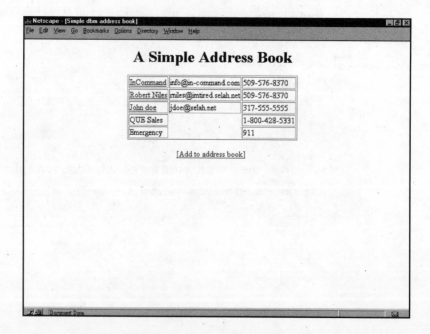

Searching a Dbm Database

You have learned how to enter information into the database and also how to retrieve information from the database. What would happen if the database starts to become extremely large? If you have 100 entries in the database, it could make for an extremely large Web page if you were to display everything within the database. Also, looking for a single name in the database would be a pain.

To solve this problem, you can enable the visitor to search through the database. For example, a visitor could enter the last name *Doe,* thus narrowing down the number of names that the visitor has to weed through. The script that provides this search utility, DBBOOKSEARCH.PL, is on this book's companion CD-ROM.

First, you provide a form in which the visitor can enter a name. The script then hunts through the database, returning anything that matches the string that the visitor entered.

You tell the script the path to Perl and then use the DB_FILE and FCNTL modules just as you did in the last two scripts:

```
#!/usr/bin/perl
# dbbooksearch.pl

use DB_File;
use Fcntl;
```

You then check to ensure that the method POST was used, and then break up STDIN:

```
if ($ENV{'REQUEST_METHOD'} eq 'POST')
{
        read(STDIN, $buffer, $ENV{'CONTENT_LENGTH'});
        @pairs = split(/&/, $buffer);
        foreach $pair (@pairs)
        {
                ($name, $value) = split(/=/, $pair);
                $value =~ tr/+/ /;
                $value =~ s/%([a-fA-F0-9][a-fA-F0-9])/pack("C",
        hex($1))/eg;
                $form{$name} = $value;


        }
}
```

You then print the Content-type and assign the variables that enable you to tie the database:

```
print "Content-type: text/html\n\n";

$file="addresses";
$database=tie(%db, 'DB_File', $file, O_READ, 0660)
    || die "can't";
```

Just as you did for the previous script, you print the Web page's top portion:

```
print <<"HTML";
<HTML>
<HEAD><TITLE>Simple dbm address book results</TITLE></HEAD>
<BODY>
<CENTER>
<H1>A Simple Address Book Results</H1>
<TABLE BORDER=1>
HTML
```

As each key/value pair loads from the database, you check whether the key matches the string that the visitor entered:

```
while (($key,$value)= each(%db)) {
if ($key =~ /$form{'name'}/i) {
```

The following line performs this magic:

```
if ($key =~ /$form{'name'}/i)
```

The /i switch allows for case-insensitive matching. Therefore, if the user enters *Bert, bErT,* or *bert,* the entry would match *Bert, bert, Robert,* or *Bertman.*

If you find a match, you print it:

```
@part = split(/:/,$value);
 if ($part[0]) {
   print "<TR><TD><A HREF=\"mailto:$part[0]\">$key</A></TD>";
   }
 else {
   print "<TR><TD>$key</TD>";
   }
 print "<TD>$part[0]</TD><TD>$part[1]</TD></TR>\n";
 }
}
```

Then you complete the Web document, untie the database, undefine the variable, and exit the script:

```
print <<"HTML";
</TABLE>
<P>
<A HREF="/dbbook.html">[Add to address book]</A>
</BODY>
</HTML>
HTML

untie(%db);
undef($database);

exit;
```

You could also search the value. Such a search gives you even more flexibility on what information is returned.

More on Database Locking

If you use any of the other db libraries, you definitely need to do your own file locking. There are various ways to lock a db database, but the following quick routine, written by Nem (Ryun) Schlecht, uses some of the functions of the file control module (FCNTL.PM).

First you set up four subroutines that define various file-locking methods:

```
sub LOCK_SH { my($s)=shift; 1; }
sub LOCK_EX { my($s)=shift; 2; }
sub LOCK_NB { my($s)=shift; 4; }
sub LOCK_UN { my($s)=shift; 8; }
```

LOCK_SH allows multiple processes to read entries from the database, but does not allow any process to write to the database. You should use this method before reading from a database so that information within that database doesn't change between the first time that you access the database and the next time that you read it.

LOCK_EX obtains an exclusive lock. This method allows the script to read and write to the database, but does not allow any other process to write to or even read from the database.

LOCK_NB is a nonblocking lock. It does not wait for the lock to be freed up. You must use this method with either LOCK_SH or LOCK_EX.

The last method is LOCK_UN, which unlocks the database.

After defining the various locking methods, you must open the database. To do so, you use the `tie()` function as follows:

```
$database=tie(%db, 'DB_File', $file, O_RDWR|O_CREAT, 0660);
```

You next check the file descriptor and open the file for reading and writing:

```
$fd = $databes->fd;
open(DESC, "+<&=$fd");
```

The open() command first opens the file for reading and writing by using +< and the file descriptor &=. In this case, the file descriptor is $fd.

After you open the database and access the file descriptors, you can lock the file and change the locking method anywhere within your script by using the flock() call, as in the following example:

```
flock(DESC, $LOCK_SH); or
flock(DESC, $LOCK_EX); or
flock(DESC, $LOCK_NB);
```

Of course, before you exit your script, you release any locking method as follows:

```
flock(DESC, $LOCK_UN);
```

By locking the database, you can ensure that two or more people don't try to write to the database simultaneously. Failing to do so can lead to disaster, possibly corrupting the whole database.

SQL Databases

Most SQL database servers consist of a set of programs that manage large amounts of data. These programs offer a rich set of query commands that help manage the power behind the SQL server. The programs also control the storage, retrieval, and organization of the information within the database. Thus, you can change, update, and remove the information within the database—after the support programs or scripts are in place.

A relational database doesn't link records together physically, like a dbm database does with the key and value pair. Instead, a relational database simply provides a field that can match information, and returns the results as though the information were organized that way.

Relational databases store information in tables. A table is like a miniature database stored within a main database that groups the information together. For instance, you can have one database that contains one, two, or many tables.

Each table consists of columns and rows. The columns identify the data by name, as in the following example:

Name	Home Phone	E-Mail
Robert Niles	555-5555	**rniles@selah.net**
Jeffry Dwight	555-5556	**jeffryd@twilight.greyware.com**
John Doe	555-5557	**jdoe@whatcha.want.com**

The name, phone number, and e-mail address are the columns, and each entry set is the row.

Although this book's purpose isn't to explain how relational databases work, you need a basic understanding of the concept. Suppose that you stored the preceding information in a table called personal. You can join information from two or more tables within your query. Suppose that the following table is called work:

Name	Work Phone	Department
Robert Niles	555-5558	sysadmin
Jeffry Dwight	555-5559	programmer
John Doe	555-5560	janitor

Within your query, you can have something like the following:

Select the name, home phone, and e-mail from the personal *table.*

Select the work phone and department from the work *table.*

Equate the name from personal *to the name from* work.

This query would print information about individuals from both tables. Keep in mind that this example is a very simple one. Queries from relational databases can get extremely complex. In fact, there are professionals whose sole job is to manage multiple databases with multiple tables and ensure that when this information is queried from a database, the results are intelligible.

You now need to understand SQL a little bit. SQL (Standard Query Language) is a query language that has become standardized. The simple language contains commands that query a database for information. The SQL language was written to be easily understandable, using simple English-like words and syntax. A SQL query reads much like it would sound if you were explaining it to another person. The preceding pseudocode example query is quite close to how SQL works, with only a few differences. Examine the following example:

```
select personal.name,personal.home_phone,personal.email,
➥ work.work_phone, work.department from personal,work
➥ where personal.name=work.name
```

Even the following example would work on most systems:

```
select * from personal,work where personal.name=work.name
```

where the asterisk is a wild card that matches everything.

To insert information into a database, you use a query as follows:

```
insert into table (name, home_phone, email) VALUES ('rniles',
➥ '555-5555','rniles@selah.net')
```

Just by examining this query, you can easily determine what it does.

A SQL database not only makes for a good Intranet application, from which members can retrieve information about their workplace, but is also a wonderful tool for normal Internet applications. You can create anything from a simple guestbook to a front-end to your company's stock of used shoes—all of which can be displayed on the Web. You could even provide up-to-date information on the price of goods or services, or a schedule of events. By creating a Web page based on the information obtained from a database, you can eliminate much of your work. Instead of having to update a Web page, all you have to do is update the information within a database.

To help you figure out which SQL server is best for your Web applications, this section lists some of the most popular servers, including links that can lead you to further information.

Oracle

Oracle, the leader of the database pack, has created its own Web server to integrate with its database engine (see fig. 11.2). Although Oracle is a commercial product with a hefty price tag, it's the most widely used database product on the market. Oracle is a good choice for large businesses that need to manage a lot of information. You can find Oracle at the following address:

http://dozer.us.oracle.com/

Figure 11.2

The Oracle Web server enables you to access Oracle's database.

Sybase

Sybase has a suite of tools to help your Web applications use Sybase's database. You can find information about these tools at the following address:

http://www.sybase.com/

Illustra

Illustra by Informix is the commercial version of Berkeley's Postgres (see fig. 11.3). You can find information on Illustra at the following site:

http://www.illustra.com/

Figure 11.3

All the Illustra Web pages are created using information from Illustra's databases.

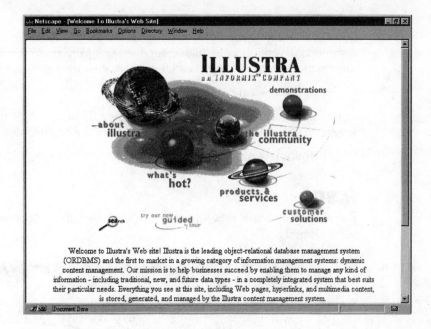

Using the DataBlade module that comes with Illustra, you can quickly incorporate information from a database into your Web pages.

Postgres

Postgres is a database developed by the University of California at Berkeley. Although the university no longer supports the database, it is stable and widely used. There are plenty of applications that help you use Postgres as a powerful backend to your Web pages.

For more information on Postgres, visit the following site:

http://epoch.cs.berkeley.edu:8000/postgres95/

Ingres

Ingres (Interactive Graphics Retrieval System) comes in both a commercial and public domain version. The University of California at Berkeley originally developed this retrieval system. Although the university no longer supports the public domain version, you can still find it on the university's Web site.

Ingres uses the QUEL query language as well as SQL. QUEL is a superset of the original SQL language, making Ingres more powerful. Ingres was developed to work with graphics in a database environment. The public domain version is available for UNIX systems. You can find that version at the following site:

ftp://s2k-ftp.cs.berkeley.edu/pub/ingres/

Computer Associates owns the commercial version of Ingres. This version is quite robust and capable of managing virtually any database application. The commercial version is available for UNIX, VMS, and Windows NT. For more information about the commercial version, visit the following site:

http://www.cai.com/products/ingr.htm

For information about both the commercial and public domain versions of Ingres, visit the North American Ingres Users Association at the following site:

http://www.naiua.org/

mSQL

David Hughes wrote mSQL, or Mini SQL, a simplified but powerful SQL database server (see fig. 11.4).

Figure 11.4

mSQL is a fantastic SQL database powerful enough for everyday use but less expensive than other SQL engines.

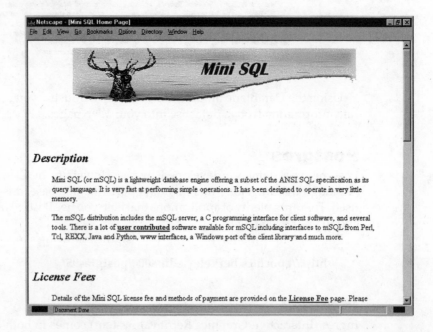

Although it doesn't support the SQL query language completely, mSQL provides enough support to help you manage your information without problems. Although free to organizations doing research, mSQL costs commercial organizations only about $170. Chapter 12, "Common Database Solutions," covers mSQL in depth, and you can find more information on mSQL at the following site:

http://www.Hughes.com.au/product/msql/

Hughes is currently working on an updated version that should make mSQL even more powerful.

Database Information

If you are still looking for other alternatives, try visiting the Database Resource information archive:

http://www.inquiry.com/techtips/thesqlpro/internet.html

You should also see the Catalog of Free Database Systems, which you can find at the following site:

ftp://idiom.com/pub/free-databases

A Web version of the catalog that you can search is available at the following address:

http://cuiwww.unige.ch/~scg/FreeDB/FreeDB.home.html

You can also find additional information at the following address:

http://www.stars.com/Vlib/Providers/Database.html

Now that the idea of using existing databases with Internet and especially intranet applications is becoming increasingly popular, the major database corporations are scrambling to integrate their technology with the Web. Various groups have already perceived this need and have begun working on methods that integrate databases with the Web.

DBI

Tim Bunce started DBI hoping to create a standard Perl-based interface to various SQL engines. Since DBI's conception, others have contributed to his work, ensuring that the DBI interface works with a multitude of database servers. Along with Oracle, the group has created interfaces for mSQL, Ingres, Sybase, and more. Currently, however, most of the database interfaces are in testing stages.

You can find the DBI interface at the following site:

http://www.hermetica.com/technologia/DBI/index.html

WOW

WOW is another product that you might want to explore. WOW expands on the PL/SQL package bundled with the Oracle7 SQL and Web server. The product contains a stand-alone PL/SQL compiler and several other utilities to help you access information from an Oracle7 database. WOW also provides you with greater flexibility to create dynamic Web pages based on the information from the SQL server.

You can find it at the following site:

http://www2.ariscorp.com/

At this site, you can find the source code to interface with the Oracle 7 server.

Cold Fusion

A company called Allaire created Cold Fusion as a system that enables you to write scripts with HTML. Cold Fusion, a database interface, processes the scripts. The interface processes commands within scripts and then returns the information within the HTML written in the script. Although Cold Fusion currently costs $495, the product is definitely worth the price. Allaire wrote Cold Fusion to work with just about every Web server available for Windows NT. Cold Fusion integrates with just about every SQL engine, including those server engines on a UNIX machine (if a 32-bit ODBC driver exists).

Cold Fusion works as follows. After you create a form that sends a request to the Web server, that server starts Cold Fusion and sends it information that Cold Fusion uses to call a template file. After reading the information that the visitor entered, Cold Fusion processes that information according to the template's instructions. Cold Fusion then returns an automatically generated HTML document to the server, which in turn returns the document to the visitor.

For example, examine the following form:

```
<HTML>
<HEAD><TITLE>Phonebook</TITLE></HEAD>
<BODY>
<FORM ACTION="/cgi-bin/dbml.exe?Template=/phone/entry/enter.dbm"
➡ METHOD="POST">
Enter your full name:<INPUT TYPE="text" NAME="name"><BR>
Enter your phone number:<INPUT TYPE="text" NAME="phone"><P>
<INPUT TYPE="submit">
</FORM>
</BODY>
</HTML>
```

The form prompts the visitor to enter a name and phone number. After the visitor clicks the submit button, the information goes to the Cold Fusion program, which then calls the template ENTER.DBM.

The template contains a small script that inserts the information into the database and then displays an HTML document to the visitor:

```
<DBINSERT DATASOURCE="Visitors" TABLENAME="Phone">
<HTML>
<HEAD><TITLE>Thank you!</TITLE></HEAD>
<BODY>
<H1>Thank your for your submission!<H1>
Your name and phone number has been entered into our database.
➡ Thank you for taking the time to fill it out.
<P>
<A HREF="main.html">[Return to the main page]</A>
</BODY>
</HTML>
```

If your organization needs a way to work with a SQL database engine, take a look at Cold Fusion. You can find Allaire at the following site:

http://www.allaire.com/

Nothing integrates a SQL server as well and as easily as Cold Fusion.

Concurrency Issues

When you open a database for writing, you usually make a connection to that database. That connection stays open until you finish, usually locking the record in which you are editing. When a visitor to your site connects to your server, the connection is *stateless*—that is, the client sends its request, waits for the reply, and then disconnects. When you make a change to a database, your CGI script connects to the database. Because your script is making the connection, you usually must ensure that other visitors using the script cannot write to the database at the same time.

You definitely want to check how the database that you are using handles multiple attempts at writing. Some of the dbm database libraries lock the file whenever there is a request to write to it. mSQL handles multiple requests by queuing each request to the database.

If the database doesn't handle multiple connections, you want to ensure that your CGI scripts do. If you fail to do so, you will regret it later when the information in the database becomes corrupt.

Database Considerations

When deciding which database to use, you want to keep a few issues in mind.

You must decide which server to run. You don't want to run a Windows-based server that cannot access a SQL server on a UNIX machine. You cannot access Microsoft's SQL database from a UNIX Web server either. When choosing a Web server, make sure that it works with your existing database or the database engine that you are considering.

You also want to consider which databases are powerful enough for your needs. You shouldn't have any difficulty finding a robust database system, but you don't want to get a database engine so powerful that you never use it at all. At the same time, you definitely want your system to allow you to grow. Some databases available commercially charge you according to the number of hits on your Web pages. Others provide special Web-related packaged deals that allow unlimited access at a substantial cost. If you have a busy site, you need to consider which scheme is cost-effective.

You might have several other important issues to consider. Are support mechanisms available for your database and Web server? If you're running on a Windows NT machine, do ODBC drivers exist to help you integrate your Web server with the database engine? Does another gateway exist?

Many companies let you try out a database before you buy it. Oracle, Microsoft, and others allow you to test drive a database engine before requiring that you fork over large amounts of money. You might also want to consider whether freely available or very reasonably priced databases such as Postgres or mSQL suit your needs.

Summary

In this chapter, you learned about the various dbm database routines and how you can use them to save information to a database. You also learned how relational databases work. The chapter also described the various SQL servers and a few of the methods that you can use to access information in a database.

Review Questions

1. What is a dbm database?

2. How is information stored to a dbm database?

3. What's the difference between a dbm database and a relational database?

4. Of what do relational databases consist?

Review Exercises

1. Write a script using a dbm database that enables a visitor to enter his or her name and a URL to the home page.

2. Adding to the previous exercise, create a script that enables a visitor to your site to enter his or her name, URL, and e-mail address. Note: Use a character other than a colon to separate each entry (\0200 would be a good choice).

3. Create a Web page that enables you to remove an entry from the database. You might want to refer to the manual pages for dbm or ndbm to figure out how to handle this exercise.

## CHAPTER 12

Common Database Solutions

All the fuss over databases and the Web is understandable. Almost every organization keeps information about something within a database.

If you want to provide a Web page with employee information (either to the Internet at large, or for internal use only), conventionally, you would have to create a Web page by hand, typing the information about each employee into the HTML document. Much of the information is redundant, and if your organization is large, you'll have sore wrists in no time!

By using databases as a back-end, you can alleviate the problem of having to enter the same information in different places and save yourself both time and money. Database back-ends aren't only for big businesses; they can serve the individual as well.

This chapter covers a few solutions that you might use to collect information and make it available over the Internet or an organization's intranet.

Microsoft's IIS Using the SQL Server

Microsoft has been playing catch-up ever since it figured out that the Internet business has a future. At first, Microsoft seemed not to want anything to do with the Internet. Then, at an incredibly fast pace, the corporation got into the race and has been trying to take the lead. Microsoft first introduced a free Web browser, and then released the Internet Information Server (ISS)—again, for free.

IIS enables people who want to provide information on the Web to integrate their existing applications as Web applications. The IIS works well with the Back Office

Suite, which is a rich set of tools for businesses. One of the items included within the Back Office Suite is Microsoft's SQL Server.

Although costly to individuals and possibly small businesses, the combination of the SQL Server and the IIS can make your Web pages stand out even more. As far as commercial products go, this combination might even be your cheapest option.

The IIS uses the Internet Database Connector (IDC), which communicates with the database Open Database Connectivity (ODBC) driver. The IDC is an Internet Server API (ISAPI) file (HTTPODBC.DLL) that reads a file. IDC files have the extension .IDC and contain commands that are sent to the SQL ODBC.

The SQL ODBC driver retrieves the information from the database and formats the output of the information by using an .HTX file (*HTX* means *HTML extension*).

The .HTX file formats the information from the ODBC driver as an HTML page. That file then returns to the Web server, which then sends the document to the client.

Suppose that you want to create a form that takes an order from a visitor and then store that order into the SQL Server for later retrieval. The form action would point to an .IDC file, such as that shown in listing 12.1. Figure 12.1 shows the resulting form.

Figure 12.1

Using a form, you can send information to Microsoft's SQL Server using an .IDC file.

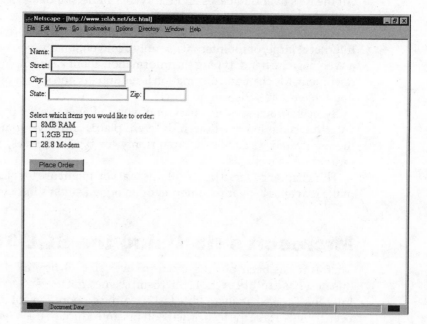

Listing 12.1   An Order Form Processed by the IDC

```
<FORM ACTION="/orders/order.idc" METHOD="POST">
Name: <INPUT TYPE="text" NAME="name"><BR>
Street: <INPUT TYPE="text" NAME="street"><BR>
City: <INPUT TYPE="text" NAME="city"><BR>
State: <INPUT TYPE="text" NAME="state">
Zip: <INPUT TYPE="text" NAME="zip" SIZE=10><P>
Select which items you would like to order:<BR>
<INPUT TYPE="checkbox" NAME="ram" VALUE="ram"> 8MB RAM<BR>
<INPUT TYPE="checkbox" NAME="hd" VALUE="hd"> 1.2GB HD<BR>
<INPUT TYPE="checkbox" NAME="modem" VALUE="modem"> 28.8 Modem<P>
<INPUT TYPE="submit" VALUE="Place Order">
```

When the user clicks the Place Order button, the information entered in the form is sent to the server, which then opens the ORDER.IDC file.

ORDER.IDC contains commands that specify the database, the .HTX template, and the SQL query. Here's the ORDER.IDC file for the preceding example:

```
Datasource: Orders
Template: orderthx.htx
SQLStatement:
+INSERT name,street,city,state,zip,ram,hd,modem
+INTO orderinfo VALUES ('%name%', '%street%', '%city%',·'%state%',
➥ +'%zip%', '%ram%', '%hd%', '%modem%');
```

IDC's Required Directives

The .IDC file contains three directives that the IDC requires. The `Datasource` directive specifies the database to which to connect. The `Template` directive specifies which .HTX file to use to create the HTML page that returns to the server and ultimately goes to the client. The `SQLStatement` directive contains the query that inserts information into the database or retrieves information from the database.

Additional IDC Directives

Along with the `Datasource`, `Template`, and `SQLStatement` directives, additional directives are available. These directives are not required, but add a bit of flexibility when dealing with HTTPODBC.DLL. The rest of this section examines each of these directives and explains how you can use them.

The *DefaultParameters* Directive

You can use the `DefaultParameters` directive to specify the default parameters to use if the visitor doesn't fill out the form completely. For example, you can set the following default in case a visitor fails to enter a name:

```
DefaultParameters: name=%John Doe%
```

You can specify more than one parameter, but you must separate each with a comma.

The *RequiredParameters* Directive

The RequiredParameters directive enables you to specify which items the visitor must fill. If you want to ensure that the visitor enters a name and address, for example, you specify the following:

```
RequiredParameters: name, street, city, state, zip
```

The *MaxFieldSize* Directive

With the MaxFieldSize directive, you can specify a record's maximum length. If you don't specify the MaxFieldSize, the default value is 8,192 bytes.

The *MaxRecords* Directive

You can use the MaxRecords directive to set the maximum amount of records that a query returns. If you don't set the MaxRecords directive, the IDC allows the return of all records that match the query. This default setting isn't a problem with smaller databases, but can be with larger ones. Set this directive to a reasonable number of records, based on the kind of information that you are retrieving.

The *Expires* Directive

If you don't set the Expires directive, the database is accessed each time for information. If you do set this directive, the query returns to the user from a cache instead of accessing the database again. This can help reduce the system's load and return information to the visitor more quickly. Using the Expires directive, you specify the number of seconds before the cache is refreshed.

The *Username* Directive

If you're not using the SQL Server's integrated security, you can specify a username for accessing the SQL Server.

The *Password* Directive

You use the Password directive only if a password is required. When specifying the Password directive, you must enter a username.

The *BeginDetail* and *EndDetail* Tags

Now all you need to do is create an .HTX file that creates the HTML document that you return to the visitor. As with the .IDC file, the .HTX file uses special commands or tags that help format the HTML document.

If a visitor to your site wants to query the database, the `<%begindetail%>` and `<%enddetail%>` tags store the returned information. For example, suppose that a visitor perusing your company product catalog enters a query to search for modems, and that your database includes a field called modem. You can format the .HTX file to report each instance that matches the field:

```
<table>
<%begindetail%>
<tr><td><%modem%><td><%price%></td></tr>
<%enddetail%>
</table>
```

This code opens the `<TABLE>` tag. For each instance of a match, the file creates a row with the modem (which could simply be a name) and the price. The `<%enddetail%>` tag specifies the end of a section. You then use the `<\TABLE>` tag to close the table. If no records are found, this section is skipped.

The *CurrentRecord* Directive

The CurrentRecord directive counts the number of times that records are processed. You can use this directive to check whether the query generated any results and then inform the visitor of any results.

Soon you'll see how to use the CurrentRecord directive, but first you examine another tag that enables you to check information and return results based on conditions.

Conditional Operators

Within the .HTX file, you can use the following simple conditional operators: `<%if%>`, `<%else%>`, and `<%endif%>`. Using these operator tags, you can check whether certain conditions are met. For example, you can check whether any records were returned, and if not, you can inform the visitor:

```
<table>
<%begindetail%>
<tr><td><%modem%><td><%price%></td></tr>
<%enddetail%>
</table>
<%if CurrentRecord EQ 0 %>
I'm sorry, but there isn't anything in the database
➡ that matches your query.
<center>
<a href="products.html">[Product Database]</a>
</center>
```

The `<%if%>` tag uses four conditional words that you can use to check information.

EQ checks whether a value is equal to the test, as in the following example:

```
<%if modem EQ "US Robotics" %>
US Robotics 28.8
<%endif%>
```

GT enables you to check whether one value is greater than another, as in the following example:

```
<%if price GT 500 %>
```

LT checks whether a value is less than another value, as in the following example:

```
<%elseif price LT 10 %>
<%endif%>
```

CONTAINS enables you to check whether a value is anywhere within another value, as in the following example:

```
<%if modem CONTAINS "Robotics" %>
US Robotics
<%endif%>
```

The *MaxRecords* Variable

The MaxRecords variable contains the value of the MaxRecords directive that the IDC file specifies, as in the following example:

```
<%if CurrentRecord EQ MaxRecords %>
Results have been abridged
<%endif%>
```

Fields

After a visitor enters fields within an HTML form, you can pass them directly to the .HTX file by adding the *idc.* prefix. For example, if you want to return information to the visitor that entered it, you could use the following code line:

```
Hello %idc.namd%. How is the weather in %idc.city%,
➥ %idc.state%?<BR>
```

HTTP Variables

You can also use HTTP variables within .HTX files. To do so, you enclose the variable within the <% %> delimiters, as in the following example:

```
You are using, <%HTTP_USER_AGENT%>
```

To continue with the order-entry example, you simply thank the visitor for entering the order and let the visitor know that you have processed it.

First, you format the beginning of the HTML document:

```
<HTML>
<HEAD><TITLE>Thank you!</TITLE></HEAD>
<BODY>
<H1> Thank you for your order!</H1>
Thank you, %idc.name%. The following items will be added to your bill:
<UL>
```

Then you want find out which items the visitor ordered:

If ram has no value, do nothing.

Otherwise, print 8MB of RAM.

If hd has no value, do nothing.

Otherwise, print 1.2GB Hard Drive.

If modem has no value, do nothing.

Otherwise, print 28.8 Modem.

The actual code is as follows:

```
<%if% idc.ram EQ "">
<%else%>
<LI> 8MB of RAM
<%endif%>
<%if% idc.hd EQ "">
<%else%>
<LI> 1.2GB Hard Drive
<%endif%>
<%if% idc.modem EQ "">
<%else%>
<LI> 28.8 Modem
<%endif%>
</UL>
```

Next, you let the visitor know where you are sending the order. Essentially, you are confirming the visitor's order.

```
These items will be sent to:
<%name%><BR>
<%street%><BR>
<%city%>, <%state%> <%zip%><P>
Again, thank you for your order, please visit us again soon!<BR>
<HR>
<P>
<A HREF="http://www.selah.net">[Return to main page]</A>
</BODY>
</HTML>
```

The .HTX file produces a page similar to that shown in figure 12.2.

Figure 12.2

By using the .HTX file, you can embed a database's information into the final HTML document.

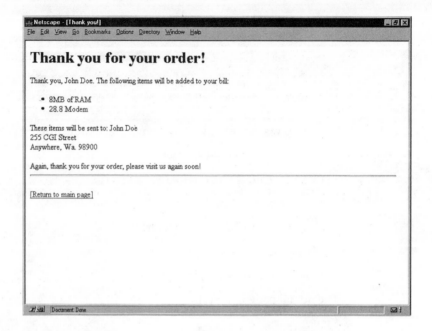

Using GSQL

GSQL, written by Jason Ng at the National Center for Supercomputing Applications (NCSA), is a gateway to SQL databases. GSQL checks a process file (called a *proc* file) that is used to create a form which, in turn, is used to query a database and return the results.

GSQL consists of three parts. The first part is the main GSQL program. GSQL does most of the work by processing the proc file and accessing the database if necessary. GSQL can be called either as part of the URI or from a shell script that wraps GSQL to the proc file. For example, you can call GSQL as follows:

```
http://www.selah.net/cgi-bin/gsql
```

You can also call GSQL with the proc file's path and name appended, as in the following example:

```
http://www.selah.net/cgi-bin/gsql?test.proc
```

Alternatively, you can create a file that contains the full path to GSQL and the proc file, as follows:

```
#!/bin/sh
/usr/bin/gsql /usr/temp/test.proc
```

This alternative gives you greater flexibility, letting you decide where you want to place files. In particular, you can choose where to place the proc file, which contains information on how your query is performed. The proc file might include username and password information.

The proc file matches SQL information to form types. Because of this matching, you can insert information directly from the database into your HTML forms. Each command line begins with a command, continues with command information, and ends with a semicolon. The syntax is as follows:

```
COMMAND command information;
```

This section covers each command in detail.

Display Commands

Using the display commands, you can control how you return information to the visitor. The proc file processes each command sequentially.

The *HEADING* Command

The HEADING command enables you to display a heading in your HTML page. GSQL doesn't interpret anything within the heading; it displays as entered.

```
HEADING <TITLE>Test page</TITLE>;
```

The *SHOW* Command

The SHOW command creates form widgets that the visitor uses to select information. The syntax for SHOW is as follows:

```
SHOW variable_name TITLE "title name" option;
```

The variable is the SQL query information that is placed within the HTML text that the option defines. TITLE specifies a name for the HTML tags. Normally you would enter the following:

```
Click me! <INPUT TYPE="checkbox" NAME="test" VALUE="clicked">
```

However, with GSQL, you enter the following:

```
SHOW test TITLE "<br>Click me!" CHECKBOX
```

Later you learn more about how you set the variables. For now, examine the options allowed within a GSQL proc file.

The option BUTTON creates a single check box. The HTML equivalent value would look like the following:

```
<INPUT TYPE="checkbox">
```

The FIELD option creates a text entry field:

```
<INPUT TYPE="text">
```

PULLDOWN creates a pull-down menu:

```
<SELECT ...>
<OPTION> Option 1
<OPTION> Option 2
<OPTION> Option 3
</SELECT>
```

With the SCROLL option, you can create a scrolling select list. Although PULLDOWN enables you to select only one item, the SCROLL option lets you select more than one.

```
<SELECT ... SIZE=3 MULTIPLE>
<OPTION> Option 1
<OPTION> Option 2
<OPTION> Option 3
</SELECT>
```

The RADIO option creates a set of radio buttons. Using the RADIO option, you can select only one item from a set of radio buttons.

```
<INPUT TYPE="radio" name="test" value="1"> Test 1
<INPUT TYPE="radio" name="test" value="2"> Test 2
```

CHECKBOX creates a set of check boxes:

```
<INPUT TYPE="radio" name="test1" value="1"> Test 1
<INPUT TYPE="radio" name="test2" value="2"> Test 2
```

Additionally, PULLDOWN, SCROLL, CHECKBOX, and RADIO can use menu options. A menu option can be a list of items that displays in the HTML text. For example, examine the following PULLDOWN option:

```
SHOW test TITLE "Days of the Week" PULLDOWN Monday, Tuesday,
➥ Wednesday, Thursday, Friday, Saturday, Sunday;
```

Another option is to use the EXEC command, with which you can insert a system command's results into a list, as in the following example:

```
SHOW test2 TITLE "finger" SCROLL EXEC (finger bert);
```

The *TEXT* Command

Using the TEXT command, you can display text within the proc file without GSQL processing it. Note the following example:

```
TEXT This is just <b>some</b> text.;
```

General Commands

In addition to the display commands, GSQL provides a variety of general commands that enable you to redefine variables, execute UNIX commands, pass information to the database as variables, and specify the file and path name of a back-end application.

The *SUB* Command

To display any information from the database, you use the SHOW command. Using the SUB command, you can define a variable to a SQL phrase. When processing the proc file, GSQL reformats the information in the defined variables as information within an HTML page.

The following is SUB's syntax:

```
SUB variable_name [LISTTYPE] AS sql-query
```

Using the SUB command, you can name the variable anything you want. The LISTTYPE is either the WHERELIST or the SELECTLIST statement. WHERELIST defines a query using the SQL WHERE clause, and the SELECTLIST statement defines a query using the SQL SELECT clause. The LISTTYPE is followed by the AS keyword and then the actual query statement.

The query statement consists of one string containing the database name, table name, and the column name. The database is followed by two periods (..) and connected to the table name. After the table name is one period and the column name. For example, take a look at the following query statement:

```
database_name..table_name.column_name
```

The following is another example:

```
bookmarks..personal.computer
```

Here's a full SUB statement:

```
SUB test SELECTLIST AS bookmarks..personal.computer like '$';
```

The like operator collects any information from the column, computer, and the table, personal, that matches the information contained in '$'. You use the dollar sign to store information that the visitor entered in the HTML form.

The *EXEC* Command

The EXEC command enables you to execute UNIX commands and display the results of the command within the form. The following example results in the form shown in figure 12.3:

```
EXEC (finger);
```

Figure 12.3

Using the EXEC command, you can execute system commands and display the results within the HTML document.

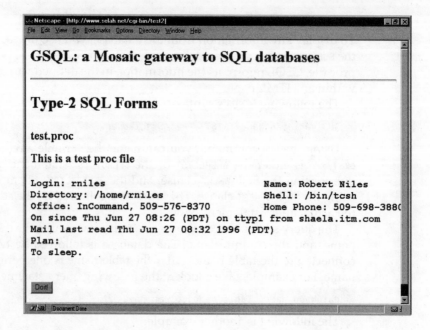

The *DEFINE* Command

Using the DEFINE command, you can pass information to the database as an argument. The command passes the information as a keyword/value pair. Suppose, for example, that your database requires the following command line:

```
sybase username rniles password test
```

With GSQL, you set these arguments as follows:

```
DEFINE username rniles;
DEFINE password test;
```

The *SQLPROG* Command

You can use the SQLPROG command to specify the full path and name of your database back-end. When the visitor fills the form, GSQL checks SQLPROG to determine which database to use, because GSQL works with various SQL databases. This command is required; your proc file cannot function without it.

Here's an example of SQLPROG in use:

```
SQLPROG /usr/local/databases/sybase
```

SQL Directives

GSQL also makes several SQL directives available. These include FROMLIST, WHERELIST, SELECTLIST, and SORT.

The *FROMLIST* Directive

The FROMLIST directive enables you to specify which databases and tables to use to create the SQL query. If you configure your proc file to retrieve information from the database, this directive is required. You separate each database and table with a comma, using the following syntax:

```
FROMLIST database..table [alias];
```

For example, if you want to pull information from the bookmarks database using the tables personal and shared, you enter the following:

```
FROMLIST bookmarks..personal p, bookmarks..shared s;
```

By using an alias, you can later shorten your query and make input more manageable. The alias is completely optional but can make things a bit easier. You don't want to type more than you have to.

The *WHERELIST* Directive

Suppose that two tables hold information about an employee. One keeps personal information, the other holds information on the department in which the employee works. The following is an example of how you might set up the fields for both tables:

Personal Table	Department Table
emp_num	emp_num
emp_name	dept_name
address	location
home_phone	work_phone

Using the WHERELIST directive, you can tie these two tables together as if they were stored in one. The following is the syntax for WHERELIST:

```
WHERELIST database..table.column = database..table.column;
```

Note the following example:

```
WHERELIST employee..personal.emp_num =
➥ employee..department.emp_num;
```

This directive provides information from both tables if the personal table's employee number matches that of the department table.

The *SELECTLIST* Directive

An optional directive, SELECTLIST enables you to query information and display it to the visitor; no matter what the visitor searches for. The syntax for the SELECTLIST directive is as follows:

```
SELECTLIST database..table[.column];
```

For example, to create a list of everyone in the employee database, you could use the following directive:

```
SELECTLIST employee.personal.name;
```

The *SORT* Directive

In relational databases, you can specify whether a list of information is in alphabetic or numeric order. Note the following SQL query:

```
SELECT * FROM personal,department WHERE personal.emp_num =
➥ department.emp_num ORDER by name
```

In the proc file, you use the SORT directive to specify how to list information.

The SORT directive enables you to display information in either ascending or descending order. The syntax is as follows:

```
SORT order by [table.]column [asc¦desc] [,[table.]column
➥ [asc¦desc]];
```

To get the same result as the previous SQL query, you add the following line to your proc file:

```
SORT order by personal.name asc;
```

This line creates a list of employee names listed alphabetically from A to Z.

GSQL's Drawbacks

GSQL might seem intimidating at first, but if you create a proc file and then start playing with it—changing a value here for a value there—you'll find that GSQL is quite easy to use.

If all you are looking for is a SQL gateway, GSQL is quite beneficial. It does have limitations, however. Controlling the HTML document's layout can be difficult. GSQL creates header information automatically, so you don't have much control over the presentation of that information. Nor do you have much control over the size at which your text displays.

Another problem with GSQL is that unless you are using Sybase or Oracle, you have to create your own back-end. Some developers might find that task difficult.

The back-end program must be in C and act as the gateway between GSQL and your database server. After the visitor fills out the form, GSQL receives that information and passes it to the database back-end application, which then creates the query to your SQL server.

For more information on the database back-end and GSQL in general, visit the following site:

http://www.ncsa.uiuc.edu/SDG/People/jason/pub/gsql/starthere.html

Using mSQL

mSQL is a SQL server that works over a TCP/IP network (see fig. 12.4). Although not as powerful as some of the commercial SQL engines, mSQL has just about everything that you might need for most everyday jobs. Some commercial SQL servers cost well over $1,000, but mSQL is free to the educational and nonprofit sectors; if you use it for commercial purposes, the cost is only about $170.

Figure 12.4

mSQL is a small but powerful SQL database server that is free for noncommercial use.

David Hughes wrote mSQL to fill the need for a freely available SQL engine. mSQL has all the main functions that you find in a SQL server and runs on most UNIX systems. The latest version is 1.015, but Hughes is currently working on release 2.0, which probably will be available by the time that you read this book. For more information on mSQL, visit the following site:

http://hughes.com.au/product/msql/

Visiting this site is well worthwhile, because it contains many programs that support the mSQL database.

Inserting Information

Suppose that you are developing a scheduling application. You want the application to make it easy to add information to a work schedule without having to create a Web page for each schedule. To do so, you can use a SQL database. The user can then enter information into a simple form, which the application then stores into the database. To retrieve the information, you use the CGI script that created the Web page.

Adding Different Schedules

To create such an application, you first need to be able to add different schedules. For each schedule, you list various activities necessary to complete the job. To accomplish this task, you create two tables within an mSQL database.

The first table holds a schedule's number and name. A simple HTML document can ask the user to enter the schedule's name (see fig. 12.5).

Figure 12.5

After the user enters a schedule name, the form goes to the CGI script, which adds the schedule name to the database.

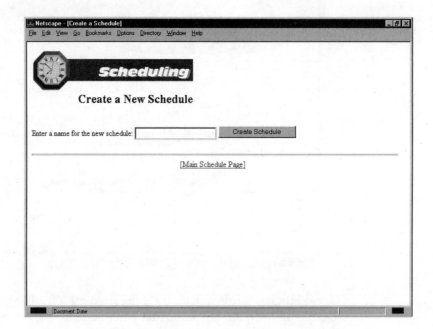

Listing 12.2 shows SCHEDNEW.HTML, the HTML document. You can find this file on the CD-ROM.

Listing 12.2   SCHEDNEW.HTML—Enabling the Visitor To Enter a New Schedule

```
<HTML>
<HEAD><TITLE>Create a Schedule</TITLE></HEAD>
<BODY bgcolor="white">
<table border=0>
<tr><td><IMG SRC="/pics/shed.gif"></td></tr>
<tr><td align=right valign=top><H2>Create a New Schedule
➥ </H2></td></tr>
</table>
<form action="/cgi-bin/schednew.pl" method="POST">
Enter a name for the new schedule:
<input type="text" name="sched_name">
<input type="submit" value="Create Schedule">
</form>
<p><hr>
<center>
<a href="/schedmain.html">[Main Schedule Page]</A>
```

Placing Information into the mSQL Database

The form calls the CGI script SCHEDNEW.PL, which is on the CD-ROM accompanying this book. This script processes the information and places it into the mSQL database. You first specify the path to Perl and then call the `MsqlPerl` module, which makes it easier to interface with the mSQL server.

```
#!/usr/bin/perl
# schednew.pl
# Creates a new Schedule

use Msql;
```

Next, you split the information:

```
if ($ENV{'REQUEST_METHOD'} eq 'POST')
{
    read(STDIN, $buffer, $ENV{'CONTENT_LENGTH'});
    @pairs = split(/&/, $buffer);
    foreach $pair (@pairs)
    {
        ($name, $value) = split(/=/, $pair);
        $value =~ tr/+/ /;
        $value =~ s/%([a-fA-F0-9][a-fA-F0-9])/pack("C",
➥      hex($1))/eg;
        $contents{$name} = $value;

    }
}
```

You then make sure that the `Content-type` goes to the Web server:

```
print "Content-type: text/html\n\n";
```

If the visitor failed to enter a schedule name, you have to notify the visitor of this omission. The next line tells the script to go to the subroutine &error if sched_name has no value:

```
&error unless $contents{'sched_name'};
```

Now you are connected to the database. Because you can use mSQL to call any system on the Internet, you can specify the server's name. To do so, you use the following line:

```
$db1 = Msql->Connect("imtired.selah.net", "schedule") or die;
```

However, because you are connecting to the server locally, you can simply omit the domain name and instead specify the database's name:

```
$db1 = Msql->Connect("", "schedule") or die;
```

Suppose that you have given the two tables the names `table1` and `table2`. `table1` has two columns. The first column is the schedule number, which you assign as sched_num. The schedule number is a required entry that the script generates. The script check finds the highest number already in the database and increments the count so that the next schedule entered has its own unique number.

When you use this technique, you are using a *primary key*. mSQL requires that the primary key be unique. Using a primary key makes searching through a database faster, which is important if your database starts to become quite large.

First, the script reads the schedule numbers from the database:

```
$sth = $db1->Query("select sched_num from table1 order
➡ by sched_num") or die;
```

Now you assign the contents of each row to the variable check. The variable sched_num holds the information of check and increments. You make this assignment for the whole database. When you finish reading the database, sched_num has the highest number contained within the database and increments. sched_num then becomes the schedule number.

```
while (@check = $sth->FetchRow) {
$sched_num = $check[0];
$sched_num++;
}
```

Creating the Query

To create your query, you assign the SQL query to the variable $query. This query tells the mSQL server to insert into `table1` the values for the schedule number and schedule name:

```
$query = qq{insert into table1 (sched_num,sched_name) values
($sched_num,'$contents{'sched_name'}')
};
```

After creating your query, you add its information to the database. Using the `MsqlPerl` module, you can accomplish this task with one code line such as the following:

```
$db1->Query($query);
```

Displaying the Schedule Number to the Visitor

After you add the information to the database, you print an HTML document that informs the visitor that you have entered the information. The document also tells the visitor the schedule number that you assigned to the schedule name.

```
print <<"HTML";

<HTML>
<HEAD><TITLE>Add a Schedule</TITLE></HEAD>
<BODY bgcolor="white">
<table border=0>
<tr><td><IMG SRC="/pics/shed.gif"></td></tr>
<tr><td align=right valign=top><H2>A new Schedule has been added
➥ </H2></td></tr>
</table>

The schedule, <b>$contents{'sched_name'}</b>, has been added to the
database as schedule number $sched_num.
<p>
<hr>
<center>
<a href="/schedmain.html">[Main Schedule Page]</a>
</center>
</BODY>
</HTML>
HTML

exit;
```

If the visitor failed to enter a schedule name, you send the `&error` subroutine. All you do at this point, however, is create a page that tells the visitor that he or she must enter a schedule name. You also provide a link so that the visitor can try to enter a schedule name.

```
sub error {
print <<"HTML";
<HTML>
<HEAD><TITLE>Error!</TITLE></HEAD>
<BODY bgcolor="white">
<table border=0>
<tr><td><IMG SRC="/pics/shed.gif"></td></tr>
```

```
<tr><td align=right valign=top><H2>Error!</H2></td></tr>
</table>
<p>
No schedule name was entered!
<p>
<hr>
<center>
<a href="/schedmain.html">[Main Schedule Page]</a>
</center>
</BODY>
</HTML>
HTML
exit;
}
```

Adding Activities to Each Schedule

You next want to add activities within each schedule. You create a schedule for InCommand Intranet, a project that requires the accomplishment of several activities. table2 holds all this information.

The table also needs a schedule number. This number is the same as the schedule number listed in table1.

You also need an activity name, a description of the activity, the date at which that section of the project is due, and a listing of the people responsible for that activity.

Again, you provide the path to Perl and then tell the script to use the MsqlPerl module. You then separate the contents of STDIN. This time, however, you have to add an additional line when you split STDIN. Notice the following line:

```
$value =~ tr/\///\/\//;
```

When the visitor enters a date in the form, he or she most likely will use a slash (/). mSQL doesn't like having a slash within a row, so you add an extra slash. This extra slash tells mSQL to ignore the original slash. Without the extra slash, the database would ignore the query, and nothing would be entered into the database. A good practice is to add an extra slash to every script that accesses the mSQL server.

Listing 12.3 shows ACTADD.PL, the script that adds activities to the database. This script is also on the companion CD-ROM.

Listing 12.3   ACTADD.PL—Adding Activities to the Database

```
#!/usr/bin/perl
# actadd.pl
# Add Activity to Schedule

use Msql;
```

```
if ($ENV{'REQUEST_METHOD'} eq 'POST')
{
    read(STDIN, $buffer, $ENV{'CONTENT_LENGTH'});
    @pairs = split(/&/, $buffer);
    foreach $pair (@pairs)
    {
        ($name, $value) = split(/=/, $pair);
        $value =~ tr/+/ /;
        $value =~ s/%([a-fA-F0-9][a-fA-F0-9])/pack("C",
    hex($1))/eg;
        $value =~ tr/\///\/\///;
        $contents{$name} = $value;

    }
}
```

After splitting STDIN, you provide the Content-type and then check whether the visitor selected one of the database names. If not, the script calls the subroutine &form, which simply prints the form.

```
print "Content-type: text/html\n\n";
&form unless $contents{'sched_num'};
```

Now you connect your query to the database and form. In the query line, you can see that you are inserting information into the database. In pseudocode, the process looks like the following:

Gather the values contained within the variables from the columns, sched_num, *activity,* description, *due, and* resp.

Insert the values into table2.

The actual code is as follows:

```
$db1 = Msql->Connect("", "schedule") or do {&error_db};
$query = qq{insert into table2 (sched_num,activity,description,
 due,resp)
values ($contents{'sched_num'},'$contents{'activity'}',
'$contents{'description'}','$contents{'due'}','$contents{'resp'}')
 };
```

After forming the query, you execute it in the following line:

```
$db1->Query($query);
```

You have now entered the information into the database and can print a statement informing the visitor:

```
print <<"HTML";
<HTML>
<HEAD><TITLE>Information Entered</TITLE></HEAD>
<BODY bgcolor="white">
<table border=0>
<tr><td><IMG SRC="/pics/shed.gif"></td></tr>
```

```
<tr><td align=right valign=top><H2>Activity Entered</H2></td></tr>
</table>
The activity has been entered into the database<p>
Thank you!
<p><hr>
<a href="/schedmain.html">[Main Schedule Page]</a>
</body>
</html>
HTML
exit;
```

The following is the form subroutine that prints the form in which the visitor can choose the schedule name. Figure 12.6 shows the form.

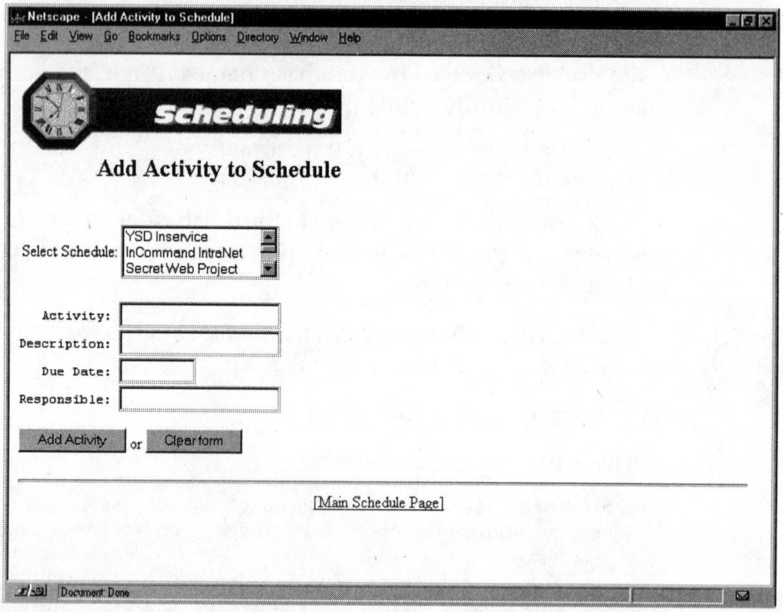

Figure 12.6

You create this form on the fly, using information that the database supplies.

```
sub form {
$db2 = Msql->Connect("", "schedule") or do {&error_db};
$query = qq{select sched_num,sched_name from table1 order
➥ by sched_num
};

$sth = $db2->Query($query);

print <<"HTML";
<HTML>
<HEAD><TITLE>Add Activity to Schedule</TITLE></HEAD>
<BODY bgcolor="white">
```

```
<table border=0>
<tr><td><IMG SRC="/pics/shed.gif"></td></tr>
<tr><td align=right valign=top><H2>Add Activity to Schedule</H2>
➡ </td></tr>
</table>
<FORM ACTION="/cgi-bin/actadd.pl" METHOD="POST">
<TABLE border=0>
<TR><TD>Select Schedule:</TD><TD>
```

Using the <SELECT> tag, you automatically create a list from which the visitor can select a schedule name. Because the information is already in a database, you can simply call the names from it. Then you don't have to edit the HTML file manually every time that a visitor adds a new schedule to the database.

```
<SELECT NAME="sched_num" SIZE=3>
HTML

while (@option = $sth->FetchRow) {
print "<OPTION VALUE=\"$option[0]\">$option[1]";
}
print "</SELECT>";
print <<"HTML";
</TD></TR>
</table>
<br>
```

After creating the list, you supply fields in which the visitor can enter the activity information. Each line has a MAXLENGTH of 255 characters or less because each field in the database can hold only that much information.

```
<pre>
   Activity: <input type="text" name="activity" MAXLENGTH=255>
Description: <input type="text" name="description" MAXLENGTH=255>
   Due Date: <input type="text" name="due" size=9 MAXLENGTH=9>
Responsible: <input type="text" name="resp" MAXLENGTH=255>
</pre>
```

After entering the information, you display submit and clear buttons to the visitor:

```
</td></tr>
<input type="submit" value="Add Activity"> or
<input type="reset" value="Clear form">
<p><hr>
<center>
<a href="/schedmain.html">[Main Schedule Page]</a>
</center>
</BODY>
</HTML>

HTML
exit;
}
```

The &error subroutine tells the visitor if a problem arose when connecting to the database:

```
sub error_db {
print <<"HTML";
<HTML>
<HEAD><TITLE>Error!</TITLE></HEAD>
<BODY bgcolor="white">
<table border=0>
<tr><td><IMG SRC="/pics/shed.gif"></td></tr>
<tr><td align=right valign=top><H2>Main Page</H2></td></tr>
</table>
Cannot connect to database\n
<p><hr>
<center>
<a href="/schedmain.html">[Main Schedule Page]</a>
</center>
</BODY>
</HTML>
HTML
exit;
}
```

Entering information into the database helps considerably. You can create dynamic HTML pages based on the information within a database. If the information in the database changes, the HTML document does as well—almost magically.

Retrieving Information

After entering information into the database, you can retrieve the information and display it to visitors.

If the visitor hasn't already entered a schedule name, the script creates a form with a list of schedules from which the visitor can choose. If the script receives a schedule number through STDIN, that schedule is printed. This script performs both functions, creating either page depending on the information (or lack thereof) received. Therefore, the script doesn't have to create a separate HTML page for both tasks.

Listing 12.4 shows SCHEDVIEW.PL, the script that retrieves information from the database. You can find this script on this book's companion CD-ROM.

Listing 12.4   SCHEDVIEW.PL—Retrieving Information from the Database

```
#!/usr/bin/perl

use Msql;


if ($ENV{'REQUEST_METHOD'} eq 'POST')
```

```
{
    read(STDIN, $buffer, $ENV{'CONTENT_LENGTH'});
    @pairs = split(/&/, $buffer);
    foreach $pair (@pairs)
    {
        ($name, $value) = split(/=/, $pair);
        $value =~ tr/+/ /;
        $value =~ s/%([a-fA-F0-9][a-fA-F0-9])/pack("C",
➥       hex($1))/eg;
        $value =~ tr/\///\/\//;
        $contents{$name} = $value;

    }
}

print "Content-type: text/html\n\n";
```

After specifying the path to Perl, you split STDIN and load the MsqlPerl module. You then check whether the visitor selected a schedule number. If not, you provide the visitor a form in which to select a schedule. The following line simply checks whether the visitor selected a schedule number; if not, Perl processes the subroutine &form:

```
&form unless $contents{'sched_num'};
```

If the visitor selected a schedule number, you connect to the database and perform your query. In this instance, you have many fields to request from the database, so you place all these fields within the string $fields:

```
$db1 = Msql->Connect("", "schedule") or do {&error_db};

$fields = "table1.sched_num,table1.sched_name,table2.sched_num\n";
$fields = $fields . ",table2.activity,table2.description,
➥ table2.due,table2.resp";
```

Next, you do the same with the tables, because you are querying both tables:

```
$tables = "table1,table2";
```

Now you form the actual query. From both databases, you want only information that matches the schedule number that the visitor chose.

```
$query = qq{select $fields from $tables where
            table1.sched_num=$contents{'sched_num'}
            AND table2.sched_num = $contents{'sched_num'}
};
```

You also form another query that retrieves only the schedule name outside of the loop that prints the activities:

```
$query2 = qq{select sched_num,sched_name from table1 where
sched_num = $contents{'sched_num'}
};
```

Next, you actually perform the query, retrieving the information from the database:

```
$sth=$db1->Query($query);
$sth1=$db1->Query($query2);
```

After querying the database, you test whether the query produced any results. If there are none, you inform the visitor. Unless you inform the visitor, he or she doesn't know what is happening and might get upset and annoyed and move on to something else.

```
$exist = $sth->numrows;
if ($exist < 1) {
print <<"HTML";
<HTML>
<HEAD><TITLE>No Activities Listed</TITLE></HEAD>
<BODY bgcolor="white">
<table border=0>
<tr><td><IMG SRC="/pics/shed.gif"></td></tr>
<tr><td align=right valign=top><H2>No Activities Listed</H2>
➥ </td></tr>
</table>
<P>There are no activities listed within this schedule<P> <p><hr>
<a href="/schedmain.html">[Main Schedule Page]</a>
</body>
</html>
HTML
exit;
}
```

If there are activities, you print the header with information obtained by the second query:

```
@head=$sth1->FetchRow;
print <<"HTML";
<HTML>
<HEAD><TITLE>$head[1]</TITLE></HEAD>
<BODY bgcolor="white">
<table border=0>
<tr><td><IMG SRC="/pics/shed.gif"></td></tr>
<tr><td align=right valign=top><H2>$head[1]</H2></td></tr>
</table>
<center>
<table border=1>
<tr><td><b>Activity</b></td><td><b>Description</b></td><td><b>Due
Date</b></td><td><b>Responsibility</b></td></tr>
HTML
```

Then you print all activities with the same sched_num selected by the visitor. The easiest way to do so is by using Perl's while loop. This structure prints one line at a time until it has printed every matching element.

```
while (@row=$sth->FetchRow) {
print "<tr>";
print "<td>$row[3]</td>";
print "<td>$row[4]</td>";
print "<td>$row[5]</td>";
print "<td>$row[6]</td>";
print "</tr>";
}
```

After printing the information, you finish the HTML document and exit the script:

```
print <<"HTML";
</table>
<p><hr>
<a href="/schedmain.html">[Main Schedule Page]</a>
</body>
</html>
HTML
exit;
```

Figure 12.7 gives you an idea of the resulting document's appearance.

Figure 12.7

The HTML document lists every activity, showing you every task that you must complete to finish the project.

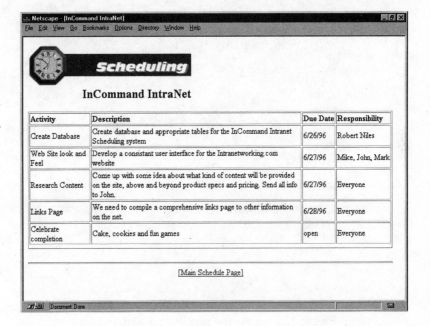

Now you create the subroutine that prints a form in which the visitor can select a schedule number if he or she hasn't already selected one:

```
sub form {
$db2 = Msql->Connect("", "john") or do {&error_db};
$query = qq{select sched_num,sched_name from table1 order
➥ by sched_num
};

$sth = $db2->Query($query);

print <<"HTML";
<HTML>
<HEAD><TITLE>List Schedule</TITLE></HEAD>
<BODY bgcolor="white">
<table border=0>
<tr><td><IMG SRC="/pics/shed.gif"></td></tr>
<tr><td align=right valign=top><H2>List Schedules</H2></td></tr>
</table>
<FORM ACTION="/cgi-bin/schedview.pl" METHOD="POST">
<TABLE border=0>
<TR><TD>Select Schedule:</TD><TD>
<SELECT NAME="sched_num" SIZE=3>
HTML

while (@option = $sth->FetchRow) {
print "<OPTION VALUE=\"$option[0]\">$option[1]";
}
print "</SELECT>";
print <<"HTML";
</TD>
<td>
<input type="submit" value="Show Schedule">
</td>
</TR>
</table>

<p><hr>
<center>
<a href="/schedmain.html">[Main Schedule Page]</a>
</center>
</BODY>
</HTML>

HTML
exit;
}
```

Figure 12.8 shows the resulting document.

Figure 12.8

By querying the database, you can generate a listing of the available schedules.

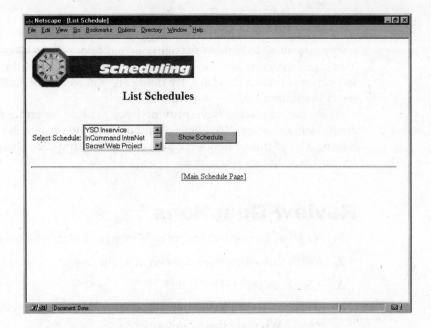

If the script cannot connect to the database, you inform the visitor:

```
sub error_db {
print <<"HTML";
Can not connect to database\n
HTML
exit;
}
```

Reviewing and Expanding the Scripts

This collection of scripts helps keep a list of every task that the user needs to complete to finish a project. By entering information into the database and creating an ever-changing form on the fly, the scripts relieve the user from having to create a Web page manually. Anything that saves time helps.

The scripts are especially useful in that they remove a big portion of the paper trail. No longer does the user have to print enough copies of each task for every person. Now everyone can obtain that information from one place. If the information changes, you needn't reprint and redistribute the information; you simply access it again through a Web browser.

Although these scripts demonstrate how to enter and retrieve information, they aren't complete. You need to create scripts that enable visitors to remove a schedule or activity or edit an activity.

Summary

Using a database to build Web pages can make your life as Webmaster much easier. You could conceivably create Web pages solely through the use of scripts and information from a database. By doing so, you avoid the tedious task of editing every document within your realm.

This chapter should have provided you with ideas and a means by which to create rich, dynamic Web pages. Don't be afraid to change the example scripts by adding a bit of this or removing a bit of that. Making such changes is the best way to learn how things work.

Review Questions

1. For what do you use Microsoft's Internet Database Connector?

2. Which three directives does an .IDC file require?

3. What does the .HTX file do?

4. In GSQL, what are the differences between the commands PULLDOWN and SCROLL? What are their similarities?

5. Which GSQL command enables you to execute system commands?

6. Using mSQL and MsqlPerl within your Perl script, how do you connect to a database?

7. What do you need to do to place a slash (/) within an mSQL database?

8. Using mSQL, how many characters are allowed in each field?

Review Exercises

1. Create a SQL database that contains two tables. The first table should contain a product number, a product name, the cost of that part, and the name of a dealer from which you would purchase that part. The second table should contain the part number, the sale price of that part, and the quantity of that part that you have in stock.

2. Using any method to access the database through a CGI script, create a form that enables the user to enter the information provided in exercise 1, ensuring that you place each field in the appropriate table.

3. Expanding on exercises 1 and 2, write a script that creates a Web page based on the information in the database. For example, your script should display something like the following:

```
3493 8MB RAM RAM_Makers_Inc. $50.00 $70.00 23
```

where the first field is the part number, the second field is the part name, the third field is the dealer, the fourth field is the store's cost, the fifth field is the sale price, and the last field is the quantity that you have of that part in your stock.

Part V

Web Indexing

## CHAPTER 13

Introduction to Indexing

If you'd ever seen my desk, you'd realize two things instantly: First, I'm highly computerized; second, I'm highly disorganized. I usually have two or three keyboards within reach, and often type on more than one at a time. I'm surrounded by monitors displaying graphs, status reports, blinking prompts, and applications. Modems, tape drives, CD-ROM drives, routers, hubs, printers, switches, mice, disks, pagers, and my coffee cup all vie for space on the desk.

Yet piled between the keyboards, on top of the monitors, in stacks on the floor beside the chair, on cabinets overhead, on shelves behind me, and—thanks to 3M Corporation—attached to anything with a flat surface, you'll find bits of paper. Yellow, white, lined, or plain—torn, whole, padded, punched, folded, spindled, or mutilated—I work within a growing mountain of flattened wood pulp. Anything will do—envelopes, sticky notes, legal pads, memo pads, napkins, or backs of receipts—as long as it has a blank area, I'll write something on it.

I write down everything. Phone numbers, names, dates, doodles, IP addresses, my to-do list—*everything*. Worse yet, people *give* me paper. Memos, time sheets, junk mail, letters, business cards, paychecks (I don't mind those), manuals, instruction sheets, and the odd bit here and there marked, "This page intentionally left blank." Yet for all the incomprehensible bulk of written material scattered around me like the debris from an explosion in Pueblo, Colorado, I do fairly well at keeping mental track of what's where.

Ask me two days after I write down your birthday, and I can reach into a pile, pull forth a crumpled napkin, turn it inside out, and triumphantly report success. That I'd written it using a felt pen on an angle across the only free space left on that napkin, and that the ink had spread throughout the fiber, making everything else on the napkin illegible, is beside the point. Out of thousands of pieces of paper, I was able to retrieve exactly the right one within moments. I'd remembered the napkin, the felt-tip pen, on which part of the napkin I'd written, and even in which pile I'd put the napkin. Pretty impressive, even if just remembering your birthday would have been simpler.

Ask me two weeks later rather than two days later and I'll scratch my head, narrow my eyes, and rummage through all the napkins, then all the papers with felt-tip pen marks, until I find your birthday. It might not be an instantaneous retrieval, but it's good enough. I've remembered two key items about your birthday—napkins and felt tips. If I couldn't find it using the first key, I'd use the second. At worst, I could iterate through all the papers matching either key, with the highest probability ranking given to those matching both keys.

But ask me two *months* afterward, and I'll say, "Who are you again?" or just pretend I didn't hear your question.

Clearly, my system is inadequate. Just as clearly, the solution is sitting on the same desk with all that confetti. The World Wide Web has the same problem, the same kind of system, and the same solution.

The Perfect Secretary

To solve my paperwork problem, I need a system to organize that information, sort it by keyword, topic, concept, or phrase; order it using some hierarchical scheme; and then correlate it with all the other bits of information already organized. I can imagine the world's best secretary—someone who would come into my office without ever disturbing me, take all of those bits of paper away, file them appropriately, and be on call 24 hours a day to retrieve anything instantly.

I might hit the intercom button and say, "I need to know the birthday of John, um, somebody—I forget his last name, but he's a member of the Elks—maybe the Moose—and he was in here sometime last week, or the week before. It might have been last month, but it was definitely after I had my wisdom teeth out."

"You mean John Peterson, 5'10", brown eyes, black hair, born on 25 December 1974? Married to your daughter?"

"Yeah, that's the one! Thanks!"

Well, maybe any good secretary could have answered that particular question, but only a robot could solve the general case. Fortunately, the Web has robots—called spiders, Web crawlers, or worms—that are on the job 24 hours a day, 365 days a year. They do nothing but wander around, picking up stray bits of paper, reading and cataloging whatever they find. They store the results of their searches in huge databases, which anyone can browse.

But just as I'll never find the perfect secretary, you'll never find the perfect search engine. Each one has its strengths and weaknesses, its admirers and detractors. What you *can* do, however, is build a team of secretaries, each one doing the particular task that he or she does best.

The WAIS and Means Committee

WAIS (pronounced *ways*) stands for Wide-Area Information Systems, and is a popular full-text indexing and retrieval engine. *Full-text* refers to the fact that each word in each document scanned becomes part of the index. Listings 13.1, 13.2, and 13.3 show three files that might be included in a WAIS index.

Listing 13.1   HOLIDAYS.TXT—Sample Text File #1

```
Holiday Schedule
New Year's Day, Monday, January 2.
Memorial Day, Monday 29 May
July 4th, Independence Day, Thursday
```

Listing 13.2   BIRTHDAYS.TXT—Sample Text File #2

```
John, Jan 17 (Thursday this year)
Mary, May 29
```

Listing 13.3   TAXES.TXT—Sample Text File #3

```
Fiscal year ends 31 December
Expect big write-off in May or June
Estimates due July 1
```

These three files roughly correspond to things that I might have scrawled on slips of paper here and there. My wonderful secretary, Mr. Ways, has swept through the room, cleaned up all the papers, and organized the information for me. Mr. Ways keeps a careful catalog of everything that he finds, and can examine it on demand.

Suppose that I ask Mr. Ways for anything with the word *Jan*. Mr. Ways would instantly hand me HOLIDAYS.TXT (which has *January*) and BIRTHDAYS.TXT (which has *Jan*). He wouldn't give me TAXES.TXT because *Jan* doesn't appear anywhere in it.

If I ask for *May*, I'll get back all three files, because all three contain the word *May*.

If I ask for anything containing either *February* or *tax*, Mr. Ways will return TAXES.TXT. Even though none of the files contains the word *February*, the TAXES.TXT file contains the word *tax* as part of the title. This satisfies my request for either the first word *or* the second word. This kind of search is called a Boolean OR.

If I ask Mr. Ways to search for both *May* and *29*, he will hand me BIRTHDAYS.TXT and HOLIDAYS.TXT, at which point I'll find out that Mary's birthday is on Memorial Day this year. TAXES.TXT contains the word *May* but not the word *29*, so the file fails the "find files with the first term *and* the second term" test. This kind of search is called a Boolean AND.

I can stretch Mr. Ways a bit, by asking him to produce only files that have both *May* and *29*, but not *Mary*. A Boolean expression might state this search as follows:

((May AND 29) AND (NOT Mary))

This search first finds files matching the first term (it must have both *May* and *29*), then excludes files having *Mary*, leaving only HOLIDAYS.TXT as the result. Suppose that the following had been the search expression:

((May AND 29) OR (NOT Mary))

Then Mr. Ways would have cheerfully given me all three files. The HOLIDAYS.TXT file gets included because it has both *May* and *29*; the BIRTHDAYS.TXT file gets included for the same reason; and the TAXES.TXT file shows up because it *doesn't* have *Mary*.

A full-text index is obviously very powerful. Even in this limited example, you can clearly see the usefulness and flexibility of this kind of tool. Yet in a large database of files, thousands might include the word *May*. If the database includes source code files, there might be hundreds of thousands of references to *29*. Wouldn't it be nice to find only *dates that look like birthdays*, or *the word May, but only if it's near the word 29, and not in any source code files*?

Fuzzy search engines go one step beyond Mr. Ways and give you the means to do more.

Warm Fuzzies

A *fuzzy* search is one that doesn't rely on exact matches. It is not based on Boolean algebra, with its mixture of AND, OR, and NOT operators, although these might come into play if appropriate. Instead, it tries to identify concepts and patterns, and deal with *information* rather than *data*.

Feel the Heat

Information is data that's been assigned *meaning* by a human. In a simple example, "It's 98 degrees" is data, whereas "It's hot" is information. As the amount of data on the Internet grows, the importance of distinguishing information from data skyrockets.

The ultimate artificial-intelligence machine would have a DWIM, or "Do What I Mean" command. Putting data in *context* with other data is one way to derive information. Human language abounds with contextual references and implied scopes.

For instance, when you say "It's hot," you probably don't mean "Somewhere in the world the temperature is such that someone might refer to it as hot," or "The global distribution of thermal energy across the planet's surface gives rise to local anomalies, with perception of the relative differences being expressed by the relevant indigenous populations as either 'hot' or 'cold,' and the area to which I now refer is one of the former."

You mean that you're feeling hot right now, regardless of the actual temperature.

The context and scope of your original statement is *implied*; the concomitant associations *derive* from both the context and your knowledge of human behavior in general, and your behavior in particular.

If I searched the Internet for *Hot Babes* (not that I would ever do so), I would be disappointed if I got back pointers to the National Weather Service's reports mingled with articles about infant care. How can search engines figure out what kind of *hot* I mean? Can DWIM ever be achieved?

This question is a *hot* topic—the basis for an ongoing and bitter debate among philologists, linguists, artificial-intelligence theorists, and natural language programmers. There are almost as many sides as there are participants in the debate, and no one view clearly outstrips the rest. If you are interested in this sort of debate, check out the **comp.ai.fuzzy** newsgroup on UseNet, or stop by your local library or favorite online search engine and find references to *AI* and *natural language*.

Much of the following material is adapted from Rod Clark's excellent discussion in *Special Edition Using CGI* (Que Publishing, 1993).

Suppose that a friend mentions a reference to "dogs romping in a field." It could be that what he actually saw, months ago, was the phrase "while three collies merrily romped in an open field." In a very literal search system, searching for "dogs romping" would turn up nothing at all. *Dogs* are not *collies*, and *romping* is not *romped*. But the query "romp field" might yield the exact reference, if the search tool understands *substrings*. A substring is just part of the a string—but figuring out which part is meaningful isn't easy.

People think and remember in imprecise terms. But conventional query syntax follows very precise rules, even for simple queries.

Concept-based engines can effectively find related information even in files that don't contain any of the words that the user specified in a search query. These tools are particularly helpful for large collections of existing documents that were never designed to be searched.

Casual users seldom use the more advanced syntax that sophisticated search tools offer. Concept-based searching offers such users a broad, reasonable search by default. This is much easier for people than phrasing several specific queries and conducting multiple searches for them.

Concept-based search tools might combine several different searching techniques, some of which are described in the following sections. The most general of those techniques is pattern matching, which is used to find similar files.

Thesauri

One way to broaden the reach of a search is to use a *thesaurus*, a separate file that links large numbers of words with lists of their common equivalents. Most thesauri let you add special words and terms, either linked to a dictionary or directly to synonyms. A *thesaurus-based* search engine automatically looks up words related to the terms in your submitted query and then searches for those related words.

Stemming

Some search engines, but by no means all, offer *stemming*. Stemming is trimming a word to its root, and then looking for other words that match the same root. For example, *wallpaper* has *wall* as its root word. So does *wallboard*, which the user might never have entered as a separate query. A stemmed search might serve up unwanted additional references to *wallflower, wallbanger, Wally,* and *walled city*, but would also catch *wall* and *wallboard* when the user entered *wallpaper*, and probably provide useful information that way.

Stemming has at least two advantages over plain substring searching. First, it doesn't require the user to mentally determine and then manually enter the root words. Second, it allows assigning higher relevance scores to results that exactly match the entered query and lower relevance scores to the other stemmed variants.

But stemming is language-specific. Human languages are complex, and a search program can't simply trim English suffixes from words in another language.

Finding Similar Documents

Several newer search engines concentrate on some more general techniques that are not language-based. Some of these tools can analyze a file even if it's in an unknown language or file format and then search for similar files. The key to this kind of search is matching *patterns* within the files instead of matching the contents of the files.

Building specific language rules into a search engine is difficult. What happens when the program encounters documents in a language that it hasn't seen before, for which the programmers haven't included any language rules? There are people who've spent their whole adult lives formally recording the mathematics of the rules for using English and other languages—and they still aren't finished. In our daily experience, we hardly think of those rules, because we've learned them in our everyday, human way—by drawing conclusions from comparing and summing up a great many unconscious, unarticulated pattern-matching events.

Even if you don't know or can't explain the rules for constructing the patterns that you see—whether those patterns are in human language, graphics, or binary code—you can still rank them for similarity. *Yes, this one matches.* Or *No, that one doesn't. This one is very similar, but not exact. This one matches a little. This one is more exact than that one.* To analyze files for content similarity, nearness, and other such qualities, some of the newer search engines look for patterns. Such engines use fuzzy logic and a variety of weighting schemes.

Leveraging Commercial Indexes

Fortunately, you don't have to be a natural-language or artificial-intelligence expert to incorporate indexing into your home page or Web site. Many fine public search engines are available. You link to some and install others. In this section, you learn about some of the more common commercial indexes and how you can use them.

Public indexes are just that—public. They are made available freely by sponsoring corporations, groups, or individuals. Usually a paired set of Web-crawling robots to collect data and a CGI program to search the index, these public indexes are accessed from an HTML form.

You don't have to rely on a list of bookmarks or your browser's setting for a search page. You can make a page of your own that links directly to your favorite search engines. You can even tailor the form so that it comes preloaded with specific search terms. Listing 13.4 shows a generic form for invoking Alta Vista's gigantic search engine. Listing 13.5 shows a modification to restrict the search to one of several predefined terms.

Alta Vista

Alta Vista provides a helpful index of Web sites and newsgroups. You can find Alta Vista at the following address:

http://www.altavista.digital.com

Figure 13.1 shows the Alta Vista Web page.

Figure 13.1

The Alta Vista Web page.

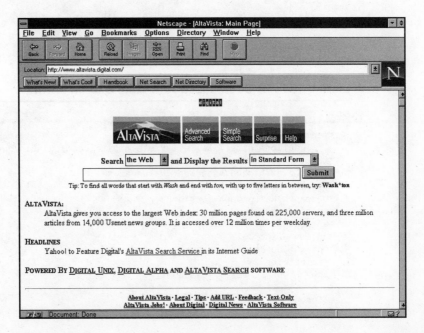

Notice how listing 13.5 takes the same form fields defined in listing 13.4 and hard-codes some of them. The result is that listing 13.5 always searches the newsgroups, and only for *CGI by Example, Using CGI,* or *Que Corporation.*

Note: HTML examples are not provided for the other sites. The concept is the same for each site—you take the HTML used by the site itself to invoke its CGI script, and then modify the HTML to suit your needs.

Listing 13.4 A Generic Alta Vista Search Form

```
<h1>Search Alta Vista</h1>
<form method=get
      action="http://www.altavista.digital.com/cgi-bin/query">
<input type=hidden name=pg value=q>
<B>Search
<select name=what>
<option value=web  SELECTED>the Web
<option value=news >Usenet
</select>
and Display the Results
<select name=fmt>
<option value="." SELECTED>in Standard Form
<option value=c >in Compact Form
<option value=d >in Detailed Form
</select></B>
<input name=q size=55 maxlength=200 value="">
<input type=submit value=Submit>
<br>
</form>
```

Listing 13.5 A Customized Alta Vista Search Form

```
<h1>Search Alta Vista</h1>
<form method=get
      action="http://www.altavista.digital.com/cgi-bin/query">
<input type=hidden name=pg value=q>
<input type=hidden name=what value=news>
<input type=hidden name=fmt value=d>
<b>Search Newsgroups for</b>
<select name=q>
<option>CGI by Example
<option>Using CGI
<option>Que Corporation
</select><br>
<input type=submit value=Submit>
<br>
</form>
```

Infoseek

Infoseek is one of my favorite search engines, because it is fast, usually up, and processes search terms in ways that make sense to me. Figure 13.2 shows Infoseek's Web page.

Figure 13.2

Infoseek's Web site.

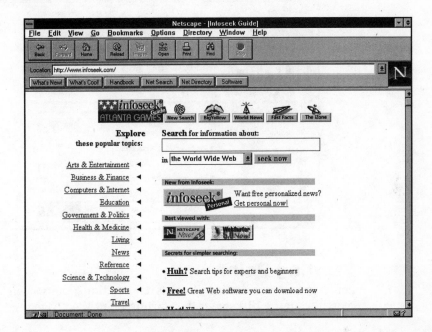

One nice touch is that you don't have to write any HTML at all if you want to include a link to Infoseek's search engine on one of your pages. Simply send a blank e-mail message to **html@infoseek.com**, and 5 to 10 minutes later you'll receive HTML ready to plug into any of your pages.

You can find Infoseek at the following site:

http://www.infoseek.com

Lycos

Lycos also provides HTML by e-mail. Figure 13.3 shows the Lycos Web page.

Stop by **http://www.lycos.com/backlink.html** and fill out the online form. Within a day or so, you'll get back some sample HTML. The backlink service from Lycos enables you to incorporate your own company logo or custom graphics so that visitors see a nicely integrated package.

Lycos is available at the following site:

http://www.lycos.com

Figure 13.3

The Lycos Web site.

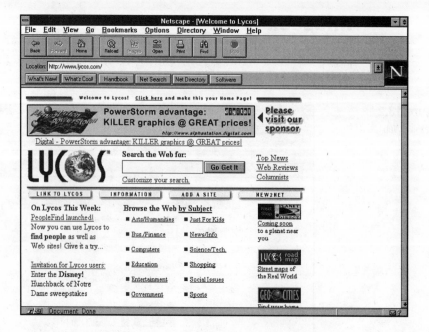

Starting Point

For many users, Starting Point is *the* starting point when they conduct Web searches. Figure 13.4 shows the Starting Point Web page.

Figure 13.4

The Starting Point Web page.

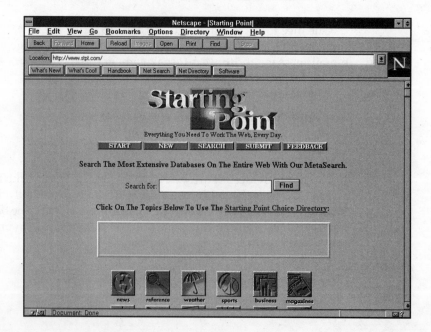

When you visit Starting Point, you can add a link for your site. Starting Point responds in e-mail with suggested HTML for linking your site with the Starting Point site.

You can find Starting Point at the following site:

http://www.stpt.com

Excite

Excite is more than a public index. Excite makes search engines that you can install on your own system, and is working closely with Web server companies to provide integrated solutions. Figure 13.5 shows the Excite Web site, which you can find at the following address:

http://www.excite.com

Figure 13.5

The Excite Web site.

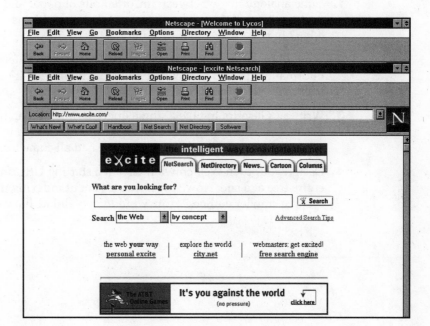

Summary

In this chapter, you learned why indexing is necessary, and saw some of the methods used to deal with the incredible mountain of information on the Internet. In particular, you learned about full-text indexing and fuzzy searches, and saw how your own site can leverage the capabilities of some of the big commercial indexes.

Review Questions

1. Does WAIS provide fuzzy searching capabilities?

2. Would the WAIS search term *Bill AND Ted* retrieve a document discussing the movie *Bill and Ted's Excellent Adventure*?

3. Would the same WAIS search term retrieve a document discussing how to bill customers for teddy bears?

4. Web crawlers, spiders, and worms collect information and store it in databases for later retrieval. What kind of program is usually used to retrieve this information?

Review Exercises

1. Is the analogy made between unsorted bits of paper and unsorted Web documents a valid one? In what ways do the problems resemble each other? In what ways do they differ?

2. Why do large commercial indexes use spiders and other tools to collect information instead of relying on visitors to provide it? Is there a better way to collect information?

3. Write a CGI script to take a single query term and search, in turn, Lycos, Excite, and Alta Vista. Collect the results of the search in your CGI program and present it to the visitor as if it had all come from one source.

4. Design your own Web crawler. Give it a starting URL and have it walk the entire tree at a site. How would you go about indexing the information that the crawler gathers? How would you validate it a week later?

## CHAPTER 14

Indexing Your Own Site

In Chapter 13, "Introduction to Indexing," you learned the theory behind site indexing, and saw some of the large commercial search engines at work. In this chapter, you study two of the smaller indexers and search engines—ones more appropriate for a single site.

Keywords

Before you start studying indexing programs and individual search engines, you need to examine the kinds of information that you can provide for the indexers to index. The examples in this section are drawn from Rod Clark's discussion of indexing in Chapter 11 of *Special Edition Using CGI* (Que Corporation, 1993).

Adding keywords to files is particularly important when using simple search tools, many of which are very literal. These tools need all the help that they can get.

Adding keywords manually to existing files is a slow and tedious process. Doing so isn't particularly practical when you are faced with a blizzard of seldom-read archival documents. However, when you first create new documents that you know people will search online, you can stamp them with an appropriate set of keywords. This stamping (or *keying*) provides a consistent set of words that people can use to search for the material in related texts, in case the exact wording in each text doesn't happen to include some of the relevant general keywords. Using equivalent nontechnical terminology that users are likely to understand also helps.

Sophisticated search engines can yield good results when searching documents with little or no intentional keying. But well-keyed files produce better and more focused results with these search tools. Even the best search engines, when they set out to catch all the random, scattered unkeyed documents that you want to find, return information that's liberally diluted with *noise*—irrelevant data. Keying your files helps keep them from being missed in relevance lists for closely related topics.

Keywords in Plain Text

To help find HTML pages, you can add an inconspicuous line at the bottom of each page that lists the keywords that you want, like this:

```
Poland Czechoslovakia Czech Republic Slovakia Hungary Romania
➡ Rumania
```

This line is useful, but ugly and distracting. Also, many search engines assign a higher relevance to words in titles, headings, emphasized text, `<a name=...>` tags, and other areas that stand out from a document's body. The next few sections consider how to key your files in more sophisticated and effective ways.

Keywords in HTML *META* Tags

You can put more information than simply the page title in an HTML page's `<head>...</head>` section. Specifically, you can include a standard `Keywords` list in a `META` tag. `Keywords` and `Expires` are officially defined components of HTTP headers, which is why they include `HTTP-EQUIV` as part of the statement in the tag.

People sometimes use `META` tags for other, nonstandard information. But search engines often pay particular attention to a `META` `Keywords` list. Here's an example of using the `META` `Keywords` tag within an HTML header:

```
<head>
<META HTTP-EQUIV="Keywords" CONTENT="George, Jungle">
<title>George's Jungle Page</title>
</head>
```

Keywords in HTML Comments

This section presents some lines from an HTML file that lists links to English-language newspapers. (These are just examples, not links to real places.) The lines aren't keyed, so to find a match, you have to enter a query that exactly matches something in either a particular line's URL or its visible text. Such matches are not too likely with some of these example lines. Only one of them comes up in a search for *Sri Lanka*. None of them comes up in a search for *South Asia*, which is the section head just above them in the source file.

```
<b><a href="http://www.lanka.net/lakehouse/anclweb/dailynew
➡ /select.html">Sri Lanka Daily News</a></b><br>

<b><a href="http://www.is.lk/is/times/index.html">Sunday Times
➡ </a></b><br>
```

```
<b><a href="http://www.is.lk/is/island/index.html">Sunday Island<
➥ /a></b><br>

<b><a href="http://www.powertech.no/~jeyaramk/insrep/">
➥ Inside Report: Tamil Eelam News Review</a></b><i> -
➥ monthly</i><br>
```

To improve the search results, you can key each line with one or more likely keywords. The keywords can be contained within `<!--comments -->`, in `<a name=...>` statements or in ordinary visible text. Some of these approaches are more successful than others. The following are examples of each.

First, add some keywords as HTML comments on each line. The following example already looks better. (Again, these are examples, not real URLs.)

```
<!--South Asia Sri Lanka --><b><a href="http://www.lanka.net
➥ /lakehouse/anclweb/dailynew/select.html">
➥ Sri Lanka Daily News</a></b><br>

<!--South Asia Sri Lanka --><b><a href="http://www.is.lk/is
➥ /times/index.html">Sunday Times</a></b><br>

<!--South Asia Sri Lanka --><b><a href="http://www.is.lk/is
➥ /island/index.html">Sunday Island</a></b><br>

<!--South Asia Sri Lanka --><b><a href="http://www.powertech.no
➥ /~jeyaramk/insrep/">Inside Report: Tamil Eelam News Review
➥ </a></b><i> - monthly</i><br>
```

You could put the keywords in `<a name=...>` statements, too, but HTML prohibits spaces in `<a name=...>` statements. Therefore, keys in an `<a name=...>` statement are limited to single keywords rather than phrases. This *might* suffice if you can always be sure of using an AND or OR search instead of searching for exact phrases. But many scripts don't support Boolean operators, and, even when Booleans are allowed, most users don't use them. So, overall, using `<a name=...>` statements for keying isn't the best choice. Nevertheless, here is an example of using an `<a name=...>` statement to provide a keyword:

```
<a name="Tamil">
```

SWISH (Simple Web Indexing System for Humans)

SWISH is easy to set up, and offers fast, reliable searching for Web sites. Kevin Hughes wrote the program in C for UNIX Web servers. SWISH is freeware, available from EIT, from the following site:

http://www.eit.com/goodies/software/swish/swish.html

You can download SWISH's source code from EIT's FTP site and compile it on your own system:

http://www.eit.com/software/swish/

Installing SWISH is straightforward. After uncompressing and untarring the source files, you edit the SRC/CONFIG.H file and compile SWISH for your system.

Configuring SWISH isn't very hard. You set up a configuration file, SWISH.CONF, which the indexer uses. Listing 14.1 shows a sample SWISH configuration file.

Listing 14.1   SWISH.CONF—a Sample SWISH Configuration File

```
# SWISH configuration file

IndexDir /home/rclark/public_html/
# This is a space-separated list of files and directories you
# want indexed. You can specify more than one of these directives.

IndexFile index.swish
# This is what the generated index file will be.

IndexName "Index of Small Hours files"
IndexDescription "General index of the Small Hours Web site"
IndexPointer "http://www.aa.net/~rclark/"
IndexAdmin "Rod Clark (rclark@aa.net)"
# Extra information you can include in the index file.

IndexOnly .html .txt .gif .xbm .jpg
# Only files with these suffixes will be indexed.

IndexReport 3
# This is how detailed you want reporting. You can specify numbers
# 0 to 3 - 0 is totally silent, 3 is the most verbose.

FollowSymLinks yes
# Put "yes" to follow symbolic links in indexing, else "no".

NoContents .gif .xbm .jpg
# Files with these suffixes will not have their contents indexed -
# only their file names will be indexed.

ReplaceRules replace "/home/rclark/public_html/"
➥ "http://www.aa.net/~rclark/"
# ReplaceRules allow you to make changes to file path names
# before they're indexed.

FileRules pathname contains test newsmap
FileRules filename is index.html rename chk 1st bit
FileRules filename contains ~ .bak .orig .000 .001 .old old. .map
➥ .cgi .bit .test test log- .log
FileRules title contains test Test
```

```
FileRules directory contains .htaccess
# Files matching the above criteria will *not* be indexed.

IgnoreLimit 80 50
# This automatically omits words that appear too often in the files
# (these words are called stopwords). Specify a whole percentage
# and a number, such as "80 256". This omits words that occur in
# over 80% of the files and appear in over 256 files. Comment out
# to turn off autostopwording.

IgnoreWords SwishDefault

# The IgnoreWords option allows you to specify words to ignore.
# Comment out for no stopwords; the word "SwishDefault" will
# include a list of default stopwords. Words should be separated
# by spaces and may span multiple directives.
```

After setting SWISH up the way that you want for your site, create the indexes by running SWISH from the command line:

```
swish -c swish.conf
```

You can use cron to update the indexes regularly, or just run the job manually when needed. Now that you have your indexes, you need some CGI to access them. You can use the WWWWAIS gateway, also available from EIT (**http://www.eit.com/ software/wwwwais/**) or you can create your own script using the WWWWAIS gateway as your model. Figure 14.1 shows the results of a search using the WWWWAIS gateway.

Figure 14.1

The results of a search using the WWWWAIS gateway against a SWISH index at EIT. Notice that the results are ranked in order of relevance and file size.

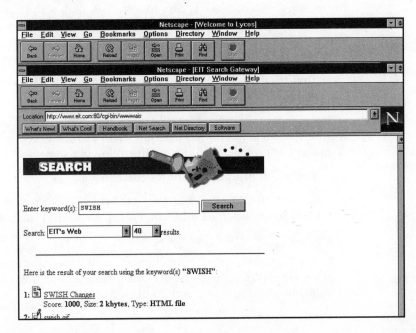

freeWAIS

Chapter 13, "Introduction to Indexing," introduced you to Wide-Area Information Systems (WAIS, pronounced *ways*). Pretty much any time that you encounter a discussion of WAIS on the Internet, *freeWAIS* is also mentioned. The term freeWAIS is fairly self-explanatory—it's a freeware version of the WAIS. Much of the material in this section is adapted directly from Bill Schongar's comprehensive discussion of WAIS in Chapter 12 of *Special Edition Using CGI* (Que Corporation, 1993).

freeWAIS on UNIX

Most WAIS tools are still primarily designed for use on UNIX servers. These tools include the servers themselves as well as the client scripts. So it only makes sense that one of the most significant public extensions to original WAIS functions showed up on UNIX servers first. *freeWAIS-SF,* designed by the University of Dortmund, Germany, takes advantage of built-in document structures to make more sense out of queries. It even enables you to specify your own document types for its use.

In addition, freeWAIS-SF piles more power at your fingertips for searching the way that you want to search. Wild cards, "sounds-like" searches, and more conditions for what matches and what doesn't are all components that make finding what you're looking for much less painful. You no longer have to worry about whether the author wrote *Color* or *Colour, Center* or *Centre.*

Unlike many things that you use with your server, especially in the UNIX world, the freeWAIS-SF package is easy to install. A shell script leads you through basic configuration by asking questions; when you finish answering the questions, you're finished installing freeWAIS-SF.

You can obtain the freeWAIS-SF package at the following site:

> **ftp://ftp.germany.eu.net/pub/infosystems/wais/Unido-**
> **➡ LS6/freeWAIS-sf-2.0/freeWAIS-sf-2.0.65.tar.gz**

If you want the original freeWAIS instead, which you can certainly use, you'll want to get it from CNDIR. To get the main distribution directory so that you can choose the appropriate build, visit the following site:

> **ftp://cnidr.org/pub/NIDR.tools/freewais/**

Whichever freeWAIS build you get will be a tarred and GNUZIPped file. Therefore, to unpack the build, you enter a command such as the following:

```
gunzip -c freeWAIS-0.X-whatever.tar.gz | tar xvf -
```

freeWAIS comes with its own longer set of installation instructions within the distribution, so double-check the latest information for the build that you've obtained to make sure that you don't skip any steps.

freeWAIS on Windows NT

A port of freeWAIS 0.3 is available for Windows NT from EMWAC (the European Microsoft Windows Academic Center) in its WAIS Toolkit. EMWAC's current version of the toolkit is 0.7, but when you're ready to obtain the toolkit, you'll want to check with EMWAC to see what its latest version is. Versions are available for all flavors of Windows NT: 386-based, Alpha, and Power PC. You can obtain the toolkit from the following site:

ftp://emwac.ed.ac.uk/pub/waistool/

After obtaining the ZIP file, decompress it to get the six files that comprise the distribution. Move them to an NTFS drive partition and then rename the file WAISINDX.EXE to WAISINDEX.EXE.

If you plan to use the entire WAIS Toolkit with your server, put all three .EXE programs into the %SYSTEMROOT%\SYSTEM32 directory (which is usually C:\WINNT35\SYSTEM32).

Tip: UNIX flavors of WAIS use a program called WAISQ to query the WAIS indexes. The query tool provided for Windows NT is called WAISLOOK. Keep this in mind when you see references to WAISQ, and simply substitute WAISLOOK if you are using Windows NT.

Building a WAIS Database

Now that you have the software installed and running, you're ready to make a database (a set of index files).

The WAISINDEX program looks through your files and creates an index that the WAIS query tool can use later. This index consists of seven distinct files that are either binary or plain text, as shown in table 14.1.

Table 14.1   WAIS index database files

File Extension	Purpose	File Type
.CAT	A catalog of indexed files with a few lines of information about each one.	Text
.DCT	A dictionary of indexed words.	Binary
.DOC	A document table.	Binary
.FN	A file name table.	Binary

continues

Table 14.1 Continued

File Extension	Purpose	File Type
.HL	A headline table, featuring the descriptive text used to identify documents that the search returns.	Binary
.INV	An inverted file index.	Binary
.SRC	A structure for describing the source. The structure includes the creation date and other similar information.	Text

The files with the extensions listed in table 14.1 all share the same first name, as in INDEX.CAT, INDEX.DCT, INDEX.DOC, and so on. You can name the first file anything you want, but if the file containing the HTML for the search form is called INDEX.HTML, then INDEX is what you should use for the database. If your HTML file is called DEFAULT.HTM (as it would be using EMWAC's HTTP server), the DEFAULT is the correct first name for your database.

> **Tip:** Many Web servers have built-in support for WAIS databases, and determine which files to look at by matching the first name of the HTML file with the first name of the database files. Therefore, naming your database files correctly is important if you expect the built-in support to function.

The command-line options that you use when executing WAISINDEX determines these database files' contents. There are a variety of different options that you might want to use, depending on your objective and the nature of the files that you want to index. The following is a simple command line to create an index:

```
waisindex -d Data\database1 Data\*.html
```

This command line uses only one option, the -d switch, which specifies that the next argument is the name that you want to give the index. The preceding command specifies that the name is DATABASE1, and that the database is to reside in the DATA directory. Arguments following the switches are the file names to index. In this example, the command indexes all the HTML files (those with an .HTML extension) in the DATA directory.

One of the more powerful features of WAISINDEX is that it enables you to index a variety of file types. To find out exactly which file types your version supports, check your version's documentation. The versions of WAISINDEX vary in the file type support that they offer. In particular, freeWAIS-SF enables you to specify your own document types, and the EMWAC Toolkit supports such formats as Microsoft's Knowledge Base.

Accessing the WAIS Database

If your Web server has built-in support for WAIS (as many Web servers do), accessing the WAIS database is quite simple. You just create an HTML file to make the query, and put the file in the same directory as the WAIS database files. (Remember that the first names of the HTML file and the database files must match.)

The HTML itself couldn't be simpler. Listing 14.2 shows a sample. All you have to do is include an `<isindex>` tag somewhere on the form, and the Web server does the rest.

Listing 14.2   a Sample WAIS Search HTML

```
<head>
<title>Sample WAIS Search</title>
</head>
<body>
<h1>Sample WAIS Search</h1>
This page has a built-in index.  Give it a whirl!
<p>
<isindex>
</body>
</html>
```

If your Web server doesn't support WAIS directly, you must use a CGI script to access the data. You might also want to use a script when you need to format the output or filter the input.

Your script must gather data from a fill-in form and run a query against the WAIS index, then format the data appropriately for the visitor.

You can have your script do exactly as Web servers that support WAIS directly: Call the WAISQ (or WAISLOOK) program. You can test this call from the command line:

```
waisq -d -http Data\database1 stuff
```

In this simple example, you run a query against the DATA\DATABASE1 index files, using stuff as the query term. The result returns to STDOUT as properly formatted HTML code, which makes the result perfect for use in a CGI script.

WAIS is so popular that dozens of scripts are available in the public domain for managing your queries. Here are the three most generic and useful scripts:

♦ WAIS.PL

   ftp://ftp.ncsa.uiuc.edu/Web/httpd/Unix/ncsa_httpd/cgi/ /wais.tar.Z

♦ Son-of-WAIS.PL

   http://dewey.lib.ncsu.edu/staff/morgan/son-of-wais.html

♦ Kid-of-WAIS.PL

   http://www.cso.uiuc.edu/grady.html

Summary

In this chapter, you learned how to include keywords and phrases within your files so that no matter what kind of indexing you use, your files will be indexed accurately and completely. You also learned how to install and configure a popular UNIX-based indexer/search engine, SWISH, and a platform-independent indexer/search engine, freeWAIS.

Review Questions

1. Will any search engines find keywords and terms inserted into your HTML documents as plain text, without any special markers or tags?

2. What kind of search engine/indexer would be affected by finding a word repeated over and over (a thousand times, for example) in a document?

3. Although many indexers give a higher priority to terms found within an `<a name=...>` tag, why can't you use this feature to index phrases?

4. What is the name of the SWISH configuration file?

5. Which files in a WAIS index database are text-based?

Review Exercises

1. Write a CGI script in C or Perl to read the data from a fill-in form and query a WAIS index. How would you go about parsing the output without using the `-http` switch?

2. Build a practice WAIS index that looks at GIF files only, and catalogs only the *names* of the files.

3. Build a practice WAIS index that looks at both GIF files and HTML files, and catalogs the names of the GIF files but the contents of the HTML files.

4. Design on paper your own ideal cataloging engine. What features would you include? How would it operate? How would you configure it for different servers and different environments?

Part VI

Server Administration Issues

## CHAPTER 15

Enabling and Configuring Servers To Use CGI

Before you can start waving around the magic wand of CGI, you need to get things straight with your fairy godmother—the Web server itself.

If you aren't your site's Webmaster, you can probably skip this chapter; it explains how to configure Web servers to allow CGI. If you are your site's Webmaster, however, and don't already know how to turn CGI on and off, or how to limit its scope on your server, you need the information in this chapter, which includes the following:

♦ Understanding key terms and concepts

♦ Configuring UNIX servers

♦ Configuring Windows NT servers

Caution: See Chapter 17, "Security Issues," for a discussion of security problems and risks associated with enabling CGI on a Web server. *Don't* ignore security issues, thinking that you are immune from security problems. They can (and do) happen to anyone.

Key Terms and Concepts

A Web server's *document root* is the directory defined as the main directory for that particular Web server. Documents in the Web server's document root are referenced with URLs such as the following example:

http://www.your.server.com/index.html

where INDEX.HTML is a file that resides within the document root of WWW.YOUR.SERVER.COM. On a UNIX system, the real directory might be something like /USR/LOCAL/ETC/HTTPD/HTDOCS, so the file's full path and name would be /USR/LOCAL/ETC/HTTPD/HTDOCS/INDEX.HTML.

Files and directories living under the document root are said to be in the *document tree*. Altogether, the document tree consists of all the documents—living either in the document root or in directories under it—that your Web server can reach.

There are some exceptions. In particular, you can expand the document tree to include directories living elsewhere on the server, or even on other servers, through redirection, aliases, UNC (Universal Naming Convention) paths, and other techniques. Usually, however, the document tree consists of the document root and everything below it.

Other files and directories on the Web server are *relative* to the document root. For instance, on a Windows NT system, if your Web server's document root is C:\PROGRAM FILES\WEB SERVER\DOCUMENTS\ and the URL that you are accessing is **http://www.your.server.com/faqs/config/cgi.html**, the Web server fetches C:\PROGRAM FILES\WEB SERVER\DOCUMENTS\FAQS\CONFIG\ CGI.HTML. Notice that the URL shows two directory levels after the root—**/faqs/ config/**—and that the Web server concatenates this path to the document root to determine the actual path.

This chapter refers to your Web server's document root as %DOCUMENT-ROOT%. Whenever you see %document-root% in an example, replace it with the name of your Web server's actual document root.

Web servers usually have a *scripts* directory, too. Again, this is a physical directory living on the Web server, and is almost always relative to the document root, usually one level away.

The following are common locations and names for the scripts directory:

- ◆ %DOCUMENT-ROOT%/CGI-BIN

- ◆ %DOCUMENT-ROOT%/CGI-WIN

- ◆ %DOCUMENT-ROOT%/CGI-DOS

- ◆ %DOCUMENT-ROOT%/CGI

- ◆ /USR/LOCAL/ETC/SCRIPTS/CGI-BIN

- ◆ %DOCUMENT-ROOT%/SCRIPTS

Note that the fifth example has a SCRIPTS directory that is not relative to the document root.

This chapter refers to the SCRIPTS directory as CGI-BIN, because this name is the most common. When you see CGI-BIN as part of a path, replace it with the correct name for your particular Web server. Note that quite often, CGI-BIN is just an alias for another directory somewhere else. Even though you form URLs by using CGI-BIN as a directory relative to the document root, the directory might in fact reside elsewhere.

> **Tip:** Some Web servers let you put the SCRIPTS directory anywhere you want and then set up an alias for it. Some servers *require* an alias. Others use the real directory name—CGI-BIN—and do not enable you to configure them differently. An *alias* is just a directory name that refers to another directory somewhere else.
>
> Aliasing enables you to put the real CGI-BIN directory somewhere safe, while still letting URLs be formed like **%document-root%/cgi-bin/someprogram.exe**. When the request references a file in the aliased /CGI-BIN directory, the Web server substitutes the actual path for the real CGI-BIN directory, wherever it might be.

Configuring UNIX Servers To Allow CGI

At first glance, Web servers running on UNIX seem to have fussy and complex configuration files, with needlessly obscure syntax and obtuse options. At second glance, they're even worse.

On the whole, UNIX Web servers fall into three main categories: NCSA, CERN, and those that are compatible with NCSA or CERN. (NCSA stands for National Center for Supercomputer Applications. The Web server designed by NCSA is called the NCSA server. CERN is the European Laboratory for Particle Physics, the birthplace of the World Wide Web. The CERN server was the first of its kind.) All of them are configured through text files. Making entries in these configuration files is a bit like praying: You try to use all the right words, and you put your heart into it, but the mechanism is a bit murky, and you're not convinced there's much cause and effect going on. You make up for your uncertainty with renewed determination and perhaps an anonymous gift to the local orphanage. Then you dust off your knees, start up the server again, and hope that you get something similar to what you sought.

Don't panic! The process isn't as bad as it seems. There's nothing that six cups of coffee, three dog-eared manuals, two aspirins, and this section won't get you through.

HTTPD from NCSA

Get a sticky note and write down this URL:

http://hoohoo.ncsa.uiuc.edu/docs/setup/Configure.html

This site explains all the NCSA configuration files and provides the latest updates. The site also provides several helpful online tutorials and samples.

To enable CGI on your NCSA server, you must modify two files: the Server Resource Map file, (usually %DOCUMENT-ROOT%/CONF/SRM.CONF) and the Access file (usually %DOCUMENT-ROOT%/CONF/ACCESS.CONF).

The SRM.CONF File

You have two choices in the SRM.CONF file: CGI by file type or CGI by location. If you enable CGI by file type, scripts can reside anywhere in the document tree (a situation that poses a security risk). If you enable CGI by location, scripts are treated as scripts only if they reside in the proper place.

Using the AddType directive, you can enable CGI by specifying the extension marking a script. For example, if you add the following line to your SRM.CONF file, any executable files with the extensions .CGI, .SH, or .PL execute as scripts:

```
AddType application/x-httpd-cgi .cgi .sh .pl
```

.SH refers to a Bourne shell script, .PL to a Perl script, and .CGI to a binary executable.

Using the ScriptAlias directive, you can enable CGI by specifying the directory in which CGI scripts must reside. Executables found on the document tree that aren't in this directory do not execute. This directive provides the most secure way to run your server, because controlling one directory is easier than controlling a dozen or a hundred. If you add the following line to your SRM.CONF file, any executables (of whatever kind) found in the /USR/LOCAL/ETC/HTTPD/CGI-BIN directory execute in response to a request referencing /CGI-BIN:

```
ScriptAlias /cgi-bin/ /usr/local/etc/httpd/cgi-bin/
```

The first parameter to the ScriptAlias directive is the alias name; the second is the definition of that alias. You could just as easily write the line as follows:

```
ScriptAlias /cgi-bin/ /usr/bin/scripts/httpd/
```

Then references to /CGI-BIN/ are instead pulled from /USR/BIN/SCRIPTS/HTTPD.

The ACCESS.CONF File

ACCESS.CONF enables you to set global limitations on how each directory under the document root gets accessed. Listing 15.1 shows a sample ACCESS.CONF file.

Listing 15.1   A Sample ACCESS.CONF File for NCSA HTTPD

```
<Directory /usr/local/etc/httpd/cgi-bin>
Options Indexes ExecCGI
</Directory>

<Directory /usr/local/etc/httpd/htdocs>
Options Indexes FollowSymLinks
<Limit GET>
order allow,deny
allow from all
</Limit>
</Directory>
```

The first line in listing 15.1, `<Directory /usr/local/etc/httpd/cgi-bin>`, is the opening directive. This directive tells the server that everything between it and the closing directive, `</Directory>`, applies to the directory /USR/LOCAL/ETC/ HTTPD/CGI-BIN. Note that this aspect of ACCESS.CONF's syntax is similar to that of HTML.

Nestled between the `<Directory...>` and `</Directory>` directives is an `Options` directive. This directive is where you actually turn CGI on or off for the referenced directory. `Options Indexes ExecCGI` specifies that both `Indexes` (displaying the contents of the directory) and `ExecCGI` (executing CGI scripts) are allowed in this directory. To turn off `ExecCGI`, just remove the word `ExecCGI` from the line.

The second directory, /USR/LOCAL/ETC/HTTP/HTDOCS, shows some other directives that help control access to the main document directory.

The line `Options Indexes FollowSymLinks` tells the server that indexing is allowed, as is the capability to follow symbolic links. Therefore, this line specifies that files residing outside your document root can be accessed. A *symbolic link* is a pointer file, like an alias, that points to a file that resides somewhere else. Such links are often convenient for referencing a directory or file from more than one location. For example, some Webmasters put symbolic links for each user within the Web server's document root.

> **Caution:** Be careful when you enable symbolic links with the `FollowSymLinks` directive. This powerful and far-reaching capability can lead to security holes. For instance, a user might link an innocuous-sounding name like `fluffy` to the `rm` command, then execute `fluffy -rf`.

The opening directive `<Limit GET>` sets the limit for how the GET method is allowed in the directory. With HTTPD, the options to the `<Limit>` directive are GET, POST, and PUT (although HTTPD doesn't yet implement PUT).

The statements between `<Limit...>` and `</Limit>` are called *subdirectives*. Subdirectives enable you to control which sites can access your pages. The line order allow,deny tells the server to parse the allow line before looking at the deny line. The next line, allow from all, tells the server to allow all sites to access the pages within that directory.

HTTP (W3C) from CERN

The CERN server is pretty easy to set up. It has two scripting interfaces—one left over from a proprietary scheme, and the more modern, standards-based CGI interface. This section doesn't discuss the proprietary scheme, and you shouldn't use it.

To enable CGI on HTTP, edit the /ETC/HTTP.CONF file. To turn on CGI, you add an Exec directive such as the following:

```
Exec /cgi-bin/* /usr/local/web/cgi-bin/*
```

The first parameter, /cgi-bin/*, is the alias for the CGI-BIN directory. You can call the alias anything you want, but CGI-BIN is the convention. The asterisk at the end of the parameter calls for any reference to the alias. The second parameter is the actual path for the script files. In the preceding example, the path is /USR/LOCAL/WEB/CGI-BIN—again, a very conventional path. When the server sees a request for /CGI-BIN/FOO.PL, it will actually look for /USR/LOCAL/WEB/CGI-BIN/FOO.PL.

It's hard to say anything negative about HTTP's CGI configuration. It's clean, simple, and logical. The only tricky part is remembering the asterisk.

Configuring Windows NT Servers To Allow CGI

Web servers running on Windows NT (and often Windows 95) are fairly easy to configure. You almost always find a sensible configuration screen, often a Control Panel applet, that enables you to set your server options without once mucking around with configuration files and their obscure, finicky syntax.

The ease of configuration is both good and bad. As any system administrator or support desk worker knows, the Windows GUI interface has done more than any other to empower the user. Things that used to require a couple of years' experience and a reference manual can now be accomplished by a complete novice, just by selecting something from a drop-down list and running a wizard.

Unfortunately, the ease with which you can configure Windows NT servers also empowers the user to screw up worse than ever before. The phenomenon also has an odd side effect: Because some complex configuration tasks are quite easy to accomplish, the user begins to believe that *everything* should be easy to accomplish. If something doesn't work, the user seldom assumes the blame, but instead suspects that the application is broken, that the help screen doesn't explain things properly, that the documentation is wrong, or that some other convenient scapegoat is to blame. Worse yet, sometimes the user can't tell which tasks are complex and which are simple, because the interface can hide the complexity.

This state of affairs, while perhaps inevitable, becomes awkward in truly complex situations because no matter how friendly the interface, the user must make intelligent, informed decisions to accomplish the task. A Web server is a very complex beast indeed, and is hardly an end-user application. Yet many novice Webmasters blithely assume that they can set up a Web server without the slightest understanding of directory paths, file-naming schemes, drives and volumes, pipes, redirection, command-line arguments, 16- versus 32-bitness, inheritance, security contexts, user privileges, or even the difference between an application and a utility.

If you *do* understand these concepts, setting up a Web server on Windows NT is like falling off a log. You have to *try* to get it wrong, and you probably can't. If these concepts sound like technical gobbledygook to you, you're in for a lot of trouble.

A beginner's book on CGI is not the place to learn about your operating system. Magical answers that make everything work are beyond this book's scope. However, if you want tips and pointers for setting up CGI on your NT server, read on. This section covers the most common Windows NT Web servers, and informs you of any known pitfalls or features.

HTTPS from EMWAC

The European Microsoft Windows NT Academic Consortium (EMWAC) produces a fine little 32-bit Web server called HTTPS. Many sites start with EMWAC and then move on as their needs expand beyond HTTPS's capabilities, or as their concerns about security mature.

Configuring HTTPS to use CGI couldn't be easier: You can't turn it off. HTTPS treats any .EXE file in the document tree as a CGI script. HTTPS doesn't recognize a CGI-BIN directory, and tries to execute any .EXE file that it finds, as long as anything points to it using a `<form...>` tag or a plain `<a href...>` link.

CGI scripts on HTTPS must have the last name .EXE and must be 32-bit console mode programs.

You can download HTTPS (which is freeware) from the following site:

ftp://emwac.ed.ac.uk/html/internet_toolchest/https/software.htm

IIS from Microsoft

Microsoft didn't do a good job of documenting the steps for enabling CGI on IIS, so most beginners end up quite frustrated. However, getting the IIS to use CGI is actually pretty simple.

Follow these steps to enable CGI on IIS:

1. Launch the Internet Service Manager.

2. Select WWW Service from the list.

3. Open the Properties menu and choose the Service Properties command.

4. Click the Directories tab.

5. Choose the Add button.

6. Add the full path to your CGI-BIN directory (that is, C:\WEBFILES\SCRIPTS or whatever other path you're using).

7. Use /SCRIPTS or /CGI-BIN as the directory alias.

8. Select the Execute check box to enable execution from this directory.

9. Choose OK to save your changes.

10. Put your CGI programs in the directory C:\WEBFILES\SCRIPTS and refer to them in your HTML as /SCRIPTS/SOMEPROGRAM.EXE or /CGI-BIN/SOMEPROGRAM.EXE, depending on the alias that you chose. Of course, you must adjust these references to use the real directory name on your server (step 6) and the correct directory alias that you've set up (step 7).

In addition, your CGI scripts probably need read access to the following directories and the files in them:

♦ %SYSTEMROOT%\SYSTEM (usually C:\WINNT35\SYSTEM)

♦ %SYSTEMROOT%\SYSTEM32 (usually C:\WINNT35\SYSTEM32)

If your CGI scripts call DLLs, OLE servers, or are VB-based, they almost certainly will need change rights to your temporary directory (usually C:\TEMP).

If any of your CGI scripts create output files (logs, counters, and so on), you must provide change rights to the CGI-BIN directory, and read rights to the document root.

Under IIS, CGI scripts run in the security context of the user account that you created during installation, not in the security context of the Web server itself. This user account is usually called IIS_USER (or something similar). Using File Manager, open the Security menu and choose Permissions to adjust access rights for the IIS user account.

You can download IIS from the following site:

http://www.iis.digital.com/infoserv/

IIS is freeware. It requires NT Server 3.51 with Service Pack 3 or later.

WebSite from O'Reilly

WebSite recognizes three kinds of CGI scripts: Windows CGI (CGI-WIN), Standard CGI, and DOS CGI.

WIN-CGI is O'Reilly's proprietary scheme for doing CGI using .INI files rather than environment variables and STDIO (that is, STDIN and STDOUT).

Standard CGI is for CGI scripts that conform to the CGI 1.3 specification and that use environment variables and STDIO to communicate with the server.

DOS-CGI is another O'Reilly proprietary scheme, reserved for the Windows version of shell scripts—the batch file.

WebSite determines how to launch each type of CGI script and configures the proper environment for it, based on the directory in which the script resides. You set up an alias for each directory—usually /CGI-WIN for Windows CGI, /CGI-BIN for Standard CGI, and /CGI-DOS for DOS CGI.

To set up CGI on WebSite, start the Server Properties applet and click the Mapping tab. In the List Selector box, click Windows CGI, Standard CGI, and DOS CGI, one at a time, modifying whatever you want to modify for each type of CGI.

In the CGI URL Path list box, select each entry in turn. After you do so, the entry appears in the CGI URL Path and Directory text boxes. The CGI URL Path text box specifies the alias that you want to use; the Directory text specifies the actual directory path—either a full path or a path relative to the document root. Use forward slashes for the alias, and backslashes for the directory path.

You can download WebSite 1.1e (which is freeware) from the following site:

http://www.ora.com

Purveyor from Process Software

Purveyor lets you turn CGI on or off, and lets you specify the name of the CGI-BIN directory, which is always relative to the document root.

To configure Purveyor, open Control Panel and double-click the Purveyor applet's icon. Click the Virtual Servers tab to display a list of all the virtual servers installed. The first server (and perhaps the only server) is always Default.

In the Virtual Servers list box, highlight the server that you want to configure. Select the Disable CGI Execution check box to turn off CGI scripts, or deselect the check box to turn on CGI scripts. In the CGI Script Directory text box, enter the name of the CGI-BIN directory. This entry should *not* be an alias, but the actual name of a directory that you want to create immediately below the document root. Scripts with the extension .EXE that reside in this directory are treated as CGI scripts; executables elsewhere are not.

After making any changes to the CGI setup, choose the Set button before clicking OK. A confirmation box then warns you that the virtual server name is already listed. This warning just indicates that you're modifying an existing server definition instead of creating a new one. The confirmation box asks whether you want to continue. Choose Yes.

You can download Purveyor from the following site:

http://www.process.com/purchase/evaluate.htp

There's no charge for an evaluation copy.

Summary

In this chapter, you learned how to enable CGI on six of the most common Web servers. You also learned about some of the fundamental concepts used in Web server configuration: the document root, the CGI-BIN directory, relative paths, aliasing, and symbolic links.

## CHAPTER 16

Server-Side Includes

Most Web servers enable you to add such information as the date or the last time that a file was modified. Such servers also often enable you to add the information from CGI scripts or even the results of a shell command within an HTML document. To incorporate the results of queries, and the output of CGI scripts within the Web page, you use a function within your Web server called Server-Side Includes (SSI).

With SSI, you can add special tags within your HTML documents. The server executes these tags as subprocesses. The HTML document then displays the information that these subprocesses provide. Before the advent of SSI, developers had to create a script to generate a Web page to display information such as the date; with SSI, you can do so by inserting only one line within your HTML document.

In this chapter, you learn how to activate SSI. The chapter also explains how to use the SSI tag, which commands are available, and finally how to use SSI to execute shell commands and CGI scripts.

Activating SSI

Not every Web server lets you use SSI, so you have to check whether your server does. The following is a list of some of the most popular Web servers and their home pages. These servers can use Server-Side Includes:

♦ NCSA HTTPd 1.5 (UNIX), at **http://hoohoo.ncsa.uiuc.edu/**

(You can find this server on the companion CD-ROM.)

♦ Apache 1.1 (UNIX), at **http://www.apache.org/**

(You can find this server on the companion CD-ROM.)

- ◆ WebQuest 2.1 (Windows NT and Windows 95), at **http://www.questar.com/**

- ◆ NetScape Communications/Commerce Server (UNIX and Windows NT), at **http://www.netscape.com/**

- ◆ Purveyor 1.2 (Windows NT and Windows 95), at **http://www.process.com**

- ◆ WebSite Pro or 1.1 (Windows NT), at **http://www.ora.com/**

SSI doesn't have an official standard, so you most likely will come across different versions of SSI. For example, you can use XSSI, which is available for the Apache server, or SSI+, which is available for the WebQuest Windows NT and Windows 95 server. Both of these versions vary a little from the original SSI, but for the most part, they work the same. They have few additional elements that are unavailable in the original NCSA SSI specification. You can find out more information about XSSI at the following address:

http://pageplus.com/~hsf/xssi/

You can find further information on SSI+, which is available for the WebQuest Windows NT and Windows 95 server, at the following site:

http://www.questar.com/ssiplus.htm

Although every server is a bit different, this section discusses how to activate SSI on the NCSA server. Before doing so, you need to make two decisions:

- ◆ Where to allow use of SSI

- ◆ Which file name extension you want the server to recognize as a parsed file

You might not want to allow the use of SSI in a user's home directories. Using SSI, a user could accidentally or even purposely provide confidential information about your system. (For example, the user might display your /usr/passwd file to the whole world.) You also must decide which directories you want to allow use of the exec command. This command, as you'll learn later, enables users to execute scripts as well as shell programs. You can control which directories can use SSI by editing the ACCESS.CONF file.

ACCESS.CONF enables you to control access to your files and directories. You can also control what can happen in each of those directories. By specifying which directories can do what, you can control access to certain areas of your Web server. Here's an example of an entry in the ACCESS.CONF file:

```
<Directory /usr/local/etc/httpd/htdocs>
Options Includes
<Limit GET POST>
order allow,deny
allow from all
</Limit>
</Directory>
```

The `<Directory>` tag enables you to specify the directory in which you want to control access. In the preceding example, you are controlling the directory HTDOCS. You can use as many `<Directory>` tags as you want. The `Options` directive is the line that you want to edit to allow the use of SSI. The following `Options` concern SSI:

♦ `Includes` enables all SSI options.

♦ `ExecCGI` allows the execution of CGI scripts, but not the execution of shell commands.

♦ `IncludesNOEXEC` allows all SSI options except for CGI scripts and shell programs.

A parsed file is a document that the script executes. The file can be an HTML document as well as a script. Normally scripts have the extensions .CGI or .PL, and you can have the server recognize these extensions by editing your SRM.CONF file using the `AddType` directive. You also can parse every file with the extension .HTML, but doing so imposes a heavy load on the system, particularly if you have a busy site. The best alternative is to use the extension .SHTML to distinguish the HTML files that you don't want to parse from those that you want to parse. To do so, you can edit your SRM.CONF file by specifying the following:

```
AddType text/x-server-parsed-html .shtml
```

However, if you aren't worried about the system load and want to parse .HTML files, you can use the following line, which configures the server to parse both types:

```
AddType text/x-server-parsed-html .html .shtml
```

The NCSA server also enables you to use a file called .HTACCESS. This file is much like the ACCESS.CONF file, except that you place the .HTACCESS file in each directory that you want to control. You don't need the `<Directory>` tag, because the .HTACCESS file only places limits on the directory in which it resides. Also, if you use the .HTACCESS file, you don't have to restart the server to enable it to recognize a change within the file.

For more information on the NCSA server's configuration files, visit the following site:

http://hoohoo.ncsa.uiuc.edu/

The SSI Format

After configuring your server to use SSI, you can include the SSI tags within your documents. The SSI tags are formatted as Standard Generalized Markup Language (SGML) comments (see Chapter 1, "The World Wide Web," for more information on SGML). In fact, except for the exclamation mark, SSI tags are the same as a comment tag. By using SGML comments, you ensure that you don't display your SSI command's contents to the visitor unparsed.

> **Note:** Unlike with the `hidden` input type, when you view a file with the browser's view source, you cannot see SGML comments. Therefore, the information within the SSI tag is not revealed.

If a server isn't set up for SSI, an SSI command (such as the following line) is completely ignored, as if it were a comment. You format the SSI tag as follows:

```
<!--#command tag1="value1" tag2="value2"-->
```

Each command varies with the number of tags allowed and the values that you can place within them. This section discusses each command and its associated tags, and explains how each one can be useful within your pages.

The *config* Command

The `config` command enables you to configure some of the output that the server processes. The tags for the `config` command are the following:

◆ `errmsg` specifies the error message returned when the server encounters a problem. For example:

```
[an error occurred while processing this directive]
```

The server returns this default error message if it cannot execute your SSI command.

Here's an example of this tag in use:

```
<!--#config errmsg="-Uhh, I think there's a problem-"-->
```

This tag displays the following message if an error occurs with any other SSI command:

```
-Uhh, I think there's a problem-
```

◆ `timefmt` reformats the output of the time. The default usually is similar to the following example:

```
Saturday, 01-Jun-96 19:25:09 PDT
```

The format for the `timefmt` tag is the same as for the `date` command on UNIX systems (check your man pages for `date`). The following is an example of this tag in use:

```
<!--#command timefmt="%d%m%y"-->
```

The output for this example looks similar to the following if you use SSI to display a date:

```
060596
```

♦ sizefmt specifies the size at which a file displays if called by an SSI command. The value of the sizefmt tag is either bytes, which displays the file's size (for example, 355,404), or abbrev, which abbreviates the file size in either kilobytes or megabytes (for example, 356K or 1.2M). The format for this tag is as follows:

```
<!--#command sizefmt="abbrev"-->
```

The *include* Command

The include command enables you to include the text of another document into the body of your parsed HTML document. You can include any type of file, including text files, HTML files, or even parsed HTML files, but you cannot include a CGI script.

Two tags are associated with the include command. The virtual tag enables you to call a file by its *virtual path*—that is, the path relative to the server. For example, /MYDOCS/MAIN.HTML refers to your SERVERROOT/MYDOCS/MAIN.HTML document.

Take a look at this example:

```
<HTML>
<HEAD><TITLE>Welcome to QUE</TITLE></HEAD>
<BODY>
<H1> Welcome to QUE </H1>
<!--#include virtual="/sections/main.html"-->
</BODY>
</HTML>
```

When called, this page displays the header information to the visitor and then instructs the SSI tag to get the SERVERROOT/SECTIONS/MAIN.HTML file. By calling a text file or portions of another HTML file when using SSI, you can save a lot of time by editing only one file, especially if you have to edit the file's contents on a regular basis.

If your document's footer includes information that changes on a regular basis, you can use something like the following instead:

```
<HTML>
<HEAD><TITLE>Welcome to QUE</TITLE></HEAD>
<BODY>
...
...
...
<!--#include virtual="/sections/foot1.html"-->
</BODY>
</HTML>
```

This code can save you much work if, for example, an address changes. Instead of editing every document on your site, you only have to edit one document.

In addition to the `virtual` tag, the only other tag that the `include` command allows is `file`. The `file` tag follows the same rules as the `virtual` tag, except that `file` specifies a file with a path name relative to the existing document. The only limitation is that you can only travel down the path tree, not up. For example, the following is not allowed:

```
<!--#include file="../main.html"-->
```

However, the following example is acceptable:

```
<!--#include file-"sections/part1/main.html"-->
```

The *echo* Command

The `echo` command prints the values of the environmental variables that the server and client share. SSI also allows for an additional set of variables that you can use:

- ◆ `DOCUMENT_NAME` displays the name of the file requested.

- ◆ `QUERY_STRING_UNESCAPED` displays the query string that the client sends. The string displays with all special characters unescaped.

- ◆ `DATE_LOCAL` displays the date local to the server. The formatting of the date and time depends on how you set the `timefmt` tag for the `config` command.

- ◆ `DATE_GMT` is the date set according to Greenwich Mean Time. The date's format also depends on the `timefmt` settings.

- ◆ `LAST_MODIFIED` shows the date when the file was last modified. The format of the date used with this variable also depends on the settings of `timefmt`.

The only tag associated with the `echo` command is `var`. In a document, the `echo` command is as follows:

```
<!--#echo var="LAST_MODIFIED"-->
```

This command is especially useful if you want to include a date within your document. By using the `echo` command with the `DATE_LOCAL` environmental variable, you don't have to write a script to include a date.

The *fsize* Command

The `fsize` command displays the size of a file within your document. The tags associated with this command are the same as those used with the `include` command. `fsize`'s output depends on the `sizefmt` tag used with the `config` command. For example, here's a list of files included in a particular document:

```
bill_of_rights.txt <!--#fsize file="bill_of_rights.txt"-->
dec_of_independance <!--#fsize virtual="txt/dec_of_ind.txt"-->
```

The *flastmod* Command

The `flastmod` command displays the date when the specified file was last modified. The following SSI command displays the date when the displayed document was last modified:

```
<!--#echo var="LAST_MODIFIED"-->
```

However, you can use the `flastmod` command to display the modification date of any file, as in the following example:

```
bill_of_rights.txt <!--#fsize file="bill_of_rights.txt"-->
 Modified on:<!--#flastmod file="bill_if_rights.txt"-->

dec_of_independence <!--#fsize virtual="txt/dec_of_ind.txt"-->
 Modified on:<!--#flastmod virtual="txt/dec_of_ind.txt"-->
```

The `flastmod` command uses the same tags as the `fsize` and `include` commands.

The *exec* Command

`exec` is the most powerful and useful command—and, if you're not careful, the most dangerous command. The `exec` command has two tags: `cmd` and `cgi`.

The `cmd` tag enables you to execute a shell command and display that command's results within your document. The usage of the `cmd` tag varies with each server, so you definitely want to check your documentation. The NCSA server enables you to add arguments with the `cmd` tag. Examine the following example:

```
<!--#exec cmd="/usr/bin/cat /etc/passwd"-->
```

This example uses the shell's `cat` command to display the contents of a UNIX system's password file (see fig. 16.1). As you can see, the `cmd` tag can be quite dangerous unless you use it carefully.

Here's another example of the `cmd` tag using the `finger` command to display information about a user:

```
<!--#exec cmd="/usr/bin/finger rniles@selah.net"-->
```

This example outputs the same information as if you entered the following within a UNIX shell:

```
% /usr/bin/finger rniles@selah.net
```

Figure 16.2 shows this example's output.

Using the `cgi` tag, you can execute a CGI script and display the results within your document. Page counters are a popular example of the `cgi` tag in use. When using the `cgi` tag, you must specify the virtual path to the CGI script. For example, if your Web server's CGI-BIN directory includes the script COUNT.PL, the SSI command would be the following:

```
<!--#exec cgi="/cgi-bin/count.pl"-->
```

Figure 16.1

If you're not careful when using the cmd tag, you can display confidential information for anyone to see.

Figure 16.2

The exec command can also be a useful tool for displaying information about a user.

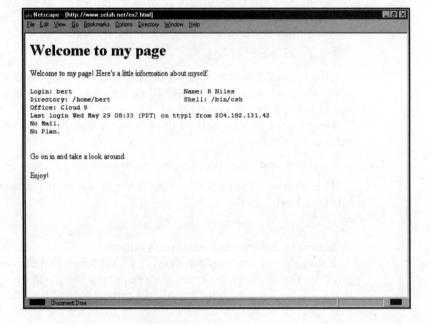

When you use the `cgi` tag, the server does not perform any error detection, so you have to do so yourself, to ensure that you do not output something like an image file.

Using SSI can definitely make some tasks a little easier, but as you have seen, you must be careful how you implement it on your server. Now that you know how to use the SSI commands, the following section takes a look at a few scripts that can enhance your Web pages.

SSI Scripts

Probably SSI's most useful capability is to add the results from scripts to your HTML documents. You can use this capability to make your pages more dynamic. Although SSI doesn't always offer the best means for creating dynamic Web documents, Server-Side Includes are definitely useful tools for doing so. In fact, with SSI you can accomplish some tasks that would be impractical, if not impossible, to attempt with normal scripts. This section presents a couple of examples that use SSI to execute scripts to perform functions not normally suited for CGI scripts.

A Counter Script

The most popular of the SSI scripts are the counters. You probably have seen them on just about every page that you encounter. It's handy to see at a glance how often users are visiting your pages. Although you can overdo the the amount of counters on your pages, counters have their use. Not only do they enable you to see how your pages are doing, they enable others to do so as well. Such counters can be beneficial when you are trying to attract sponsors who might want to know whether your pages are worth their interest.

In this section, you create a script that stores in a text file the document URI along with the number of hits received. Before you start, you need to determine what must happen within the script:

Read the count file.

Separate each line at the colon, providing the URL and the count.

Increment the count belonging to the URL.

Write to the count file, recording the count.

Display the count to the visitor.

Your first step is to display the path to Perl:

```
#!/usr/bin/perl
# simplecount 1.0
# count.pl
```

The best way to find out the document's URI is to use the environmental variable DOCUMENT_URI, which you assign to the variable $uri:

```
$uri = $ENV{'DOCUMENT_URI'};
```

You next want to specify the count file. By assigning it to a variable, you can easily change where your script is looking for the file. Therefore, if you want to change the file's name, you can edit this variable and all pointers to your file change within the script. With this particular script, defining the location of the count file by using a variable isn't so important because the script is called only once, but it's nice to have it just in case you expand the script later.

You must ensure that the counter file resides at a location to which the server has permission to write. If the server doesn't have permission to write to the directory, it cannot create the file. If you want to prevent the server from creating files (which is a good idea), you must create the file and enable the server to write to it. With UNIX, you can do so by using the chmod command.

You give the variable $countfile the value count:

```
$countfile = "count";
```

Therefore, the script looks for and writes to the file count, which resides in the directory from which you execute the script.

You also must ensure that the Content-type prints:

```
print "Content-type: text/html\n\n";
```

Now you need to open the counter file. If the file cannot open the counter, you must tell the visitor that a problem has occurred:

```
open(COUNT, "+<$countfile") || do{print "Can't open count file"; die; };
```

For a script in which multiple people write to a file, it is very important to lock the file so that two or more people cannot write to the file at the same time:

```
flock(COUNT, 2);
```

Now you read the file. As you will see, you format each line with URI:count, where URI is the virtual path to the file, and count is the number of times that the URI has been hit. A colon separates the URI from the count. Your script must read through the file, split the contents of each line at the colon, and assign the value of each URI to an array:

```
while (<COUNT>) {
        chop;
        ($file, $count) = split(/:/, $_);
        $counts{$file} = $count;
}
```

Now increment the URI's count:

```
$counts{$uri}++;
```

Next use Perl's seek() command to position the pointer:

```
seek(COUNT, 0, 0);
```

Then you write to your count file, separating the URI and the count with a colon:

```
foreach $file (keys %counts) {
        print COUNT $file, ":", $counts{$file}, "\n";
    }
```

After you finish writing to the file, you must close the file handle:

```
close(COUNT);
```

Finally, you display the count to the visitor and exit the script:

```
print $counts{$uri};
exit;
```

Now you just need to set the executable bit to the COUNT.PL file and add an SSI command to your HTML document. Here's an example of an HTML document using your counter script:

```
<HTML>
<HEAD><TITLE>Count with me</TITLE></HEAD>
<BODY>
...
...
...
This document has been hit <!--#exec cgi="/cgi-bin/count.pl"--> times.
</BODY>
</HTML>
```

Figure 16.3 shows this script's output.

This script is available on the companion CD-ROM, under the file name COUNT.PL.

Figure 16.3

By using a counter within your pages, you can give yourself and your pages' visitors an idea of how popular your pages are.

A Random Picture Script

A script that randomly displays an image or URL is another good example of SSI in use. You've probably seen quite a few sites that display an advertisement that consists of a small image file and some information about the advertiser. Often a site has several advertisers, each with its own logo. Instead of having the page display all advertisements at the same time, you can create a CGI script that picks one at random and then displays it within your page. Then the next time that a visitor hits your page, a different advertisement displays (see fig. 16.4).

This capability's usefulness isn't limited to only those sites that display advertisements. A script that displays a random image can make any site much more dynamic and interesting. You can also create a script that displays a random URL rather than a random image.

Suppose that your site must provide advertisements for four different sponsors. You have an image and a URL from each of your sponsors. Now you want to create a script that randomly picks and displays one of the images. You also want to use each sponsor's URL so that the visitor can transfer to the sponsor's Web page by clicking the displayed image.

Figure 16.4

A random image displayer is one of the most popular CGI scripts used within an HTML document.

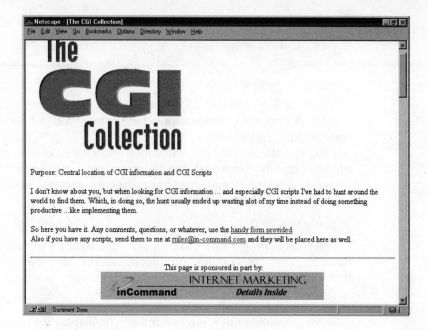

Before you start, you need to figure out exactly what your script needs to do:

Generate a list of the images to display.

Pick a random number based on the number of images.

Display the picture along with the URL associated with the image picked in HTML.

First, you need to specify the path to Perl:

```
#!/usr/bin/perl

# randpic.pl
# A simple random picture generator
```

Next you create an array that contains the virtual path to each image. List the images as IMG1.GIF, IMG2.GIF, and so on:

```
@pics= ("pics/img1.gif",
        "pics/img2.gif",
        "pics/img3.gif",
        "pics/img4.gif");
```

You then create an array that holds the URL for each sponsor's Web page:

```
@url= ("www.somewhere.com/",
       "www.another.place.com/griffon/",
       "www.someplace.com/",
       "www.advert.com/advert.html");
```

You must list each URL in the same order as the images. Therefore, IMG1.GIF should correspond to **www.somewhere.com**, IMG2.GIF to **www.another.place. com/griffon/**, and so on.

Next you should create a *seed*, which creates the random number based on the time. Because the time constantly changes, a seed ensures that the selected number is always random. (Computers have difficulty creating random numbers, so the seed gives your script a starting point.)

```
srand(time ^ $$);
```

After generating a random number, you assign it to $picnum. The rand(@pics) function generates a random number depending on the amount of pictures specified in the @pics array:

```
$picnum = rand(@pics);
```

After generating this random number, you display the randomly selected image within the document. First you make sure to print the Content-type:

```
print "Content-type: text/html\n\n";
```

Then you open an anchor that prints the URL:

```
print "<a href=\"http://$url[$picnum]\">";
```

The anchor then prints the image:

```
print "<IMG SRC=\"$pics[$picnum]\" border=0>";
```

Then you close the anchor:

```
print "</A>";
```

Now the visitor can click the image to go to the advertiser's Web page. Finally, you exit the program gracefully:

```
exit;
```

After you set the permissions so that the Web server can execute the script, you must edit your HTML document using the SSI command:

```
<!--#exec cgi="/cgi-bin/randpic.pl"-->
```

This command specifies where to display the image within your HTML document.

This script is available on the companion CD-ROM under the file name RANDPIC.PL.

Summary

After reading this chapter, you can understand why SSI is important and why you would want to use it. Most Web servers, both on UNIX and Windows NT (and sometimes Windows 95), can use SSI. SSI enables you to add information, generated on the fly, to your HTML documents. You now know how to use the SSI tags within your documents. You also have an idea of the kinds of scripts for which SSI is most useful.

Review Questions

1. Within the SRM.CONF file, what `Addtype` type do you use to tell the server that a particular extension is to be parsed?

2. For what do you use the `config` command?

3. How can you change the format for the date and time output?

4. For what do you use the `include` command?

5. Which tags are available with the `echo` command?

6. What is the difference between the `echo` command's `cmd` and `cgi` tags?

7. Name four environmental variables used only with SSI.

Review Exercises

1. Design a footer that can be used with a few HTML documents. Save the the footer as a file and use SSI to place the footer within an HTML document.

2. Expand the COUNT.PL script so that you can control whether the count displays on the Web page. Hint: Use the environmental variable `QUERY_STRING`.

3. Expand the RANDPIC.PL script so that a short line of text displays underneath the advertisement.

## CHAPTER 17

Security Issues

Chapter 1 of *Special Edition Using CGI* begins with these words: "The *Common Gateway Interface (CGI)* specification lets Web servers execute other programs."

Consider this statement for a minute. When does a server execute a CGI script? At a browser's behest. Where does the script get its input? Directly or indirectly, the input comes from the user operating the browser. When you enable CGI on a server, you are letting other people run programs on your machine. Whether a visitor's intent is malicious or not, you are ceding a great deal of power. Under ordinary circumstances, you wouldn't let people stop by your server's console and run any program they wanted to run. What if the program that they chose was `rm -rf` or `del *.* /s`?

You might think that because all the visitor can do is run the script that you set up, you aren't giving away complete access. However, if you aren't careful, you might in fact give away complete access.

This chapter helps you learn how to spot and avoid the common security pitfalls in CGI. Specifically, you'll learn about the following:

♦ Validating input

♦ Executing external programs safely

♦ Guarding files, directories, and programs

♦ Using someone else's scripts

Validating Input

If everything goes as planned, visitors to your Web site fill out your forms using the type and length of data appropriate to each field, then submit the form to your CGI script for processing. But what happens when the input from the visitor is longer than expected? What if the user pastes a 7M file into the Street Address field?

The GET method has a practical data-length limit of about 1K, and all the user input passes to your CGI program in a single environment variable called QUERY_STRING. The POST method, on the other hand, has no such data-length limitation. The information from the visitor feeds in to your CGI script through STDIN, with the environment variable CONTENT_LENGTH reflecting the length.

In languages such as C, where you must explicitly allocate memory to hold variable data, your script runs the chance of having its buffers overflow. Other languages have similar constraints. Either the program crashes in a peculiarly ugly fashion, or complacently writes the data into memory locations beyond the bounds that you have allocated for the input.

The infamous Internet Worm program took advantage of this particular vulnerability. Specifically, when Robert T. Morris wrote the Internet Worm, he attacked the UNIX sendmail program's input buffers, purposely overflowing them. The extra data—which just happened to be executable machine instructions—were written into sendmail's stack space. Suddenly sendmail wasn't running its own code any more—it was running Morris's Worm program.

Because Morris made this hacking technique so well known, it has become a favorite method for malicious users to try to gain unauthorized access to supposedly secure machines. Sometimes pranksters send huge amounts of data just for the fun of watching your CGI script break.

Fortunately, guarding against this sort of attack is pretty easy, as the next section explains.

Sources of Bad Data

Not all bad data comes from hackers trying to break your system. In fact, more often than not, bad data comes from visitors misinterpreting (or not bothering to read) your instructions and entering something wildly inappropriate.

Most CGI scripts are designed to work hand-in-hand with the HTML forms that invoke them. If you are the author of both the script and the HTML, you *know* what the data should look like, and take reasonable steps in your script to handle the expected data.

Never Trust Data Sent by *POST*

Visitors can copy your HTML easily, then run it from somewhere else, still pointing to your CGI script. During the process, they can change the HTML so that your carefully designed data formats are no longer valid. Or, if your script expects only the GET method, visitors can invoke your script and use the PUT or POST methods to flood it with bytes.

Suppose that the visitor is using your own HTML form and simply not reading the instructions. In the ZIP-code field (for which you've allocated 11 bytes in the CGI script, expecting this allocation to suffice), the visitor enters a phone number with the area code, which requires 12 bytes. If your script doesn't check the length, not only of the overall data sent with POST but of each individual field, you run the risk of corruption.

As another example, suppose that a visitor copies your CGI script's HTML so that he can use it as a template and write his own script. Unfortunately, he changes all the names of the text fields, adds a bunch of differently named radio buttons, and changes the text of the options in the option list. Even more unfortunately, he forgets to edit the action URL before testing his spiffy new script. Suddenly your CGI is being run with completely unexpected input—with potentially disastrous results.

The *GET* Method Isn't Safe, Either

The GET method relies on passing data appended to the URL, usually as several name and value pairs. Many scripts use this information to specify the name of the file to be read or another important parameter. As long as your HTML sends the request, it will be formatted correctly. But browsers have a quirk—they put the full URL on their location line. The visitor could resubmit the CGI request simply by clicking the reload button.

The following example illustrates how such a resubmittal can cause trouble. Suppose that you've written a simple script that does nothing but retrieve a variable called `filename` and then return that file's contents to the browser. You display some HTML for visitors to use:

```
<a href="http://www.mysite.com/cgi-bin/readfile.exe?filename=/usr
➥ /tom/stats.txt">Read the Stats file</a>
<p>
```

After clicking the link and viewing **/usr/tom/stats.txt**, the visitor's browser displays the following on its location line:

```
http://www.mysite.com/cgi-bin/readfile.exe?filename=/usr/tom/stats.txt
```

Consider what happens if the visitor deliberately changes the name and value pairs before clicking the reload button:

```
http://www.mysite.com/cgi-bin/readfile.exe?filename=/etc/passwd
```

In this admittedly unlikely example (you would never write such a script that doesn't check the file name), your script delivers the contents of **/etc/passwd** to the visitor.

Verifying File Names and Paths

Whenever a visitor can potentially modify or even see an actual file name on your system, take a few precautions to restrict access to those areas that are appropriate for that script:

♦ Use the operating system's security. The CGI script always runs in a particular *security context*—a set of file permissions, volume mappings, port access permissions, and operating system authorizations usually associated with a user account. The server launches CGI scripts, which thus inherit the server's security context. In UNIX systems, the account is often the user nobody. In Windows NT, the user can be a system account or a special user account created by you (or the Web server). Whatever user account you use, make sure that account doesn't have read, list, execute, or write permissions in any directories other than those associated with your script.

♦ Force your script to reject any file reference that doesn't reside in the script's own directory or a directory below it. For instance, if your script resides in /CGI-BIN, the script should be capable of reading files only in /CGI-BIN, /CGI-BIN/DATA, /CGI-BIN/GFX, and so forth.

♦ Parse file references to catch relative paths. For example, even though you've set up your script to read a particular directory, the visitor could enter a file name in the form of ..\..\..\etc\passwd and bypass your default directory entirely.

♦ Parse file references to catch absolute paths. On Windows systems, don't let users enter drive letters. On any kind of system, don't let the file name start with a slash (indicating that the file is relative to the root), dots, or double-dots (indicating that the file is relative to the current directory or the parent). Of particular concern on Windows NT systems is the Universal Naming Convention (UNC) syntax. For example, if your Web server's name is BARNEY and your accounting data is stored on another server named FRED, a visitor could enter \\FRED\accounting\salary.xls and pluck data from a machine that's not even related to your Web server except that it is on the same internal network.

Checking Data Lengths

To validate the length of incoming data, follow these steps:

1. Allocate a reasonable amount of buffer space.

2. Read the REQUEST_METHOD variable to see whether the incoming data is the result of a POST operation.

3. If the data was sent with POST, read the CONTENT_LENGTH variable, compare it to the size of the buffer that you've allocated, and then go to step 6.

4. If the data came from GET, retrieve the length of the QUERY_STRING variable and compare it to the size of the buffer that you've allocated.

5. If the data came from some other method, return an error code to the visitor and then exit.

6. If the size of the incoming data (either from POST or GET) is longer than the buffer size, copy (from STDIN if by POST, or from the QUERY_STRING variable if by GET) only as much as fits in your buffer.

7. For each name/value pair in the data, perform a similar length check, rejecting or truncating anything falling outside the bounds that you expected.

Listing 17.1 shows actual C code that you can paste into your own programs to read data safely from STDIN.

Listing 17.1   Reading *STDIN* Safely

```
// This code fragment shows how to retrieve characters from
// STDIN after you've determined that your script was
// invoked with the POST method.

char * pContentLength;  // pointer to CONTENT_LENGTH
char InputBuffer[1024]; // local storage for input
int  ContentLength;     // value of CONTENT_LENGTH string
int  i;                 // local counter
int  x;                 // generic char variable

// First retrieve a pointer to the CONTENT_LENGTH variable
pContentLength = getenv("CONTENT_LENGTH");

// If the variable exists, convert its value to an integer
// with atoi()
if (pContentLength != NULL) {
    ContentLength = atoi(pContentLength);
}
else
{
    ContentLength = 0;
}

// Make sure specified length isn't greater than the size
// of our statically allocated buffer
if (ContentLength > sizeof(InputBuffer)-1) {
    ContentLength = sizeof(InputBuffer)-1;
}
```

continues

Listing 17.1   Continued

```
// Now read ContentLength bytes from STDIN
i = 0;
while (i < ContentLength) {
    x = fgetc(stdin);
    if (x==EOF) break;
    InputBuffer[i++] = x;
}

// Terminate the string with a zero
InputBuffer[i] = '\0';

// And update ContentLength
ContentLength = i;
```

Verifying That Data Meets Field Criteria

A guestbook program often stores visitor input in a file for later display. Suppose that your script has the file name and path hard-coded, and you've tried to ensure that the lengths are all within bounds. You assume that all your script does is place a name into a file, and thus can't go wrong.

Suppose that an unscrupulous visitor, instead of entering **Jamie Smith** in the name field, enters **<h1>HOT SEX!!!<hr> <font size="+12">HOT SEX!!!</font> </h1>**. Somehow, you probably wouldn't want to show off your guestbook to your boss or your mother after this visitor filled out your form.

Inappropriate data isn't always just annoying. Sometimes it can pose an actual security risk. For instance, if your server has Server-Side Includes (SSI) enabled, the visitor could enter **<!—#include file="/etc/passwd" —>** as his name and reveal your password file to every person who looks at your guestbook.

If your SSI also allows program execution, and the user enters **<!—#exec cmd="rm -rf /"—>** as his name, your hard disk might not have anything left on it by the time you catch on to the problem.

You must validate the data supplied for each field against the type of data appropriate for that field.

There are two generally accepted ways of dealing with this situation:

◆ Disallow the greater-than and less-than signs in any text input (by replacing the characters with spaces when you find them). This technique disables all special HTML formatting and SSI commands, because the syntax requires that you enclose these operations in angle brackets.

◆ Replace angle brackets with the HTML display codes associated with them; that is, for every less-than sign (<) that you encounter, substitute a **&lt**, and for every greater-than sign (>), a **&gt**. This technique requires a bit more work and doesn't provide much of an advantage, unless you want to enable the visitor to enter stuff that looks like HTML but isn't.

Executing External Programs Safely

Perl and UNIX shell scripts often call other workhorse programs, such as awk, grep, mail, and cat, to help accomplish CGI's task. Windows programs do this sometimes, too, although far less often, and when they do, they seldom pose as great a security risk as under UNIX.

Although validating data coming into your CGI script is important, it is *absolutely vital* that your script validate any data that it passes to an external program. Here's why:

In the UNIX environment, the semicolon character is a command separator. The UNIX shell executes the first command, then moves on to execute the second one. For example, if your script takes a user name from an HTML form and passes the name to the mail program for processing, you could be in a world of trouble. A visitor entering **pat@somemail.drop.com** causes no problem. But if the visitor enters **pat@somemail.drop.com;rm -rf /** instead, a hidden command executes. The mail still gets processed, but your entire hard drive is erased too.

The UNIX system is full of characters that can get you into trouble. For example, the asterisk (*) and question mark (?) perform file globbing (wild-card matches); the semicolon (;) allows multiple commands on one line; and the exclamation point (!) and back-quotation mark (") can reference or run jobs. In fact, just about any character with special meaning to the program that you call could create trouble. For instance, the mail program treats any line starting with a tilde (~) as one of its internal commands to execute. The visitor could supply **~r /etc/passwd** in the body of the e-mail message and end up mailing your password file to himself.

Some script authors let these metacharacters go through to other scripts, either after escaping them (so that the shell interprets them as characters rather than commands) or by enclosing the command line within quotation marks (so that the shell treats the command line as one argument). However, these methods are not foolproof.

You are far better off filtering the data to remove any potential problem. Names sent to mail should contain alphanumeric characters, plus the *at* sign (@). You must strip anything else first. Likewise, you should validate data for other programs before passing it on. UNIX has far too many holes for you to ever catch them all.

You usually shouldn't write a script that expects to receive data containing special characters unless you prepare your script to handle every potential eventuality. Another security hole is the usually innocuous vertical bar character (|). Many people use this character—along with hyphens, underscores, and slashes—as part of their *signature* line. But if your script passes a parameter containing the vertical bar to an external program, that program is likely to interpret the vertical bar as a pipe symbol—and just about anything could happen then. Even the mostly harmless hyphen can cause trouble. For instance, if your script uses grep to perform a pattern search and the visitor enters a term that contains a hyphen followed by a valid letter, grep interprets this combination of characters as a switch, producing unexpected results.

Self-contained scripts are much easier to secure. If you have the time to write your own routines, you're better off using them than shelling out to the operating system to run something like cat or grep. If you can't avoid using an external program as part of your processing, make sure that the input and output are well-defined and completely filtered, and that the directories and files on which the commands will work are appropriate for your script.

You should remove any nonalphanumeric characters, except for the *at* sign (@) for mail and a few similar exceptions. In other words, write your filter to exclude *everything* not alphanumeric unless you specifically instruct it to allow a special character in a special circumstance.

Guarding Files, Directories, and Programs

So far this chapter has focused on visitors entering troublesome input, either maliciously or innocently. Now take a look at your *friends*—the people sharing your server.

Your server is far more vulnerable to attack from within than from without. This is because, in all but the most trivial cases, a user with valid access to the system can much more easily monkey with your Web server's setup, toss executables or scripts into the SCRIPTS directory, or change your HTML.

Particularly on UNIX systems, the security context in which the server runs is a weak point. Most UNIX systems restrict access to the first 1,024 ports (0 to 1,023) to the user root. Therefore, your Web server must run as root to listen to the standard HTTP port, port 80. For this reason, your Web server has all the powers associated with the root user, and unless you take specific steps to avoid the situation, so do all your CGI scripts.

Most UNIX Web servers enable you to specify a second user account for the server to impersonate while running scripts. You should set this *CGI user* to use the nobody account, or another account with similarly restricted privileges.

Another UNIX pitfall—a strength in other circumstances—is the *setuid bit*. This bit, when set on a CGI script, makes the executable run in the security context of the user owning the file, rather than the security context of the user executing the script. Webmasters usually restrict access to the CGI-BIN directory to themselves (root), so if you set the setuid bit, the scripts run as root no matter what CGI user you have set up.

Tip: Use the UNIX command chmod a -s on your CGI scripts to ensure that you turn off the setuid bit.

Using the Operating System's Permissions Facility

Under Windows NT, you use File Manager to set the security for all the files and directories that the CGI user can reach. You can select the following rights individually: read, write, execute, list (directory contents), and delete. Usually, the CGI user should not have any access to any directories outside the CGI-BIN directory itself or any directories under it. Further restrictions within the script itself help limit potential damage. If a script can't even see a file elsewhere on the system, no amount of user hacking can make the script do anything with the file or program.

UNIX keeps track of permissions much the same way as Windows NT does, but you have to think in octal and use chmod and umask() to control the security.

Administering Windows NT and UNIX security is beyond this book's scope; much longer books have been written about just those aspects of each system. If you don't understand your operating system's security model and how to make it do what you want, refer to your manual or online help, or ask your system administrator for assistance.

Using Explicit Paths to External Programs

A common hack is for a user to replace a standard UNIX program with another one that has the same name. Even though you can set your operating system's permissions so that the hacker can't replace the original program, you often have no way to prevent a hacker from putting his program earlier in the path than the original program. Thus, a simple shell script that uses echo (an external UNIX command) could execute anything at all—as long as the hacker has created an executable called echo.

The solution to this problem is to use full, explicit path names when invoking external programs.

For example, the following script is insecure, even though it accepts no input from the visitor:

```
#!/bin/sh
echo "Content-Type: text/html"
echo ""
echo "Today's fortune is:"
fortune
```

All a hacker has to do is place a program called either fortune or echo somewhere in your executable path prior to your original fortune or echo.

Rewritten with explicit path names, the script becomes almost invulnerable:

```
#!/bin/sh
/usr/bin/echo "Content-Type: text/html"
/usr/bin/echo ""
/usr/bin/echo "Today's fortune is:"
/usr/bin/fortune
```

Now the only way for a hacker to interfere with this script is to replace files in the /USR/BIN directory itself—something that you or the system administrator should have disallowed with the operating system's security.

Using Someone Else's Scripts

A wealth of information is available on CGI—from the Internet, from your college library, from books such as this one, from UseNet groups, and from friends and coworkers. But you not only can get information, you also can get actual programs and libraries. Why do all the work yourself when someone else has already done it?

Just as you shouldn't blindly follow someone else's instructions for how to manage your finances, strengthen your marriage, or handle other aspects of your life, you shouldn't blindly run someone else's code on your server.

And, just as someone else's advice about your investments or romance might actually provide good guidance, scripts that you get off the Internet might actually be good scripts—but they also might not be.

You should take time to consider the source of the script, and the reliability of the site from which you got the script.

Some Webmasters won't even consider running a public-domain, shareware, or commercial script if they can't see and puzzle through the source code. These Webmasters are probably excessively paranoid. If a reputable firm sells a well-documented and widely used script, it's more likely to be safe than one that you write yourself, for two reasons. First, professionals are aware of the common security holes and how to avoid them. Second, companies are in business to make money, and they can't do so if they get a reputation for shoddy or malicious work.

On the other hand, if on a UseNet group you see a compiled executable that was posted by someone of whom you've never heard, that provides little or no documentation, and that lists no users that you can check, hesitate a long time before putting it on your server. Chances are good that the program is a perfectly legitimate offering from another CGI programmer like yourself, who wants to share his programmatic children with the rest of the world. But the programmer might also be a malicious 15-year-old with a warped sense of humor, who just wants to see how many people he can dupe into wiping their disks.

When evaluating public-domain, shareware, or commercial offerings, look for these features:

◆ Does the script come from a reputable site? Has the site been around for a long time? Is it well-maintained? Does the Webmaster vet files before releasing them?

◆ Is there adequate documentation indicating how the program works and how you should use it?

♦ How many other users have downloaded the script? Is the site willing to provide references of customers on request? (Ask only if you have reason to be suspicious; Webmasters can't spend all day answering this type of question.)

♦ Is anyone talking about the script in UseNet? If so, are users saying good things or bad? If you can't find any mention of the script, ask for comments. Chances are pretty good that several people will respond with their experiences.

> **Tip:** Check these UseNet groups when evaluating scripts: **comp.security.announce**, **comp.security.unix**, and **comp.infosystems.www.authoring.cgi**. Also drop by the Computer Emergency Response Team (CERT) at **ftp.cert.org** to get a comprehensive history of security problems, workarounds, and attack-prevention software.

♦ Does the script's author have other scripts with well-established (and good) reputations?

♦ Is the source code available, either for free or for a price?

♦ Does the author make extravagant claims about the program's capabilities? If so, you might have stumbled onto either a scam or a novice programmer.

♦ Does the site have the script running itself? If not, why not? Can you find any site running the script?

Summary

In this chapter, you learned how visitors to your Web site can cause mischief, either intentionally or unintentionally, when they access your scripts. Sometimes the only thing that happens is that your script crashes; other times, you might end up giving the visitor the power to delete all the files on your server.

You also learned how to write scripts to reduce or eliminate these risks, and you saw how to write scripts that deal with incorrect input gracefully and safely.

Review Questions

1. Why is it important to know the length of incoming data before you read all of it?

2. What is the average maximum length of data that you can send using GET?

3. What is the security context of a script running as root on UNIX systems, or as administrator on Windows NT systems?

4. Name at least three characters that are dangerous for your UNIX shell script to send to another program as command-line arguments.

Review Exercises

1. Create a set of routines for generic input data validation. Make them robust enough to handle wildly invalid data by rejecting it, and "probably okay" data by parsing it and eliminating potentially dangerous character sequences. Make three routines: one to validate e-mail addresses, one to validate URLs, and one to validate text sent to sendmail in the body of a letter.

2. Write a script that does nothing but take the QUERY_STRING data from a GET operating and save it to a text file. Then try to break the script by feeding it incorrect or badly formatted information. What sort of security risks does this kind of script pose?

3. Write a script that takes the name of a file from the QUERY_STRING variable and prints the file's contents on the browser. Revise the script as necessary until, no matter what a visitor types, the script displays only files in one particular directory. Revise the script again so that it can display only files with the extension .H, but from any directory on the system. What security holes have you opened? What permissions will your script need to handle this kind of function?

Part VII

CGI Alternatives

## CHAPTER 18

JavaScript

JavaScript is an object-based scripting language developed by Netscape for its Navigator 2.x and later browsers. JavaScript has proved popular enough that other browsers, including Microsoft's Internet Explorer, are beginning to incorporate support for it. Because Netscape by itself already owns the lion's share of the browser market, and because Microsoft covers all but a tiny percentage of the remainder, JavaScript is (or shortly will be) compatible with most browsers. Those using Lynx or other older technologies will not be able to take advantage of JavaScript.

Tip: If you design your pages using JavaScript—or any of the new technologies—remember to include alternate functions for visitors with older, text-based browsers. Just as you use `alt` in your `<IMG>` tags, provide a way for text-only visitors to know what's going on.

The primary advantage of JavaScript over regular CGI is that the script, including all subroutines, declarations, event triggers, and event handlers, is contained within otherwise-standard HTML. The browser sees and recognizes the JavaScript, and executes it as appropriate. This means there are no run-time modules to distribute, no class modules to download, and no code running on the server to support the script.

JavaScript statements embedded in an HTML page can recognize and respond to user events such as mouse clicks, form input, and page navigation. For example, you can use JavaScript to validate input before letting a form be submitted, or you can use JavaScript to perform an action (execute a Java Applet, start a new browser window, play a sound, pop up an alert message, and so forth) in response to user actions.

Netscape (**http://www.netscape.com**) provides excellent, up-to-date tutorials on JavaScript, along with links to sites using JavaScript in interesting ways. Much of the theoretical and technical information about JavaScript in this chapter is adapted directly from Netscape's online documentation.

In this chapter, you learn about the following:

♦ The fundamentals of JavaScript

♦ Gizmos and doodads

♦ Concerns and cautions

Fundamentals of JavaScript

JavaScript is an interpreted language; there is no compile step and no directly executable code, pcode, or byte-code. A JavaScript program is a collection of textual statements representing instructions to the browser to do various things. The browser works through these instructions one by one, from the top down (that is, from the beginning of the HTML file), and interprets them on the fly.

JavaScript supports most of Java's syntax for forming expressions and controlling program flow. JavaScript uses a small number of built-in data types—numeric, Boolean, and string—for all operations. JavaScript's object model is called instance-based, which means that the objects are created and manipulated as needed, for each instance of a JavaScript program. This simple yet powerful mechanism is ideal for integration into HTML.

JavaScript supports functions, or subroutines (either provided by you as part of your JavaScript program, or built in to the JavaScript interpreter) to manipulate objects and their properties. Functions can be either properties of objects (that is, *methods*) or regular subroutines.

Unlike Java programs, which consist exclusively of classes and their methods, JavaScript is procedural as well as class-based, making it closer to C than C++. Java programming is significantly more complex than JavaScript authoring. Table 19.1 shows some of the significant differences between JavaScript and Java.

A JavaScript author doesn't have to understand or worry about class functions such as instantiation, extension, overloading, or inheritance. Instead, the author uses built-in components with rather high-level properties and methods.

Table 19.1   JavaScript versus Java

JavaScript	Java
Interpreted (not compiled) by client.	Compiled on server before execution on client.

JavaScript	Java
Object-based. Code uses built-in, extensible objects, but no classes or inheritance.	Object-oriented. Applets consist of object classes with inheritance.
Code integrated with, and embedded in, HTML.	Applets distinct from HTML (accessed from HTML pages).
Variable data types not declared (loose typing).	Variable data types must be declared (strong typing).
Dynamic binding. Object references checked at run time.	Static binding. Object references must exist at compile time.

Browser Objects

When you load a page in the browser, the JavaScript interpreter creates a number of *objects*—named entities with properties, methods, and scope.

Every page always has the following objects:

- ◆ *Window.* The top-level object, containing properties that apply to the entire window. If the page uses frames, there is also a window object for each frame window.

- ◆ *Location.* This object's property is the current URL.

- ◆ *History.* This object contains properties representing URLs the user has previously visited.

- ◆ *Document.* This object contains properties for the content and layout of the current document, such as title, background color, and forms.

The properties of the document object are based, mostly, on the content of the document. For example, the document object has a property for each form and each anchor in the document.

Here are some examples of objects and their properties. The actual contents of the properties will vary, of course, based on the document's actual location, its title, the colors used, and so forth. The properties are examples only:

- ◆ location.href = **http://www.greyware.com/javascript.htp**

- ◆ document.title = Sample JavaScript Page

- ◆ document.fgColor = #000000

- ◆ document.bgColor = #ffffff

- ◆ history.length = 7

If the document contained a named form called form1, which included a check box called check1, a button called button1, and a text field called text1, the following objects would also be created:

- document.form1
- document.form1.check1
- document.form1.button1
- document.form1.text1

The properties for these objects might look something like this:

- document.form1.action = **http://www.greyware.com/jtest.exe**
- document.form1.method = POST
- document.form1.length = 5
- document.form1.button1.value = Submit
- document.form1.button1.name = button1
- document.form1.text1.value = JavaScript Test Form
- document.form1.text1.name = text1
- document.form1.check1.defaultChecked = True
- document.form1.check1.value = On
- document.form1.check1.name = check1

Notice that each of the preceding property references starts with document, followed by the name of the form (form1), and then the property name (for form properties) or the name of the form element. This is a hierarchical naming scheme, consistent with most class-oriented languages.

The *document* Object

One of the most useful of the browser objects is the document object, because its write and writeln methods can generate HTML. These methods are the way that you display JavaScript expressions to the user.

The only difference between write and writeln is that writeln adds a carriage return at the end of the line. However, because HTML ignores carriage returns, this only affects preformatted text, such as that inside a <PRE> tag.

The document object also has onLoad and onUnload event handlers to perform functions when a user first loads a page and when a user exits a page.

There is only one document object for a page, and it is the ancestor for all the form, link, and anchor objects in the page.

The *form* Object

The browser creates a form object for each form in a document. You can name a form with the name attribute, as in this example:

```
<FORM NAME="form1" METHOD="POST" ACTION="...">
Your Shirt Size? <INPUT TYPE=TEXT NAME="Size">
...
</FORM>
```

JavaScript creates a form object and names it form1. The form object contains a text object called UserName. You refer to this text object as document.form1.Size, and to the value property of this object as document.form1.Size.value.

The forms in a document are stored in an array called forms. The first (topmost in the page) form is forms[0], the second forms[1], and so on.

So the preceding references could also be as follows:

```
document.forms[0].Size
document.forms[0].Size.value
```

Likewise, the elements in a form, such as text fields, radio buttons, and so on, are stored in an elements array.

The *window* Object

The window object is the *parent* object for all other objects in the browser. You can always omit the object name in references to window properties and methods.

window has several very useful methods that create new windows and popup dialog boxes:

♦ open and close: Opens and closes a browser window.

♦ alert: Pops up an alert dialog box.

♦ status: Lets you set the message in the status bar at the bottom of the client window.

♦ confirm: Pops up a confirmation dialog box.

The window object has properties for all the frames in a frameset. The frames are stored in the frames array. The frames array contains an entry for each child frame in a window. For example, if a window contains three child frames, these frames are reflected as window.frames[0], window.frames[1], and window.frames[2].

Document Parsing

HTML documents are parsed by the browser in a top-down fashion; that is, from beginning to end. Because your JavaScript program is embedded in the HTML, your JavaScript program is also parsed and interpreted this way.

How the browser accomplishes the interpretation really isn't important to this discussion, with one exception: Because the browser goes from top to bottom through the HTML file, at any given point in the process, it knows *everything* about what it has seen so far, and *nothing* about what's yet to come.

This means you cannot use forward references in your JavaScript program. A *forward reference* is the mention or use of a variable, property, function, or method, which is defined later on in the script.

For this reason, it's best to put your variable declarations and subroutines at the top of your JavaScript program, and the main functions and event handlers at the bottom.

Values, Names, and Literals

JavaScript recognizes the following types of values:

♦ Numbers, such as 42 or 3.14159

♦ Logical (Boolean) values, either True or False

♦ Strings, such as This is a string literal.

♦ null, a special keyword denoting a null value

JavaScript makes no distinction, from the programmer's point of view, between real numbers and integers. The internal format used by the JavaScript interpreter is not exposed.

Note that although there is no explicit data type for storing date/time information, there is a date object with appropriate built-in functions for manipulating date information.

Type Conversions

JavaScript is a *loosely typed* language. That means that you do not have to specify the data type of a variable when you declare it, and data types are converted automatically as needed during the course of script execution. So, for example, you could define a variable called answer as follows:

```
var answer = 42
```

Later, you could assign the same variable a string value:

```
answer = "Thanks for all the fish..."
```

Because JavaScript is loosely typed, this will not cause an error message, although it may cause unexpected results if you don't pay attention.

In general, in expressions involving numeric and string values, JavaScript converts the numeric values to strings. For example, consider the following statements:

```
x = "The answer is " + 42
y = 42 + " is the answer."
```

The first statement will return the string The answer is 42. The second statement will return the string 42 is the answer.

Variable Names

You use variables to hold values in your application. You give these variables *names* by which you reference them, and there are certain rules to which these names must conform.

♦ Names must start with a letter or underscore (_) character. A letter is defined as the characters A through Z and a through z.

♦ Subsequent characters can be either digits (0 through 9) or letters. Spaces are not permitted.

♦ Names are *case-sensitive*. Case-sensitive means that Yes, yes, and YES are three different names.

Literals

Literals are the way you represent constant values in JavaScript. These are fixed values that you provide in your application source and are not variables.

♦ **Integers** Integers can be expressed in decimal (base 10), hexadecimal (base 16), or octal (base 8) format. A decimal integer literal consists of a sequence of digits (optionally suffixed as described later) without a leading zero. An integer can be expressed in octal or hexadecimal rather than decimal. A leading zero on an integer literal means it is in octal; a leading 0x (or 0X) means hexadecimal. Hexadecimal integers can include digits (0–9) and the letters a–f and A–F. Octal integers can include only the digits 0–7.

♦ **Floating point** A floating-point literal can have the following parts: a decimal integer, a decimal point, a fraction (another decimal number), an exponent, and a type suffix. The exponent part is an e or E followed by an integer, which can be signed (preceded by a + or -). A floating-point literal must have at least one digit, plus either a decimal point or exponent. Some examples of floating-point literals are 3.1415, -3.1E12, .1e12, and 2E-12.

♦ **Boolean** The Boolean type has two literal values: True and False.

♦ **Strings** A string literal is zero or more characters enclosed in double quotation marks (") or single (') quotation marks. A string must be delimited by quotation marks of the same type; that is, either both single or both double.

◆ **Special Characters** You can use several special character sequences in JavaScript to represent meanings that would otherwise be hard to type. For example, `Column 1\tColumn 2` would produce `Column 1`, then a tab character, and then `Column 2`. The complete list of special character sequences is as follows:

Constant Expression	Meaning in JavaScript
\b	Backspace
\f	Form feed
\n	Newline
\r	Carriage return
\t	Tab

Gizmos and Doodads

Okay, that's enough theory for now. It's time to put some gizmos and doodads on the screen! Figure 18.1 shows a page put together to demonstrate the most common JavaScript functions. Listing 18.4 shows the complete HTML used to create this page, but before looking at the whole thing, take a look at some of the parts.

Figure 18.1

This page demonstrates over a dozen JavaScript functions. Notice the text on the status line, caught in mid-scroll.

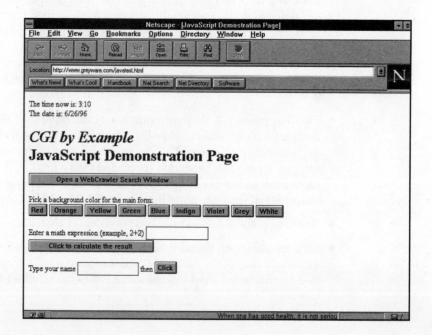

Time and Date

Figure 18.1 shows the current time and date in the upper-left corner of the screen. This is the actual time and date that the screen was loaded. Listing 18.1 shows the JavaScript code to produce the date and time.

Listing 18.1   JavaScript Code To Print the Date and Time

```
<html>
<head><title>JavaScript Demonstration Page</title>
<script language="JavaScript">
<!-- Beginning of JavaScript Applet ------------------

// The following code gets executed when the page first loads

    // create an instance of the date object
    Today = new Date();

    // write a plain string
    document.write("The time now is: ");

    // write out a value from the date object,
    // using the getHours method.  This
    // statement also shows how you can
    // write more than one thing per statement;
    // simply separate the items with commas
    document.write(Today.getHours(),":");

    // write out the minutes
    document.write(Today.getMinutes());

    // make the HTML pretty, with a <br> tag
    document.write("<br>");

    // and so forth, for the date.  Note that
    // the getMonth method returns a month
    // number relative to zero (0=Jan, 1=Feb,
    // etc.), so we add one to it

    document.write("The date is: ");
    document.write(Today.getMonth()+1,"/")
    document.write(Today.getDate(),"/");
    document.write(Today.getYear());

// -- End of JavaScript code --------------->
</script>
</head>

<body bgcolor=#FFFFFF
      text=#000000>
```

continues

Listing 18.1   Continued

```
<h1><i>CGI by Example</i><br>
JavaScript Demonstration Page</h1>

</body>
</html>
```

Listing 18.1 includes all the HTML to display the date and time, whether concerned with JavaScript or not. The listing does it this way so that you can see not only the JavaScript code, but how JavaScript fits into the structure of an HTML document.

All JavaScript code gets placed in the HTML header, between the `<head>` and `</head>` tags. The JavaScript itself is identified by the `<script language="JavaScript">` and `</script>` tags.

Browsers that don't understand the `<script...>` tag will ignore it, as with any unknown HTML tag. However, the script statements themselves will show up—unless you hide them. The easiest way to hide them is to enclose the entire script within a comment. This is what the `<!-- Beginning of JavaScript Applet ---------` `---------- and // -- End of JavaScript code ------------- -->` lines do.

After the header comes the normal `<body>` tag and the document's main HTML. I won't show the JavaScript structure again.

The date and time are produced by creating an instance of the JavaScript's built-in date object, and then printing out the properties. The code itself is heavily documented and doesn't need any further explanation.

The WebCrawler Window

Figure 18.2 shows how the screen looks after the visitor has clicked the button labeled Open a WebCrawler Search Window. Listing 18.2 shows the code to invoke the WebCrawler window.

Listing 18.2   JavaScript To Create the WebCrawler Window

```
Insert this function into the <script> section:

// OpenSearchWindow -- opens window to search engine

    function OpenSearchWindow() {
        var SearchWindow;
        var SearchLocation;
        var SearchWindowSettings;

        SearchWindowSettings = "toolbar=0,"
                            + "resizable=0,"
                            + "scrollbars=0,"
```

```
                                    + "width=290,"
                                    + "height=150";

        SearchLocation = "http://www.republic.se/"
                        + "search/webcrawler.html";

        SearchWindow=open("",
                        "SearchWindow",
                        SearchWindowSettings);

        SearchWindow.location = SearchLocation;
}
```

Insert this code into the \<body> of the document:

```
<form name=DemoStuff>
<input type="button"
    value="Open a WebCrawler Search Window"
    onClick="OpenSearchWindow()">
</form>
```

Figure 18.2

The WebCrawler search window open on top of the main page. Notice that the text in the status area has scrolled on to a new quotation since figure 18.1.

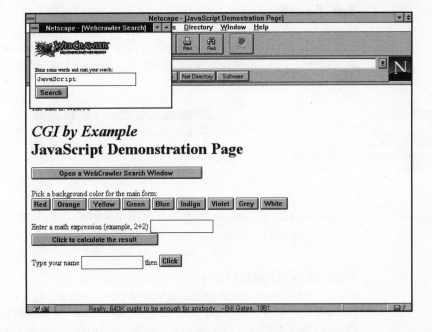

Listing 18.2 uses a form within the \<body> of the HTML document. The form includes only one element, an input of the type `button`. The button's `onClick` property calls the function `OpenSearchWindow()`.

A Confirmation Dialog Box

Figure 18.3 shows the confirmation dialog box after the visitor has filled in an expression to be calculated and clicked the calculate button. The confirmation dialog box is another built-in JavaScript function. It returns a Boolean value (True if the visitor clicks Yes, and False if the visitor clicks No or presses Esc). The code to invoke a confirmation dialog box is quite simple:

```
if (confirm("Ready to do some math?"))
    // do something
else
    // do something else
```

Figure 18.3

A confirmation dialog box.

An Alert

Figure 18.4 shows the use of an alert. An alert doesn't return a value, and you can't change the alert's title bar or first caption. This makes the alert rather ugly and unsatisfying, because you can't keep it from saying "Alert!" even when your message is purely informative.

Figure 18.4

An alert displaying the results of the calculation entered on the main screen.

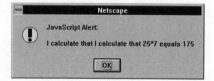

The alert() function takes exactly one parameter, the message of the alert text:

```
alert("Something alarming has happened!");
```

Input Validation

Figure 18.5 shows a prompt dialog box. A prompt dialog box takes two parameters: the text for the prompt caption, and the name of the variable to hold the result. Figure 18.6 shows another alert, this time used to indicate an error condition, in this case, where the visitor didn't enter a name before clicking the button.

Figure 18.5

A JavaScript prompt dialog box in action. The prompt caption includes information supplied by the visitor on the main screen.

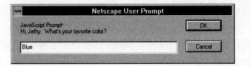

Figure 18.6

A JavaScript alert box informing the user that he didn't enter his name.

Listing 18.3 shows the JavaScript function that produced both figures 18.5 and 18.6. The `PromptUser()` function first checks to make sure the passed variable, `VisitorName`, isn't null. Remember that *null* is a special value in JavaScript meaning either uninitialized or set to nothing. The implied comparison in `if (VisitorName)` is to null; if `VisitorName` is not null (that is, if it has been filled in by the visitor), then the routine goes ahead and uses it. If `VisitorName` is null, however, the routine just pops up an alert.

Listing 18.3 JavaScript Code That Validates Its Input

```
// PromptUser -- function to prompt user for input

    function PromptUser(VisitorName) {
        if (VisitorName) {
            var VisitorColor = "Blue";
            var PromptText = "Hi, " + VisitorName
                         + ".  What's your favorite color?";
            if ((VisitorColor=prompt(PromptText,VisitorColor)))
                alert("\nReally?  "+VisitorColor+"?")
            else
                alert("\nDidn't want to say, huh?");
        }
        else
        {
            alert("\nYou didn't enter your name!");
        }
    }
```

The JavaScript Demonstration Page

Listing 18.4 contains the complete HTML to produce the JavaScript Demonstration page shown in figure 18.1. The code is also on the CD-ROM that came with this book, and available online at **http://www.greyware.com/cgi/javademo.htm**.

Look through listing 18.4 carefully, noting how all the JavaScript functions are placed within the HTML header. The functions are called either by user action (clicking a button) or by timer events.

The scrolling text across the status line is produced with a *timer*, a built-in JavaScript function. The ScrollText() function is invoked right after the form loads, without any user intervention required. The <body> tag includes two JavaScript calls: onLoad and onUnload.

```
<body bgcolor=#FFFFFF
     text=#000000
     onUnload="window.alert('\nThanks for visiting!')"
     onLoad="TimerOne=window.setTimeout('ScrollText(100)',500);">
```

The onLoad event is triggered by the JavaScript interpreter automatically when the page is first loaded. The onUnload event is triggered when the user leaves the page. Note that the onUnload event has no equivalent in standard CGI. Only the visitor's browser knows when the visitor decides to go elsewhere, so only code running on the browser itself could trigger this kind of event.

Listing 18.4 JAVADEMO.HTM—the Complete HTML To Produce the JavaScript Demonstration Page

```
<html>
<head><title>JavaScript Demonstration Page</title>
<script language="JavaScript">
<!-- Beginning of JavaScript Applet ------------------

// ComputeValue -- function to compute an expression

    function ComputeValue(form) {
        var result;
        if (confirm("Ready to do some math?")) {
            result = "\nI calculate that "
                    + form.expression.value
                    + " equals "
                    + eval(form.expression.value);
            alert(result);
        }
    }

// PromptUser -- function to prompt user for input

    function PromptUser(VisitorName) {
        if (VisitorName) {
```

```
                  var VisitorColor = "Blue";
                  var PromptText = "Hi, " + VisitorName
                                    + ".  What's your favorite color?";


alert("\nReally?  "+VisitorColor+"?")
else
                  alert("\nDidn't want to say, huh?");
          }
          else
          {
              alert("\nYou didn't enter your name!");
          }
      }

// OpenSearchWindow -- opens window to search engine

      function OpenSearchWindow() {
          var SearchWindow;
          var SearchLocation;
          var SearchWindowSettings;

          SearchWindowSettings = "toolbar=0,"
                                + "resizable=0,"
                                + "scrollbars=0,"
                                + "width=290,"
                                + "height=150";

          SearchLocation = "http://www.republic.se/"
                          + "search/webcrawler.html";

          SearchWindow=open("",
                          "SearchWindow",
                          SearchWindowSettings);

          SearchWindow.location = SearchLocation;
}

// ScrollText -- scrolls text across the status line
      function ScrollText(delaytime) {
          var msg = "When one has good health, it is not "
                  + "serious to be ill.  --Francis Blanche"
                  + "                                      "
                  + "Really, 640K ought to be enough for "
                  + "anybody.  --Bill Gates, 1981"
                  + "                                      "
                  + " ------>  CGI by Example! <------";
          var out = " ";
          var c = 1;

          if (delaytime > 100){
```

continues

Listing 18.4 Continued

```
            delaytime--;
            var cmd="ScrollText(" + delaytime + ")";
            TimerTwo=window.setTimeout(cmd,100);
        }

        else if (delaytime <= 100 && delaytime > 0) {
            for (c=0 ; c < delaytime ; c++) {
                out+=" ";
            }
            out+=msg;
            delaytime--;
            var cmd="ScrollText(" + delaytime + ")";
            window.status=out;
            TimerTwo=window.setTimeout(cmd,100);
        }

        else if (delaytime <= 0) {
            if (-delaytime < msg.length) {
                out+=msg.substring(-delaytime,msg.length);
                delaytime--;
                var cmd="ScrollText(" + delaytime + ")";
                window.status=out;
                TimerTwo=window.setTimeout(cmd,50);
            }
            else
            {
                window.status=" ";
                TimerTwo=window.setTimeout("ScrollText(100)",75);
            }
        }
    }

// ChangeBackground -- Changes the background color
    function ChangeBackground(hexNumber){
        document.bgColor=hexNumber
    }

// The following code gets executed when the page first loads
    Today = new Date();
    document.write("The time now is: ");
    document.write(Today.getHours(),":");
    document.write(Today.getMinutes());
    document.write("<br>");
    document.write("The date is: ");
    document.write(Today.getMonth()+1,"/")
    document.write(Today.getDate(),"/");
    document.write(Today.getYear());

// -- End of JavaScript code -------------- -->
</script>
</head>
```

```
<body bgcolor=#FFFFFF
      text=#000000
      onUnload="window.alert('\nThanks for visiting!')"
      onLoad="TimerOne=window.setTimeout('ScrollText(100)',500);">

<h1>
<i>CGI by Example</i>
<br>
JavaScript Demonstration Page
</h1>

<form name=DemoStuff>
<input type="button"
       value="Open a WebCrawler Search Window"
       onClick="OpenSearchWindow()">

<p>Pick a background color for the main form:<br>
<input type="button"
       value="Red"
       onClick="ChangeBackground('#FF0000')">
<input type="button"
       value="Orange"
       onClick="ChangeBackground('#FF8000')">
<input type="button"
       value="Yellow"
       onClick="ChangeBackground('#FFFF00')">
<input type="button"
       value="Green"
       onClick="ChangeBackground('#008000')">
<input type="button"
       value="Blue"
       onClick="ChangeBackground('#0000FF')">
<input type="button"
       value="Indigo"
       onClick="ChangeBackground('#0000A0')">
<input type="button"
       value="Violet"
       onClick="ChangeBackground('#8000FF')">
<input type="button"
       value="Grey"
       onClick="ChangeBackground('#C0C0C0')">
<input type="button"
       value="White"
       onClick="ChangeBackground('#FFFFFF')">

<p>

Enter a math expression (example, 2+2)
<input type="text"
       name="expression"
       size=15>
```

continues

333

Listing 18.4 Continued

```
<br>
<input type="button"
       value="Click to calculate the result"
       onClick="ComputeValue(this.form)">
<p>
Type your name
<input type="text"
       name="VisitorName"
       size=15>
then
<input type="button"
       value="Click"
       onClick="PromptUser(this.form.VisitorName.value)">

</form>

</body>
</html>
```

Concerns and Cautions

For all the fun you can have with JavaScript, you must remember that it is a new and relatively unblooded technology. If you are planning to use JavaScript to spruce up your pages with doodads and gizmos, be prepared for complaints from visitors that your code made their browsers crash.

If you are planning to use JavaScript to process form input, perhaps to validate orders before sending it on to a Java or regular CGI application, be prepared to lose a lot of business from those who (a) can't use JavaScript because their browsers don't support it, or (b) have JavaScript turned off because they're tired of it crashing all the time. If you need something reliable, try using regular CGI until JavaScript (and for that matter, Java) matures a bit more.

Netscape is swatting bugs quickly, but the number of bugs reported keeps mounting, and each new release of the Netscape Navigator introduces new problems. This is as much a design and marketing problem as an almost-unavoidable concomitant of the technology's youth. To stay on top of the market, Netscape must fix bugs and issue new releases as fast as possible. This, combined with rapidly evolving hacker sophistication, makes both security holes and plain old programming mistakes inevitable.

Netscape intended JavaScript to be secure from the start, and did a credible job in designing the basic environment. Unfortunately, clever users keep figuring out ways to outwit Netscape's precautions. At the moment, most of the risks are minimal, and they concern privacy only. It is possible, under some special circumstances, and with the right (wrong) version of Netscape, to yield up the contents of files on your hard disk without knowing it. It is also possible for malicious JavaScript authors to obtain your browser's history list—including information on what sites you've visited, what search terms you used at various indexes, and so forth.

This chapter won't go into more detail now because by the time this book sees print, these particular security holes surely will be closed. Unfortunately, new ones will doubtlessly have opened by then, too. If you are curious or concerned about the security risks posed by Java and JavaScript, browse the newsgroups or search for "Java security" on your favorite search engine. You'll find many long, detailed, and highly technical discussions on the subject.

Summary

JavaScript is a fun, easy-to-learn scripting language with features specifically designed for Internet applications. It is a new technology, and therefore it is both changing rapidly and full of minor annoying problems.

JavaScript uses Java-like syntax, but doesn't use class modules or downloaded run times. JavaScript is contained completely within the HTML of the page being accessed.

JavaScript gives your pages more interactivity than ever before, and can be used in conjunction with Java or CGI to produce powerful applications where the browser does part of the work.

Review Questions

1. Where does JavaScript execute? On the Web server, the browser, or both?

2. JavaScript won't work with Lynx browsers. Why not?

3. Do JavaScript objects support inheritance?

4. Could you use JavaScript to write a finger, Telnet, or chat client? Why or why not?

5. How many data types does JavaScript support? What are they?

6. Which object is considered the parent of all other objects in the browser?

7. When does the `onLoad` event execute?

8. Why is the JavaScript code kept inside HTML comments as well as inside `<script> </script>` tags?

Review Exercises

1. How could you validate that the input to the ComputeValue() function is nonblank? That it is a valid expression consisting only of numbers and operators? That the operands and result don't exceed the JavaScript interpreter's precision?

2. Write a function to convert numbers from one radix to another, using an input text box, three radio buttons for decimal, hex, and octal, and an alert to display the results.

3. Write JavaScript code to display a running clock on the status line, but *only* when the user's mouse isn't over a link.

## CHAPTER 19

Using PHP/FI

Whether you can use JavaScripts depends on which browser you are using. Some browsers cannot use JavaScripts. PHP/FI, on the other hand, is not browser-dependent, so no matter who visits your site, your PHP/FI scripts will work.

PHP/FI was developed by Rasmus Lerdorf, who needed to create a script that enabled him to log visitors to his page. The script replaced a few other smaller ones that were creating a load on Lerdorf's system. This script became PHP, which is an acronym for Rasmus' Personal Home Page tools. Later Lerdorf wrote a script that enabled him to embed commands within an HTML document to access a SQL database. This script acted as a forms interpreter (hence the name *FI*), which made it easier to create forms using a database. These two scripts have since been combined into one complete package called PHP/FI.

PHP/FI grew into a small language that enables developers to add commands within their HTML pages instead of running multiple smaller scripts to do the same thing. PHP/FI is actually a CGI program written in C that can be compiled to work on any UNIX system. The embedded commands are parsed by the PHP/FI script, which in turn prints the results through another HTML document.

How PHP/FI Works

Suppose that you have a form in which visitors to your site can enter a name and telephone number. When the visitor submits the form by calling another HTML document, PHP/FI first processes the entered information and then presents that information to the visitor in the called HTML document.

For example, suppose that you have the following form within an HTML document:

```
<FORM ACTION="/cgi-bin/php.cgi/result.html" METHOD="POST">
Name:<INPUT TYPE="text" NAME="name"><BR>
Phone number:<INPUT TYPE="text" NAME="phonenum"><BR>
<INPUT TYPE="submit">
```

The visitor completes the form and then clicks the submit button. The entered information initially goes to the PHP.CGI script. The path is sent within the environmental variable PATH_INFO to the HTML file. The PHP.CGI script then interprets the form's information and places it into variables. PHP/FI then sends that information to the HTML file, RESULT.HTML.

> **Note**: PHP/FI can also be compiled as an Apache server module. Such compiling eliminates many of the inefficiencies of CGI scripts. Also, you can configure PHP/FI to run as a FastCGI persistent CGI process (see **www.fastcgi.com**) to enable non-Apache servers to achieve performance similar to that of a server module.

Within the RESULT.HTML file you can embed commands that display the information originally entered by the visitor. The following example displays output similar to figure 19.1:

```
<HTML>
<HEAD><TITLE>Results</TITLE></HEAD>
<BODY>
<?echo "<H1> Hello $name</H1>">
Your name is <?echo "$name"> and your phone number is
➥    <?echo "$phonenum">.
<P>
Welcome to our site!
</BODY>
</HTML>
```

The commands embedded within your HTML document start with <? and end with >.

> **Tip:** Some HTML editors do not like the opening tag <?. To avoid this problem, PHP/FI can also use <!?. If you are having problems with one tag, try the other.

Within the tags you can have your script do a wide variety of things. The tags can include variables, if and while functions, as well as a full set of conditional operators. Take a look at the following example:

```
<?
if ($num != 4 && $num > 5);
 echo "The number is too large!<P>";
endif;
>
```

Figure 19.1

PHP/FI interprets the PHP/FI commands embedded within a document and then displays the interpreted message to the visitor.

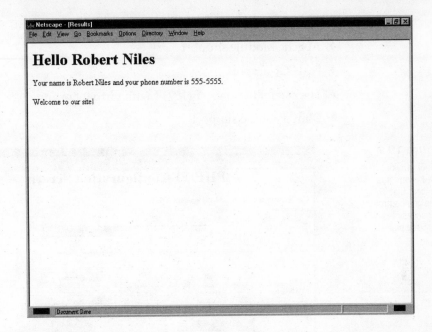

PHP/FI also has other built-in options that can make your job as Web developer easier. You can use the PHP/FI language to configure how your pages are accessed. This capability enables you to add password protection and special log functions, to restrict certain visitors from your site. To add such features, you use an HTML form such as that shown in figure 19.2. Access control is based on the owner of the file; each owner can supply his or her own password to the access control form. For example, if Fred owns the file, the password that Fred uses to modify or protect the script through PHP is initially based on Fred's system password. If you were to create a script called PHONE.CGI while logged on to the system under the username of `fred`, you see something like the following when you list the file:

```
-rwxr—r-x  1 fred  html    43060 Aug  1 09:32 phone.cgi
```

The file PHONE.CGI belongs to Fred. PHP/FI sees this and asks you for your system password, which enables you to access or configure your pages or scripts without enabling anyone else to do so.

Here are some other features available with PHP/FI:

♦ Access logging

♦ File uploads through the Web (by using a browser that complies with RFC 1867)

♦ Tom Boutell's GD graphics library support

♦ Mini SQL (mSQL) support

◆ Postgres95 support

◆ Apache Module support

◆ FastCGI support

◆ The capability to use PHP/FI with virtual hosting

◆ Dbm database support

Figure 19.2

PHP/FI provides a built-in configuration form that gives you control over access to your Web pages.

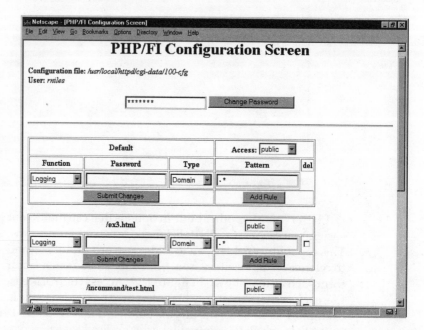

To cover all aspects of PHP/FI would be beyond this book's scope. Instead, this chapter covers quite a few of the commands, and demonstrates how you can use PHP/FI within your Web pages. For the complete documentation, visit the PHP/FI home page at the following address (see fig. 19.3):

http://www.vex.net/php/

The PHP/FI site provides plenty of examples on how to use the PHP/FI to its fullest advantage. Although this book's companion CD-ROM includes the current version of PHP/FI, you can always find its latest version at the PHP/FI Web site.

Figure 19.3

The PHP/FI page contains the complete documentation along with plenty of examples that demonstrate how to use PHP/FI.

A Simple Guestbook

Rasmus Lerdorf wrote this guestbook program, which the PHP/FI package includes. After prompting the visitor to enter information, the program stores the information in a dbm database.

First the program lays out the HTML page, including the colors and background images:

```
<html><head><title>GuestBook</title></head>
<body bgcolor="#ffffff" text="#000000" link="#0000FF"
➥ vlink="#000090" alink="#ff000000">
<p align=center><img src="/php/gifs/phpfi-blk.gif">
<center><h1>GuestBook</h1></center>
```

Next the program generates a file name for the guestbook. The name is based on the name and the path of the HTML file.

```
<?

$fn = $PATH_TRANSLATED;
$fn = $fn - "\.phtml";
```

Now you want to check whether the PHP/FI page was called with the `read` variable set. Suppose that a visitor called the page as follows:

```
<a href="/cgi-bin/php.cgi/guestbook?read+1">
```

You would then assign the first argument, read, to $argv[0], and assign 1 to $argv[1].

As you can see in listing 19.1, the script checks whether the guestbook database exists. If not, the script reports this and exits.

Listing 19.1 PHPGUEST.HTML—Checking Whether the Guestbook Database Exists

```
if ($argv[0]=="read");
        /* Check if the file exists */
        $err = fileinode($fn);
        if($err<0)>
                Guestbook is empty!<p>
                <?include "footer">
                </body></html>
                <?exit;
        endif;
```

Now you check how many days have been requested for viewing. You do so with $argv[1] (see listing 19.2). If the number of days requested equals zero, you display a form in which the visitor can select a time period.

Listing 19.2 PHPGUEST.HTML—Displaying Entries in the Database

```
$days = intval($argv[1]);

if(strtoupper($DAYS)=="ALL");
        $days=0;
elseif ($DAYS > 0);
        $days = $DAYS;
endif>
<form action="<?echo $PHP_SELF>?read" method="POST">
<center>Show entries for the past
<?if($days==0)>
        <input type="text" name="DAYS" value="All" size=4
➥       maxlength=4>
<?else>
        <input type="text" name="DAYS" value="<?echo $days>" size=4
➥       maxlength=4>
<?endif>
days. (0 = All entries)</center></form><hr>
<?
echo "<center><strong>";
/* Title switch */
switch($days);
case 0;
        echo "Showing all entries";
        break;
case 1;
```

```
        echo "Showing today's entries";
        break;
case 2;
        echo "Showing entries for today and yesterday";
        break;
default;
        echo "Showing entries for the past $days days";
        break;
endswitch;
echo "</strong></center>";
echo "<hr>";
```

Next you open the database and look for the entries that match the requested number of days. The pseudocode for this process is as follows:

Open the database.

Check whether the key matches the number of days requested.

If the key matches, assign it to the key array.

Go to the next key and perform the same check until you find GUESTBOOKPASS.

Listing 19.3 shows how you code this process.

Listing 19.3   PHPGUEST.HTML—Checking Whether the Key Matches the Request

```
dbmopen($fn,"r");
$i=0;
$getkey = dbmfirstkey($fn)>
<?while($getkey);
        if($getkey!="GUESTBOOKPASS");
                $keyday = intval(date("Y",
            $getkey))*365+date("z",$getkey);
                $today = intval(date("Y"))*365+date("z");
                if(($today - $keyday < $days) ¦¦ $days==0);
                        $key[$i] = $getkey;
                        $i++;
                endif;
        endif;
        $getkey = dbmnextkey($fn,$getkey);
endwhile;
```

Now you sort each entry in reverse order, using the $j variable to keep track of the number of keys:

```
sort($key[0]);
 $j=$i-1;
```

As you can see in listing 19.4, you next separate each field with an ESC character and assign each field to its own variable.

Listing 19.4 PHPGUEST.HTML—Fetching and Separating Each Entry

```
while($j>=0);
/* Look up the key */
$entry = dbmfetch($fn,$key[$j]);
/* Fields are separated by ESC chars, so tokenize on char 27 */
$name = strtok($entry,27);
$email = strtok(27);
$comment = strtok(27)>
```

In listing 19.5, you finally print the results, which should look similar to figure 19.4.

Figure 19.4

The program displays the results with the specified time period.

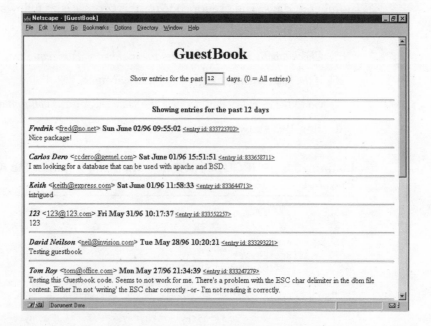

Listing 19.5 PHPGUEST.HTML—Printing the Results

```
<b><i><?echo $name></i></b>
            &lt;<a href="mailto: <?echo $email>"><?echo $email>
➥        </a>&gt;
<b><?echo date("D M d/y H:i:s",$key[$j])></b>
            <font size=-1><a href="<?echo $PHP_SELF>?edit+
➥        <?echo $key[$j]>">
            &lt;entry id: <?echo $key[$j]>&gt;</a></font>
            <br><?echo $comment><hr>
            <?$j--;
    endwhile;
    /* Don't forget to close the dbm file */
    dbmclose($fn)>
    <center>
```

```
        <a href="<?echo $PHP_SELF>"> [Top] </a>
        <a href="<?echo $PHP_SELF>?read+1"> [Read] </a>
        <a href="<?echo $PHP_SELF>?admin"> [Admin] </a>
        </center>
        <?include "footer">
        </body></html>
        <?exit>
<?endif;
```

Now check whether the visitor is trying to change the password. In listing 19.6, the script first checks the $GUSTBOOKPAS variable to see whether the visitor has requested the admin page. If so, you tell the visitor that a password already exists.

Listing 19.6 PHPGUEST.HTML—Checking Whether a Password Exists

```
$a=$argv[0];
if(strlen($GUESTBOOKPASS) && $a!="admin");
        dbmopen($fn,"w");
        $gp = dbmfetch($fn,"GUESTBOOKPASS");
        if($gp)>
                Sorry, this guestbook already has a password<p>
                <center>
                <a href="<?echo $PHP_SELF>"> [Top] </a>
                <a href="<?echo $PHP_SELF>?read+1"> [Read] </a>
                <a href="<?echo $PHP_SELF>?admin"> [Admin] </a>
                </center>
                <?include "footer">
                </body></html>
                <?exit;
        endif;
```

If a password doesn't exist because the guestbook database has been recently created, your script needs to take the password entered by the visitor into the guestbook database:

```
dbminsert($fn,"GUESTBOOKPASS",$GUESTBOOKPASS)>
Password registered!<p>
<?dbmclose($fn);
```

If there isn't a password, you need to inform the visitor and provide an opportunity to enter a password:

```
elseif($GUESTBOOKPASS);
        dbmopen($fn,"r");
        $gp = dbmfetch($fn,"GUESTBOOKPASS");
        dbmclose($fn);
        if(!$gp)>
                There is no password set for this guestbook.
            Please set one.<p>
                <form action="<?echo $PHP_SELF>" method="POST">
                <center><input type="password" name="GUESTBOOKPASS">
                <input type="submit" value=" Ok "></center>
                </form>
        <?endif;
```

If the visitor is trying to administer the guestbook, you must check whether the password is correct. If not, you tell the visitor and exit the script.

```
if($gp!=$GUESTBOOKPASS)>
        Sorry, wrong password.<p>
        <center>
        <a href="<?echo $PHP_SELF>"> [Top] </a>
        <a href="<?echo $PHP_SELF>?read+1"> [Read] </a>
        <a href="<?echo $PHP_SELF>?admin"> [Admin] </a>
        </center>
        <?include "footer">
        </body></html>
        <?exit;
endif>
```

At this point you display the administrative screen (see listing 19.7). This screen consists of a series of forms created by the script. The administration screen enables the administrator to change the password, delete entries, or edit entries.

Listing 19.7   PHPGUEST.HTML—Displaying the Administration Page

```
<?if (!$GUESTBOOKFUNC)>
<center><h2>Administrative Screen</h2></center>

<center>
<form action="<?echo $PHP_SELF>?admin" method="POST">
<input type="hidden" name="GUESTBOOKPASS"
➡  value="<?echo $GUESTBOOKPASS>">
<input type="hidden" name="GUESTBOOKFUNC" value="clear">
<input type="submit" value="Clear all entries">
</form>
</center>

<center>
<form action="<?echo $PHP_SELF>?admin" method="POST">
<input type="hidden" name="GUESTBOOKPASS"
➡   value="<?echo $GUESTBOOKPASS>">
<input type="hidden" name="GUESTBOOKFUNC" value="delete">
Delete all entries older than
<input type="text" name="GUESTBOOKARG" value="30" size=4
➡  maxlength=4> days.
<input type="submit" value=" Ok ">
</form>
</center>

<center>
<form action="<?echo $PHP_SELF>?admin" method="POST">
<input type="hidden" name="GUESTBOOKPASS"
➡  value="<?echo $GUESTBOOKPASS>">
<input type="hidden" name="GUESTBOOKFUNC" value="edit">
```

```
entry id: <input type="text" name="GUESTBOOKARG">
<input type="submit" value="Edit Entry">
</form>
</center>

<center>
<form action="<?echo $PHP_SELF>?admin" method="POST">
<input type="hidden" name="GUESTBOOKPASS"
➥    value="<?echo $GUESTBOOKPASS>">
<input type="hidden" name="GUESTBOOKFUNC" value="change_password">
Change password to: <input type="password" name="GUESTBOOKARG">
<input type="submit" value=" Ok ">
</form>
</center>
<?else;
switch($GUESTBOOKFUNC);
```

If the administrator elects to clear the guestbook, you open the database and delete everything inside. Because you're not deleting the database itself, and don't want someone else to start administering your guestbook, the script must place the password back into the database. Finally, you tell the administrator that you have deleted everything.

```
case "clear";
            dbmopen($fn,"w");
            $dkey=dbmfirstkey($fn);
            while($dkey);
                    dbmdelete($fn,$dkey);
                    $dkey = dbmfirstkey($fn);
            endwhile;
            dbminsert($fn,"GUESTBOOKPASS",$GUESTBOOKPASS);
            dbmclose($fn);
            echo "All Guestbook entries deleted<p>";
            break;
```

If the administrator elects to delete entries older than specified, you need to check the database and delete those entries within the specified time period (see listing 19.8).

Open the database and assign its contents to $dkey.

Read through the database's contents.

Delete the keys that match your criteria.

Loop back and read the next line until you have deleted all matched items.

Listing 19.8   PHPGUEST.HTML—Deleting the Older Entries

```
case "delete";
        dbmopen($fn,"w");
        $dkey=dbmfirstkey($fn);
        $i=0;
        while($dkey);
                $age = intval(date("Yz")) - intval(date("Yz",$dkey));
                if($age > $GUESTBOOKARG);
                        $dead[$i] = $dkey;
                        $i++;
                endif;
                $dkey = dbmnextkey($fn,$dkey);
        endwhile;
        $j=0;
        while($j<$i);
                dbmdelete($fn,$dead[$j]);
                $j++;
        endwhile;
        dbmclose($fn);
        echo "$i entries deleted<p>";
        break;
```

If the administrator requests to edit the password, you open the database and use dbmreplace to exchange the new password with the old one:

```
case "change_password";
        dbmopen($fn,"w");
        dbmreplace($fn,"GUESTBOOKPASS",$GUESTBOOKARG);
        dbmclose($fn);
        echo "Password changed<p>";
        break;
```

If the administrator requests to edit a guestbook entry, you first check whether the string that the administrator entered matches a value in the database. If not, you must tell the administrator.

```
case "edit";
        dbmopen($fn,"r");
        $entry=dbmfetch($fn,$GUESTBOOKARG);
        dbmclose($fn);
        if(!$entry);
                echo "Entry not found<p>";
        else;
```

If you find the entry, you create a form that enables the administrator to edit the contents (see listing 19.9). When the administrator finishes, he or she clicks the submit button, which calls the script again and replaces the information in the database.

Listing 19.9 PHPGUEST.HTML—a Small Form Used to Edit an Entry

```
$name = strtok($entry,27);
            $email = strtok(27);
            $comment = strtok(27)>
            <form action="<?echo $PHP_SELF>?admin"
        method="POST">
          <input type="hidden" name="GUESTBOOKPASS"
        value="<?echo $GUESTBOOKPASS>">
          <input type="hidden" name="GUESTBOOKARG"
        value="<?echo $GUESTBOOKARG>">
          <input type="hidden" name="GUESTBOOKFUNC"
        value="editsave">
            <font size=-1><tt><b>Name</b></tt></font><br>
            <input type="text" name="EditGuestName"
        value="<?echo $name>"><br><br>
            <font size=-1><tt><b>E-Mail</b></tt></font><br>
            <input type="text" name="EditGuestEmail"
        value="<?echo $email>"><br><br>
            <font size=-1><tt><b>Comment</b></tt></font><br>
            <textarea name="EditGuestComment" rows=8 cols=70>
        <?echo $comment></textarea><br><br>
            <center><input type="submit"
        value=" Submit Changed Record "></center>
      <?endif;
      break;
case "editsave";
      dbmopen($fn,"w");
      dbmreplace($fn,$GUESTBOOKARG,"$EditGuestName^
    [$EditGuestEmail^[$EditGuestComment");
      dbmclose($fn);
      echo "Changed record saved.<p>";
      break;
endswitch;
endif>
<center>
<a href="<?echo $PHP_SELF>"> [Top] </a>
<a href="<?echo $PHP_SELF>?read+1"> [Read] </a>
<a href="<?echo $PHP_SELF>?admin"> [Admin] </a>
</center>
<?include "footer">
</body></html>
<?exit;
```

Now check whether a visitor is trying to enter into the administration screen. If so, you need to prompt the visitor for a password.

```
elseif($argv[0]=="admin" || $argv[0]=="edit")>
        Please enter your guestbook admin password:
        <form action="<?echo $PHP_SELF>?admin" method="POST">
        <?if ($argv[0]=="edit")>
                <input type="hidden" name="GUESTBOOKFUNC" value="edit">
                <input type="hidden" name="GUESTBOOKARG"
            value="<?echo $argv[1]>">
        <?endif>
        <input type="password" name="GUESTBOOKPASS">
        <input type="submit" value=" Ok ">
        </form>
        <?include "footer">
        </body></html>
        <?exit;
endif;
```

If the visitor hasn't requested anything specific, you simply supply the visitor with a form to enter something into the guestbook, along with links to the script's other functions:

```
if (!$GuestComment)>
Fill in the fields below to leave an entry in the guestbook. Or you
might <a href="<?echo $PHP_SELF>?read+1">Read the Guestbook</a>.
The owner of this guestbook may <a href="<?echo $PHP_SELF>?admin">
Adminstrate the Guestbook</a>.
<hr>
<form action="<?echo $PHP_SELF>" method="POST">
<font size=-1><tt><b>Name</b></tt></font><br>
<input type="text" name="GuestName"><br><br>
<font size=-1><tt><b>E-Mail</b></tt></font><br>
<input type="text" name="GuestEmail"
 value="<?echo $EMAIL_ADDR>"><br><br>
<font size=-1><tt><b>Comment</b></tt></font><br>
<textarea name="GuestComment" rows=8 cols=70></textarea><br><br>
<center><input type="submit" value=" Submit Comment "></center>
<?include "footer">
<?else>
<?
```

If the visitor has entered information, you must check whether the guestbook is new. If so, you need to create the database.

```
$err = fileinode($fn);
if($err<0);
        /* if file doesn't exist, make a new one */
        dbmopen($fn,"n")>
        This is a new guestbook. Please select an administrative
        password for this guestbook. You will need this password
        to manipulate the guestbook later on.<p>
        <form action="<?echo $PHP_SELF>" method="POST">
        <center><input type="password" name="GUESTBOOKPASS">
        <input type="submit" value=" Ok "></center>
        </form>
        <?include "footer">
        </body></html>
        <?exit;
else;
```

Otherwise, you open the database to write to, using `dbminsert()` to enter the information that the visitor entered into the database:

```
                dbmopen($fn,"w");
        endif;
        /* insert the guestbook data */
        dbminsert($fn,time(),"$GuestName^[$GuestEmail^[
    $GuestComment");
        dbmclose($fn);
>
Thank you, your entry has been added.<p>
<center>
<a href="<?echo $PHP_SELF>"> [Top] </a>
<a href="<?echo $PHP_SELF>?read+1"> [Read] </a>
<a href="<?echo $PHP_SELF>?admin"> [Admin] </a>
</center>
<?include "footer">
</BODY><HTML>
```

The guestbook program is a good example of how PHP/FI integrates with HTML to create applications that you can use within your Web pages. PHP/FI is flexible enough to enable you to consolidate of many of your smaller Perl scripts, which can cause a significant load on your system—especially if your server is a busy one.

A Phonebook Using mSQL and PHP/FI

Using PHP/FI to integrate with a SQL server can speed up your database applications considerably. PHP/FI contains a full set of functions that enable you to process information much more quickly and much more flexibly than a dbm database. This section explores a simple phonebook application that uses PHP/FI to query the database for information.

First you need to create a database. For this example, you need four fields:

♦ `fname` holds the first name of the person entered into the phonebook.

♦ `lname` holds the last name of the person entered into the phonebook.

♦ `phone` holds the telephone number.

♦ `email` holds the person's e-mail address.

The database created for this example is called `myphone`, and the table in which each field belongs is called `phonebook`. You could create additional tables within the database to expand your PHP/FI scripts.

The first page that you create is ADD.HTML. You can find this script on the companion CD. This page enables you to add entries into the `phonebook` table, which you can later call up with another HTML page.

The script first prints the header information for the HTML file:

```
<?
echo "<HTML>";
echo "<HEAD><TITLE>Add to phonebook</TITLE></HEAD>";
echo "<BODY>";
>
<H1>Add to the phonebook</H1>
```

You then assign your database to a variable. Therefore, if you later want to change your database's name, you can do so simply by editing one line.

```
<?
$database = "myphone";
```

Now you want to check whether this script has been called to add information into the database. If so, you must connect to the database and check whether the name entered already exists. The process is as follows:

Get the first and last name from the database and assign the results to $result.

If the names match those already in the database,

Tell the visitor and provide a form for reentering the names.

If the names do not match,

Enter the information into the database.

You check whether the value of the form's hidden input type is 1:

```
if($ADD == 1);
```

If so, you connect to the mSQL server:

```
msql_connect("localhost");
```

You then retrieve the first and last names from the database. These names are equal to the names that the visitor wants to enter into the database. You then assign that value of the first and last name to $result:

```
$result = msql($database,"select fname,lname from phonebook where
➥   fname='$fname' and lname='$lname'");
```

If the first and last names already exist in the database, tell the visitor and provide the form so that the visitor can try again:

```
  if($fname == msql_result($result,0,"fname") && $lname ==
➥ msql_result($result,0,"lname"));
  echo "$fname $lname already exists<p>";

>
<?else>
```

Otherwise, add the first name, last name, phone number, and e-mail address to the database:

```
<?
msql($database, "insert into phonebook (fname,lname,phone,email)
➥ VALUES ('$fname','$lname','$phone','$email')");
>
<?endif>
<?endif>
```

In any event, you print the form:

```
<FORM ACTION="/cgi-bin/php.cgi/phonebook/add.html" METHOD="POST">
<INPUT TYPE="hidden" name="ADD" value="1">
<PRE>
First name:<INPUT TYPE="text" name="fname" maxlength=255>
 Last name:<INPUT TYPE="text" name="lname" maxlength=255>
     Phone:<INPUT TYPE="text" name="phone" maxlength=11>
     Email:<INPUT TYPE="text" name="email" maxlength=255>
</PRE>
<P>
<INPUT TYPE="submit">
<HR>
<CENTER>
<A HREF="phone.html">[Phonebook]</A>
</CENTER>
</FORM>
</BODY>
</HTML>

<?exit>
```

Now that you can enter information into the database, you need to create a script to *retrieve* information from the database. You can find the following HTML file on the companion CD-ROM under the file name PHONE.HTML.

Again, you first print the HTML header information:

```
<HTML>
<HEAD><TITLE>My Phonebook</TITLE></HEAD>

<BODY>
<H1>My Phonebook</H1>
```

Then you connect to the database. You don't have to worry about disconnecting from the database, because PHP/FI handles disconnecting for you when you exit the script. After connecting to the database, you assign the database name to the variable $database, just as you did with the previous script:

```
<?
msql_connect("localhost");
$database="myphone";
```

Next you select all fields from the phonebook table, and assign the value of the result to $result:

```
$result = msql($database, "select * from phonebook");
```

The next line takes the number of rows from the variable $result and assigns that number to $num. You need to do so to find out how many rows exist in the table. Then you set the variable $i to zero. This variable keeps track of the while loop.

```
$num = msql_numrows($result);

$i=0;
```

Use the HTML <TABLE> tag, which helps align the output neatly:

```
echo "<TABLE>";
```

Now display the results of the query. While the $i variable is less than the amount of $rows, you print the result:

```
while($i < $num);
    echo "<TR><TD>";
```

The next line essentially specifies the following:

Print the value of row $i (the row that keeps track of which line you are on), where the name of the row is fname.

Go to the next entry within the row, which is lname, the last name.

Continue until you finish printing the row.

After incrementing the value $i, the process starts all over again until $i equals $num. Here is the actual code:

```
    echo msql_result($result,$i,"fname");
    echo " ";
    echo msql_result($result,$i,"lname");
    echo "</TD><TD>";
    echo msql_result($result,$i,"phone");
    echo "</TD><TD>";
    echo msql_result($result,$i,"email");
    echo "</TD></TR>";
    $i++
  endwhile;
>
```

When you finish, you close the tags:

```
</TABLE>
</BODY>
</HTML>
```

Your script is finished, and you have a working phonebook application; figure 19.5 shows an example of the phonebook's output. The script generates a page that shows each person along with his or her phone number and e-mail address.

Figure 19.5

You can use PHP/ FI to create an application that retrieves a person's name, telephone number, and address from a SQL database.

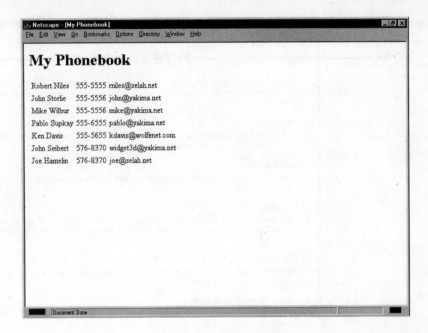

Of course, this application is only a simple example of what you can accomplish with PHP/FI and a SQL database. You doubtlessly can think of other applications that you can use PHP/FI to create. If not, move on to the next section, which points you to a place where you can see how others have put PHP/FI to use.

Exploring Other PHP/FI Examples

Exploring every conceivable way that you can use PHP/FI is beyond the scope of this chapter. To learn more, visit the following site:

http://www.vex.net/php/examples.phtml

Figure 19.6 shows the site, which lists several examples of applications written with PHP/FI.

Figure 19.6

This page shows what other people have accomplished with PHP/FI.

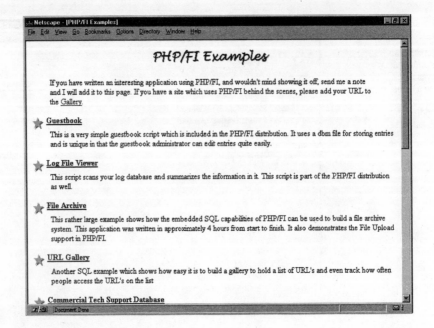

Summary

Although PHP/FI probably can't accomplish everything that you want, you can do quite a bit with the language. At the same time, you can consolidate your scripts within your HTML pages, possibly saving space as well as decreasing the load on your system.

In this chapter, you have learned how PHP/FI can be useful. You learned how to use PHP/FI to create a dbm database for a guestbook script. You also learned how to integrate PHP/FI with mSQL to create a phonebook.

Review Questions

1. Does PHP/FI require that you use a particular browser to run PHP/FI scripts?

2. On what systems can PHP/FI run?

3. How can you use the password-protection features of PHP/FI?

4. Which tags designate the beginning and ending of a PHP/FI command?

Review Exercises

1. Following as an example the PHP/FI phonebook script provided in this chapter, write a script that enables a visitor to enter a first or last name, and have the script search through the database and print any matching results.

2. Write a PHP/FI script that enables a visitor to edit an entry into the phonebook database.

3. Write a PHP/FI script that enables a visitor to remove an entry from the phonebook database.

## CHAPTER 20

Using Visual Basic

Microsoft's Visual Basic programming language (*VB*) is powerful, flexible, extensible, and easy to use. It removes or hides much of the complexity behind creating a Windows application and lets developers get their products up and running quickly.

Although amateurs and dabblers embraced VB enthusiastically when it first appeared, professional programmers saw it mainly as a prototyping tool and fancy toy rather than a serious application development system. When version 3.0 (called *VB3* by those in the know) came along, however, it quickly proved itself equal to the task of making robust commercial applications while losing none of its ease of use. Professionals found that their prototypes could be developed into real applications instead of thrown away. Amateurs who never thought themselves able to write a lick of code suddenly became Windows programmers.

VB is not a cross-platform development environment. It uses precompiled DLLs and other extensions, and relies heavily on the Windows event-driven paradigm. Microsoft made a half-hearted attempt to create VB for DOS, but gave up after version 1.0 because the environment wouldn't support either the tool or the applications created with it. There are VB-like tools for UNIX and the Mac, but they aren't nearly as popular or as robust as VB itself.

VB and CGI: Problems

The Web started out primarily as a UNIX phenomenon, and CGI scripts were typically shell scripts somewhat like DOS batch files. In fact, CGI scripts are still called *scripts* because of this early bias toward using UNIX scripting languages for the task. Although much of the CGI you'll encounter will indeed be scripts (written in sh, Perl, or other UNIX-derived scripting languages), just as much will be programs (written in C, VB, PowerBuilder, and so on). Of these options, pretty much only the C programs and the Perl scripts are portable across platforms, and then only with some attention to inconsistencies and platform-dependent utilities.

By the time Web servers written for Windows NT became popular, there were tens of thousands of programmers who were comfortable with VB, but had no idea how sh or Perl scripts worked. This legion of new Webmasters wanted to use their own tools to write CGI, and, not unreasonably, were upset to find out that VB and CGI were incompatible.

Because the CGI standard was written with shell scripts in mind, it uses the good old UNIX text-based standby of STDIN and STDOUT to communicate with the Web server.

Standard Input and Output

STDIN and STDOUT are mnemonics for *Standard Input* and *Standard Output*, respectively, two predefined stream/file handles. Each process inherits these two handles already open. Command-line programs that write to the screen usually do so by writing to STDOUT. If you redirect the input to a program, you're really redirecting STDIN. If you redirect the output of a program, you're really redirecting STDOUT. This mechanism is what allows pipes to work. If you do a directory listing and pipe the output to a sort program, you're redirecting the STDOUT of the directory program (DIR or LS) to the STDIN of the sort program.

For Web servers, STDOUT is the feed leading to the script's STDIN. The script's STDOUT feeds back to the server's STDIN, making a complete route. From the script's point of view, STDIN is what comes from the server, and STDOUT is where it writes its output. Beyond that, the script doesn't need to worry about what's being redirected where. The server uses its STDOUT when invoking a CGI program with the POST method. For the GET method, the server doesn't use STDOUT. In both cases, though, the server expects the CGI script to return its information via the script's STDOUT (the server's STDIN).

This standard works well in the text-based UNIX environment in which all processes have access to STDIN and STDOUT. In the Windows and Windows NT environments, however, STDIN and STDOUT are available only to non-graphical (console-mode) programs. To complicate matters further, NT creates a different sort of STDIN and STDOUT for 32-bit programs than it does for 16-bit programs. Because most Web servers are 32-bit services under NT, this means that CGI scripts have to be 32-bit console-mode programs. That leaves popular languages such as VB3 and Delphi 1.0 out in the cold.

Some NT servers, notably Bob Denny's WebSite, use a proprietary technique using .INI files to communicate with CGI programs. This technique, which may well become an open standard soon, is called CGI-WIN. A server supporting CGI-WIN writes its output to an .INI file instead of STDOUT. Any program can then open the file, read it, and process the data. Unfortunately, using any proprietary solution like this one means your scripts will only work on that particular server.

For servers that don't support CGI-WIN, you can use a *wrapper* program. Wrappers do what their name implies: they *wrap* around the CGI program like a coat, protecting it from the unforgiving Web environment. Typically, these programs read STDIN for you and write the output to a pipe or file. Then they launch your program, which reads from the file. Your program writes its output to another file and terminates. The wrapper picks up your output from the file and sends it back to the server via STDOUT, deletes the temporary files, and terminates itself. From the server's point of view, the wrapper *was* the CGI program. For more information on wrappers, or to download one that works with the freeware EMWAC server, visit the following site:

http://www.greyware.com/greyware/software/cgishell.htp

Unfortunately, programs written in VB3 don't have access to the server's STDIN and STDOUT. This wasn't an oversight so much as a design decision; the VB3 environment is for creating *visual* applications. The world of text streams, piped output, intricate text scripts, and command-line redirection was left behind like a bad dream. Developers and end-users could now point and click, use drop-down boxes, embed OLE applets, and a hundred thousand other things that text streams just can't provide. The only thing developers *couldn't* do was use the text streams required by the CGI specification.

VB and CGI: Solutions

The problem of getting VB to work with CGI has been addressed in several ways over the years, each solution with its own advantages and disadvantages. In this next section, you'll look briefly at some of those solutions.

CGI-WIN

Bob Denny, creator of the popular *WebSite* server for Windows NT, took the bull by the horns and created the CGI-WIN specification. CGI-WIN isn't specifically a solution for VB, but rather a way of letting practically any Windows-type application provide CGI services for the WebSite server.

WebSite implements CGI-WIN by creating Windows .INI files on the fly any time a CGI-WIN application is invoked. Instead of having to read environment variables and STDIN, the CGI-WIN application only has to read the .INI file. The .INI file contains, among the rest of the variables, the name of the output file WebSite is expecting to be filled in by the CGI-WIN application.

The entire process therefore goes something like this:

1. A visitor clicks a link or submits a form that invokes a CGI-WIN application.

2. WebSite creates an .INI file and launches the CGI-WIN application, passing the name of the .INI file to the application as the command tail.

3. The CGI-WIN application reads the .INI file to find its variables, and then writes its output to the output file.

4. The CGI-WIN application terminates.

5. WebSite notices that the CGI-WIN application has ended, and shovels the contents of the output file back to the visitor who initiated all the action.

6. WebSite cleans up the temporary files.

You can get all the information you want about WebSite and CGI-WIN from either

http://website.ora.com/wsdocs/

or

http://www.website.ora.com/devcorner

WebSite is maintained and distributed by O'Reilly Software, and has progressed significantly since its first release. CGI-WIN now supports either 16-bit or 32-bit VB, and there are hundreds, if not thousands, of programs written to the CGI-WIN specification.

CGIShell

Like CGI-WIN, CGIShell uses files to handle the communication between the Web server and the Windows CGI application. Unlike CGI-WIN, however, CGIShell is a true 32-bit CGI application in its own right, and therefore will work with almost every Windows NT server available, including WebSite, the freeware EMWAC HTTPS, Microsoft's IIS, and dozens of others.

CGIShell uses the PATH_INFO variable to determine what secondary program to run. A typical link using CGIShell might be **http://www.greyware.com/cgi/cgishell.exe/cdemo**. From the Web server's point of view, CGISHELL.EXE is the CGI program. CGIShell turns around and launches CDEMO (or whatever program name you supply) without the Web server being any the wiser.

1. A visitor clicks a link or submits a form that invokes a CGIShell application.

2. The Web server processes the CGI request in the usual way, funneling information into environment variables and/or STDOUT, and then launching CGISHELL.EXE.

3. CGIShell creates two temporary files: one to hold the input to your application, and one to hold the output from your application. While creating the

file with your application's input, it also decodes all encoded URLs and does some other housekeeping on your application's behalf.

4. CGIShell launches your application, with the names of the input file and output file passed to your application as the command tail.

5. Your application looks at the information supplied in its input file, and then writes its output to the output file. When finished, it deletes the input file and terminates.

6. CGIShell shovels the contents of the output file back to the Web server, which passes it on to the visitor who initiated the action.

7. CGIShell deletes any left-over temporary files and terminates.

Almost every Windows NT server that supports standard CGI will work with CGIShell. In addition, CGIShell will work with any 16-bit or 32-bit application that can read and write files.

CGIShell is maintained and distributed by Greyware Automation Products. The online documentation, including many working samples, is at the following site:

http://www.greyware.com/greyware/software/cgishell.htp

A copy of CGIShell, along with several example programs, is included on the CD-ROM that accompanies this book.

VB4-32

With a little bit of effort on the programmer's part, Visual Basic version 4.0 32-bit (*VB4-32*) *can* read and write the 32-bit STDIN and STDOUT used by Web servers. This ability eliminates the need for proprietary solutions such as CGI-WIN, or wrapper programs such as CGIShell.

If you are using the 16-bit VB3, or even VB4's 16-bit environment (*VB4-16*), you must still rely on CGIShell, WIN-CGI, or another such solution. But if you're ready to move into the world of true 32-bit programming, you can use VB4-32 to talk directly to the Web server.

VB4-32 also lets you create OLE applications that can be invoked through some of the new, DLL-based solutions such as the Internet Server Application Programming Interface (ISAPI). ISAPI and OLE are beyond the scope of this chapter. If you are interested in these solutions, stop by Microsoft (**http://www.microsoft.com/**) or Process Software (**http://www.process.com**) and read about ISAPI and other new technologies.

How To Use VB4-32

CGI-WIN and wrapper programs like CGIShell don't need much more discussion. Until recently, these were the only solutions available, so most of the books or articles focus almost exclusively on them (naturally enough).

The remainder of this chapter will concentrate on using VB4-32 for CGI—something you probably can't find *anywhere* else right now. The techniques that this section presents are simple, yet almost unheard-of in the CGI programming community. The situation is sure to change shortly, as more and more people become aware that VB4-32 can interface directly with Web servers.

This chapter will present and explain VB4CGI.BAS, a set of routines and functions you can incorporate directly into your VB4-32 programs. The complete source code for VB4CGI.BAS is included on the CD-ROM accompanying this book. In this section, you examine some of the important features found in this file.

Talking the Standard Talk

VB4-32 can use the Win32 API functions `ReadFile()` and `WriteFile()` to communicate with all files—*including the STDIN and STDOUT streams*—on the system.

Listing 20.1 shows the declarations your program needs to access these APIs.

Listing 20.1   Declarations for VB4-32 To Use *STDIO*

```
' ----- Constants for STDIO

Public Const STD_INPUT_HANDLE = -10&
Public Const STD_OUTPUT_HANDLE = -11&


' ----- Functions for STDIO

Declare Function GetStdHandle _
    Lib "Kernel32" _
    ( _
    ByVal nStdHandle As Long _
    ) As Long

Declare Function ReadFile _
    Lib "Kernel32" _
    ( _
        ByVal hFile As Long, _
        lpBuffer As Any, _
        ByVal nNumberOfBytesToRead As Long, _
        lpNumberOfBytesRead As Long, _
        lpOverlapped As Any _
    ) As Long

Declare Function WriteFile _
```

```
    Lib "Kernel32" _
    ( _
        ByVal hFile As Long, _
        ByVal lpBuffer As String, _
        ByVal nNumberOfBytesToWrite As Long, _
        lpNumberOfBytesWritten As Long, _
        lpOverlapped As Any _
    ) As Long
```

As you can see from the declarations in listing 20.1, using VB4-32 to talk to the standard streams is simply a matter of using the standard API file-handling routines. Listing 20.2 shows a subroutine you can use for printing to STDOUT. A more robust version of this routine would check the return code from the API call.

Listing 20.2   Printing to *STDOUT* from VB4-32

```
Sub Out(txt As String)
    Dim lResult As Long

    WriteFile _
        GetStdHandle(STD_OUTPUT_HANDLE), _
        txt, _
        Len(txt), _
        lResult, _
        ByVal 0&

    ' Debug.Print txt ' if desired
End Sub
```

Reading STDIN is a bit trickier, but not much. The only real difference is that your routine must (a) know how many bytes to read, and (b) allocate storage for the bytes before calling the API. Listing 20.3 shows a code fragment that reads from STDIN.

Listing 20.3   Code Fragment Demonstrating Reading from *STDIN*

```
Content_Length = Val(cgiGetEnv("CONTENT_LENGTH"))
If Content_Length > 0 Then
    lpszBuf = String$(Content_Length + 1, 0)
    lBytesRead = Content_Length
    lResult = ReadFile( _
        GetStdHandle(STD_INPUT_HANDLE), _
        ByVal lpszBuf, _
        Content_Length, _
        lBytesRead, _
        ByVal 0& _
        )
```

continues

Listing 20.3 Continued

```
    If lResult Then
        lpszBuf = Left(lpszBuf, lBytesRead)
    Else
        lpszBuf = ""
    End If
End If
```

Listing 20.3, unlike listing 20.2, shows error checking in action. The `ReadFile()` API routine returns True if the function succeeds, and sets the `lBytesRead` variable to the number of bytes read.

Listing 20.3 obtains the number of bytes to read from STDIN from the CGI environment variable CONTENT_LENGTH, using another VB subroutine called `cgiGetEnv()`. Later you explore the `cgiGetEnv()` routine, but the important thing here is that the fragment in listing 20.3 uses this value to allocate buffer space with the `lpszBuf = String$(Content_Length + 1, 0)` statement. This statement allocates string storage (a sequential buffer of bytes) long enough to hold CONTENT_LENGTH bytes plus one. It also initializes the buffer by filling it with binary zeros.

Listing 20.3 then goes on to make the API call, reading in as much as (but no more than) CONTENT_LENGTH bytes. The number of bytes actually read is used to truncate `lpszBuf` as necessary.

Unraveling the Input

Listing 20.4 shows the complete VB4-32 code to read the input, create an array of environment variables, and parse out and decode any form or QUERY_STRING variables. This listing is part of a larger routine called `cgiStartup()`, and it references other subroutines, such as `cgiGetEnv()` and `cgiURLDecode()`, which are explained later on.

Listing 20.4 Getting and Normalizing All the Input

```
' initialize the Env() array
ReDim Env(0)
EnvCount = 0

' fill in first variables with real environment variables
Do
    Tmp = Environ$(EnvCount + 1)
    If Tmp = "" Then Exit Do
    EnvCount = EnvCount + 1
    ReDim Preserve Env(EnvCount)
    Env(EnvCount) = Tmp
Loop
```

```
' now retrieve anything in the query string or stdin
lpszBuf = ""
Select Case UCase(cgiGetEnv("REQUEST_METHOD"))

    Case "POST"
        Content_Length = Val(cgiGetEnv("CONTENT_LENGTH"))
        If Content_Length > 0 Then
            lpszBuf = String$(Content_Length + 1, 0)
            lBytesRead = Content_Length
            lResult = ReadFile( _
                GetStdHandle(STD_INPUT_HANDLE), _
                ByVal lpszBuf, _
                Content_Length, _
                lBytesRead, _
                ByVal 0& _
                )

            If lResult Then
                lpszBuf = Left(lpszBuf, lBytesRead)
            Else
                lpszBuf = ""
            End If

        End If

    Case "GET"
        lpszBuf = cgiGetEnv("QUERY_STRING")

    Case Else
        cgiErrExit "Request_Method must be either GET or POST"

End Select

' parse out lpszBuf into separate variables
Do
    x = InStr(lpszBuf, "&")
    If x Then
        EnvCount = EnvCount + 1
        ReDim Preserve Env(EnvCount)
        Env(EnvCount) = cgiURLDecode(Left(lpszBuf, x - 1))
        lpszBuf = Mid(lpszBuf, x + 1)
    End If
Loop While x

If Len(lpszBuf) Then
    EnvCount = EnvCount + 1
    ReDim Preserve Env(EnvCount)
    Env(EnvCount) = cgiURLDecode(lpszBuf)
End If
```

Listing 20.4 puts all of the applications input—whether from environment variables, from POSTed data arriving via STDIN, or from the QUERY_STRING variable—into a single string array called Env(). Env() has an arbitrary number of members, and is dimensioned (allocated) dynamically. The current count of members is kept in the EnvCount variable.

Variables can be retrieved from the Env() array by name, using the cgiGetEnv() subroutine presented in listing 20.5. To retrieve the value of the HTTP_REFERER variable, for instance, you would issue a statement such as Debug.Print cgiGetEnv("HTTP_REFERER").

Listing 20.5   Getting *Env()* Variables

```
'
' Returns value of env variable 'var'
'

Function cgiGetEnv(var As String) As String

    Dim x As Integer
    Dim QV As String

    On Error Resume Next

    ' env variables are stored as token=value, so set up QV
    ' to match the token= part

    QV = Trim(UCase(var) + "=")

    ' Loop through each env variable until match is found,
    ' or array exhausted

    For x = 1 To UBound(Env, 1)
        If Left(UCase(Env(x)), Len(QV)) = QV Then
            cgiGetEnv = Mid(Env(x), Len(QV) + 1)
            Exit Function
        End If
    Next x

End Function
```

Listing 20.6 shows all the subroutines used to manage the input processing. This code makes up the bulk of VB4CGI.BAS. The routines have been reformatted slightly to fit the requirements of this book; however, the functionality is identical to VB4CGI.BAS on the CD-ROM.

Listing 20.6   Routines To Handle the Input

```
'
' Main CGI startup routine.  Your program's Sub Main()
' should call this routine at startup, and call
' cgiShutdown or cgiErrExit to terminate.
```

```
' There are two variables your Sub Main() may set before
' calling cgiStartup():
'     ContentType -- if non-blank, cgiStartup will use
' this as your content-type header
'     PragmaNoCache -- if TRUE, cgiStartup will tell
' browsers not to cache your page
' You may leave these variables alone and accept the
' defaults most of the time.
'

Sub cgiStartup()
    Dim x As Integer                ' generic local counter
    Dim EnvCount As Integer         ' local count of env vars
    Dim Tmp As String
    Dim Content_Length As Long
    Dim lpszBuf As String
    Dim lBytesRead As Long
    Dim lResult As Long

    On Error Resume Next

    ' output the standard headers unless told otherwise

    If ContentType = "" Then
        ContentType = "Content-Type: text/html"
    End If


    ' start with Content_Type always!
    Out ContentType + vbCrLf

    If PragmaNoCache Then
        Out "Pragma: no-cache" + vbCrLf
    End If

    Out "" + vbCrLf                 ' terminate header with blank!

    ' define constants & such
    CWD = App.Path                  ' Current Working Directory
                                    ' (not necessarily CurDir$)

    If Right(CWD, 1) <> "\" Then
        CWD = CWD + "\"
    End If

    ' initialize the Env() array
    ReDim Env(0)
    EnvCount = 0

    ' fill in first variables with real environment variables
    Do
```

continues

Listing 20.6   Continued

```
        Tmp = Environ$(EnvCount + 1)
        If Tmp = "" Then Exit Do
        EnvCount = EnvCount + 1
        ReDim Preserve Env(EnvCount)
        Env(EnvCount) = Tmp
Loop

' now retrieve anything in the query string or stdin
lpszBuf = ""
Select Case UCase(cgiGetEnv("REQUEST_METHOD"))

    Case "POST"
        Content_Length = Val(cgiGetEnv("CONTENT_LENGTH"))
        If Content_Length > 0 Then
            lpszBuf = String$(Content_Length + 1, 0)
            lBytesRead = Content_Length
            lResult = ReadFile( _
                GetStdHandle(STD_INPUT_HANDLE), _
                ByVal lpszBuf, _
                Content_Length, _
                lBytesRead, _
                ByVal 0& _
                )

            If lResult Then
                lpszBuf = Left(lpszBuf, lBytesRead)
            Else
                lpszBuf = ""
            End If

        End If

    Case "GET"
        lpszBuf = cgiGetEnv("QUERY_STRING")

    Case Else
        cgiErrExit "Request_Method must be either GET or POST"

End Select

' parse out lpszBuf into separate variables
Do
    x = InStr(lpszBuf, "&")
    If x Then
        EnvCount = EnvCount + 1
        ReDim Preserve Env(EnvCount)
        Env(EnvCount) = cgiURLDecode(Left(lpszBuf, x - 1))
        lpszBuf = Mid(lpszBuf, x + 1)
    End If
Loop While x
```

```
        If Len(lpszBuf) Then
            EnvCount = EnvCount + 1
            ReDim Preserve Env(EnvCount)
            Env(EnvCount) = cgiURLDecode(lpszBuf)
        End If

End Sub


'
' searches through string 'source' replacing every instance of
' 'char1' with 'char2' -- char1 and char2 may be any length
'

Sub cgiSwapChar(source As String, char1 As String,
➥char2 As String)
    Dim x As Long
    Dim tmp1 As String, tmp2 As String

    ' make sure char1 and char2 are different
    If InStr(char2, char1) = 0 Then
        Do
            x = InStr(source, char1)
            If x Then
                tmp1 = Left(source, x - 1)
                tmp2 = Mid(source, x + Len(char1))
                source = tmp1 + char2 + tmp2
            End If
        Loop While x
    End If
End Sub



'
' Decodes %xx escapes and plus signs; does NOT change / to \
'

Function cgiURLDecode(iTxt As String) As String
    Dim x As Integer, i As Integer
    Dim oTxt As String
    On Error Resume Next

    oTxt = iTxt    ' work on a copy of the string

    ' first fix all the plus signs
    Do
        x = InStr(oTxt, "+")
        If x Then Mid(oTxt, x, 1) = " "
    Loop While x

    ' now fix the %xx escapes
    x = 0
    Do
```

continues

Listing 20.6   Continued

```
        x = InStr(x + 1, oTxt, "%")
        If x Then
            i = Val("&H" + Mid(oTxt, x + 1, 2))
            If i Then
                oTxt = Left(oTxt, x - 1) + Chr$(i) + Mid(oTxt, x + 3)
            End If
        End If
    Loop While x
    cgiURLDecode = oTxt
End Function
```

Managing the Output

VB4CGI.BAS includes several handy functions and routines for managing CGI output, too. You don't need to examine them all, but here are a few of them:

- ◆ `Sub cgiDumpEnv()` creates a nicely formatted listing of all environment variables and input variables. Useful for debugging purposes.

- ◆ `Sub cgiErrExit(ErrMsg As String)` outputs an error message and terminates the application. Useful for fatal errors.

- ◆ `Function cgiGetScript() As String` returns the name of the currently executing script in a format suitable for `<a href...>` links.

- ◆ `Sub cgiHeader(txt As String, Optional Level As Variant)` outputs an `<hnn>...</hnn>` header, with the text you supply as the text between the tags. The header level is optional. If you omit this routine, the header will be level 1 (`<h1>...</h1>`).

- ◆ `Sub cgiTitle(txt As String)` outputs the standard CGI `<head><title>...</title></head>` sequence, using the text that you provide between the tags.

- ◆ `Function cgiURLEncode(iTxt As String) As String` returns the text you provide as a URL-encoded string, suitable for use in `<a href...>` links.

- ◆ `Sub Out(txt As String)` sends the text you provide to STDOUT. All output goes through this routine, whether called explicitly by your code or by the other subroutines listed in this section.

Building a CGI Application with VB4CGI.BAS

At this point, you know enough about both CGI and VB4CGI.BAS to build your first application using it. You may be surprised how simple it is.

Copy VB4CGI.BAS from the CD-ROM and put it somewhere safe on your hard disk. It's a good idea to mark it read-only to prevent accidental errors and to force you to add your code to your own modules.

Now fire up VB4 and create the framework for your CGI project:

1. Start a new project in VB by opening the <u>F</u>ile menu and choosing <u>N</u>ew Project.

2. Choose the <u>F</u>ile menu's <u>R</u>emove File command to remove Form1 and any other files present in the project.

3. Choose the <u>F</u>ile menu's <u>A</u>dd File command to add VB4CGI.BAS to the project.

4. Open the <u>I</u>nsert menu and choose <u>M</u>odule to create and insert Module1.

5. In Module1, type Sub Main() and press Enter. VB creates a subroutine called Main() and positions the cursor for you to begin typing your code.

That's the basic framework all your CGI applications will have. Sub Main() is the startup point for the application, and VB4CGI.BAS is sitting in the background, ready to provide support.

Now type a simple program, using only routines from VB4CGI.BAS, to display the environment variables:

```
Sub Main()
    cgiStartup
    cgiDumpEnv
    cgiShutdown
End Sub
```

To compile the program, open the <u>F</u>ile menu and choose <u>M</u>ake EXE File. Name the program VB432TEST.EXE. If you want, compile it directly into your Web server's CGI-BIN directory. If you don't have direct access to your Web server's CGI-BIN directory from your development workstation, compile the file in a temporary directory, then manually copy it to its proper home on the Web server.

Don't put VB away just yet. Pull up your browser and type **http://www.yoursite.com/cgi-bin/vb432test.exe** on the location line. Press Enter and watch your VB4-32 program in action.

You should end up with something resembling the screen shot in figure 20.1.

All your CGI programs will have a structure similar to the program you just created. In particular, your CGI programs must have these features:

1. Start with Sub Main().

2. Sub Main() should immediately call cgiStartup().

3. Sub Main() can then perform whatever code is appropriate to your script, using any of the subroutines and functions provided in VB4CGI.BAS, or any subroutines and functions you create.

4. Sub Main() must end with a call to either cgiShutdown() or cgiErrExit().

Figure 20.1

The output from
VB432TEST.EXE.

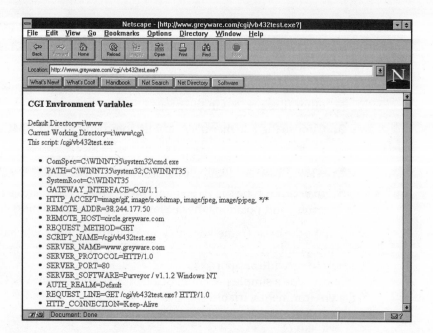

You can modify VB4CGI.BAS to suit your needs, but it's a good idea to keep it in a library of other included files, marked read-only most of the time.

Error Checking

Because VB is primarily a visually oriented environment, Microsoft programmed run-time errors to pop up message boxes with error text. This is handy during development, and somewhat embarrassing in a finished application. If an error message pops up in a finished application, it means you didn't trap errors and test for them correctly in your code.

The run-time environment of a CGI program isn't a desktop. When you create a CGI program using VB, it runs like a background task. Depending on your Web server, any error messages may or may not pop up on the Web server's screen—they certainly won't pop up on the visitor's screen!

In short, you can't rely on VB's built-in error messages while debugging your code, or to discover those nasty run-time errors that you never thought to check for. An untrapped error may leave your CGI program running, waiting patiently for the Web server operator to hit OK before terminating. Again, depending on which Web server software you use, the message box and OK button may not be visible even on the Web server's console.

When this happens, you can usually figure out what's happening because the .EXE file will be locked and the process will still be running.

An even more ugly situation, though, is when you have error trapping turned on, but don't handle all of the errors that might crop up. In this case, your CGI program may blithely continue processing, ignoring the error condition, or may terminate without notice, leading to invalid results or a "hung" browser.

It's a good idea to turn on error trapping with the On Error Resume Next function. Then, after any operation that might produce an error, check the contents of the built-in Err or Error$ variables. (Err will hold a numeric error code; Error$ will hold the corresponding text explanation of the error.)

Use the cgiErrExit() subroutine to report errors back to the browser and to make sure the application quits completely. For example, to trap errors during a file open, you might use code like this:

```
Sub OpenDataFile(DataFileName as String)
    Dim hFile as Long

    On Error Resume Next

    hFile = FreeFile
    Open DataFileName for Input as #hFile
    If Err Then cgiErrExit Error$


    ...

    ' Do something with the open file
End Sub
```

If the file open fails for any reason, the cgiErrExit() routine gets invoked with the proper error message text.

Startup Parameters

Listing 20.6 mentions that there are a couple of optional startup parameters your Sub Main() can set before calling cgiStartup().

These parameters are PragmaNoCache and ContentType. PragmaNoCache defaults to False, and ContentType defaults to Content-type: text/html.

If, for instance, your CGI program wanted to send text/plain instead of text/html, do this:

```
Sub Main()
    ContentType = "Content-type: text/plain"
    cgiStartup
    ....
    cgiShutdown
End Sub
```

Setting the global ContentType variable to anything other than blank forces cgiStartup() to use ContentType for the Content Type HTTP header.

Similarly, if you don't want the output of your CGI program cached by the browser or any caching proxy servers along the way, just include the following line before your call to `cgiStartup()`:

```
PragmaNoCache = True
```

Summary

Visual Basic is a powerful, flexible, easy-to-learn programming language. With the 32-bit version of VB4, you can read and write the standard input/output streams with only a modest amount of effort. CGI scripts written using VB4-32 can do anything any other type of CGI can do, including server push.

VB3 and the 16-bit version of VB4 require an intermediary to sit between them and the Web server. Bob Denny's CGI-WIN (for use with WebSite and compatibles) and Greyware's CGIShell (for use with any server) enable you to use VB3 or VB4-16 for CGI scripts.

This chapter presented you with VB4CGI.BAS, a VB4-32 module that you can incorporate into your own VB4-32 programs to turn them into CGI scripts.

Review Questions

1. Why are CGI programs called *scripts* even when compiled?

2. What is the biggest problem traditional VB programs have talking to Web servers?

3. Can VB3 programs, or VB4-16 programs, use VB4CGI.BAS?

4. How many environment variables can VB4CGI.BAS handle, and how long can the longest one be?

5. How does `cgiStartup()` avoid buffer overflow when reading STDIN?

Review Exercises

1. Write a program using VB4CGI.BAS that accepts the input from a fill-in form and echoes back to the browser (a) the contents of a form variable called `VisitorName`, or (b) an error message saying that `VisitorName` wasn't filled out.

2. Write a program using VB4CGI.BAS that reads the SGB2.DAT file created in Chapter 7, and prints out the guestbook entries as a bulleted list.

3. Can you do a "server push" using either CGIShell or WebSite's WIN-CGI? Why or why not? Would the same restrictions apply to a VB4-32 application using VB4CGI.BAS?

4. How would you modify VB4CGI.BAS to provide global error checking and reporting for *any* project to which it's attached? Would you have to use VB4CGI.BAS differently in such projects?

5. Draw a chart outlining the data flow of a CGI application using CGIShell, starting at the browser issuing the request and showing a complete circuit.

Part VIII

CGI Resources Online

## CHAPTER 21

Finding Help on the Internet Itself

> Know thyself, presume not God to scan; the proper study of mankind is man.
> —*Alexander Pope (1688-1744)*

When Alexander Pope penned the famous lines above, the Internet was not even a bright dream on the horizon. No one imagined the kind of intercourse and connectivity that would appear by the end of the 20th century. And we in the late 20th century are having a hard time keeping up ourselves, let alone understanding what the 21st or 22nd century will bring. Nevertheless, Pope's insight could well have been written as part of the Internet's own credo, for the Internet community likes nothing so much as talking about the Internet.

The first and best place to find documentation, helpful examples, tutorials, and discussions about the Internet is on the Internet itself. This chapter shows you some of the most interesting places.

UseNet

The Internet is far more than just the World Wide Web. If you haven't yet dived into the newsgroups, it's time to take the plunge.

UseNet is a collection of hierarchical *newsgroups*, or discussion topics, maintained on thousands of machines around the world. Newsgroups are said to *propagate* from one server to another—that is, when you make a post to a newsgroup on your local server, that server passes it on to another, which passes it on to another, and so forth. Eventually (and theoretically), all the servers have the same posts, no matter where the posts originated.

It doesn't work out quite that neatly in real life, but most of the time, most of the posts in the primary groups get distributed widely. There are tens of thousands of newsgroups, each concentrating on a particular subject. (My local server offers *only* 17,243 newsgroups!)

This system of distributed newsgroups creates an almost universal bulletin board system. Here's a typical post from one of the newsgroups:

```
Joe Newbie <jnewbie@somewhere.com> writes:

> How can I make an A HREF link do a POST instead of
> a GET to my CGI program?

I'm afraid you can't.  The POST method is only supported
for fill-in forms.  Sorry about that!

- j.
```

The lines starting with greater-than signs (>) indicate that the post's author is quoting an earlier post. In this case, someone had asked a question, and the author was quoting the question and then answering it.

UseNet can be an absolutely priceless treasure trove of information. People make posts around the world, around the clock. Busy newsgroups can rack up a thousand posts a day (although most active groups get only a few dozen to a few hundred).

UseNet newsgroups are mostly *unmoderated*. This means that anyone with access to a news server can participate in the discussion—experts with PhDs in the field, beginners eager for a few pointers, salty old-timers with more opinions than information, and 12-year-olds using Daddy's account. Unmoderated newsgroups have a high signal-to-noise ratio (lots of static, very little information). In general, the comp groups are better than the alt groups, but from day to day, you pay your money and take your chances.

In a *moderated* newsgroup, a person known as the *moderator* approves or rejects each post before it propagates. This greatly reduces the noise and irrelevant chatter, but it also slows down the process considerably. Moderated groups are used mainly for official announcements, publications of specifications, and press releases.

Here's a list of some of the most helpful groups in the comp hierarchy. There isn't much reason to explain what each group discusses, as the hierarchical naming scheme makes it pretty plain:

- **comp.infosystems.gopher**
- **comp.infosystems.wais**
- **comp.infosystems.www.advocacy**
- **comp.infosystems.www.announce** (moderated)
- **comp.infosystems.www.authoring.cgi**
- **comp.infosystems.www.authoring.html**

- comp.infosystems.www.authoring.images

- comp.infosystems.www.authoring.misc

- comp.infosystems.www.browsers.mac

- comp.infosystems.www.browsers.misc

- comp.infosystems.www.browsers.ms-windows

- comp.infosystems.www.browsers.x

- comp.infosystems.www.misc

- comp.infosystems.www.servers.mac

- comp.infosystems.www.servers.misc

- comp.infosystems.www.servers.ms-windows

- comp.infosystems.www.servers.unix

The World Wide Web FAQ

Since November 1993, Thomas Boutell has shepherded one of the largest and most
ambitious FAQs on the Web. (A *FAQ* is a list of frequently asked questions, with
answers, too.) The World Wide Web FAQ covers just about every aspect of the Web,
including CGI programming and debugging. The FAQ is a marvelous continuing
work in progress, and you'll find it quite helpful.

The following is a small excerpt from the World Wide Web FAQ's table of
contents:

```
 1. Overview: how to create web documents
 2. Writing HTML documents yourself
 3. HTML editors
 4. Converting other formats to HTML
 5. Checking web pages for errors
 6. How can I "include" one HTML document in another?
 7. How can I include a "back" button in my web page?
 8. How can I create a background and choose my own text colors?
 9. Generating web pages from a program (CGI)
10. How can I keep "state" information between CGI calls?
11. How can I identify the user accessing my CGI script?
12. My CGI script doesn't work! What's wrong?
13. How can I keep my document from being cached?
14. How can users send me comments and/or email?
15. How can I create fill-out forms?
16. Are HTML 3.0 tables ready? Are there other options?
17. How can I use inline images without alienating my users?
18. Can I create animations in my web page?
19. How can I distribute audio through the web?
20. How can I generate inline images on the fly?
```

```
21. What is HTML 3.0?
22. How do I comment an HTML document?
23. How do I create clickable image maps?
24. How can I create transparent and interlaced GIFs?
    What are they?
25. Why do my transparent GIFs look (grainy, chunky,
    not so transparent)?
26. Which is better for the web, JPEG or GIF?
27. What is a progressive JPEG? How can I produce progressive
    JPEGs?
28. Can I lease space on an existing server?
29. Can I make a link that doesn't load a new page?
30. How can I redirect the browser to a new URL?
31. How can the user download binaries from my server?
32. How can I mirror part of another server?
33. Does mailto: work in all browsers?
34. How can I serve [Word documents, Excel spreadsheets...]
    through my server?
35. How do I publicize my work?
36. Hey, why can't I write a web-exploring robot?
37. Where can I get an access counter for my page?
```

Here's a sample question and answer session from the FAQ:

```
HOW CAN I MAKE MY WEB SITE SEARCHABLE BY THE USER?

    Both free and commercial tools are available for this task.
    A brief list of such tools follows. Thanks to John K. Hinsdale
    for contributing the original list.

  Free Web Site Search Engines

  freeWAIS-sf
          The well-known freeWAIS-sf engine offers an HTTP front
          end,sf-gate, with which users can explore indexed
          documents on your site. <URL:http://ls6-www.informatik.
➤         uni-dortmund.de/freeWAIS-sf/freeWAIS-sf.html>

  glimpse
          From the University of Arizona, the glimpse engine can
          be used to easily search large numbers of HTML documents.
          <URL:http://glimpse.cs.arizona.edu:1994/index.html>

  Harvest
          Harvest, from the University of Colorado, is a powerful
          but somewhat complex information search and replication
          system. Used properly, Harvest can be a powerful tool to
          distribute your documents.
           <URL:http://harvest.cs.colorado.edu>
```

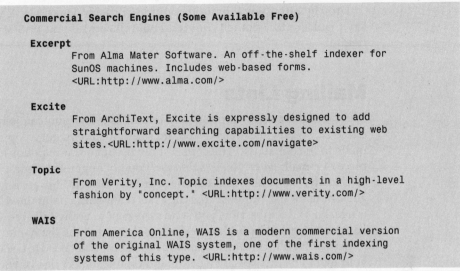

```
Commercial Search Engines (Some Available Free)

Excerpt
        From Alma Mater Software. An off-the-shelf indexer for
        SunOS machines. Includes web-based forms.
        <URL:http://www.alma.com/>

Excite
        From ArchiText, Excite is expressly designed to add
        straightforward searching capabilities to existing web
        sites.<URL:http://www.excite.com/navigate>

Topic
        From Verity, Inc. Topic indexes documents in a high-level
        fashion by "concept." <URL:http://www.verity.com/>

WAIS
        From America Online, WAIS is a modern commercial version
        of the original WAIS system, one of the first indexing
        systems of this type. <URL:http://www.wais.com/>
```

This book's companion CD-ROM includes the full text version of the World Wide Web FAQ (with Thomas Boutell's kind permission). You'll find it in two formats: WWWFAQ.ZIP, an MS-DOS format ZIP file (use PKUNZIP to extract), and WFAQ_TAR.Z, for UNIX platforms. WFAQ_TAR.Z is really WWWFAQ_TAR.Z, renamed to be compatible with the CD-ROM's requirements.

Even better than the text files included on the CD-ROM, the entire World Wide Web FAQ is *online*, set up with proper hypertext links, so that you can find things quickly and easily (see fig. 21.1).

Figure 21.1

The front page of the World Wide Web FAQ.

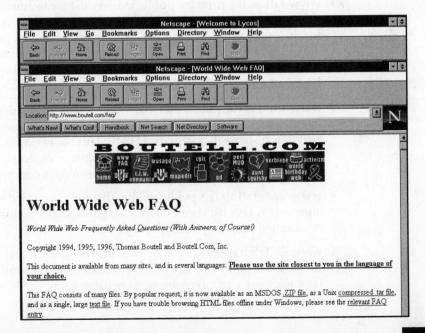

Drop by **http://www.boutell.com/faq/** today and take a look around. Be sure to say thanks to Mr. Boutell (**boutell@boutell.com**) if you find any of the answers helpful.

Mailing Lists

Several organizations support free e-mail lists that you can join. Joining a list is called *subscribing*. As long as you are subscribed, you get a copy of every posting made to the e-mail list. The copies show up in your e-mail box just like any other piece of e-mail. After you *unsubscribe*, you no longer get copies.

Usually, subscribing is simply a matter of sending an e-mail to the robot governing the list. Suppose that the list is **www-talk**, maintained by **w3.org** (which is a real list). To subscribe, you send an e-mail to **www-talk-request@w3.org**. The address is formed by adding *-request* to the end of the list name.

Because you're sending e-mail to a robot, you don't need to be fancy or remember your manners. Just specify a command on the Subject line of your e-mail:

◆ `subscribe` subscribes you to the list.

◆ `unsubscribe` removes you from the list.

◆ `help` gets information about the list.

◆ `archive help` gets information about the list's archives.

Here are some of the lists maintained by **w3.org** that you might find interesting:

◆ **www-talk** is the primary public mailing list for technical discussion among those developing World Wide Web software. This list is explicitly intended for the collaborative design of new systems, software, protocols, and documentation that might be useful to the WWW developer community. General questions from nondevelopers should go to the newsgroup, and topics relating to HTML should go to **www-html**.

◆ **www-html** is the public mailing list for technical discussion among those interested in enhancing the HyperText Markup Language (HTML) or building systems that support HTML. This list is explicitly intended for the collaborative design of new systems, software, protocols, and documentation that might be useful to the HTML developer community.

◆ **www-annotation** is a public mailing list for technical discussion on annotation. This list continues the work originally begun on the W3C Annotation Working Group mailing list.

◆ **www-collaboration** is a public mailing list for technical discussion on the use and further development of Web technology for collaboration, particularly wide-area and asynchronous collaboration.

♦ **www-lib** is the public mailing list for discussion about the W3C Reference Library (libwww). This list is the proper location for discussing bug reports, patches, enhancements, and public contributions to libwww.

♦ **www-style** is the mailing list for technical discussion on Web style sheets. This list is a focused discussion area; all posts to this list must be about style sheets.

♦ **www-font** is a mailing list that discusses fonts and the Web.

♦ **www-next** is a mailing list for general discussion among those using (or thinking of using) the World Wide Web with NeXT machines or with the NeXTSTEP environment.

♦ **www-speech** is a mailing list for discussion among those interested in using (or developing) World Wide Web clients with speech-enabled interfaces.

Online Tutorials

The Web is chock-full of online tutorials for CGI programming. Chapter 22, "The Best CGI Collections on the Web," points out some of the most useful sites, along with collections of libraries and working code that you can snitch.

A good place to start when looking for online tutorials is the World Wide Web Consortium (**http://www.w3.org/**). At **http://www.w3.org/pub/WWW/CGI/**, you can find a fine little section on CGI pointing to various authoritative sources for overviews, examples, and specifications.

Summary

If this chapter continued to provide the URLs of every site relating to CGI, the list would continue for several pages. Chapter 22 provides some of the best sites, but that's no substitute for going out there yourself and getting your feet wet. Hop into your browser, visit your favorite search engine, and search on *cgi, cgi tutorial, cgi script*, or whatever particular subclassification of CGI interests you. You'll find enough to keep you busy—reading, coding, and having fun—for weeks.

The Best CGI Collections on the Web

In a world in which the objective of writing CGI is to publish immediately, it makes sense to provide you with a list of public pages that demonstrate some of what this book has discussed so far. After all, knowing that you *can* accomplish something is sometimes all that's necessary to inspire you to do it for yourself.

This book lists sites that are outstanding for one or more of several reasons. Each site demonstrates a superb and elegant use of CGI, has good CGI reference materials, or offers CGI tools you can download or buy. In recognizing for such excellence, this chapter doesn't consider whether the software is freeware, shareware, or a commercial application. The only objective is to show you how to use CGI correctly and effectively. You might find cheaper ways (and almost certainly more expensive ways) to accomplish your CGI objectives, but the sites described in this chapter are accomplishing them with excellence, and accomplishing them *now*. There's no reason that you can't also achieve the same excellence.

This list is an updated version of the one that appeared in Que's *Special Edition Using CGI*. Undoubtedly, you will note great sites omitted from this chapter, or that a product listed as available from one corporation for a cost is available from another corporation as freeware. This chapter intentionally omits some well-known and excellent sites, often because the sites are too busy to be useful. The worst catch-22 of the Web is that if you produce something very clever or popular, visitors are likely to overwhelm your server. WWW should stand for *World Wide Web*, not *World Wide Wait*. For this reason, the chapter features sites that offer a reasonable response time, and that are dependable rather than fashionable. Of course, this chapter might overlook other great sites simply because the Web changes so quickly.

In this chapter, you explore sites that provide information and examples of the following:

♦ Programming tutorials and sample code

♦ CGI and SSI freeware and shareware

♦ Fun stuff that exemplifies excellent use of CGI

♦ Indexing

♦ Connecting SQL databases

♦ Spiders, worms, crawlers, and robots

♦ CGI interactive games

You'll also study three companies—CalWeb, Internet Concepts, LLC, and RealCom—that are using CGI programming to great effect.

This Ever-Changing URL in Which We Live

URLs change. Sites come and go. Some last for years, others for days or hours. Sometimes a popular site becomes temporarily unavailable due to excessive traffic. Sometimes a router fails between you and the site. Sometimes the site's server goes down. Sometimes a site just disappears.

Any book that provides current information runs the risk of becoming outdated. A chapter such as this one, however, is almost certain to list expired links—pointers to sites that have either moved or gone on to the Great Bit Bucket in the Sky.

We made every effort to ensure that, as of the date of manuscript preparation, the URLs provided throughout this book are correct and working. By "correct," we mean that the site's URL is accurate and that the site's content is described accurately. There's no guarantee, especially when referring to subpages on a site, that the Webmaster hasn't shuffled things around—or even decided to give up CGI information in favor of spotlighting the latest interactive smut fiction. Such is the way of the Web. By "working," we mean that we tested the link and determined that it was both reliable and reasonably responsive.

Programming Tutorials and Sample Code

You can find a variety of online tutorials on the Web, many of which include sample code. Some are meant to be tutorials; others are just such good examples of programming, or such simple code, that they become lead-by-example instruction sheets. Because this book is itself one long CGI tutorial, this section doesn't list too many of these online tutorials. However, even a book as comprehensive as this one can't cover everything, so here are pointers to some fundamental or esoteric tutorials that you might find useful.

♦ The Common Gateway Interface (**http://hoohoo.ncsa.uiuc.edu/cgi/**). If your high school teachers did their jobs, you know that you must return to original sources when doing research. You'll make your teachers and yourself happy by reading this tutorial from NCSA. Starting at ground zero and working up to a library of examples, this hypertext document gives the proper foundation for further exploration.

♦ University of Utah's Introduction to CGI Programming (**http://ute.usi.utah.edu/bin/cgi-programming/counter.pl/cgi-programming/index.html**). This document contains an introductory tutorial on CGI programming, including some example CGI programs. If you are already an accomplished programmer, this tutorial provides the basic information that you need to develop your own CGI programs. The example programs are in UNIX Bourne shell language (sh) and Perl. The programs are relatively simple and should be understandable to anyone familiar with the UNIX environment and the C programming language.

♦ W4 Consultancy (**http://sparkie.riv.net/w4/software/counter/**). This site offers a digital-counter script for UNIX. From this page, you can download a GZIP of the counter and also access a frequently asked questions (FAQ) document about the counter. If you haven't previously worked with CGI, this might make a good first project. This site is listed here rather than in "CGI and SSI Freeware and Shareware," because the code and documentation make an excellent primer.

♦ Gates-o-Wisdom Software (**http://www.neosoft.com/~dlgates/home/dggeneral.html**). This NCSA-based SSI page counter provides tips and tricks for UNIX. The page also contains a great tutorial on general SSI and CGI techniques for NCSA servers.

♦ Teleport CGI Scripts (**http://www.teleport.com/toc/**). This page is a compendium of Perl and shell scripts for users of Teleport Internet Services. The individual script documentation sections usually include the source code. The scripts are short and sweet, and provide a good idea of how to accomplish many common tasks.

♦ WebSite CGI (**http://website.ora.com/techcenter/**). If you use WebSite, you won't find a better reference than Bob Denny's own documentation (after all, he wrote the server). WebSite is one of the most popular and successful NT servers. It attacks the GUI problem directly by providing built-in support to link the Web server with Visual Basic, Delphi, or other Windows development environments. This particular page provides starting points for technical papers, server self-tests, CGI programming, and related information.

♦ Developer's Corner (**http://website.ora.com/techcenter/devcorner/**). This site explains the peculiarities and strengths of WebSite CGI, and gives you step-by-step instructions for using WebSite's support for Visual Basic, Delphi, and Perl.

♦ Bob Denny (**http://solo.dc3.com/wsdics/db-src/**). At this site, the author of WebSite can entertain and enlighten you further.

♦ CGI Scripting with MacHTTP and AppleScript (**http://152.1.24.177/ teaching/manuscript/1800-0-cgi.html**). Although this site can be difficult to reach, it offers a wealth of information about scripting for the Macintosh.

♦ CGI and AppleScript (**http://www.ddj.com/ddsbk/1995/1995.11/ simone.htm**). This site features a *Dr. Dobb's Journal* article by Cal Simone, founder of MainEvent software. Written by a gifted author and programmer, this wonderful tutorial teaches the essentials of how AppleScript interfaces with your Macintosh system, and how you can use AppleScript to perform CGI magic.

♦ Writing CGI Scripts for WebStar (**http://www.hotwired.com/staff/ userland/aretha/writingcgiscriptsforwe_227.html**). This site offers support for the Macintosh's WebStar server through UserTalk in the Frontier environment. You'll find a good explanation of how to use Frontier to create dynamic HTML on your WebStar server. If you use this platform, this site has your tutorial.

♦ The Amiga HTTP Common Gateway Interface (**http://www.phone.net/ amiga-docs/**). Mike Meyer takes time out to explain the tips you need to run CGI scripts on an Amiga Web server. He includes several useful examples in a link at the bottom of the page.

CGI and SSI Freeware and Shareware

As you wander through the online world looking for samples of scripts for tips on technique, you might find some ready-to-run scripts that do exactly what you want. This section presents some sites that offer freeware or shareware CGI, SSI, and Java scripts. You won't find anything wild or strange here; you can put these workaday programs right to work performing useful tasks.

You've probably already encountered many of these software offerings without knowing it. If you've visited a Windows NT server with a graphical counter, for instance, chances are good that the site is using Kevin Athey's creation, or at least the GD library component of it. For that matter, you'll find that most CGI scripts that produce on-the-fly GIFs, regardless of platform, use the GD library. Likewise, most of the programs in this section are proven products in widespread use. Fill your coffee cup, clear some space on your hard disk, and get ready to download.

Here are some of the best freeware and shareware tools available to spice up your Web pages and make your site more powerful:

♦ Examples of Perl CGI Scripts, with Source Code (**http://www.panix.com/ ~wizjd/test.html**). This no-nonsense page demonstrates six useful utilities, all built with Perl. The utilities include a clickable imagemap, ways to maintain state information and design a self-scoring questionnaire, demonstrations of generating random numbers and finding names in a phone book, and a client-pull demonstration.

Each utility includes the source code, which usually has a helpful header explaining the script's function, but absolutely no documentation thereafter. Fortunately, these scripts are short and simple enough that you can probably figure out what they are doing and how they work.

♦ Mooncrow's CGI/Perl Source Page (**http://www.seds.org/~smiley/cgiperl/ cgi.htm**). Mooncrow is Carl M. Evans, a long-time computer professional with BSEE and MSEE degrees, several commercial applications, and a textbook to his credit.

Also to Mooncrow's credit is Aeyrie, which includes Mooncrow's CGI/ Perl Source Page. Evans says

> When I decided to create and run my own Web pages, I had trouble locating adequate resources on the Internet concerning CGI/Perl programming, so I created my own. While scripts can be written in a number of languages, I prefer to use Perl 4 or Perl 5. It doesn't matter what platform the server is being run on as long as the server supports Perl 4 and/or Perl 5 compliant scripts.

Evans ended up with probably the most complete reference set of Perl programs available on the Internet. With over 50 links to tutorials, sample programs, reference materials, and source code, Evans' site provides a wonderful resource for anyone considering using Perl for CGI scripting.

♦ gd 1.2 Library (**http://www.boutell.com/gd/**). If you're planning to create on-the-fly GIFs, don't miss Thomas Boutell's wonderful C library. You can incorporate this code directly into your own programs to give them spontaneous GIF creation powers.

♦ Greyware Automation Products (**http://www.greyware.com/greyware/ software/**). Greyware provides a good selection of freeware and shareware CGI and SSI programs for Windows NT and Windows 95.

Greyware's CGIShell program is of particular interest if you want to do CGI with Visual Basic, Delphi, or another 16-bit GUI development language on EMWAC (European Microsoft Windows NT Academic Consortium). CGIShell comes with a handful of fully functional demonstration programs, including source code and a guestbook program written in Visual Basic 4 that you can put to work immediately. The online documentation often provides a good explanation of what goes on behind the scenes.

◆ Windows NT Web Server Tools (**http://www2.primenet.com/~buyensj/ ntwebsrv.html**). Jim Buyens has put together a great resource covering programs that provide server extensions, connectivity, Domain Name Service (DNS), finger, firewall, File Transfer Protocol (FTP), Gopher, HyperText Transport Protocol (HTTP), log analysis, mail, news, Network File System (NFS), Perl, publishing, search engines, software suites, Telnet, Tiny FTP (TFTP), Wide Area Information Service (WAIS), and X Window clients. The category "Other Resources" covers features that Buyens couldn't fit into the other groups.

If you're running Windows NT, put this site in your bookmark file. You'll find yourself returning to it again and again.

◆ The Windows NT Resource Center (**http://backoffice.bhs.com/scripts/ dbml.exe?template=/scripts/wntrc.dbm**). This site's URL is long, but worth typing. The site is probably the most comprehensive repository of Windows NT software on the Internet. The site includes a little bit of everything, and many features that you won't find elsewhere. You'll notice this site featured again in the following section, "Fun Stuff: Examples of Things Done Right."

Fun Stuff: Examples of Things Done Right

This section lists a collection of sites that demonstrate stylish, informative, creative, or intriguing uses of CGI on the Web. You'll find plain old CGI and SSI mixed in with Java, real-time audio, real-time video, and other features.

This list starts small, with a simple page counter, and works its way toward the bizarre and fanciful. The chosen sites demonstrate technique and taste. If you don't find any ideas for programs in this section, check your pulse; you might already be dead.

◆ Voyager, Publisher of Interactive Media (**http://www.voyagerco.com/**). This site's presentation is tasteful and elegant. Pay particular attention to the current date and the quote of the day, which are carefully blended into the page's overall theme.

◆ The Amazing Fishcam! (**http://www.netscape.com/fishcam/fishcam.html**). No list of sites is complete without including the one, the original, the Amazing Fishcam! This site is nothing more than two cameras focused on a tank of fish. Nothing more? Well, as the site explains in gleeful detail, there's a lot more. You can look at the fish in low resolution or high, and if you're running Netscape, you can visit the Continuously Refreshing Fish Cam—a wonderful example of server push technology. Although the idea of watching fish in near real time isn't particularly exciting, this site is one of the first to demonstrate the power of the Web to provide electronic photos. Just in case you care about the fish as well as the technology, this page happily refers you to 12 other aquatic sites.

♦ The Amazing Parrot-Cam! (**http://www.can.net/parrotcam.html**). If fish aren't enough, here's Webster, the parrot, on a live camera feed for your viewing pleasure. In addition to good camera work, this page features a nice explanation of how its camera is set up and connected to the computer.

♦ Autopilot (**http://www.netgen.com/~mkgray/autopilot.html**). This site takes you on a whirlwind tour of the Internet. Offering a choice of over 8,000 sites in its list of URLs, Autopilot can help you find interesting and surprising places that you never would have chosen to visit otherwise. Autopilot relies on Netscape's client pull function to whisk you from site to site every 12 seconds. This site is also a good demonstration of random URL generation.

♦ Background Generator (**http://east.isx.com:80/~dprust/Bax/index.html**). This handy site lets you build an image file to use as a background. It starts with some stock images, then takes you through a customization phase where you can edit the colors until you get exactly what you want. This UNIX magic comes to you from a program written by **dprust@isx.com**.

♦ bsy's List of Internet-Accessible Machines (**http://www.cs.cmu.edu/afs/cs/usr/bsy/www/iam.html**). This page is an exhaustive source for Internet gadgets. Want to find a Coke machine that responds to a ping? Or change the track on a CD player at Georgia Tech? Do you care about Paul Haas's current refrigerator contents? Want to play with a remote-control model railway over the Internet? Are you craving some real-time Internet Talk Radio from NRL? Or did you ever wonder how to find the infamous Ghostwatcher home page? This site points you to all the cool places for gadgets, machines, and goofy things on the Internet. It's great for helping you think of new ways to use the Web!

♦ Dr. Fellowbug's Laboratory of Fun & Horror (**http://www.dtd.com/bug/**). This site features great examples of games and general interactivity, with a macabre twist that's as much fun as the games themselves. This site doesn't offer any software to download, just hours of entertainment and perhaps an idea or two for the terminally twisted mind. The animated Hangman game is particularly well done.

♦ The Electric Postcard (**http://postcards.www.media.mit.edu/Postcards/**). This site uses CGI and e-mail in a clever way. The Electric Postcard lets you choose from a variety of amusing (or just plain strange) postcard stock, and then enables you to personalize your postcard.

♦ The Windows NT Resource Center (**http://backoffice.bhs.com/scripts/ dbml.exe?template=/scripts/wntrc.dbm**). You saw this site earlier in the section on freeware and shareware programs. This section lists the site as well, because it's the cleanest example on the Web of interfacing a back-end database with a software library. The site is well indexed, carefully categorized, and easy to use. Kudos to Beverly Hills Software for providing such a well-designed and useful site.

♦ Nanimation of the Week (The Vertex Award) (**http:// weber.u.washington.edu/~stamper/notw/animate.cgi?far.txt**). Although often almost intolerably slow, this site is nevertheless important enough to mention here; it happens to be worth the wait. A Nanimation is a Netscape animation. This page lists the Vertex Award winners for best Nanimation on the Internet. Even the introduction to the award lets you know that you're in for something special. The pages that win awards are spectacular.

♦ The Netscape Engineering Sign (**http://www.netscape.com/people/mtoy/ sign/**). This CGI-machine interface enables you to type a message to be displayed in huge green letters on a sign in the Netscape office's engineering pit.

♦ The Web in Pig Latin (**http://voyager.cns.ohiou.edu/~jrantane/menu/ pig.html**). This site could easily win the award for the most bizarre idea ever to grace the Internet. In fact, the site has won several awards: *Business Weekly*'s "As a Time Out" Site of the Week; The Stick's Misc Surf Site; a Hot Site in Internet World; and "a site that 'does stuff' by the Center for the Easily Amused." Basically, you enter a URL on a provided form. The CGI program then fetches the page and presents it to you in Pig Latin. This section lists the site because the CGI does more than create HTML on the fly for you; it actually fetches a page, playing a browser role, to generate the HTML.

♦ Talk to My Cat (**http://queer.slip.cs.cmu.edu/cgi-bin/talktocat**). This site, says author Michael Witbrock, features a speech synthesizer connected to the computer. You type in a sentence, and the speech synthesizer says it aloud to Michael's cat—if the cat happens to be around, that is. And awake. And listening. Who knows? Who cares? Is this any different from talking to a cat in person?

♦ WebChat Broadcasting System (**http://www.irsociety.com/wbs.html**). WBS, or WebChat Broadcasting System, is one of the cleanest examples of real-time chatting using the Web. With hundreds of "channels" (separate discussion areas) from which to choose, WebChat offers something for everyone. And it seems that everyone has been on WebChat once or more. WebChat boasts over 35 million hits per month. WBS offers to sell its software to run on your own server or to lease you space on its server. A freeware version of WebChat with limited features is also available. You'll need a UNIX machine to run this version, although a port to NTPerl is under way.

♦ Xavier, the Web-Controlled Robot (**http://www.cs.cmu.edu/afs/ cs.cmu.edu/Web/People/Xavier/**). Xavier isn't a toy. He has three onboard 486 computers, a Sony videocam, and enough engineering guts to rebuild the atom bomb from scratch. Well, maybe not, but he *can* tell knock-knock jokes! Users can issue commands to Xavier and, by tapping into this video eye, watch him execute those commands. Xavier communicates to the rest of the world with wireless Ethernet.

Indexing

Many Web sites do indexing well, and this section lists several of the best and brightest searchable sites on the Internet. For the sake of contrast and instruction, this section lists one site that actually makes the content harder to find than if it were buried at sea in a locked cabinet. This kind of egregious irresponsibility is rare, however. This list begins with examples of small sites and works its way up to the behemoths at Infoseek and Alta Vista.

♦ The UBC Facility of Medicine Home Page (**http://www.med.ubc.ca/ home.html**). A good example of a site (really a collection of pointers to sites) with a static index. UBC (University of British Columbia) demonstrates how to handle manually this type of project, in which full-text indexing is either impossible or impractical. If you haven't visited this site before, be sure to make a bookmark for it. The information presented on this site is invaluable.

♦ Site-Index.pl (**http://www.ai.mit.edu/tools/site-index.html**). This site presents Perl code for preparing your site to participate in the Aliweb master index and search engine. Site-Index.pl is useful even if you don't plan to participate in Aliweb, because you can examine the Perl code to see what kinds of information are used to create a site index.

♦ Technical Discussion of the Harvest System (**http://harvest.cs.colorado. edu/harvest/technical.html**). This site offers a thoughtful and complete overview of the problems inherent in current indexing systems, along with the rationale behind the new Harvest System's approach. For information on getting the Harvest software, or to sample sites already using it, see Harvest's main page at **http://harvest.cs.colorado.edu/**.

◆ Newsgroup-Related Indexes (**http://www.ncsa.uiuc.edu/SDG/Software/ Mosaic/Interfaces/wais/NewsGroupsRelated.html**). This site contains a list of pointers to several other WAIS engines maintaining full-text indexes for several popular UseNet newsgroups. If for no other reason, you can visit these sites to see how efficient WAIS can be. Often overlooked in favor of large relational database back-ends, WAIS can be quite useful for appropriate tasks. If you need a full-text search engine to handle a reasonable amount of data, WAIS can handle the job quickly and efficiently.

◆ Greyware Site Index (**http://www.greyware.com/index/**). Here's an example of using WAIS to catalog all the HTML on a site. The WAIS catalogs are rebuilt daily and stored in one directory. Static HTML documents in that directory enable you to select the database, then execute the actual search using Boolean operators and keywords. This site proves that WAIS is alive and well on the Windows NT platform. You can search over 18M of index in less than a quarter of a second, on average. The cataloging itself takes about 15 minutes a day to run.

◆ Social Security Handbook 1995, from the United States Social Security Administration (**http://www.ssa.gov/handbook/ssa-hbk.htm**). This URL is the best example I've found of exactly the *wrong* way to index a site. A database engine could easily organize the material; even FreeWAIS could handle it without much effort. Instead, this "index" is nothing more than a list of links—"Index letter A," "Index letter B," and so on. When you choose an index letter—roughly corresponding to the first word of the subject rather than the key idea of the subject—you'll find a bunch of static links to documents by an inscrutable SSA document number. Good luck ever finding anything on this site. A better strategy would have been to list everything in one directory and then rely on keyword retrieval. Study this page carefully so you know how *not* to handle indexing. If you're ever tempted to organize your site this way, be prepared to deal with angry e-mail from your bewildered and abused visitors.

◆ Infoseek Guide (**http://guide-p.infoseek.com/**). Here's an example to balance the Social Security Administration's abomination. This search engine shows how indexing *should* be done. It's clean, fast, easy to use, and remarkably useful. Infoseek's award-winning engine not only brings you speedy results, but offers advanced users a great deal of flexibility. If you're writing your own search engine from scratch, take a close look at Infoseek's specifications and capabilities first. When you realize the size of the task and the sanity that Infoseek brings to it, you'll find the site even more impressive.

◆ Alta Vista (**http://www.altavista.digital.com/**). Another example of how to handle indexing the right way. Using some frighteningly powerful DEC workstations and servers, Alta Vista brings you an incredibly fast, incredibly large index of Internet sites and newsgroup contents. Digital's research laboratory personnel developed this proprietary 64-bit search software inhouse. The indexer software can crunch a gigabyte of text per hour. Scooter, DEC's Web spider, collects information and can visit as many as 2.5 million sites each day. Although the presentation isn't as slick as Infoseek's, the search engine's breadth of knowledge simply staggers the mind. This search engine is a technology to watch.

♦ Indexes and Search Engines for Internet Resources (**http://www.well.com/ user/asi/netndx.htm**). A useful list of search engines and indexes maintained by Jan Wright, this site can help you find the proper search engine for your site.

Connecting SQL Databases

Many Web servers, especially recent entries into the field and those designed for the Windows NT platform, have database connectivity built in to the server. Even those servers that don't talk to databases directly (through ODBC, or Open Database Connectivity) usually include a CGI module of some sort that does. Although this allows the advertisers to claim that the server comes packaged with database functionality, often the level of database support is only good enough to demonstrate connectivity, not to build a real application. In any case, older servers, especially in the UNIX world, usually have no database support at all.

This section looks at a few third-party products designed from the ground up to help you connect your Web server to a back-end database. Although many products are available, the ones that this section discusses are clear leaders in the field, either because of outstanding performance or general availability and widespread use.

♦ Cold Fusion (**http://www.allaire.com/**). Cold Fusion is a full set of connectivity tools that enables your Web server to work seamlessly with your SQL back-end database server. The tools work with O'Reilly WebSite, Netscape HTTPD, or Process Software's Purveyor. Support for other platforms is coming soon.

Users don't need to program in C, Perl, or any other programming language. Cold Fusion provides the power automatically through HTML, using high-level database commands and a general-purpose CGI scripting language.

Cold Fusion's heart is DBML.EXE, a CGI script tailored for ODBC access to the back-end database of your choice. Cold Fusion dynamically generates HTML pages containing the results of queries or submissions, and lets you freely mix `if-then-else` conditional processing and multiple SQL statements with your regular HTML.

◆ **W3-mSQL** (**http://Hughes.com.au/product/w3-msql/**). W3-mSQL is an interface package that enables you to use mSQL (a freeware, lightweight UNIX SQL engine) with your Web server. W3-mSQL is a CGI script that works by interpreting enhanced HTML on the fly. Using a variation on HTML comments to embed W3-mSQL commands, you connect to, query, update, and close a back-end database entirely within your HTML.

If you're planning to use mSQL on your UNIX machine and don't want to write the interface code yourself, check out W3-mSQL.

◆ mSQLJava Home Page (**http://www.minmet.uq.oz.au/msqljava/ index.html**). This site offers a library of HotJava classes suitable for use with an mSQL back-end database. The package is copyrighted by Darryl Collins, but you can use, copy, and redistribute it under the terms described in the GNU General Public License. This site provides links to FTP sites in which you can download the class library, links to pages with documentation, and links to pages with sample programs and source code.

◆ mSQL (MiniSQL) (**http://Hughes.com.au/product/msql/**). If all this talk about mSQL tools has you wondering about the back-end database itself, this site presents the official source of information and code. Although the site is occasionally quite slow to respond, you should get information about mSQL directly from its source.

mSQL is a lightweight, freeware SQL engine for UNIX machines. Although fully ANSI-compatible, mSQL implements only a subset of SQL commands. For Web developers, this subset is ideal, because it includes only those commands that you'll need and discards those that you'll never use.

◆ Tango (**http://www.everyware.com/Tango_Info/**). Tango Solutions, from Everyware, is a complete CGI package for the Macintosh to connect HTML to Everyware's own back-end database, ButlerSQL. Development is under way to enable Tango to talk to other SQL engines, but currently Tango supports only ButlerSQL. The ButlerSQL version of Tango is free; versions that connect to other databases might eventually require a fee.

On the Tango home page, you'll find links to demonstration programs—some of them rather slick—for online shopping, conferencing, and other useful ways to take advantage of Tango on your Macintosh server. You'll also find a nonsearchable FAQ page with links to individual questions and answers and generic product information. (Curiously, Everyware didn't choose to store this information in a ButlerSQL database and enable users to search for keywords using Tango.) You can download the Tango software directly from this page.

CGI *By*
EXAMPLE

♦ Oracle World Wide Web Interface Kit Archive (**http://
dozer.us.oracle.com:8080/**). If you're using Oracle as your back-end
database, look no further than this page for your interface software. Oracle
meticulously provides information for interfacing most common Web
servers with its database product. The site even examines cross-platform
connectivity issues and third-party products, and offers complete working
examples of useful programs, including one that enables you to do a
keyword search of NCSA's documentation.

♦ DB2 World Wide Web Connection, Version 1 (**http://
www.software.ibm.com/data/db2/db2wannc.html**). With typical IBM
verbiage and charts, this page shows you how to connect your OS/2 or
AIX Web server to a DB2 back-end database. You'll find demos showing
how DB2 WWW Connection V1 (the site's abbreviated name) can generate
Netscape tables to hold query results. You can download the software
directly.

If your platform is OS/2 or AIX, and you're trying to talk to an IBM
database, this package is probably your best bet.

♦ WWW-DB Gateway List (**http://flower.comeng.chungnam.ac.kr/
~dolphin/WWWDB.html**). Here's a handy site maintained by KangChan
Lee. Lee has gathered in one place links to dozens of Web-to-database
gateway programs, methods, and tutorials.

If you're using a back-end database other than the ones that this chapter
has already mentioned, take a glance at Lee's page. You'll probably find
your database, along with a helpful link to available software for it.

Spiders, Worms, Crawlers, and Robots

If you're just looking for information from the Internet, use one of the publicly
available search engines. You'll probably never have the resources to duplicate the
mighty Alta Vista, for example, and even if you did, you would need more help than
this section could possibly give. Besides, all the really good robot code has
commercial value, and hence isn't freeware.

On the other hand, if you want to build a small, special-purpose spider, worm,
crawler, or robot, some code is available to help you get started. More important
than how to build such an application, however, is how *not* to do it. That's why the
first link listed is to an article that you *must* read if you're going to build a Web
automaton. Also be sure to check Chapter 13, "Introduction to Indexing," for more
information about this topic.

♦ Ethical Web Agents (**http://www.ncsa.uiuc.edu/SDG/IT94/Proceedings/
Agents/eichmann.ethical/eichmann.html**). This white paper by David

Eichmann discusses the ethics of using automata on the World Wide Web. If you don't want to be inundated by angry letters from systems administrators, read this paper carefully before you write the first line of code for your nifty new robot.

This article is highly informative, with hot links to references and other papers pertinent to the subject. By reading this paper, you'll arm yourself with all the knowledge necessary to build a Web-safe robot.

◆ MOMSpider (**http://www.ics.uci.edu/WebSoft/MOMspider/**). MOMSpider is a UNIX-based Perl 4 program. You can use or modify this code, subject to the generous licensing restrictions from the University of California, Irvine. If nothing else, you can use the code as a starting point when building your own automaton.

◆ Checkbot (**http://dutifp.twi.tudelft.nl:8000/checkbot/**). Checkbot is a link-verification tool written in Perl, using libwww (a collection of Perl utilities). Written by Dimitri Tischenko and Hans de Graaff, this robot collects links (starting from a given URL) and then validates them. Although this tool is handy as written, you'll probably want to modify it for your particular needs.

◆ WebCopy (**http://www.inf.utfsm.cl/~vparada/webcopy.html**). Victor Parada's WebCopy program receives a URL's command-line argument and then fetches the document. WebCopy can run recursively, fetching all links that a document references. You can download the code right from the site and start using it immediately (although to do so, you also need Perl). By design, this program doesn't follow links across multiple servers, to protect you from endless recursion and retrieving more than you bargained for.

◆ WebWatch (**http://www.specter.com/**). WebWatch is a commercial program for Windows 95, but you can download an evaluation copy. (The evaluation copy has a built-in expiry feature, and does not let you view the source code.) The documentation says that the program doesn't currently work on Windows NT, but will soon.

WebWatch is a personal-use spider that monitors your bookmarks, updates lists of sites, checks for changed information, and so on. You'll find step-by-step installation instructions and a short FAQ. Although you might not find this product useful, it certainly demonstrates some smart thinking and slick marketing. You could do worse than to build a robot with this kind of user interface and intelligence.

CGI Interactive Games

If you want to play games on the Internet, you have thousands from which to choose. This section selects a few that demonstate CGI techniques particularly well. Some are incredibly complex, others very simple, but all maintain state information to provide interactivity.

♦ Real Virtual, Incorporated (**http://www.realvirtual.com/**). Real Virtual does far more than simply enable users to play Dungeons and Dragons (D&D) on the Web, although it handles D&D exceptionally well. For the CGI student, Real Virtual provides much to study (and, if you like fantasy role-playing games, you can have a great time). Pay particular attention to the way that Real Virtual maintains state information as you move through the setup screens. View the document source and notice all the hidden fields containing your selections, plus information that tells the CGI program what to do next.

Real Virtual spent much time and care developing this project. From the user's perspective, the Fantasy Worlds adventure looks much like a PC-based game, but with all the advantages of being real-time and multiplayer.

♦ Netropolis (**http://www.delphi.co.uk/netropolis/**). Netropolis makes you the CEO of a corporation located in or around England. The goal is to win lots of cash and taunt the other players.

Of special interest is the slick use of imagemaps to provide a sense of location, plus the integration of e-mail into the game. If you like stomping on the business competition, you might also enjoy this game.

♦ S.P.Q.R. (**http://alaska.net/~apearson/GRPandy.html**). When you visit S.P.Q.R., you should first notice that the URL at the top of your browser changes to something like **http://pathfinder.com/ @@awinfjG8TwMAQHSK/twep/rome/**. This vile concoction isn't something you would want to type manually, but the URL displays for a purpose. If you go to S.P.Q.R. with that URL, you can resume the game wherever you left off. S.P.Q.R. (from Time Warner Electronic Publishing) generates a fake URL for you on the fly when you walk through the front door. Thereafter, throughout the game, that URL marks you as a player so that the game can preserve state information.

The game itself is visually simple, but intriguing. You wander through Rome collecting scrolls (which you can then read) and keys (which you can use to unlock things). Your mission is to save Rome from disaster. The game doesn't miss a beat when it comes to maintaining state information or showing you, with graphics, the results of your actions.

♦ QIN: Tomb of the Middle Kingdom (**http://pathfinder.com/twep/products/qin/**). This cool game from Pathfinder also uses an artificially mangled URL to keep track of each player. The game is a visual version of a text-based adventure game, with low-key but nevertheless impressive graphics. In the game, you wander around a virtual 3-D world by clicking the view presented. The game presents the views by using imagemaps, so one of the game's inherent failings is that you can click anywhere, not just areas that do something.

This failing isn't the fault of the game design. It's a problem with using imagemaps for features without clear boundaries. For example, a toolbar or row of icons clearly has places to click. The trivial case occurs when the user mistakenly clicks a boundary or the background. In a game in which you click areas of a 3-D picture to govern motion, however, most clicks are null. The trivial case becomes the few areas of the image that actually *do* something. This problem can lead to the user doing a lot of clicking just to find out which areas of the imagemap are hotspots. Keep this problem in mind when designing your own game.

♦ The Barney Fun Page (**http://ugweb.cs.ualberta.ca/~gerald/barney/die.cgi/init**). If you really hate Barney (the big purple dinosaur), you'll love this page. Gerald Oskoboiny lets you vent all your angst against the Purple One with a knife, a gun, an axe, an Uzi, a shotgun, a motorcycle, or a cannon. You select your weapon and fire away, changing weapons as needed. Each time that you attack, the picture of Barney changes to show the wounds, and you get a caption such as, "Barney has been grazed. You can do better than that," or "Barney has been slightly wounded," until, at last, Barney dies.

Gerald thoughtfully keeps on file morgue photos from the last 10 Barney killings, so that you can view the corpses and celebrate.

This site is sometimes slow (probably due to all the crazed Barney hunters), but instructive for CGI programmers. Although the subject matter is just plain silly, the site demonstrates well how to make static drawings become interactive.

A Brief Case Study: CalWeb

CalWeb (**http://www.calweb.com**) uses O'Reilly's WebSite server on Windows NT. The main server is a 75-mHz Pentium with two 1G drives, 64M of RAM, and ISDN modems. CalWeb writes CGI and SSI software using Visual Basic, C++, Delphi, Perl, and PowerBuilder.

Frank Starsinic of CalWeb says

> Most of our CGI started out with Microsoft Access database programming, processing SQL queries and outputting the results to the Web. We soon won a contract to write a storefront application, and chose VB and MS Access because the client wanted it ASAP.

CalWeb is noteworthy for two reasons. First, it has an excellent selection of Visual Basic, PowerBuilder, and Perl tutorials. Second, it is the home of the now-famous Guestbook Server.

Starsinic wrote the Guestbook Server as a CGI experiment, using Visual Basic and Microsoft Access, but soon switched to Perl to increase the application's speed. The Guestbook Server is growing at a rate of approximately 100 new guestbooks each day, with no end in sight.

CalWeb also offers applications in Visual Basic and Perl that do fuzzy searching (or *soundexing*), server-side push animation, WWW yellow pages, page counters, random quote of the day, and more. You should be able to find many useful scripts in CalWeb, and see well-designed scripts in operation.

A Brief Case Study: Internet Concepts, LLC

Internet Concepts, LLC, knows that content and presentation are the two things that make one site stand out from another. The company has created several award-winning sites that you might have already encountered, including the following:

♦ WritersNet (sm): The Internet Directory of Published Writers (**http://www.writers.net/**)

♦ PrinterNet (sm): The Internet Directory of Commercial Printers (**http://www.printer.net/**)

♦ The Directory of Microscopists on the Net (**http://www.bocklabs.wisc.edu/imr/microscopists.html**)

♦ The Directory of Virologists on the Net (**http://www.bocklabs.wisc.edu/phonebook.html**)

♦ InnSite (sm): The Internet Directory of Bed & Breakfasts (**http://www.innsite.com/**)

These sites not only are well-designed and visually appealing, but take an unusual approach to the development of site content: They rely on the user to provide it.

Using a framework of hand-crafted CGI scripts written in Perl 5 and running on a Sun SPARCstation, Internet Concepts lets users submit an entry on a fill-out form.

A CGI script then processes that entry, adding it to the database and making it immediately available on the Web.

Stephan Spencer of Internet Concepts says

> Some consider this real-time updating risky, but since December 1994 when we first implemented this practice we have had no notable problems. Nonetheless, we'll probably change this in the near future to a policy of holding submissions in a "pending" area until we have reviewed them.

The database is based on Perl dbm. The script that processes new entries requires the user to assign a password, too. The user can then make changes to that entry later. A root or master password enables site supervisors to change individual passwords, edit entries, or delete entries. Another script allows browsing. It displays the database sorted by name, organization name (if applicable), category or genre, and location. Most of these sites are also keyword-searchable.

InnSite even offers a geographical search interface that responds to user clicks by zooming in indefinitely on a region ("drilling down," or peering more intently at a subregion), returning images in real time from the Xerox PARC Map Viewer (**http://www.xerox.com/map/**).

Internet Concepts provides many of these sites as a public service to the Internet community. The company also, however, designs and implements many commercial sites. One of the most interesting is the Online Catalogue at Seton Identification Products (**http://www.seton.com**). This site offers the Workplace Safety Home Page and a searchable online catalog of thousands of signs, labels, tags, pipe markers, and other identification products. The site supports online ordering of over 6,000 items.

If you're interested in learning more about Internet Concepts, its home page is at **http://www.netconcepts.com**, or you can send the company e-mail at **infodesk@netconcepts.com**.

The wizards at Internet Concepts have used CGI to create their enchantments. With what you've learned in this book, you can invoke the magic of CGI, too.

A Brief Case Study: Real Time Internet Services

Real Time Internet Services (RTIS) (**http://www.rtis.com/**) was formed in October 1994; shortly after that, the RealCom Web site went online. As of June 1996, the RealCom Web site had hosted thousands of unique documents, all maintained by their clients.

The RealCom server is running Microsoft Windows NT Server 3.51 with Netscape Communications Server 1.12. A second server is running Microsoft SQL Server on Windows NT. All interactive applications on the server are built with CGI PerForm and CGI PerForm Pro. PerForm Pro provides interconnectivity between the Web site and the SQL server. RealCom does not use Perl, because "it can become a serious security risk, especially if you allow your clients to use it freely for their own applications." Chapter 17, "Security Issues," discusses the reason that RTIS takes this position, and how you can minimize or eliminate the risks.

Every night, the RealCom server examines all its Web pages for invalid local links, generates a list of all root documents and all accessible documents, rebuilds search indexes from the list of accessible documents, regenerates the root home page to include a drop-down list box of all the root documents (each of which is a unique Web site), compiles usage statistics for the previous day, and then e-mails them to all clients.

RealCom uses a variety of inhouse and public-domain utilities to perform the link validation and indexing. For a search engine, RealCom uses FreeWAIS from EMWAC, modified slightly to work with Netscape Server. The root page uses CGI PerForm to redirect users to specific sites on the server.

RealCom uses CGI and back-end processing effectively to produce a robust and easy-to-use Web site. Check out RealCom's CGI PerForm utility and the rest of the site.

Glossary

.gz   A file that has been compressed with GZIP. GUNZIP is usually used to decompress the file.

.tar   A file, or files compressed (archived) using tar. (See also *tar*.)

.Z   A compressed file using the same compression algorithm as GZIP.

.zip   A compressed file, using the zip compression method commonly associated with PKWare's PKZIP.

/r   Used within various scripting languages to indicate a carriage return.

/n   Used within various scripting languages to indicate a new line.

ACTION   Used within a <FORM> tag to specify the CGI script that the information within the form will be handed to.

Apache Web Server   A free UNIX-based Web server that is meant to enhance security, speed, and reliability. It was developed by various individuals who wrote patch files for the NCSA 1.3 Web server, hence the name APACHE (A PAtCHy).

API   Application programming interface, of which CGI is one of many. API is an interface that provides a set of functions allowing one program to work with another.

argc   A variable used to store the argument count.

argv   A variable used to store the argument values.

associative array   Scalars as a key/value pair, where the scalar key is associated with the scalar value.

back end   A program that works in the background in conjunction with another program, server, or service that runs on a machine located elsewhere on a network.

bash   A GNU-derived Bourne shell commonly found on UNIX systems. Also referred to as the Bourne Again shell.

Bourne shell   The Bourne shell is the standard shell found on most UNIX systems. The UNIX command for the Bourne shell is sh.

browser   A program that interprets HTML documents and displays them to the user. Used to "browse the Web."

buffer   Saves information that is to be written to a file as a block of information instead of directly writing each bit to a file. Buffering also works with output to a terminal, where information is buffered to the end of the line (often referred to as *line buffering*).

C   A programming language developed by Dennis Ritchie and Brian Kernighan.

C++   An object-oriented (OO) version of C written by Bjarne Stroustrup.

call (noun)   A method in which information is passed to a function or procedure.

call (verb)   The act in which information is passed to a function or procedure.

CD-ROM   Compact Disc Read-Only Memory. A medium that contains information that is read by the use of a laser.

CERN   The European Particle Physics Laboratory located near Geneva. CERN is the birthplace of the World Wide Web and the name of the original Web server.

CGI   The Common Gateway Interface that is used to execute programs used in conjunction with a Web server.

check box   An HTML widget. When selected, it means the value of that widget is sent to the CGI application for processing.

child process   A process or task that another process or task created.

class   A set of objects that share a common structure and behavior.

client   Half of the client/server process, the client acts as a front-end application that requests data or information from a server (see also *server*), receives the information from the server, and processes that information. A client often manages how information is displayed, validates incoming information, interacts with the user, and so on.

concatenate   To link together, or join strings or files to a single string or file.

compiler   A program or set of programs that convert human readable programming code into machine language, which can be used by the computer system.

Content-type   The MIME type used to transfer information.

counter   A program that counts the number of hits that a page has received. See also *hit*.

crawler   Also referred to as a Web spider or robot, a crawler is a program that catalogs information on the Web.

CrLf   Short for carriage return/line feed.

daemon   A program that sits in the background, listening to a port and waiting for a connection. See *server*.

database   A system in which information is stored in a method that can be used for easy retrieval.

debug   To remove problems or errors from an application.

document root   The top level in which HTML documents are stored on a Web server.

DTD   Document Type Definition. A set of rules that describe what commands or tags are allowed within a document.

e-mail   Electronic mail, also referred to as email or Email. It's used to send a message to another individual electronically.

environment variable   A variable that is inherited by a child process. See *child process.*

escape character   A character used to encode information. For example, using \r, the backslash becomes the escape character and informs the interpreter to read the next character as a carriage return.

field   Information stored as a separate item along with a value. A field within HTML could be the value for the name attribute. Within a database, a field could be an employee's name within the column titled name.

finger   A UNIX command that allows you to see the statistics of another individual, locally or remotely.

fixed-length   A variable or string whose size remains the same.

flat file   A method of storing information in which the information is not indexed in any manner.

Gateway   An application that works as a "middleman" between two other programs.

GET   A method of sending information to the server in which the information is sent within the variable QUERY_STRING or as an argument.

GUI   Graphical user interface. A graphical interface in which objects are manipulated or programs are run by selecting an item with an onscreen pointer and then clicking the mouse.

hash   A method in which information is stored and retrieved by the use of an identifier that points to the associated data.

header   Information passed to the server or to the client that contains information about the data packet, information about the server, or information about the client. This information is usually stored in variables and can be used within CGI scripts.

heap   A writeable area whose size is determined by the ever-changing needs of the program.

hit   A slang word for a Web client's request of a Web page.

home directory   A directory assigned to a user as his own so he can store files, user-specific configuration files, and so on.

home page   The top-level page of a subject, organization, or individual. For example, an organization's home page could be something like the following:

http://www.wolfenet.com/

However, a user on that site could also have a home page as follows:

http://www.wolfenet.com/~rniles/

HTML   HyperText Markup Language. A subset of SGML used for Web documents that describes the logical structure and attributes of a document.

HTTP   HyperText Transfer Protocol. Describes how information is to be passed between the World Wide Web client and server.

hypertext   A system for linking text to parts of a document or other documents.

IETF   Internet Engineering Task Force. A group responsible for meeting the needs of the Internet and creating standards that allow the Internet to work efficiently. The IETF is a part of the Internet Architecture Board (IAB).

imagemap   An image that has been divided into sections using coordinates so that specific sections of the image are linked to specific documents.

inheritance   One process passing information (variables) to a subprocess.

Internet   A collection of networks connected together to form a worldwide system using the TCP/IP protocol suite.

intranet   A group of local area networks connected together. An intranet is not necessarily connected to the Internet.

invoke   To start up a new process or subproccess.

IP   Internet Protocol. The most widely used network protocol, IP is the main network layer for TCP/IP, providing packet delivery services between nodes.

ISDN   Integrated Services Digital Network. ISDN sends digital signals over a standard copper phone line, providing faster connections.

ISP   Internet service provider. A company that provides Internet connections to end-users or businesses.

Java   An object-oriented programming environment from Sun Microsystems.

JavaScript   A programming language used within HTML documents that was developed by Netscape Communications, Inc., and Sun Microsystems.

keyword   A string or word used to point to data within a database. A keyword is also a word that is used to search for information within a database.

language   In relation to computers, language is a means by which humans can communicate with the computer, removing the need to learn machine-specific code. Perl, C, and BASIC are platform-independent and relatively easy to learn, and thus easier for humans to use.

mark-up   A text command placed within a document that describes how elements of a document are structured, presented, laid-out, or delivered.

metalanguage   A language used to describe other languages. SGML is a common example of a metalanguage. (See also *SGML*.)

method   The manner in which information is passed between the client and the server (and vice versa) using the HTTP protocol. The most common methods are GET and POST.

MIME   Multipurpose Internet Mail Extensions. MIME is an extension of the mail message format providing the ability to send audio, images, and so on, via electronic mail. MIME is also used extensively within HTTP.

Mozilla   Netscape Communication's Web browser, commonly known as the Netscape browser.

MSIE   Microsoft Internet Explorer. Microsoft's Web browser.

NCSA   National Center for Supercomputing Applications. Located at the University of Illinois at Urbana–Champaign, Illinois. NCSA created the most popular Web server along with the first widely used graphical Web browser, which is called Mosaic.

NT   Short for Windows NT. See also *Windows NT*.

octet stream   A stream of data using eight character bytes. It's used within the HTTP protocol to send binary data.

overrun   A situation in which data arrives faster than it can be used.

Perl   Practical Extraction and Report Language. Designed by Larry Wall, Perl was originally intended to extract information from files and create formatted reports. It has grown to be a full-fledged interpreted language popular with CGI.

PHP/FI   Personal Home Page/Forms Interpreter. A scripting language written by Rasmus Lerdorf that can be used within HTML documents.

POST   A method in which information from a form is sent to the server (and on to a CGI script) through a datastream using STDIN and STDOUT.

process   A file or program running in conjunction with other programs. This term is common on multitasking systems.

protocol   A set of rules that describes how to transmit data.

pseudocode   A way of explaining a section of code with an understandable English-language description.

radio button   A widget used in forms that usually allows the user to select only one option from a group of radio buttons at a time (unlike check boxes).

real-time   Information that is accurate at the point at which it is retrieved.

record (noun)   Common within databases, a record contains a set of information in the form of fields. For example, a record on one employee may contain many fields, such as his name, employee number, telephone number, and so on.

response   Information from the server sent to a client containing data requested by the client.

robot   Usually referred to as a mechanical device used to simplify burdensome tasks. On the WWW, a robot (or *bot*) is used to browse the WWW, retrieve findings, and catalog the information.

script   A text file that is executed by an interpreter or shell that performs a function. With CGI, all programs, whether written in Perl or C, are often referred to as scripts.

SELECT   An HTML tag used to allow the visitor to select options from a list.

server   The half of the client/server process that acts as a back-end application to provide specific services, receive requests from a client (see *client*), perform the service, and return the information or data requested to the client. On a UNIX system, you can usually find the system's servers by looking at the file /ETC/SERVICES. The NCSA server, Apache, Microsoft's Internet Information Server, and the Netscape commerce server are examples of HTTP servers.

Server-Side Includes   See *SSI*.

service (NT daemon)   The Windows NT equivalent to a server.

SGML   Standard Generalized Markup Language. A metalanguage used to describe other markup languages, including HTML.

sh   The standard shell found on most UNIX systems. See also *Bourne shell*.

shell   A command-line interface (CLI) used to allow users access to the operating system.

SMTP   Simple Mail Transfer Protocol. A method used to send electronic mail from one host to another over a TCP/IP network (see *TCP/IP*). Unlike most Internet protocols, SMTP is a server-to-server protocol. RFC 821 covers the guidelines for SMTP.

spawn   The act in which a process starts a subprocess.

specification   Guidelines or rules that govern how a specific standard works.

Spider   See *robot*.

SQL   Structured Query Language. A language that allows the interaction between a user and a relational database system originally developed by IBM. It is currently an ISO and ANSI standard and widely used by both private and government organizations.

SSI   Server-Side Includes. A method by which a script can be executed and the information returned and placed into the HTML document in which it was called.

stack   A data structure for storing items that are to be accessed in a "last-in, first-out" (LIFO) order.

state information   The status of a process—whether it is running, waiting, on standby, and so on.

stateless   A method in which the server treats each request as a separate transaction. A WWW server is a stateless server.

STDIN   A "channel" in which a program or device receives information.

STDOUT   A "channel" in which a program or device sends out information.

string   A set of characters.

symbolic link   A file that points to the location of another file or directory.

tag   A formatting command included within a DTD (such as HTML). Examples of HTML tags are <PRE>, <HEAD>, and <SELECT>.

tar   Short for Tape Archive, tar is a program that archives files (although it does no compression of the archive), allowing you to store many files within one file.

TBL   Tim Berners-Lee, the creator of the World Wide Web.

Tcl   Tool Command Language (pronounced "tickle"), developed by John Ousterhout at the University of California at Berkeley, is a string processing language for issuing commands to interactive programs.

TCP/IP   The Transmission Control Protocol/Internet Protocol, a set of standards for transmitting data and correcting errors. TCP/IP enables computers connected to the Internet to communicate with each other.

TEXTAREA   An HTML tag that allows you to create a large area used for visitor input.

UNIX   A multiuser, multitasking operating system originally developed in 1969. UNIX has been one of the most popular multiuser operating systems.

URI   Uniform Resource Indicator. A string that points to a specific document or file (called a resource).

URL   Uniform Resource Locator. A string that specifies an object on the Internet. The URL consists of the protocol used, the hostname in which the resource is located, and the path to the resource. An example is **http://www.mcp.com/index.html**.

URL-encoded   The method by which information is sent to the server (and on to the CGI script). The special characters within a string are escaped using the percent sign (%).

variable-length   The size of a variable, usually noted in bytes.

VB3   Visual Basic version 3. This is the 16-bit version of Visual Basic, which VB4 has now mostly superseded. However, VB3 enjoys a wide base of programmers, and many custom utilities and even full-blown applications have been written in VB3. VB3 also has a wide variety of third-party add-ins.

VB4-16   Visual Basic 4, the 16-bit version. Visual Basic version 4 comes in two distinct flavors (packaged together): 16-bit and 32-bit. The 16-bit version is backward-compatible with Windows 3.1, and produces executables that run on Windows 3.1, Windows 95, and Windows NT. Although VB4-16 supports most of the new VB4 features, it is nevertheless limited by its 16-bit heritage. It can call only 16-bit DLLs, does not support long file names directly, and runs as a Windows 3.1 application on the Windows 95 and Windows NT platforms. VB4-16 is used primarily to develop applications that must run on all versions of Windows.

VB4-32   Visual Basic 4, the 32-bit version. Visual Basic version 4 comes in two distinct flavors (packaged together): 16-bit and 32-bit. The 32-bit version produces executables exclusively for Windows 95 and Windows NT. It has none of the 16-bit limitations, and is far more robust and powerful than its 16-bit cousins. The Enterprise Edition supports remote data objects and several other new features with the same astounding flexibility and power. VB4-32 features tight integration with 32-bit OLE; the familiar VBX files from VB3 are now OLE objects named OCX.

Visual C++   A C and C++ programming environment sold by Microsoft Corporation.

Visual Basic   A basic programming language designed to make pro-gramming graphical objects easier.

W3   Short for WWW or the World Wide Web.

W3C   World Wide Web Consortium. A group of organizations that main-tain standards for the World Wide Web, Web browsers, and other related software.

WAIS   Wide Area Information Service. A service allowing access to site indexes. WAIS allows you to access indexes either locally or on a remote network.

wanderer   See *robot*.

Web   Short for the World Wide Web.

Webmaster   A person or group that controls or develops the contents of that site's Web pages. The Webmaster is most likely the server adminis-trator.

Web root   See *document root*.

Web site   A site that contains a server that processes HMTL documents using HTTP.

white space   A space that is void of characters and between text.

widget   Geek-speak for a item that can be clicked on or can have informa-tion entered into. Radio button and check boxes are examples of widgets.

Windows   Microsoft's popular operating system. Windows is also the common name for a graphical user interface (GUI).

Windows 95   Microsoft's latest operating system introduced in 1995.

Windows NT (Windows New Technology)   Microsoft's 32-bit operating system. The technology was originally developed to be used in IBM's OS/2 3.0. Unlike Windows 3.1, in which the Windows environment rides on top of the DOS operating system, Windows NT is a complete operating system.

World Wide Web (WWW)   A global hypertext system based on a set of protocols (*HTML* and *HTTP*) that enable a visitor to click a link which then carries the visitor to another document. The document can be local or remote.

Answers to the Review Questions

Chapter 1

1. The connection, the request, the response, and the closure. HTTP uses the same steps to help the server and the client to communicate.

2. 80.

3. GET, POST, and HEAD.

4. A URL consist of a protocol method, the server's domain name or IP address, and the path to the document, file, directory, and so on. (URI.)

5. By using the method POST, you can pass more than 255 characters to the server.

6. You get an error 400, Bad Request, because the method SEND isn't a valid METHOD.

7. A status line, the response header fields, the entity type, and the entity body.

8. The current official HTML DTD is version 2.0.

Chapter 2

1. To use environment variables, you call them using the syntax ENV{'*VARIABLE_NAME*'}.

2. The query fails. The string name=john passes to the environmental variable QUERY_STRING.

3. An <ISINDEX> query.

4. A CGI script's STDIN originally is from the Web server. The server receives a CGI script's STDOUT unless it is redirected elsewhere.

5. You can pass to the server only a string that contains 255 characters or less.

Chapter 3

1. <FORM>, <SELECT>, and <TEXTAREA>.

2. The method GET is the default for most Web servers.

3. text, hidden, password, submit, reset, radio, and checkbox.

4. You must specify the NAME attribute.

5. The SELECTED attribute.

6. The NAME, SIZE, and MULTIPLE attributes.

7. There is no limit.

Chapter 4

1. It doesn't. Visitors can enter anything they want in the e-mail field.

2. SGB1 reads only as many bytes as fit into szBuffer, no matter what the CONTENT_LENGTH variable indicates.

3. SGB1 examines the REQUEST_METHOD variable and displays the form only if the request method is GET.

4. No, because the file name and location are hard-coded into the script.

5. The file is called SGB1.DAT, and resides in whatever is the current default directory when the script executes. For most servers, this directory is the document root.

6. The SCRIPT_NAME environment variable.

7. Name, email, and comments.

Chapter 5

1. Use the string `$ENV{'CONTENT_LENGTH'}` to find the length of the data being sent.

2. In Perl, `\n` represents a carriage return and line feed.

3. The ampersand (&).

4. The equal sign (=).

Chapter 6

1. You should have your scripts check whatever is necessary to ensure that the visitor's entry is what your script expects. The capability to do this varies depending on the script and its purpose.

2. To report errors.

3. One method is to have your script create a Web document that contains a form, where each input type has the value that the visitor passed previously. Note the following example:

```
<input type="text" name="name" value="$form{'name'}
```

This script enables a visitor to view the information that he or she previously entered. You can also pass these values transparently by using the `hidden` input type.

4. No, the input type `text` is also a popular input type to use.

Chapter 7

1. To allow random access to the data file, and therefore an arbitrary retrieval sequence.

2. SGB2 uses the visitor-supplied `howmany` parameter as long as it is greater than zero and less than 999.

3. About 4.2 million. SGB2 looks only at the lower 32 bits (hexidecimal FFFFFFFF, or decimal 4,294,967,295) of the file size when calculating file length and record offsets. Each record is 1,024 (hexidecimal 400) bytes long, and you can fit exactly 4,194,303 (hexidecimal 3FFFFF) such records into the lower 32 bits.

4. `first`, `howmany`, and `op`.

5. Print an error message and exit.

6. MYGUESTBOOK.INI.

7. Read, write, and create access.

8. None. SGB2 doesn't reference any directory except the one in which it resides.

9. The visitor's comments are truncated to the first 512 bytes.

Chapter 8

1. Absolutely nothing.

2. Exactly one.

3. Hidden form fields and magic cookies.

4. All the buttons in ShopCart are named Choice, and the value of each button is its caption. ShopCart examines the caption to figure out which button the visitor clicked and therefore which action to take.

Chapter 9

1. The IP address of the visitor, the user agent (the name and version of the Web browser), the requested URI, and other information that varies depending on the request and the browser.

2. The version of the HTTP protocol, the version of the Common Gateway Interface, the server software, the server name, and more.

3. No, the visitor could possibly forge the information sent by the client.

4. The types of logs that the server creates depend on the server, but the most common logs generated by the server are the access log, the agent log, and an error log.

Chapter 10

1. A record is a collection of fields.

2. Yes.

3. Characters, or bytes.

4. No, an integer can be one, two, or four bytes, depending on your computer, your operating system, your development environment, and your syntax.

5. No, this name is too long.

6. No, an unsigned integer holding up to 65,535 is always two bytes long, no matter what value it has assigned at the moment.

7. Variable-length, because it has to store only the exact number of bytes for the string, plus a delimiter or length count.

8. No, you cannot open a file in sequential mode for both read and write access simultaneously.

9. Compaction, compacting, or compressing.

10. File and/or record locking, and semaphore files.

Chapter 11

1. A database created with the use of database libraries. Most dbm databases use hash routines to store information using a key/value pair.

2. You store information in a dbm database by using a key that points to a value, as in the following example:

```
name: John Doe
```

3. A dbm database stores information based on a key/value pair. A relational database stores information in fields much like a spreadsheet that matches values. Relational databases use a powerful language, such as SQL, that enables a programmer to communicate with the database easily.

4. Relational databases consist of tables that contain columns and rows.

Chapter 12

1. The IDC is an interface between the Web server and a database.

2. The DataSource, Template, and SQLStatement directives.

3. An .HTX file creates the Web page based on the information from the SQL server and the information from the .IDC file.

4. The PULLDOWN directive creates a pulldown window and enables the visitor to select only one item from the list. The SCROLL directive creates a scrolling list of items from which you can select more than one item. Both directives create variations of HTML's <SELECT> tag.

5. The `exec` command.

6. Using mSQL and MsqlPerl within your Perl script, you would use the following syntax to connect to a database:

```
$variable = Msql->Connect("hostname", "database_name");
```

7. You need to escape the slash by using the backslash (`\`).

8. Each mSQL field allows as many as 255 characters.

Chapter 13

1. No, WAIS uses simple word searches, and uses Boolean algebra to combine multiple terms.

2. Yes. The AND is part of the search logic, not a search term itself. The document contains both *Bill* and *Ted,* so it would match.

3. Yes.

4. CGI, using an HTML fill-in form.

Chapter 14

1. Yes. Any full-text indexer will index the entire contents of a document.

2. One that relied solely on the word *frequency* to determine relevancy.

3. HTML doesn't allow the space character in an `<a name=...>` tag.

4. SWISH.CONF.

5. The .CAT and the .SRC files.

Chapter 16

1. `AddType text/x-server-parsed-html .html .shtml`.

2. You use `config` to change the output of various items, including the date and the file size format.

3. To change the format for the date and time output, you can use the `timefmt` tag, as in the following example:

```
<!--#command timefmt="%d%m%y"-->
```

4. You use the `include` command to include information from another document.

5. The var tag is the only tag used with the echo command.

6. The cgi tag executes a CGI script. The cmd tag executes a system command, such as finger.

7. QUERY_STRING_UNESCAPED, DATE_LOCAL, DATE_GMT, and LAST_MODIFIED.

Chapter 17

1. A visitor could flood your buffer areas with far more data than you were expecting, leading to buffer overruns, stack corruption, and possible security risks.

2. The maximum length is browser-dependent, but usually 1K (1,024 bytes).

3. The root or administrator account has full privileges everywhere on the system.

4. Anything except A–Z and 1–9 is suspect, and even these need to be checked for appropriateness in the particular situation.

Chapter 18

1. Browser only.

2. Because text-only browsers don't support event triggers, popup boxes, and other Windows-like objects.

3. No.

4. No. JavaScript doesn't have access to the machine's TCP/IP ports.

5. Three: string, number, and Boolean.

6. The window object.

7. After the page has loaded, but before any other code.

8. To keep non-JavaScript browsers from displaying the JavaScript code.

Chapter 19

1. No.

2. UNIX systems.

3. The echo command prints information to the visitor.

4. The <? operator starts a PHP/FI command, and the > operator marks the end of a PHP/FI command.

5. Just as you would in Perl—by specifying a value for a variable, as in the following example:

```
<? $I=45>
```

Chapter 20

1. Because the earliest CGI programs *were* scripts, and the name stuck.

2. Sixteen-bit programs like VB3 or VB4-16 cannot read STDIN or write to STDOUT.

3. No, VB4CGI.BAS works only in the 32-bit VB4-32 environment.

4. The number of members in the Env() array is limited practically only by available memory. The size of each element in the array is limited to approximately 2 billion (2^{31}) bytes.

5. cgiStartup() reads the CONTENT_LENGTH variable first, and allocates a string long enough to hold the entire input.

APPENDIX *B*

Contents of the CD-ROM

The CD-ROM that you find on this book's inside back cover includes many applications that can help you create and enhance your Web pages using CGI scripts. Although this CD doesn't contain every CGI or Web application available, it has been carefully prepared to help you get on your way to creating great CGI scripts.

You can access the contents of the CD-ROM directly, in which case table B.1 provides you with the CD's layout and describes what each directory contains. Alternatively, you can access the CD using your favorite Web browser. (The CD includes a browser, just in case you don't have one.) Load your browser and click the LOADME.HTM file. The first page leads you to additional pages, where you can choose what you would like to see next.

Table B.1   The contents of the companion CD-ROM

Directory	Contents
AUDIO	Programs that add audio capabilities to your browser or Web pages.
BOOK	Scripts created for each chapter.
BROWSERS	Web browsers.
DATABASE	Databases and related files.

continues

Table B.1   Continued

Directory	Contents
GRAPHICS	Graphics, viewers, and graphics manipulation tools.
HTML	HTML-creation utilities.
HTMLUTIL	Various Web utilities.
JAVA	Sun Microsystems' Java.
OTHUTILS	Miscellaneous tools and utilities.
SCRIPTS	Additional CGI scripts.
SERVERS	Web servers.
VIDEO	Programs for viewing video images.
WEBUTILS	Various tools, archivers, languages, and so on.

Many programs on the CD are beta versions—works in progress. Although each of the programs is fully functional, some might not have all the bugs worked out, or some of the functions might not be activated.

Also, most of the programs on the CD are shareware. You can try these programs for free, but if you like one of them and use it regularly, then you must pay a small fee. By registering a shareware program, you are supporting the continuous effort of those who make these applications available to you.

Apache Web Server

Directory: \SERVERS
Platform: UNIX

Another popular free Web server for UNIX systems, Apache is based on NCSA's Web server. Apache is becoming one of the most popular Web servers on the Internet.

This Web server was written by the Apache Group, which you can reach at the following address:

http://www.apache.org

Chapter 15, "Enabling and Configuring Servers To Use CGI," includes information on the Apache Web server.

Berkeley Db Library

Directory: \DATABASE
Platform: UNIX
The Berkeley db library consists of dbm database routines written by Margo Seltzer, Keith Bostic, and Ozan Yigit. You can easily find the Berkeley db libraries on the Internet.

Chapter 11, "Storing Information in Databases," provides information on the Berkeley db libraries.

formmail.pl

Directory: \SCRIPTS
Platforms: Written for UNIX, but should be easily portable to other platforms
This file is a simple mailing script.
Written by Matt Wright, formmail.pl can be found at the following site:

http://www.worldwidemart.com/scripts/formmail.shtml

FreeWAIS

Directory: \OTHUTILS
Platform: UNIX
FreeWAIS is a popular wide area information server (WAIS) search engine.

This search engine was written by the CNIDR (Center for Networked Information Discovery and Retrieval), which you can reach at the following site:

http://www.cnidr.org

You can find information on FreeWAIS in Chapter 14, "Indexing Your Own Site."

GSQL

Directory: \DATABASE
Platform: UNIX
GSQL is a gateway between a script and SQL databases such as Microsoft's SQL Server, Oracle, Sybase, Illustra/Postgres, and Ingres.

GSQL was written by NCSA's Jason Ng, who you can reach at the following address:

http://www.ncsa.uiuc.edu/SDG/People/jason/pub/gsql/starthere.html

You can find information on GSQL in Chapter 12, "Common Database Solutions."

Microsoft's Internet Information Server

Directory: \SERVERS
Platform: Windows NT

Microsoft's Internet Information Server (MS IIS) is a free Web server for use with Windows NT. You can find additional information on the MS IIS at the following site:

http://www.microsoft.com/

For more information on MS IIS, see Chapters 12 and 15.

mSQL

Directory: \DATABASE
Platform: UNIX

mSQL, or Mini-SQL, although smaller than most SQL servers, is a powerful SQL server for UNIX systems. mSQL doesn't have all the features that most popular SQL servers offer, but is powerful enough to handle most common, everyday database applications. The price for mSQL is also more appropriate for the budget-conscious person or business.

mSQL was written by David Hughes, who you can reach at the following site:

http://www.hughes.com.au/product/msql

Chapter 12 includes information on mSQL.

NCSA's Web Server

Directory: \SERVERS
Platform: UNIX

The most popular free Web server, NCSA's server is tried and true. It comes with example CGI scripts.

This Web server was written by the NCSA HTTP Development Team, which you can reach at the following site:

http://hoohoo.ncsa.uiuc.edu

You can find information on NCSA in Chapters 2, "The Common Gateway Interface (CGI)" and 15.

Perl 5.003

Directory: \WEBUTIL
Platforms: UNIX, VMS, OS/2, Amiga, Microsoft operating systems

Perl, written by Larry Wall, is a programming language widely used in CGI scripting.

You can find updates to Perl and additional information on the Perl Web site:

http://www.perl.com/

Although you can find information on Perl throughout this book, Chapter 2 introduces the language.

PHP/FI

Directory: \WEBUTIL
Platform: UNIX

A wonderful scripting language that you can write into your HTML pages, PHP/FI is quite a bit like JavaScript, but not client-dependent.

Written by Rasmus Lerdorf, PHP/FI can be found at the following address:

http://www.vex.net/php/

Chapter 19, "Using PHP/FI," covers this language in detail.

SWISH

Directory: \OTHUTILS
Platform: UNIX

The Simple Web Indexing System for Humans (SWISH) enables you to index your Web directories.

Written by Kevin Hughes, SWISH can be found at the following address:

http://www.eit.com/software/swish

To find information on SWISH, see Chapter 14.

WebSQL

Directory: \DATABASE
Platform: UNIX

WebSQL is a simple Web interface to an mSQL server. With WebSQL, you can manipulate all mSQL databases, tables, and data from your browser.

Written by Universal Access Inc.'s Henry Minsky (**hqm@ua.com**), WebSQL can be found at the following address:

http://www.ua.com/websql/index.html

W3-mSQL

Directory: \DATABASE
Platform: UNIX

W3-mSQL is a CGI script that interprets special scripts, goes into HTML documents, and performs queries on an mSQL database.

W3-mSQL was written by David Hughes, who you can find at the following site:

http://www.hughes.com/product/w3-msql

Index

E

F

literals (JavaScript), 323-324

LOCK_EX subroutine, 209

LOCK_NB subroutine, 209

LOCK_SH subroutine, 209

LOCK_UN subroutine, 209

locking

    databases, 209

    files, 296

log files

    accessing, 171-175

    creating, 170-171

LOG.PL (log files) script, 171

loosely typed languages, 322

LT conditional, 224

Lycos Web site, 261

M

Macintosh AppleScript, 37

    Web sites, 392

mailing lists, 386-387

    subscribing, 386

    users

        adding, 106-107

        confirming subscriptions, 117

    w3.org lists, 386-387

MAILLIST.PL script, 106-110

$mailprog string, 96

main( ) function, 62-67, 127, 148

Make EXE File command (File menu), 373

mark-up, 414

MaxFieldSize directive, 222

MAXLENGTH attribute, 47

MaxRecords variable, 222-224

messages (error), creating, 109

    duplicate information, 116

    invalid e-mail addresses, 114-115

    invalid user names, 113

<META> tags, 266

metalanguage, 414

METHOD attribute, 45

methods, 318, 414

    alert, 321

    checking, 94

    close, 321

    confirm, 321

    GET, 15, 33, 412

    HEAD, 15

    open, 321

    POST, 15, 33-35, 94, 415

    status, 321

    write, 320

    writeln, 320

Microsoft

    IIS (Internet Information Server), 219-225, 432

        configuring, 283-284

        .HTX files, 222-225

        .IDC (Internet Database Connector) files, 221

    Internet Explorer (MSIE), 415

    Web site, 284, 363, 432

MIME (Multipurpose Internet Mail Extensions), 414

    headers, printing, 67-68

    types

        BUYCAR.PL script, 99

        Content-type, 411

        text/html, 164

mini SQL, *see* **mSQL**

Minsky, Henry (WebSQL software), 433

moderated newsgroups, 382

modifying ShopCart script, 158-159

installing, 268
Web site, 267, 433
switching UNIX streams to binary mode, 65-67
Sybase, 212
symbolic links, 417

T

\t (tab escape sequence), 324
tags
HTML (HyperText Markup Language), 417
<!?>, 338
<?>, 338
<CENTER>, 22
<FORM>, 44-45, 93
<%if%>, 223-224
<INPUT>, 46-51
<META>, 266
<OPTION>, 51-53
<PRE>, 91
<SELECT>, 51-53, 90, 241, 416
<TEXTAREA>, 53, 418
IIS (Internet Information Server)
BeginDetail, 222
EndDetail, 222-223
SSI (Server-Side Includes), 289
cgi, 293
cmd, 293
errmsg, 290
file, 292
sizefmt, 291
timefmt, 290
var, 292
virtual, 291
Talk to My Cat Web site, 396
Tango Web site, 400
tar (Tape Archive), 417
TBL, *see* **Berners-Lee, Tim**
Tcl (Tool Command Language), 36, 417
TCP/IP (Transmission Control Protocol/Internet Protocol), 418

Technical Discussion of the Harvest System Web site, 397
Teleport CGI Scripts Web site, 391
Template directive, 221
testing
forms, 169-170
scripts, 110
text boxes
default values, 47
hiding text, 48
sizing, 46
text fields (flat files), 180-181
delimiting, 183
fixed-length, 181-183
numeric, 183-198
text value (TYPE attribute), 46-47
text/html MIME type, 164
<TEXTAREA> tag, 53, 418
thank-you notes, scripting, 100
thank-you page (SGB2), 141
thesauri, 258
three-dimensional files, 190
tie( ) function, 203-205, 209
tilde (~), 309
time, printing (JavaScript), 325-326
timefmt tag (SSI), 290
timers, 330
Tool Command Language (Tcl), 36
Transmission Control Protocol/Internet Protocol (TCP/IP), 418
tutorial Web sites, 387, 390-392
two-dimensional files, 190
TYPE attribute values, 46-51
checkbox, 48-49
hidden, 48
password, 48
radio, 50
reset, 50
submit, 50-51
text, 46-47
type conversions (JavaScript), 322-323

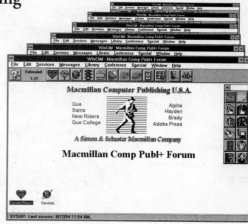

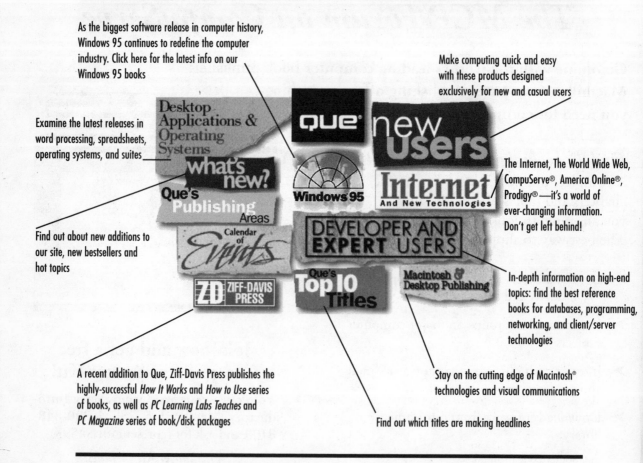
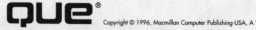

Complete and Return this Card for a *FREE* Computer Book Catalog

Thank you for purchasing this book! You have purchased a superior computer book written expressly for your needs. To continue to provide the kind of up-to-date, pertinent coverage you've come to expect from us, we need to hear from you. Please take a minute to complete and return this self-addressed, postage-paid form. In return, we'll send you a free catalog of all our computer books on topics ranging from word processing to programming and the internet.

Mr. ☐   Mrs. ☐   Ms. ☐   Dr. ☐

Name (first) [_____] (M.I.) ☐ (last) [_____]

Address [_____]

[_____]

City [_____] State [__] Zip [_____]

Phone [___] [_____] Fax [_____]

Company Name [_____]

E-mail address [_____]

1. Please check at least (3) influencing factors for purchasing this book.

Front or back cover information on book .... ☐
Special approach to the content .... ☐
Completeness of content .... ☐
Author's reputation .... ☐
Publisher's reputation .... ☐
Book cover design or layout .... ☐
Index or table of contents of book .... ☐
Price of book .... ☐
Special effects, graphics, illustrations .... ☐
Other (Please specify): _____ ☐

2. How did you first learn about this book?

Saw in Macmillan Computer Publishing catalog .... ☐
Recommended by store personnel .... ☐
Saw the book on bookshelf at store .... ☐
Recommended by a friend .... ☐
Received advertisement in the mail .... ☐
Saw an advertisement in: _____ ☐
Read book review in: _____ ☐
Other (Please specify): _____ ☐

3. How many computer books have you purchased in the last six months?

This book only .... ☐   3 to 5 books .... ☐
books .... ☐   More than 5 .... ☐

4. Where did you purchase this book?

Bookstore .... ☐
Computer Store .... ☐
Consumer Electronics Store .... ☐
Department Store .... ☐
Office Club .... ☐
Warehouse Club .... ☐
Mail Order .... ☐
Direct from Publisher .... ☐
Internet site .... ☐
Other (Please specify): _____ ☐

5. How long have you been using a computer?

☐ Less than 6 months   ☐ 6 months to a year
☐ 1 to 3 years   ☐ More than 3 years

6. What is your level of experience with personal computers and with the subject of this book?

	With PCs	With subject of book
New	☐	☐
Casual	☐	☐
Accomplished	☐	☐
Expert	☐	☐

Source Code ISBN: 0-0000-0000-0

7. Which of the following best describes your job title?

Administrative Assistant .... ☐
Coordinator .... ☐
Manager/Supervisor .... ☐
Director .... ☐
Vice President .... ☐
President/CEO/COO .... ☐
Lawyer/Doctor/Medical Professional .... ☐
Teacher/Educator/Trainer .... ☐
Engineer/Technician .... ☐
Consultant .... ☐
Not employed/Student/Retired .... ☐
Other (Please specify): _____ ☐

8. Which of the following best describes the area of the company your job title falls under?

Accounting .... ☐
Engineering .... ☐
Manufacturing .... ☐
Operations .... ☐
Marketing .... ☐
Sales .... ☐
Other (Please specify): _____ ☐

9. What is your age?

Under 20 .... ☐
21-29 .... ☐
30-39 .... ☐
40-49 .... ☐
50-59 .... ☐
60-over .... ☐

10. Are you:

Male .... ☐
Female .... ☐

11. Which computer publications do you read regularly? (Please list)

_____
_____
_____
_____
_____
_____
_____
_____

Comments: _____
_____
_____

Fold here and scotch-tape to mail

Fold here and scotch-tape to mail

BUSINESS REPLY MAIL
FIRST-CLASS MAIL PERMIT NO. 9918 INDIANAPOLIS IN

POSTAGE WILL BE PAID BY THE ADDRESSEE

ATTN MARKETING
MACMILLAN COMPUTER PUBLISHING
MACMILLAN PUBLISHING USA
201 W 103RD ST
INDIANAPOLIS IN 46290-9042

NO POSTAGE
NECESSARY
IF MAILED
IN THE
UNITED STATES